JUSTICE THE TRUE
AND
ONLY MERCY

JUSTICE THE TRUE
AND
ONLY MERCY

Essays on the Life and Theology of Peter Taylor Forsyth

Edited by
Trevor Hart

T&T CLARK
EDINBURGH

FOR

DONALD MACKENZIE MACKINNON

1913–1994

T&T CLARK LTD
59 GEORGE STREET
EDINBURGH EH2 2LQ
SCOTLAND

First published 1995

ISBN 0 567 09703 X

British Library Cataloguing-in-Publication Data
A catalogue record for this book is available from the British Library

Typeset by Trinity Typesetting, Edinburgh
Printed and bound in Great Britain by Bookcraft, Avon

CONTENTS

LIST OF CONTRIBUTORS

Jeremy Begbie is Vice Principal of Ridley Hall, Cambridge.

Clyde Binfield lectures in History in the University of Sheffield.

Keith Clements is Coordinating Secretary for International Affairs to The Council of Churches for Britain and Ireland.

Colin Gunton is Professor of Christian Doctrine at King's College, University of London.

George Hall lectures in Systematic Theology in St Mary's College, the University of St Andrews.

Trevor Hart lectures in Systematic Theology in the University of Aberdeen.

Leslie McCurdy lectures in Systematic Theology in Emmanuel Bible Institute, Oradea, Romania.

Donald MacKinnon† was Professor Emeritus of Divinity in the University of Cambridge.

Stanley Russell lectures in Theology in the Northern College and the University of Manchester.

Alan Sell is Professor of Systematic Theology in The United Theological College, Aberystwyth.

Stephen Sykes is Bishop of Ely, and formerly Regius Professor of Divinity in the University of Cambridge.

John Thompson is Professor of Systematic Theology in The Union Theological College, Belfast.

Iain Torrance lectures in Practical Theology and Systematic Theology in the University of Aberdeen.

Gordon Wakefield is now retired. He was formerly Principal of The Queens' College, Birmingham.

PREFACE

On March 30th 1895 the Senate of the University of Aberdeen honoured one of its own graduates with the award of the degree of Doctor of Divinity. Peter Taylor Forsyth was born and raised in the city, and took his M.A. (an outstanding first class honours in the Department of Classical Literature) at King's College in 1869, spending the subsequent academic session as teaching assistant to the university professor of Latin. In 1872, on the advice of his close friend William Robertson Smith, Forsyth travelled to Göttingen to spend a semester studying under the great German theologian Albrecht Ritschl. It was to be a period which Forsyth later acknowledged as among the most formative factors in his intellectual development. He returned to Britain to train for the ministry of the Congregational churches. By 1895 he had already established a reputation as a bright star in the firmament of Congregationalism, occupying one of its most prestigious pulpits in Cambridge. The decision to award the honorary degree was to prove both prophetic and providential, paving the way as it did for a glittering teaching and writing career as Principal of Hackney College, London. A. M. Hunter records two notable judgments on Forsyth's life and work: that of the agnostic Chancellor of the University of Manchester John Morley, that his was 'one of the most brilliant minds in Europe', and that of the Swiss theologian Emil Brunner, for whom Forsyth ranked as 'the greatest of modern British theologians'. In view of the calibre and achievements of the man, it is both surprising and disappointing that Forsyth's name is not more familiar and his writings more widely consulted by students of theology in the present day.

Forsyth was the invited preacher at a service to mark the University of Aberdeen's quatercentenary celebrations in 1906. In 1995 the university will celebrate its official quincentenary. Fittingly, this will also be the centenary of the award to Forsyth of his D.D. To mark this dual anniversary, and to stimulate and foster renewed interest in Forsyth's theology, the university's Department of

Theology and Church History convened a colloquium on Forsyth's life thought in June 1993. Scholars and research students from across the globe with a particular interest in Forsyth were in attendance. This collection of essays contains many of the papers read at that colloquium. They appear here in the order in which they were originally delivered.

In 1887 the young Forsyth preached a provocative sermon entitled 'Mercy the true and only justice'. It was a striking affirmation of the Ritschlian gospel. God, Forsyth insists here, has no need to meet the demands of any supposed code of justice in order to forgive and to reconcile his creatures. It is God's nature to forgive and, being God, he may do so at his pleasure. Indeed, the only just thing for God to do is to forgive freely and unconditionally, as he himself urges us to do with regard to our enemies. There are many insights in Ritschl's thought which Forsyth was to treasure and to build into his own theology throughout his long career. But the point at which the pupil rebels most notably against the teacher is here at the very centre of things. Justice, Forsyth came in time to believe, must be taken absolutely seriously even by God, for in fact it is nothing other than an expression of God's own eternal nature as the Holy. If God has forgiven us our sins, he insists, then it is in a way which meets the demands of justice and does not ignore or override these. Indeed, a mercy which set aside the demands of holiness would in truth be no real mercy at all, for it would itself be a contradiction both of the being of God and of the being of his creature, rather than a genuine healing and reconciliation between them. Anything less than the realization of God's own righteousness in his creature is cheap grace, and falls short of the biblical gospel. For the mature Forsyth (whose thought this volume explores), in other words, justice is the true and only mercy.

Neither the colloquium nor this volume would have been possible without the support and help of many different people. The Evangelical Fellowship of Congregational Churches, the Unaffiliated Congregational Churches Charities, and the Diocese of Aberdeen and Orkney were generous in their financial support. The University of Aberdeen's Institute for Cultural Studies kindly made its premises available for our use. Particular thanks must go to Dr Leslie McCurdy whose extensive bibliography will be an invaluable tool for those engaged in research on Forsyth and his work, and who has been closely involved in both the planning of the colloquium and the editing of this volume. My thanks are also due to T&T Clark for their willingness to undertake the publication of the essays and for their encouragement and support along the way. Finally, special mention is reserved for one without whose constant personal encouragement and advice the P. T. Forsyth collquium might never have happened, who honoured us by agreeing to prepare and read a paper, and whose presence and participation in the discussions enriched the whole event: the late Professor Donald MacKinnon in memory of whom this book is dedicated.

Trevor Hart
Aberdeen
July, 1994

FOREWORD

Peter Taylor Forsyth has always been taken seriously by some people in some places, but the price paid has often been an oversimplification of his achievement. Perhaps the label of a 'Barthian before Barth' is the most famous, or rather notorious, for it categorises him by means of only one point of comparison, the reaction against certain patterns of nineteenth-century liberalism which he did indeed share, although in a very different way. By contrast, one recent writer who has reappropriated part of Forsyth's legacy, the late Peter Fuller, did so for his art criticism, and that reveals only a beginning of the riches to be mined from this highly distinctive and not easily categorised theologian.

For theologian he was, and it is that above all which the papers in this collection celebrate. The conference from which they come was one of the hardest-working and most interesting I have attended, distinguished above all in the range and depth of the man's interests and reading which the papers revealed. Those who would compare or dismiss Forsyth along with Barth should read especially the account of his predilection for Wagner, and, indeed, his presence at Bayreuth for one first performance. And, as the papers show, he was a systematic theologian only in a rather occasional way, and if he is so judged, appears to operate over a rather restricted range of topics.

What kind of theologian will the reader of this collection encounter? Forsyth was a man of wide culture whose reading was highly eclectic, or perhaps better, catholic. As well as music and painting, there is appeal to drama and other literature – ancient, Shakespearean and modern – to psychology, including that of William James; and to philosophy, above all that of Hegel, the man whom Barth interviewed for the post of the Protestant Aquinas. Nietzsche, too, that paradigm of disillusioned modernity, is taken with the greatest seriousness – unlike the Fathers, who receive rather scant attention.

Despite, or perhaps by means of, his catholicity, there is a kind of personal unity to Forsyth's work, and it is one which derives from the predominance of a theology of the cross. But of this, two things must be said. In the first place, it is very different from the theology of the cross of some recent German theology, dominated as that is by apologetic concerns. There is an apologetic in Forsyth, but as Donald MacKinnon, whose loss we have so recently mourned, demonstrates, it is an apologetic shaped by a highly active conception of a saving God, and thus one which belongs firmly in the tradition of the Christian theology of atonement. Not one inch is conceded to suggestions that God is in some way constrained by suffering, either his own or that of the creation.

In the second place, despite the centre in Christ's atoning death to which Forsyth returns again and again, there is an openness in his thought which contrasts with the single-mindedness of some theologians who are more apparently diverse in their dogmatic interests. Here we return to the question of his eclecticism. There is something distinctive about the freedom of this theologian to read widely, where he felt led, in all kinds of directions, and yet without loss of control. He rarely cites his sources and rarely prints a bibliography, but the breadth and purposefulness of interest is there for all to see. He is thus the best kind of Christian intellectual, the one for whom nothing in heaven or earth is irrelevant to the theological task.

The most mysterious and fascinating of all the questions about Forsyth, the man and the eclectic, concerns his relations with Germany. As the reader will discover, one third of his library was in German, and he was, if not broken, then shaken to the roots of his being by the outbreak of the First World War. This points us to the fact that while much of the British theological tradition had, at that time, been imprisoned by a fear of continental scepticism, in parts of the church the conversation continued, without loss of either intellectual vigour or robust Christian confession. Similarly, we cannot understand this man without some appreciation of his Scottish origins and career as one of the representatives of a tradition of English Dissent then entering a period of decline that has since continued. Nor should we ignore his relation to politics, which has much to say in a day when liberal certainties are still all-pervading and yet increasingly discredited.His sometimes apparently inconsistent position may show us that the options are far wider and more interesting than current political debate usually suggests.

Several of the papers in this collection illuminate the life without ever plumbing the depths of the man. That is as it should be. No human being is fully plumbable, particularly a man of whom the overused word, genius, may be employed without exaggeration. In any case, it is the thought that is likely to be Forsyth's real agency to our and later times. Like all great thought, it bears the marks of its era – was ever a writer more truly particular than Forsyth? – and yet contains treasures that will always be worth seeking out. I hope that the readers of this collection will find a guide to some of the depths that can long continue to be plumbed, but above all, that it will inspire them to read the works of this sometimes perplexing but always remarkable writer.

Colin Gunton
King's College, London
April, 1994

ABBREVIATIONS

The following abbreviations are used in footnotes throughout the volume:

1. Forsyth's books:

Art	Religion in Recent Art: Being Expository Lectures on Rossetti, Burne Jones, Watts, Holman Hunt and Wagner
Authority	The Principle of Authority in Relation to Certainty, Sanctity and Society: An Essay in the Philosophy of Experimental Religion
Charter	The Charter of the Church: Six Lectures on the Spiritual Principle of Nonconformity
Cruciality	The Cruciality of the Cross
Father	God the Holy Father
Freedom	Faith, Freedom and the Future
Justification	The Justification of God: Lectures for War-time on a Christian Theodicy
Life	This Life and the Next: The Effect on This Life of Faith in Another
Marriage	Marriage: Its Ethic and Religion
Missions	Missions in State and Church: Sermons and Addresses
Parables	Pulpit Parables for Young Hearers
Parnassus	Christ on Parnassus: Lectures on Art, Ethic, and Theology
Person	The Person and Place of Jesus Christ
Prayer	The Soul of Prayer
Preaching	Positive Preaching and the Modern Mind
Reunion	Congregationalism and Reunion: Two Lectures
Revelation	Revelation Old and New: Sermons and Addresses
Rome	Rome, Reform and Reaction: Four Lectures on the Religious Situation

Sacraments	[Lectures on] the Church and the Sacraments
Services	Intercessory Services for Aid in Public Worship
Socialism	Socialism, the Church and the Poor
Society	The Church, the Gospel and Society
Theology	Theology in Church and State
War	The Christian Ethic of War
Work	The Work of Christ

2. Other:

| CYB | Congregational Year Book |
| DNB | Dictionary of National Biography |

NB. Footnote references are provided in full in the first instance *except* in the case of any work referred to in the P. T. Forsyth Bibliography (chapter 14).

Chapter 1

P. T. FORSYTH ON THE CHURCH

Stephen Sykes

I accept the challenge of conducting a conversation with P. T. Forsyth's doctrine of the church all the more readily because it appears to be a neglected area. John Rodgers' 1965 study, *The Theology of P. T. Forsyth* specifically admits that the doctrine of the church lies beyond the limits of the work – though for no very obvious reason – and directs the reader to Forsyth's book, *The Church and the Sacraments* (1917). Even in that book, which is essentially the publication of lectures to students, Forsyth states that he proposes to offer a fuller 'theory of the Church' elsewhere.[1] So far as I know he never did so, and died four years later. In effect, therefore, we do not have the systematic treatment of the subject which might have encouraged more critical study and reflection. As it is, Forsyth is largely known for his kenotic theory, and for that most dubious of accolades, on which Professor Thompson has enlightened the conference, 'a Barthian before Karl Barth'.[2]

In this paper, I shall concentrate on his late work, *The Church and the Sacraments*, which has every claim to be his most considerable utterance on ecclesiology. For the understanding of this work, we need to take seriously the remark of his daughter that 'the outbreak of war in 1914 distressed him beyond measure'.[3] As she testifies, one third of his library consisted of German books; he was a regular reader of the German religious press, and loved the German people and nation. Yet he was unrelenting, even fierce in his justification of

---

[1] *Sacraments*, 1st ed., 29.
[2] See Professor Thompson's essay in this volume.
[3] Jessie Forsyth Andrews, 'Memoir', in Forsyth, *Work*, 2nd ed., xxii.

1

the War, and denounced the 'shameful sacrifice of moral to elemental passion'[4] which he claimed to detect in the German enemy.

Of importance for his theology was his sense that the events of this warfare plunged the world into moral chaos. 'Civilisation', he maintained, 'has gone to pieces in the Great War.'[5] Indeed 'the great antithesis of Christianity in the world is "civilisation"'.[6] The experience of the War is of an 'unprecedented revelation of the evil power, the man of sin, the prince of this world'.[7] He continues:

> This discovery means the real end of the Victorian Age, of the comfortable, kindly, bourgeois, casual Victorian age, so credulous in its humanism... . We are in the kind of world-crisis in which creeds are reborn for history. Saint Augustine wrote *The City of God* amid the sack of Rome. We shall therefore need, as none living have ever before felt the need, a religion which shows that it possesses the innate power of the Holy to deal with the wild beast which a high and Christless civilisation shows itself to be.[8]

In many respects the War had a specific and calamitous impact upon English Nonconformity. The early years of the century had seen the high point of its political influence. In 1906, 185 Nonconformist MPs had been elected to Parliament, apparently demonstrating the strength of the 'holy alliance' between political liberalism and the Free Churches. P. T. Forsyth himself had been a passionate defender of Gladstone in his Leicester days. But as Adrian Hastings points out, most of the leading men in that group were lapsed, rather than convinced and practising churchmen, and disillusionment was rapidly setting in.[9] He writes:

> By 1920 the whole experiment was essentially over. If the War had done anything to religion, it had generated such disillusionment as to end decisively a state of politics in which

[4]Andrews, 'Memoir', xxiii.
[5]*Sacraments*, 10.
[6]*Sacraments*, 10.
[7]*Sacraments*, 34.
[8]*Sacraments*, 34.
[9]Adrian Hastings, *A History of English Christianity*, 1920–1985 (London: Collins, 1986), chapter 6.

a religious cause, preached by ministers, could somehow inflame a large part of the nation: but it was not only the War, the inherent contradiction of the alliance ensured that it could not last.[10]

A reading of *The Church and the Sacraments* informed by such an understanding makes sense of those passages which comment explicitly on the Free Churches' 'loss of influence'.[11] Forsyth's reaction is to recall the church to the source of its own authority. He wants it to turn from a 'breezy charity' to 'something more radical, more searching, more permanent, more creative'.[12] It is almost as a direct challenge to the lapsed that he writes:

> We must urge submission to that Gospel – and submission to it we must ask, and not only sympathy. A Gospel which is not exclusive will never include the world, for it will never master it. No religion will include devotees which does not exclude rivals. Half Gospels have no dignity, and no future.[13]

The tone is peremptory, but also anxious; and he knows well enough that he sounds like a 'common scold'.[14] But what he sensed, I believe rightly, is that Protestantism cannot be doing without a strong dogmatic witness; and his resource is plainly central themes of Calvinism, grace, atonement, sacrifice and authority, to construct the foundations of living church practice. The church is the social and practical response to grace.[15] There is therefore but one way of recovering the idea of the church. It is by regaining, on a scale worthy of it, the evangelical faith which made and makes the church always.[16] It is this project of re-gaining, renovation and re-formation that explicitly defines his goal, confronted with the 'crisis in righteousness' which has burst upon history with the War. One senses his agony about the insufficiency of the pulpit rhetoric of revival ('It is,' he says, 'the standing refuge of the feeble to say we

[10]Hastings, 128.
[11]*Sacraments*, 14ff.
[12]*Sacraments*, 15.
[13]*Sacraments*, 15–16.
[14]*Sacraments*, 15.
[15]*Sacraments*, 31.
[16]*Sacraments*, 31.

need a revival').[17] Nonetheless, 'we need a reformation of faith, belief and thought to make the churches adequate to the nation, the world and the age, a bracing up and a coupling of our churches, and a renovated theology as the expression of the church's rich and corporate life'.[18] So far none of the churches have adequately responded, but a 'new theology is on its way'.[19] It is a theology, according to Forsyth, which returns to what makes the church, the church. In so doing, he believes that Christianity will, in effect, rediscover itself as it will come to understand the nature of God's righteousness in the world. In this sense, ecclesiology provides the route into social renewal, and quite properly so, in his view, because of the intrinsic relationship between church and society.

Before we embark on a closer account of the leading features of Forsyth's ecclesiology, I wish to draw attention to the extensive deployment of the word 'power' and its cognates. It would perhaps be too simplistic to speak of a compensatory over-use of power-terms, but recent research has clearly demonstrated in another theologian of the period, Adolf von Harnack, the unacknowledged centrality of power language and power claims.[20] The loss of social prestige and political influence appears to elicit from theologians of the period two types of response. The first is an explicit distancing of the Christian faith and of the church from the exercise of secular power, coupled with criticism of the misuse of such power in earlier centuries; and the second is a reinvestment in, and reinforcement of, the claims for 'the power of the gospel' to transform lives and, perhaps, communities. In both forms of apologetic, there is a certain amount of self-deception. Writers seem unaware both that their perspective on the history of the church may be influenced by their social location in the church's progressive marginalization; and also, that their reinvestment in 'spiritual' power is itself a renewed claim to exercise ideological power, a form of political power, at one remove.

With these considerations in mind, we might analyse some pages of Forsyth which immediately follow the claim that 'a new theology

---

[17] *Sacraments*, 70.

[18] *Sacraments*, 104.

[19] *Sacraments*, 104.

[20] Janet Brigland Pritchard, 'The Theme of Power in the Theology of Adolf von Harnack', Ph.D. thesis, Durham University, 1990.

is on its way'. The argument relates to ecumenism, and Forsyth specifically asserts that there is evidence of ecumenical convergence upon the fundamentals of the gospel, 'the church-making truths'.[21] This is, he claims, bringing into being a tangible and organized unity of churches capable of confronting the organized power of Mammonism. Mere spiritual unity is not sufficient. The tremendous pressure of the world requires a church, animated by a supernatural faith, but possessing 'some collective means of making God's will felt on the historical scale'.[22]

As things stand at the present, Forsyth says he is 'more impressed with the church's impotence in that world of morals and affairs than with its effect'.[23] Apart from their voting power, the Free Churches are 'much too negligible' in the weight of their moral word and of their moral leaders. 'I mean,' he says, 'our power to leaven with Christian ideas the English nation [sic!] as a section of human civilisation'.[24] The problem is our divided, part-Aristotelian, part-Christian mind, which does not have 'the catholic, imperial note of a power more than adequate to the moral redemption and leadership of Humanity'.[25] Forsyth regrets the dominance of talk of social ideals over insight into Christian ethic, and misses any ethical critique on what he calls 'the real crux of the War', namely 'national self-consciousness' and 'national honour'.

Forsyth depicts the declining impact of the Free Churches, who are at home with evangelism, less convincing on labour or education, and at sea with the scale of the 'national question'.

> Are we afraid enough of our inadequacy to it? Do we duly dread a congeries of denominations with no Church feeling or force equal to the evil catholicity of the world spirit and the Church of the degenerate? Our type of religion is not false, but has it that note? If not, our Church idea so far fails the Kingdom of God and knows but a province of it – with the provincial and not the royal note.[26]

---

[21] *Sacraments*, 105.
[22] *Sacraments*, 106.
[23] *Sacraments*, 106.
[24] *Sacraments*, 106.
[25] *Sacraments*, 106–7.
[26] *Sacraments*, 107.

No one, I submit, considering these paragraphs can miss the wrestling with the question of the power of the church in history and society. I sense here a changed tone compared with the earlier volume, *The Principle of Authority* (1913). Here the personal and the institutional are sharply contrasted. (Consider the following passage where the church's authority is said to be created by the gospel, not 'in the sense of a miraculous, hierarchical, statutory, prescriptive, institution, whether curial, conciliar or consistorial, which has come to be a thaumaturgic shrine for the Gospel'.[27] Even by P. T. Forsyth's formidable standards, that strikes one as an over-protestation). By 1917, it seems to me, there is a note of real regret at the Free Churches' 'impotence', in the ordinary meaning of that term, and a desire to reverse it by ecumenical federation – surely an institutional form – with the consequent recapturing of the 'catholic, imperial note'. It is a startling perspective, and perhaps disconcerting in its realism when compared with the pallid embracing of powerlessness beloved of more recent theology. If it lacks the hermeneutics of suspicion as regards its own social location, it breathes a certain authenticity in its bold prescription for its own disjointed times, and is not without relevance to ours.

We turn now to the substance of Forsyth's doctrine of the church, and note in the first place the quite self-conscious refusal of a merely incarnational foundation for ecclesiology. In a work devoted to eucharistic theology, Charles Gore, in 1901, had referred to the well-known formula which speaks of the church as the 'extension of the incarnation'. It was a phrase he repeatedly used, and indeed popularised,[28] but Forsyth would have none of it. Picking up the terms of an earlier tractarian hymn, Forsyth wrote:

> The Church's foundation, and the trust of its ministry, is not simply Christ, but Christ crucified.... . The Church rests on the Grace of God, the judging, atoning, regenerating Grace of God, which is His holy Love in the form it must take with human sin.[29]

As a consequence, the church, Forsyth insists, has a more direct

[27] *Authority*, 2nd ed., 325.
[28] See James Carpenter, *Gore* (London: Faith Press, 1960), 222.
[29] *Sacraments*, 31.

connection with the redemption than with the incarnation. The argument is phrased in a familiar Ritschlian form: 'Only by experience of Redemption has it religious knowledge of what Incarnation means.'[30] Behind the proposal that the church is the extension of the incarnation, Forsyth spies 'the engaging fallacy of liberalism that Christ is but the eternal God-in-man, supremely revealed and carried to a luminous head in Him, but forming always the spirit of Humanity and looking out in every great soul'.[31] The church is founded on the gospel and its relation to Christ derives from his atoning work.

Having distanced himself from what he believes to be the evolutionary optimism of recent Anglican incarnationists, he also decisively separates himself form the liberal Protestants. What he terms 'the Church-building' element in Christ is not his character or his teaching, but his work. The cross, indeed, is his 'condensed word and summary work'.

> As the Holy One He went wholly into His work of the Cross for the sin of the world. The whole value of Christ's Person for the world entered it by that strait gate. He is our God because He is our Redeemer. Our approach to Christology is through the office of Christ as Saviour. We only grasp the real divinity of His person by the value for us of His Cross.[32]

The Ritschlian epistemology is put to work in refutation of exemplarist doctrines of the atonement. To use a distinction which I helpfully learnt from Professor Donald MacKinnon, Forsyth is concerned not just with a doctrine of redemption, but with a real atonement.[33] The language of crisis is thus natural. The cross is 'the crisis of God's righteous judgment, holy grace and new creating conquest of the world'; it is '*the* creative moral crisis of history'.[34]

In the second place, Forsyth specifically identifies holiness as the redemptive moral power of the cross, and thus of the church. God's act in the cross of Christ is an act of judgement, as we have seen. Holiness means judgement, and is the form which grace takes in the

---

[30] *Sacraments*, 76–77.
[31] *Sacraments*, 75.
[32] *Sacraments*, 30.
[33] See, in criticism of Ritschl, the same distinction, *Sacraments*, 81.
[34] *Sacraments*, 3 and 32.

context of sin. Again, Forsyth makes the connection between the gospel and the church's power in the social order totally explicit:

> We need more religion of the kind that gathers about a holy Cross; the kind of religion that goes to the roots of the moral soul, both in God and in man, and does not soften the issue; the kind of religion whose intrinsic nature and property is, by its very origin, to cope finally with the last evil of the world, to turn all that tragedy to victory in our hands, and to make such power, by a real Church, unmistakable to the public.[35]

Surveying the ineffectiveness of high church Anglicanism, Independency and the ethical movements such as Quakerism, he sees the recapturing of the holiness of God as that which will supply a religion 'that provides its public ethic from the same authority in Christ as creates its public worship'.[36]

In Forsyth's opinion, Quakerism's failure is attributable to the fact that 'it has founded on the Sermon rather than the Cross, and on the character of Christ in His life rather than on His person gathered into critical historic action in His death'.[37] Similarly the sacramental tradition has incorporated an ethic of conduct rather than of atonement, and 'has been more concerned with kindly sanctity in men than with the tragic holiness of love in God'.[38] It is the message and power of the crucified Christ which 'at once creates the Church and moralises it'.[39] Moralization, moreover, is what specifically removes the character of the church from the merely natural or psychological. This argument is marshalled against the doctrine that the church is the extension of the incarnation. Christ's presence in the church and the sacraments is neither a human nor a material presence, but a presence 'as in moral beings who in grace left nature behind, and have risen from forces, and laws and psychologies to become wills and consciences that baffle psychology'.[40]

---

[35] *Sacraments*, 33.
[36] *Sacraments*, 33.
[37] *Sacraments*, 56.
[38] *Sacraments*, 56.
[39] *Sacraments*, 47.
[40] *Sacraments*, 70.

It is specifically holiness, in the third place, which provides us with a standpoint from which to criticize democracy. In *The Church and the Sacraments*, Forsyth returns to his earlier insistence that Congregationalism's basic instinct was obedience to Jesus Christ in the face of all the powers and majorities about it, and that it was the mother of political democracy not its child.[41] Indeed he repeats and again italicizes a proposition which encapsulates his objection to the establishment of democracy in the Church: '*Democracy will recognise no authority but what it creates, the Church none but what creates it*'.[42] Forsyth evidently sees democracy as the 'civil religion' of freedom. However, in his view all freedom is to be judged by the Word, which is no 'vassal or colleague of the world'.[43] That proposition is as true for the Free Churches who mistakenly glory in the word 'free', as it is of political democracies. The slavish celebration of freedom and democracy robs the Church of its fulcrum outside the world.[44]

To some of these criticisms there are Nietzschian overtones. Democracy, we read, 'tends to resent excellence, to be at home with mediocrity, to idolise comfort as the rich do luxury, to be suspicious of the king, the competent, and the prophet'.[45] In due course, there is bound to be a great struggle between the church and the natural democracy.[46] But Forsyth is content to let democrats off with a warning. If democracy is not itself the kingdom of God, it offers the 'most possibility for the Kingdom if taken in hand'.[47] His real aim, however, is to establish the legitimacy and self-confidence of a 'rebuking and demanding church'. Democracy was 'made by a Calvinism which did not humour human nature, and did not believe in it till God had done with it'.[48]

---

[41] *Freedom*, 193.
[42] *Freedom*, 192. *Sacraments*, 109, reads: 'whereas a Church has no authority but what creates it'. Compare also: 'A democracy recognises no authority but what arises from itself, and a Church none but what is imposed on it from without.' *Authority*, 253.
[43] *Sacraments*, 7.
[44] *Sacraments*, 5.
[45] *Sacraments*, 11.
[46] *Sacraments*, 10.
[47] *Sacraments*, 11.
[48] *Sacraments*, 12.

So Forsyth will have no truck with the suggestion that the church is, or should be, a democracy. The church is not based, he asserts, 'on natural right, or natural fraternity, or natural ideals. It is based on total surrender to an absolute monarch and owner in Christ'.[49] And because the church is not a fraternity, a minister is an apostle to the church, a servant of the Word; a prophetic and sacramental officer, not an employee, a secretary or a president.[50] Passages of this kind lead directly, of course, to the discussion of apostolic succession in ministerial office to which we shall have to return.

Fourthly, the Church is not, insists Forsyth, a 'religious club', though some of its members plainly use it as such. He recognizes that Congregationalism, with its principle of voluntary association, lends itself to this distorted perspective, and he admits that Episcopalian critics are justified in urging the need for 'a more clear, arresting, guiding, and commanding theory of the Church and its ministry'.[51] Such a theory of the church he has already provided in his insistence on the foundational quality of the atoning act of Christ. His theory of the ministry has corresponding force in its emphasis on the sacramental bearing of the active Word of God. But to meet the persisting individualism of Protestantism, Forsyth unequivocally asserts the corporate nature of the church. In words which confound the classic distinction between the allegedly opposed principles of Catholicism and of Protestantism formulated by Friedrich Schleiermacher, Forsyth insists: 'To enter Christ is in the same act to enter the Church which is in Christ. Faith in Christ is faith in One whose indwelling makes a Church, and who carries a Church within His corporate Person.'[52] Thus fellowship in the community of the church is not an adjunct to the spiritual, inward religion of the individual. The church was the body of Christ long before it was an organization; it is in fact the organism which Christ is, so that '*the same act which sets us in Christ sets us also in the society of Christ*'.[53]

It is out of such a theological conviction that the necessity of ecumenism derives. A principal thrust of Forsyth's ecclesiology is to

[49] *Sacraments*, 11.
[50] *Sacraments*, 123ff.
[51] *Sacraments*, 27.
[52] *Sacraments*, 40.
[53] *Sacraments*, 57.

urge the need and possibility of a united church through a federation of churches in which each respect, honour and accept the polity of the others. The basis of such a federation would be agreement in the gospel and not the imposition of a uniform polity. The agreement is objective, not subjective or the result of sympathies and affinities. 'It would be no contractual thing, a matter of covenant, a thing of which the ecclesiastics would be the engineers and not the ministers.'[54]

It is striking how close to Eastern Orthodoxy is Forsyth's vision of the church's unity, in the relation of local to universal. Far from seeing the Great Church as a coagulation of local churches he, rather, insists on seeing the Great Church as the prior reality, of which the local churches are but outcrops.[55]

As regards organization or structural unity, he strongly resists the development whereby, as in Catholicism, the church came to be identified with a statutory polity. On the contrary, for the New Testament church leadership is charismatic, and 'if the element of polity became necessary in history, it must always be in such a way as to keep this idea uppermost, and not smother it as Catholicism does'.[56] In reading Forsyth on this topic, one is immediately reminded of the work of Arthur Michael Ramsey, *The Gospel and the Catholic Church* (1936), with its broad acceptance (indeed quotation) of Forsyth's principle, but its argument that the outward order of the church is related to the church's inner meaning, indeed to the gospel itself. Ramsey's words are worth quoting:

> The good news that God has visited and redeemed His people includes the redeemed man's knowledge of death and resurrection through his place in the one visible society and through the death to self which every member and group has died. And in telling of this one visible society the Church's outward order tells indeed of the Gospel. For every part of the Church's true order will bear witness to the one universal family of God and will point to the historic events of the Word-made-flesh... . A Baptism, a Eucharistic service, an

[54] *Sacraments*, 58.
[55] This particular expression is found in the summary paragraphs introducing chapter 3.
[56] *Sacraments*, 63.

Apostle, in themselves tell us of our death and resurrection and of the Body which is one.[57]

Forsyth plainly sees the force of the claim for the episcopate, but resists it. It is the Word of God which creates the apostolate, and to the few original apostles there are strictly speaking no successors. Neither did the apostolate have a monopoly, since the same Word created a great company of others, prophets, enthusiasts and preachers, who also were regarded as vehicles of the Spirit. Forsyth realizes that judgement was needed in distinguishing true from false prophets, but on the basis of the Johannine epistle denies that the judgement of the local bishop was invoked as decisive. Rather it was 'the Church *of the gospel*' which had this responsibility. 'The Church had ... the duty and power to recognise or refuse the new message as a God-given charisma of evangelical truth.'[58]

This discriminating or selective power is strongly affirmed by Forsyth, who, as we have seen, is concerned to maintain the apostolic gift of the ministry to the church. But he will not allow 'successors' to the apostles, preferring the term 'surrogate'. What made the original apostle in the first place, namely the Word, likewise makes the ministerial surrogate for the apostolate:

The ministry is ... not the canonical prolongation of the Apostolate any more than the Church is the prolongation of the Incarnation. The Church is the product of the Incarnation, and the ministry is a gift to the Church. It is not the prolongation of the Apostolate but a substitute, with a like end, and on its base. The prolongation of the Apostolate and the legatee of its unique authority (I have said) is the New Testament, as the precipitate of the apostolic preaching at first hand.[59]

---

[57] A. M. Ramsey, *The Gospel and the Catholic Church*, 2nd ed. (London: Longmans, Green, 1956; orig. pub. 1936), 50. This inclusion of apostolic order within the gospel has further commended itself, we should note, to Cardinal Ratzinger and the Congregation for the Doctrine of the Faith, in its most recent letter on the subject of 'Communion', to the Bishops of the Roman Catholic Church ('Some Aspects of the Church as Communion', 1992).

[58] *Sacraments*, 127.

[59] *Sacraments*, 129.

This rather surprising assertion – surprising in so far as it is resolutely the text of the New Testament, not the 'Word' in Forsyth's more habitual sense, which is identified as the successor of the apostolate — is not phrased with complete consistency in an earlier passage:

> The strict successor of the Apostles [says Forsyth] is the New Testament, as containing the precipitate of their standard preaching. It is not the ministry that is the successor of the Apostolate, but the ministry *plus* the true apostolic legacy of the Bible – the ministry *of the Word.* The ministry is the successor of the Apostles only as the prolongation of their Bible – as the nervous system spreads the brain.[60]

Is it then *both* the ministry *and* the Bible, or just the New Testament, which is the successor of the apostles? Forsyth's imprecision at this point is frustrating. Had Forsyth elucidated more fully a view of the Scriptures as kerygma, the written Word being the precipitate of the 'event' of preaching then he might not have seemed so confusing in his attempt to show that the succession to the apostles is found when the 'event' is renewed in the contemporary act of preaching by the ministry.[61]

It is here that I would like to engage Forsyth in a conversation. It is one conducted on my side with the greatest appreciation and respect. The catholic Calvinism of Forsyth's dogmatics, together with his perceptive and trenchant moral criticism of some of the fruits of the European Enlightenment, I find deeply attractive. He is, of course, a scold and knows it, and his rhetoric leads to unclarity. But repeatedly there are shafts of intuitive brilliance, and his theological and exegetical instincts are of a very high order.

At the same time there are doubts which rise quite sharply from the unquestionable fact that this is second article ecclesiology. It is not for nothing that he repeatedly challenges the hymn-line 'the Church's one foundation is Jesus Christ her Lord' with the insistence that the *crucified* Lord is the foundation of the church. But what of the first article, and of the third? The work of the Holy Ghost, when referred to, is nearly always reduced solely to the work

---

[60] *Sacraments*, 128.
[61] I am indebted to Professor John Thompson for his clarification of P. T. Forsyth at this point.

of regeneration. The dangers of creation-immanentism and romantic spirituality have so strongly steered Forsyth away from any alternative to redemption-centred ecclesiology that a legitimate trinitarianism has been sacrificed. This is evident in the curious insistence that the presence of Christ in the church and sacraments is at the level of a moral order in which grace has left nature behind.[62] There is here a challengeable negativity about creation, which makes the construal of the life of the actual, historic church puzzling and frankly implausible. The created order is fallen, and capable of appalling evil. But Forsyth's impressionistic brush occasionally does not scruple to represent the whole by its worst features, perhaps particularly in this book, written under the shock of the Great War. The condemnation of 'civilisation' and the 'world' on the basis of the worst to which it stoops is an example of this tendency. There is much to be said on the other side, which ought to be said, and not taken as evidence for an equally implausible, credulous humanism.

A trinitarian ecclesiology would insist, I believe, on the existence of a created sociality, a being of humankind with one another, a natural *koinonia* productive of many forms of human good, though without the means to rescue humankind from great and pervasive evils. A trinitarian ecclesiology would not be so fearful, or reticent about, the work of the Spirit within and outside the church, both creative and subversive of order and discipline. Here one wants to express dissatisfaction with Forsyth's handling of the theme of the development of church structures, especially as sketched in *Faith, Freedom and the Future*. He correctly sees that none of the modern church orders are strictly embodied and taught in the New Testament. He has read his Sohn, Hatch and Harnack; but he does not seem to have taken adequate account of Loisy. The New Testament documents reveal churches in process of being obliged to organize themselves with specific concrete structures. On the necessity for visible unity Forsyth is admirable, as he is on the authority of the ministry. But at the points where one imagines that he will grant that the episcopate fulfils these conditions, he relapses into polemics; Catholicism is simply discussed as a stifling bureaucracy or 'supernatural spiritualism', and the episcopate, monopolistic and anticharismatic. Then there is the puzzling imprecision about whether

---

[62] *Sacraments*, 70.

the Bible, the New Testament, or both, together with the ministry
constitute a true succession to the apostles. All these features I trace
to a lack of confidence in a fully trinitarian ecclesiology which can
embrace the created order, the redemption, and the eschatological
gift of new life, within a visibly united, but not uniform church.

At the same time, justice requires me to say that many of his
critical remarks about Anglicanism and Episcopalianism were thoroughly appropriate in his day, and subsequently. In many of the
difficulties which he identified, both in culture and in the church,
we are still perceptibly embroiled. No one can fail to read his work
without profit, and the attention we give him in this conference is
to a man conscious that he was ordained to be a sacrament to his
church, and not only to his church.

Chapter 2

MORALITY, ATONEMENT AND THE DEATH OF JESUS: THE CRUCIAL FOCUS OF FORSYTH'S THEOLOGY

Trevor A. Hart

1. Introductory

The substance and structure of this paper is summed up in the tripartite division in the first part of my title. The second part of the title indicates, as it were, the umbrella topic; the cross as a focal point in Forsyth's theology. This is, of course, a very big umbrella! I seriously doubt whether Forsyth had more to say on any topic, or returned more frequently to any facet of Christian faith, than the cross. There can hardly be a book or an article within his extensive corpus in which some reference or allusion to it is not made, and in most it dominates page after page, whether the ostensible theme be the doctrine of God, the church, ethics, the sacraments, society, or whatever. All is concluded *sub specie crucis*. Thus a paper on Forsyth's theology of the cross opens itself to the temptation of becoming a paper on his theology as a whole, a temptation which I have resisted. Our focus is to be on Forsyth's theology of atonement in particular.

Even this more narrowly defined field, however, presents a significant challenge to the assiduous scholar. For while the larger body of Forsyth's theology lives and breathes only as it is supplied with oxygen by the capillaries which lead ultimately to and from its heart in the crucified Jesus, it is, nonetheless, virtually impossible to isolate any comprehensive or coherent system from the living body of his thought even about this most central of concerns. The occasional and *ex tempore* nature of many of his works and his

16

frequently passionate and rhetorical style defy such cold and calcu-
lating analysis. He himself refused the attempt to map the complex
logical connections which lay tacit in his theological unconscious,
thereby presenting any would-be commentator with the challenge
of attempting to do so for him. Again, I have resisted this temptation; partly because it has been attempted by others, and partly
because even this task would occupy more time than the confines of
a paper such as this can reasonably afford.

An alternative approach might have been to seek to trace the
development of Forsyth's thinking about the cross through the forty
years or so of his publishing career. But if my reading in the field has
convinced me of anything, it is that while there is certainly some
development to be charted, in broad terms his understanding
changed relatively little from the mid-1880s until the time of his
death in 1921. There is a change of emphasis and expression to be
discerned, but little, I think, of theological substance. There was, of
course, that one determinative change of direction which saw him
part company with the Ritschlian theological education he had
received in Göttingen and which during his early parish ministry
shaped his preaching decisively. The one significant piece dating
from this period of his life, a sermon preached in his first charge in
Shipley, Bradford in 1877, and entitled 'Mercy the True and Only
Justice' reads like a manifesto for the very theological liberalism
which he was to attack so fiercely in later years, and is hardly
recognizable as the work of the same man. By the time of the
appearance of *The Old Faith and the New*, in 1891, the theological
Rubicon had clearly been crossed, and Forsyth was already engaged
in that programmatic recanting of the Liberal Protestant gospel
which was to occupy him for the rest of his life. Somewhere, in the
decade which separates these two pieces of writing, Forsyth had
undergone something resembling a conversion experience, a profound discovery of the moral reality of his circumstances under
God, a transition, as he himself would have it, 'from a Christian to
a believer, from a lover of love to an object of grace'.[1] It was a
transition which was to colour all that followed and to drive it with
an existential passion.

The way from love to grace lay across a deep chasm of natural
human resentment and theological repentance, a chasm bridged

---

[1] *Preaching*, 3rd ed., 193.

only at one point, across which Forsyth himself had stumbled, and to which he henceforth sought to lead his readers and fellow travellers – namely the cross of Christ and all that it signified. Across the ravine lay a 'strange new world' in which this same cross dominated every horizon, and which Forsyth spent the rest of his life seeking to map and to describe for the benefit of those who had not yet been there for themselves.

In this paper, then, what I want to do is to touch briefly on some of the more significant landmarks in his account. I shall look firstly at the ultimate interpretive key for making sense of the cross – the moral order; secondly, at the necessity for an atonement arising out of this context; and thirdly, at the place of the death of Jesus within this atonement, and just what this reveals to us about the nature of the atonement itself.

2. The Ethical as the Ontological

Perhaps the most striking facet of the universe as viewed through the eyes of an 'object of grace' is its irreducibly moral structure. There is, according to Forsyth, a 'moral order' which is just as surely woven into the fabric of God's creation as that other 'order' which is investigated by the natural sciences. Indeed, in terms of the status of our knowledge, the moral must be said to be more ultimate and more reliable than either the physical or the intellectual.[2] With more than a century and a half of the back and forth of the philosophical quest for epistemic certainty in his sights, Forsyth insists that it is in the practical reason alone, and not the pure, that real authority is to be had;[3] and that the moral order, unlike the physical, lays hold of us through the organ of conscience in a direct manner, rather than being at best an inference (however trustworthy) from data rendered by our sensory apparatus.[4] As fundamentally moral beings, we find ourselves engaged more naturally and immediately with this stratum of reality than with the bodily world of our spatial and temporal

---

[2]See e.g. *The Old Faith and the New* (1891), 25.
[3]'The Cross as the Final Seat of Authority' (1899), in *The Gospel and Authority*, 165.
[4]*Preaching*, 48.

intercourse. Forsyth does not develop this latent dualism but he is quite adamant that, whether we recognize it or not, ultimate reality is moral[5] and the questions which really matter concerning human life are moral questions. 'The last reality', he writes, 'is a moral reality … it has to do with a moral situation.'[6] 'The last reality, and that with which every man has willy-nilly to do, is not a reality of thought, but of life and conscience, and of judgment. We are in the world to act and to take the consequences.'[7] 'That is the final human question – how to face the eternal moral power. What is it making of us? What is He doing with us? What is He going to do? That is the issue of all issues.'[8]

This conviction that as human beings we inhabit a moral, as well as a physical, universe and not a multiverse, that a universal and objective moral structure is given to our experience just as surely as the 'laws' of gravitation and thermodynamics, that our actions and their consequences are plottable within a moral and not just a physical framework of cause and effect, is a function of Forsyth's supreme emphasis on the holiness of God. This holiness, Forsyth protests in the face of certain contemporary uses of the term, consists not in some aesthetic quality, the sublime and mysterious remoteness of a snowy alpine peak,[9] but in absolute moral authority[10] and a passionate and unswerving opposition to sin and evil in all its forms. It is holiness, and not love (at least, love only in the distinct form of *holy* love) which is most fundamental to God's nature. That this same God should invest his creation with so direct a reflection of his own being, then, ought not to surprise us unduly. To say 'ultimate reality is moral' is in effect to say God is holy love.

It is interesting to note that while the theme of the *imago Dei* finds little explicit treatment or development in Forsyth's theology (a fact which reflects his relative neglect of the doctrine of creation as a whole), it is here if anywhere that the idea enters in, as he refers repeatedly to conscience not just as that in humans which keys them directly into the moral order and in and through which God

---

[5]'Christ's Person and His Cross' (1917), 15.
[6]*Cruciality*, 1st ed., 121.
[7]*Cruciality*, 121.
[8]*Cruciality*, 119.
[9]*Preaching*, 207–8.
[10]Cf. *Society*, 19.

addresses them, but as something which both share in common. 'What is the atonement,' he asks, 'but the "satisfaction" of the conscience – God's and man's – the adjustment, the pacification, of conscience, and especially God's?'[11] Reconciliation is not, as the Ritschlians would have it, a matter of two hearts making up, or of an adjustment in which humans open themselves and their lives to God, but a mater of two consciences making good.[12] Our conscience would demand a satisfaction for our sin, says Forsyth, even if God did not,[13] a fact of our moral psychology 'the root of [which] is really in God's, who so made man in his image that the transgressor's way is hard'.[14] Conscience, Forsyth observes elsewhere, may be thought of as the moral nature of God in the constitution of human beings.[15]

This perception of the moral as the real, the ethical as the ontological, finds further expression in Forsyth's description, contra Hegel, of the ultimate cosmic and eschatological scheme of things not as the self-realization of *Geist* but of the Holy in history. 'The great object of things is not the self-expression of the Eternal in time,' he writes, 'but His self-effectuation as holy in a Kingdom.'[16] 'Holiness is the eternal moral power which must do, and do, till it sees itself everywhere.'[17] In biblical terms, this is articulated in the command of the Lord to Israel 'be holy, for I am holy' (Lev 11.45); a command which, Forsyth insists, expresses a concern proper to the very nature of God, and without the satisfactory resolution of which he cannot rest. Thus we might say that the realization or effectuation of the kingdom is that alone which can 'satisfy' God. Certainly, as we shall see, the sense in which Forsyth applies the term 'satisfaction' to the atonement is determined by this specific framework of understanding. In an important sense, as we shall see also, this self-realization, for Forsyth as for Hegel, ultimately entails self finding itself in the other: although in this case, it is not in the realization of any latent principle within the other, but of God's self becoming the

[11] *Cruciality*, 116.
[12] 'Christ's Person and His Cross', 8.
[13] *The Preaching of Jesus and the Gospel of Christ* (1987; orig. pub. as articles, 1915), 88.
[14] 'Christ's person and His Cross', 8; cf. *Work*, 166.
[15] *The Atonement in Modern Religious Thought* (1900; orig. pub. 1899), 86.
[16] *Preaching*, 209.
[17] *Preaching*, 240.

other in the kenotic act of incarnation, and 'realizing' his own holiness *in* the other through atoning action.[18] This could be achieved, Forsyth notes, 'only by bringing to practical effect an answering and trusting holiness on a world scale amid the extremest conditions created by human sin.'[19] If one wanted a concise statement of Forsyth's understanding of just what was achieved in the atonement, one would have to search long and hard to find a better formulation than this.

God's nature as the Holy, then, of which the moral structuring of reality and the moral constitution of human beings as those who exist under its jurisdiction are but created reflections, or expressions, is the supreme concern which underlies and drives all existence towards its goal, God's and ours. It is that with which God himself is, and must inevitably be, chiefly concerned;[20] and it is the question which is set uncomfortably over against each of us as we live our lives: just how do we stand here? What will be our fate or our destiny? All in all, the text inscribed on the portals of God's universe (and the one which Forsyth never tires of citing) is 'Hallowed be Thy Name'.[21]

When all this is borne in mind, it is hardly surprising to find Forsyth suggesting over and over again that the liberalism of his theological youth, with the rather naïve, sentimental and optimistic account of the nature of the moral relationship between God and humanity which it proffered, must be abandoned as a dangerous substitute for Christianity of the apostolic and evangelical sort. To get it wrong *here* was inevitably to get it wrong throughout. And get it wrong Forsyth believed they had: not only the theologians, but the whole ethos of the age was, he suggested, one caught up in a crisis of moral direction and authority which made the intellectual despair of the eighteenth and nineteenth centuries seem trivial by comparison. Having all but lost any sense of God's holiness, the age had lost sight of its moral bearings, and lost sight, above all, of the reality of the human situation as one of guilt and liability to judgement and wrath, terms which Forsyth never shies away from, although the

---

[18]See 'The Preaching of Jesus and the Gospel of Christ: The Meaning of a Sinless Christ' (1923): 298.
[19]'The Preaching of Jesus', 299.
[20]See *Justification*, 1st ed., 3.
[21]*Father*, 5.

meaning with which he invests them is somewhat sanitized, or at least refined, by comparison with their use in the Protestant orthodoxy of earlier centuries.

To some extent, Forsyth argues, what his generation faced was the problem of Christianity having to be rescued from its own moral success.[22] After more than a millennium of the saturation of society by Christian moral precepts and attitudes, 'man's devilry' had become well-disguised, overlaid by a thin but effective veneer of moral respectability and social norms. Too many generations had been 'born good',[23] born and baptized into the church with its moral code and expectations. The boundary between the redeemed and the unredeemed, grace and nature, had become difficult to discern. Compounded by a theology which viewed God in essentially aesthetic rather than moral terms and presented Christianity as 'just human nature at its best' and the kingdom of God as 'just our natural spirituality and altruism developed',[24] the net result was a complete and utter loss of perspective on the reality of the human situation. 'So much of our religious teaching betrays no sign that the speaker has descended into hell, been near the everlasting burnings, or been plucked from the awful pit. He has risen with Christ ... but it is out of a shallow grave, with no deepness of earth, with no huge millstone to roll away.'[25] Again, 'it was not Galahad or Arthur that drew Christ from heaven. It was a Lancelot race. It was a tragic issue of man's passion that called out the glory of Christ. It is a most tragic world, this, for those who see to the bottom of it and leave us their witness to its confusion, as Shakespeare did in *Hamlet, Lear* and even *The Tempest*'.[26] Needless to say, Forsyth does not consider the tragedians of the literary world to have had the final say. The gospel, he insists, is precisely the story of the *transformation* of the human tragedy into God's great *commedia*.[27] But the actual moral situation of the race, considered apart from Christ, is one of tragic dimensions. In order to see things as they really are, we must recapture a

[22]'The Cross as the Final Seat of Authority' (1899), in *The Gospel and Authority*, 152.

[23] *The Gospel and Authority*, 152.

[24] *Work*, 10.

[25] *Society*, 100.

[26] *Society*, 102.

[27] *Preaching*, 234.

due sense of God's holiness, or lay hold of the moral order with its absolute demands, and consider ourselves in its light. The starting point for such a re-evaluation must be the cross of Christ since 'We only learn the Christian measure of our sin when we see what the sin of our sinful race means for Christ'.[28]

There can be little doubt that in all this we hear Forsyth speaking powerfully from the depths of his own personal experience. Yet he is not merely insisting that all Christian experience should be like his. He fervently believes the realization of guilt and its accompanying factors to be proper to the experience of salvation,[29] and believes that in objective terms all humans are united at this one point at least – that all have breached that moral order which must not be breached,[30] have challenged the very holiness of God, and thereby stand liable to judgement. 'Love in the face of sin,' he writes, 'can only assert itself as holy love; but that means as stung and wounded love. But assert itself it must … by really judging and subjugating once for all the unholy thing everywhere, killing it in its eye, and replacing Satan's Kingdom by the Kingdom of God.'[31] To fail to face up to the reality of this situation, to pretend that it is otherwise than this with God and human beings, is to fail to take seriously enough either sin or (therefore) grace, and to fail to do justice to the reality of moral personality in either God or humanity.[32]

Two further elements in Forsyth's thinking about the place of the moral are worthy of brief mention before we turn our attention to the atonement. First, while he sets human existence clearly within the framework of a universal and objective moral order, and while he speaks of conscience as that aspect of our nature which is keyed directly into this order,[33] as our bodies key us, *mutatis mutandis*, into the physical order, Forsyth entertains no optimism about the ability of humans by virtue of natural capacities to grasp what is the good in any given context, let alone to do it. In fact there is a manifest tension in his thinking here. On the one hand, he can speak of

---

[28] *Society*, 115.
[29] See e.g. *Preaching*, 45.
[30] See e.g. *Father*, 10.
[31] 'The Preaching of Jesus', 298–9.
[32] 'Christ's Person and His Cross', 8.
[33] See e.g. *Work*, 122.

conscience as speaking to us of the moral order,[34] as a moral power within us yet in a sense other than us,[35] as the Word of God within us,[36] yet immediately he qualifies this so as to undermine any of the moral optimism which so characterized the liberal accounts in the wake of Kant (most of which were far more optimistic, it must be said, than Kant himself). 'We must take man in his actual historic situation,' Forsyth writes, 'and if we do this the so-called natural conscience does not exist. It is an abstraction; and what exists is the historic product, the sinful conscience.'[37] Here we hear a theme which is sustained throughout his theology. The relationship between the natural and the redeemed, between nature and grace, is one not of continuity and evolution but of radical discontinuity and revolution. Redemption comes, when it comes, to each of us as a crisis in which we discover ourselves to be called into question. The 'natural' response to the gospel message, therefore, is not one of welcome but of rejection:[38] the drawing near of the holy in human form to the sinful results in his crucifixion. And in a sense it is ever thus.[39] We are not merely wayward or naughty children, but prodigals. We need not to be improved or developed, but put to death and recreated.[40] In Forsyth's own inimitable rhetoric, God's reconciling revelation 'does not come to grout the gaps in nature, not simply to bless nature, but to change it, to make a new earth from a new foundation in a new heaven'.[41]

This is so much the case that, Forsyth insists, we are not even capable of perceiving the need for the atoning work of Christ, let alone of responding appropriately to it, apart from the power of that work itself acting upon us. 'The death of Christ,' he writes, 'had to redeem us into power of feeling its own worth. Christ had to save us from what we were too far gone to feel.'[42] 'Before the revealing act is complete we must by the act be also put in a position to receive it and appreciate it. The word must not return void, else it is but a

---

[34] *Work*, 123.
[35] *Cruciality*, 131.
[36] *Cruciality*, 132.
[37] 'The Cross as the Final Seat of Authority', 173.
[38] *Work*, 28.
[39] *Work*, 23.
[40] *Justification*, 80.
[41] *Justification*, 77.
[42] *Work*, 18.

sound. The circle must be closed for the spark.'[43] The message of the cross, we might say, creates its own point of contact.

Secondly, Forsyth speaks frequently of the moral order in such a way as to differentiate it from the moral condition of humankind as that is evident at the empirical level. He refers to 'the real world unseen',[44] a mystical or hidden realm in which the kingdom is already a reality,[45] the holy has already achieved self-realization through the ministry of Christ. 'It is,' Forsyth writes, 'a solemn and fortifying thought that interior to all space, time, and history there is a world where God's name is perfectly hallowed, His will fully done, and His Kingdom already come.'[46] This hidden realm is the world of the 'real', as opposed to the world of the 'actual',[47] and the purpose of God is that which has been achieved in reality should now be 'followed up and secured in actuality'. It is tempting to lose patience with such talk, asking irritably precisely where this other world is to be found, and supposing it to be some quaint rhetorical way of asserting something which is better couched in eschatological terms. But, to return to our starting point, we must recall that for Forsyth the moral order is the most ultimate reality, being, as it were, the extension of God's moral personality into the creaturely realm. Hence what he seems to be insisting here, and it is a view which his doctrine of atonement goes on to develop, is that in Christ something happens in the historical sphere which yet has meaning and value discernible only when we cast our gaze beyond that sphere; that Jesus' saving activity, rooted as it is in history, was not confined to the theatre of the human story, but, supremely at the point of the cross, has its deepest meaning only within the telling of God's story.[48] Something happened there which, whatever its impact on humans, and whatever its historical consequences, had decisive consequences for God himself, 'establishing the kingdom' in the very life of God which is the moral order, bringing the Holy to an effective self-realization which must subsequently work itself out

---

[43] *The Old Faith and the New*, 17.
[44] So, e.g., Society, 10.
[45] *Society*, 12, 21.
[46] *Justification*, 156.
[47] See *Work*, 77.
[48] *Cruciality*, 111, 204.

more widely in the historical realm. What we have here, then, is something akin to the eschatological tension between the 'already' and the 'not yet' in the New Testament theology of the kingdom, in which the 'already' is understood as referring to an adjustment made within the very nature or life of God, and the 'not yet' to its eventual actualization in the human sphere.

3. Atonement – Justice the True and Only Mercy

Let me embark on this section with a lengthy citation:

> Judicial punishment can never be inflicted simply and solely as a means to forward a good, other than itself, whether that good be the benefit of the criminal, or of civil society; but it must at all times be inflicted on him, for no other reason than *because he has acted criminally....* He must first of all be found to be *punishable*, before there is even a thought of deriving from the punishment any advantage for himself or his fellow-citizens. The penal law is a categorical imperative; and woe to that man who crawls through the serpentine turnings of the happiness-doctrine, to find out some consideration, which, by its promise of advantage, should free the criminal from his penalty, or even from any degree thereof ... If justice perishes, then it is no more worth while that man should live upon the earth.

The words are not those of Forsyth, but of Kant, cited by F. H. Bradley in his essay on 'the vulgar notion of responsibility'.[49] The sentiments, however, express admirably Forsyth's attitude towards the relationship between human sin and divine judgement, argued in the face of what had come to be an unspoken assumption of the theology of his day, namely, that punishment, where it existed, was acceptable only if reformative rather than retributive, and that God was of such a sort as had no final *need* to exact judgement on sin, but could simply forgive it in a supreme act of voluntaristic mercy. For

---

[49]F. H. Bradley, *Ethical Studies*, 2nd ed. (Oxford: Clarendon, 1962; orig. pub. 1876), 28.

Forsyth judgement, and thereby atonement, is an absolute necessity as the basis for reconciliation between God and humankind.[50]

This insistence rests on Forsyth's assertion of the moral order as the real. This order, he insists, is objective and universal, and is not to be tampered with. It is not a bylaw arbitrarily imposed and therefore readily suspended;[51] it is an eternal and unchangeable ordinance the demands of which must be met.[52] It inheres in the very nature of reality, is as much a part of the fabric of the universe as the molecular structure of hydrogen or the force of gravity, and it cannot be set aside or indeed broken without the moral structure of reality being placed at risk.[53] Thus, when its laws are broken, restitution must follow; holiness, says Forsyth, must assert itself in the face of evil, must *heal* itself.[54] In more traditional soteriological terms, sin creates a situation of guilt, and judgement must follow, otherwise the structure of our existence, and with it the very meaning of what it is to be human, begins to disintegrate. In Kant's words, 'if justice perishes, then it is no more worthwhile that man should live upon the earth'. 'The dignity of man,' Forsyth insists, 'would be better assured if he were shattered on the inviolability of this holy law than if for his mere happy existence it were ignored.'[55] God, he suggests, is more concerned for our dignity as his creatures than for our happiness[56] – or, again, the chief concern of the Holy is to find his holiness reflected and reciprocated in his creature. God, therefore, could not waive his moral order, but must honour it,[57] for the guilt of humanity is no mere matter of private and personal affront, but rather of a public justice,[58] a public truth, in which God must

[50]Forsyth acknowledged his debt to Kant in this regard in a short article in *The Christian World*, 24 September 1908: 'In respect of the place of law.... If Hooker was my first teacher ... my second was Burke, ... But my greatest was the father of modern thought – Kant.... I will add that to my mind the thing most needful in our theological education, after a knowledge of the Bible, is that each student should be examined in Kant, "the philosopher of Protestantism", before he begins the study of theology at the plastic time when mind is made or not at all.'

[51]*Preaching*, 243.

[52]*The Atonement in Modern Religious Thought*, 66.

[53]*Father*, 9–10.

[54]'The Preaching of Jesus', 298.

[55]*The Atonement in Modern Religious Thought*, 66.

[56]*Preaching*, 118.

[57]*Preaching*, 213.

[58]*Preaching*, 213.

safeguard not his own honour or his own feelings, but truth itself. It is in this sense, I think, that Forsyth insists that the cross is the *crisis* of the moral universe:[59] he plays on the underlying Greek meaning, but exploits the ambiguity of the English word to the full. The judgement is a crisis point because without it, apart from it, the very nature of things would be put at risk. The cross, as the point where God's judgement is effective once and for all, is thus the moral Armageddon of the race,[60] the longed-for Day of the Lord, the Last Judgement,[61] which safeguards the moral soul and future of humanity, reorganizing the very structure of the universe at its most real level.[62]

But we must not lose sight in all this of what, for Forsyth, is the most significant fact of all. Since, as we have already seen, the moral order is really nothing other than the holy nature of God viewed in relation to, and expressed within, the fabric of his creature. To say that the moral law is eternal and inviolable is not to set some third entity over against God and the universe, but precisely to say that it is God's holy being which necessitates judgement, that the cross is a crisis for God as well as for his creature, and that in a profound sense, it actually safeguards God's own existence, since it deals with that which puts his very being under threat. Forsyth is not afraid of such strong language or such radical conclusions. 'The holy law,' he writes, 'is not the creation of God but His nature, and it cannot be treated as less than inviolable and eternal, it cannot be denied or simply annulled unless He seems false to Himself. If a play on words be permitted in such a connection,' he adds, 'the self-denial of Christ was there because God could not deny Himself'.[63]

> Sin is the death of God. Die sin must or God. Its nature is to go on from indifference to absolute hostility and malignantly to the holy; and one must go down. There is no compromise possible between the holy and the sinful when the issue is seen from the height of heaven to the depth of hell, and followed into the uttermost parts of the soul. And that is the nature of the issue as it is set in the cross of Christ. It is the eternal

---

[59]E.g. *Justification*, 136.
[60]'The Cross of Christ as the Moral Principle of Society' (1917): 11.
[61]*Justification*, 130, 171; *Work*, 160–61.
[62]*Father*, 8.
[63]*The Atonement in Modern Religious Thought*, 79.

holiness in conflict for its life. In the Son of God the whole being of God is staked upon this issue. It is a question of a final, salvation both for man and for God.[64]

Such statements make it quite clear that for Forsyth the atonement is not a matter of any arbitrary vindictiveness, or of addressing some sort of abstract legal code. It is a matter of God satisfying the law of his own being,[65] of meeting conditions internal to his own nature, of preserving his own life in the face of threat to it. Of 'doing justice' to himself as well as to his creature. The cross, then, as the focus of his own atoning activity, is in a profound sense crucial for God's own existence.[66] Far from being unnecessary to the redemption of the race, or being merely an incidental visual aid or stimulus to human response, the death of Jesus on the cross, was, quite literally, the most necessary thing in the world. For the redemption of the race was at the same time the self-rescue of God from a potentially fatal circumstance.

Nothing could be further from all this than the Ritschlian account which Forsyth himself had advocated with zeal in that early sermon of 1877. From the mid-1880s onwards, and with increasing vigour as the years passed, he stood its title on its head and insisted that justice, the self-realization of the Holy in the creature, the establishment of the kingdom, is the true and only mercy, as well as the only possible course of action for a truly holy God.

Atonement, then, we should note, is addressed first and foremost *not* to the moral or legal status of individual human persons, nor to that abstraction of atonement theologies 'the human race', but to the objective and universal moral order within which all humans 'live and move and have their being'. Only secondarily, and as inhabitants of this same order, do particular persons come into consideration, a fact which Forsyth never tires of emphasizing. Viewed thus, he writes, 'the work of Christ was ethical, final and positive. It was something which had a completeness of its own before human experience, and apart from it'.[67] Thus Forsyth sets himself apart from what he would have considered the unduly

[64] *Justification*, 152.
[65] *The Old Faith and the New*, Appendix, ii.
[66] *The Old Faith and the New*, 17.
[67] *Society*, 12.

anthropocentric emphasis in much contemporary atonement theology which insists on asking *first* about the significance of the atonement for, and its impact upon, the actual here and now existence of particular people. Thus, for example, Paul Fiddes objects to traditional juridical interpretations of the cross because their narrow focus on the historical event of Golgotha, while furnishing an account of salvation in terms of the supposed release of individuals from debt or guilt, cannot adequately explain how we are *actually* released from the power of sin in our lives, an aspect of experience which is therefore generally treated as a second and separate stage in God's saving work, a distinct activity of regeneration, rather than an integral part of atonement itself. Forsyth, on the other hand, because he sees atonement primarily not as a matter of either the status or the experience of individual persons, but an adjustment of the cosmic order of things which thereby inevitably has universal implications (just as surely as if the molecular structure of oxygen were to be adjusted tomorrow), presents both aspects under the one rubric of the self-realization of the Holy: first in the order of reality, and secondarily, as that 'reorganization of the universe' works itself out in actuality and history. We do not have time to address the distinction between objective and subjective atonement here, save to mention briefly that it is a distinction which Forsyth dislikes and prefers not to use. Its terms presuppose an anthropocentric focus, whereas Forsyth's focus is ever upon God's purpose of the establishing of his kingdom in human history, and the cross of Jesus as the surety both to humans and to God of the completion of that goal.

4. The Death of Jesus – the Self-Realization of Holiness in the Sphere of the Human

How precisely, then, does the death of Jesus on the cross fit into this scheme of things and realize, as Forsyth suggests, this divine purpose? First, we must return to the language of the cross as the judgement of God upon human sin. In the light of the cross, Forsyth insists, we must confess that we live in a saved world precisely because we live in a judged world.[68] In the cross, we see 'a work

[68] *Missions*, 72.

historic yet timeless and final' in which 'the absolute and irreversible judgement was passed upon evil. There, too, the judgement of our sins fell once for all on the Holy One and the Just'.[69] 'God', writes Forsyth, 'must either inflict punishment or assume it. And He chose the latter course, as honouring the Law while saving the guilty. He took His own judgment.'[70] Again, 'God must either punish sin or expiate it, for the sake of His infrangibly holy nature.'[71] Thus Forsyth is content to employ all the dark imagery of the forensic metaphor, of Christ's death as a curse, a bearing of the wrath of God, an exhausting of the punishment due to human sin. Yet he makes a decisive distinction which qualifies this language: Christ's death may be described as *penal* because it relates directly to that which we could only experience as punishment – namely, the consequence of our sin in its collision with God's holy nature. But God did *not* punish Christ on the cross.[72] It is only a sense of personal guilt which transforms the experience of that which is the consequence of human sin into punishment, and Christ, in experiencing death, knew no such guilt. Thus while 'it was the punishment of sin that fell on Him,'[73] he did not experience it as punishment, and His Father cannot be thought to have been angry with him as he bore it.[74]

In fact, the precise opposite was true. It was because Christ voluntarily submitted in obedience to the death of the cross, because he placed himself in the way of his own judgement and acknowledged it as righteous in his bearing of it that this same death has the atoning value which redresses the moral order of the universe. Thus, in a supreme paradox, the attitude of the Father towards his Son on the cross is simultaneously one of enormous grief and pain and one of great joy and delight.[75] What it never is, is an attitude of anger. Forsyth anticipates Moltmann here in a profound passage from *God the Holy Father*: 'Love, loss, fatherhood, motherhood, wifehood, widowhood, home, country, and the heroisms that renounce these

[69] *Missions*, 73.
[70] *Cruciality*, 203.
[71] *Cruciality*, 205.
[72] Cf. *Work*, 162–3.
[73] *The Atonement in Modern Religious Thought*, 84.
[74] *The Atonement in Modern Religious Thought*, 85, 68.
[75] 'Preaching of Jesus' (1923): 301.

are ... embalmed forever in the heart of the infinite Father, once bereaved of His Son, and the Eternal Son, once orphaned of His Father.'[76]

This leads us on directly to the question of the nature of satisfaction in God. Forsyth employs the Anselmian terminology, but interprets it consistently within the framework of his idea of the overall divine purpose as the self-realization of the Holy. Satisfaction, therefore, is no mere matter of an excess of merit obtained through supererogatory obedience, although Anselm's model is in many ways closer to Forsyth than traditional theories of a penal exaction. Rather, satisfaction is almost an aesthetic quality: it is that which God feels when he finds himself in the world through the presence of a reciprocal holiness. It is divine self-fulfilment in relationship with a holy other.[77] It is the satisfaction of a job well done, a sense of well-being, a delight. It might be supposed to be (although Forsyth, to the best of my knowledge, never makes this comparison) that which God felt at the creation when he saw that 'it was good'. It is certainly that which God expressed at the baptism of his Son in whom he was well-pleased. For Forsyth, this self-same attitude extends all the way to the cross, and, having ruptured its darkness, manifests itself in the resurrection.

This understanding of satisfaction in essentially positive, rather than negative and retrospective, terms finds a parallel in Forsyth's description of judgement. Judgement, he argues, is no mere matter of inflicting a punishment upon sin: viewed in terms of the larger scheme of things it is 'the actual final establishment of righteousness upon the wreck of sin'.[78] In referring to the death of Jesus as the decisive judgement of God, therefore, Forsyth intends us to understand this moment as the decisive invasion of the kingdom of this world by the kingdom of God, of the arena of sin and evil by the presence of an unprecedented and radical holiness. 'There is only one thing that can satisfy the holiness of God,' Forsyth writes, 'and that is holiness',[79] holiness offered, of course, from the human side.

---

[76] *Father*, 25–6; cf. *The Atonement in Modern Religious Thought*, 64: 'The Son could not suffer without the Father suffering'.

[77] Cf. *Work*, 204, 205.

[78] *Missions*, 52.

[79] *Work*, 126; cf. *Society*, 82.

'The holiness of love's judgment must be freely, lovingly, and practically confessed from the side of the culprit world.'[80] The ancient word to Israel, 'You shall be holy as I am Holy' must be fulfilled. Only in this is there genuine satisfaction for a holy God. And its achievement, the establishment of the kingdom, of righteousness, from within the sphere of sin, by God himself, is the judgement of God upon sin.

It is for this reason that Forsyth repeatedly insists that the atoning thing in the death of Christ was obedience rather than suffering and death *per se*.[81] It was the voluntary *submission* to suffering the death, and the acknowledgment of them as the righteous judgement of God upon human sin which was the holy, and therefore the satisfying, thing. Christ's death was no mere death, but rather death as 'a decisive moral achievement',[82] the homologation of God's judgement upon human sin,[83] the adjustment of God's conscience and man's,[84] and thereby the renewal of the image of God in humanity and the establishment of the kingdom of God. God, Forsyth writes, 'must satisfy His being's law. And he did so by uniting with that law the concrete reality of history in the life, passion, and death of Jesus Christ'.[85]

In other words, the death of Jesus had atoning significance not in and of itself as death, nor even as the punishment due to human sin (note that for Forsyth it *is* such, although interestingly he does not pursue the question *why?*), but rather in that *knowing* it to be such, Christ willingly submitted to it, and thereby sealed a perfectly holy life which alone could constitute an adequate satisfaction to a holy God. In him, we might simply say, reverting to more biblical language, the covenant promise is fulfilled: You shall be my people and I shall be your God. Reciprocally, the motif which runs through Jesus' life as the Son beloved of his Father is 'Hallowed be Thy Name'. It is as the concrete expression and climax of a life driven by that same concern for God's holiness, or, viewed differently, as the climax of God's entry into the life of the other in order to find and

---

[80] *Justification*, 172.
[81] Cf. *The Atonement in Modern Religious Thought*, 67.
[82] *Cruciality*, 181.
[83] *Work*, 157.
[84] *Cruciality*, 116.
[85] *The Old Faith and the New*, 14.

to realize his own holiness there, that the cross of Calvary has satisfying and atoning significance. It was simply 'the enthronement of the Holy in the arena of human experience, under the conditions of a historic situation concrete with the soul of the race'.[86] Christ, Forsyth writes, 'set up the Kingdom in his own person and work'.[87] This, then, is the judgement of the world, a judgement which asserts itself not merely negatively in punishment 'but positively in righteousness; so that judgment is not a terror but a hope, and the day of the Lord is not convulsion and catastrophe, but creation, a new heaven and earth, wherein dwell the peace of righteousness and assurance for ever'.[88]

In closing, I want simply to hint at the direction which Forsyth's thought takes from here. For, of course, the question remains to be answered concerning the nature of the relationship between this decisive moment of history, and the history of our experience, this new creation and established kingdom, and the still convulsing and catastrophic world in which we live. There can be no question of God resting content with a judgement, an atoning holiness, a new creation manifest in Christ and Christ alone. If there is a distinction to be drawn between the real and the actual they must, nonetheless, not be allowed to drift apart into a dualism which denies redemption to the historical, and leaves Forsyth's God open to the charge that he is concerned with his own holy being to the exclusion of the sort of passionate concern for the creature of which the New Testament speaks so clearly. No such dualism is permitted to open up in Forsyth's theology. Christ's death has its final value, he affirms, only when its effect in us is taken into account.[89] Indeed, Christ's response to God in the cross is not one which excludes us, but in which our response is already present, latent in the power which pours out from the cross itself, the power which itself directly creates and generates our holiness.[90] 'Whatever we mean, therefore, by substitution,' he writes, 'it is something more than merely vicarious. It is certainly not something done over our heads ... it is a matter not so much of substitutionary expiation (which, as these words are commonly understood, leaves us too little committed), but of

[88]'The Preaching of Jesus', 298.
[89]*Work*, 195.
[90]*Work*, 192.

solidary confession and praise from amid the judgement fires, where the Son of God walks with the creative sympathy of the holy among the sinful sons of men.'[91] Christ, he notes, 'is not only the pledge to us of God's love, but the pledge to God of our sure response to it in a total change of will and life.'[92]

In some sense, in other words, the 'objective' aspect of the atonement in Christ is precisely the vanguard, the firstfruits, the security of the ultimate return, the 'subjective' realization of holiness in us, the historical or eschatological manifestation of the kingdom in the world. Only then will God truly be satisfied. Only then will his joy be complete. Only then will God have done justice to himself, and to his decision to create.

This is the question to which Forsyth addressed himself brilliantly in one of his latest and best-known books, *The Justification of God*, or, in his own preferred title, simply *Theodicy*. And I want to end by citing at length from this book and thereby provide an anticipatory hint of Forsyth's vision of a universal restoration, a realization of what has already been secured in reality in *actuality*,[93] the manifestation of God's kingdom on earth, the realization of holiness not just in Christ's life, but in ours, when God will be all in all:

> There never was such a fateful experiment as when God trusted man with freedom. But our Christian faith is that He knew well what He was about. He did not do that as a mere adventure, not without knowing that He had the power to remedy any abuse of it that might occur, and to do this by a new creation more mighty, marvellous, and mysterious than the first. He had means to emancipate even freedom, to convert moral freedom, even in its ruin, into spiritual. If the first creation drew on His might, the second taxed His all-might. It revealed His power as moral majesty, as holy omnipotence, most chiefly shown in the mercy that redeems and reconciles.[94]

[91] *Work*, 226.
[92] *Work*, 195.
[93] *Work*, 130.
[94] *Justification*, 125.

There is an Eye, a Mind, a Heart, before Whom the whole bloody and tortured stream of evolutionary growth has flowed... . And in the full view of it He has spoken. As it might be thus: 'Do you stumble at the cost? It has cost Me more than you – Me who see and feel it all more than you who feel it but as atoms might... . Yea, it has cost Me more than if the price paid were all Mankind. For it cost Me My only and beloved Son to justify My name or righteousness, and to realise the destiny of My creature in holy love. And all mankind is not so great and dear as He. Nor is its suffering the enormity in a moral world that His Cross is. I am no spectator of the course of things, and no speculator on the result. I spared not My own Son. We carried the load that crushes you. It bowed Him into the ground. On the third day He rose with a new creation in His hand, and a regenerate world, and all things working together for good to love and the holy purpose in love. And what He did I did. How I did it? How I do it? This you know not now, and could not, but you shall know hereafter. There are things the Father must keep in His own hand. Be still and know that I am God, whose mercy is as His majesty, and His omnipotence is chiefly in forgiving, and redeeming, and settling all souls in worship in the temple of a new heaven and earth full of holiness. In that day the anguish will be forgotten for joy that a New Humanity is born into the world.'[95]

---

[95] *Justification*, 169–170.

Chapter 3

THE REAL AS THE REDEMPTIVE: FORSYTH ON AUTHORITY AND FREEDOM

Colin Gunton

1. The Question of Context

Peter Taylor Forsyth has about him something of the capacity of Kierkegaard to utter the kind of lapidary judgement that both breaks through cliché and comes, upon reflection, to appear to be undeniably true.[1] As a rule they are 'fireworks in a fog', according to one notorious and foolish characterization,[2] only if their relation to the remainder of Forsyth's thought is ignored. Whether or not Forsyth is a systematic theologian is partly a matter of definition, but there is an overall unity and coherence to his thought of the kind that justifies its claim to be systematic after the manner of Brunner's fine description of Irenaeus: 'if this is what it means to be a systematic theologian: to perceive connections between truths, and to know which belongs to which'.[3] It is fortunate that Brunner's definition does not centre on tight coherence, for one of the things that becomes apparent from this collection of papers is that there are some fundamental tensions within Forsyth's corpus. The general contention that I would make is that his is an integrating mind, bringing together in an overall vision, if one with at times rather misty outlines, a wide range of intellectual, cultural and practical considerations.

---

[1] That is not to deny that sometimes his dicta come to appear obviously false.
[2] D. J. G. Stevenson, letter to *British Weekly*, 31 January 1907, 22.
[3] Emil Brunner, *The Mediator: A Study of the Central Doctrine of the Christian Faith*, trans. Olive Wyon (Philadelphia: Westminster, 1947), 262.

Nowhere is there likely to be a better test of overall consistency than in a theologian's – or, for that matter, in any thinker's – grasp of the relation between authority and freedom. In the modern world, they are widely thought to be in some form of opposition: freedom is to be achieved in freedom from authority, at least so far as that is conceived, after the manner of Kant's celebration of enlightenment, in terms of traditional forms of authority. According to this, any authority that is not in some way self-imposed is inherently suspect. On the other hand, the ever-present threat of authoritarian orders arising from the chaos bred by modern autonomy appears equally to make a choice between the two in some way necessary. But the best accounts bring them into some kind of positive relation, and it is here that the real test of consistency is to be sought; for the modern fashion, against which Forsyth repeatedly directs polemic, is right to the extent that they have come at least to appear to represent incompatible values, or at least values to be traded off one against the other.

The first judgement that I want to cite from Forsyth is germane to this enquiry. 'There is only one thing greater than Liberty, and that is Authority.' In the decades after the ruinous careers and defeat of two similar but rival systems of authoritarian politics, each in its own way a reaction to modern libertarianism, we may think that Forsyth had failed to read the signs of his own times. But that would be to mistake his point, for he knew only too well that the drift to those systems of oppression derived from the failure and not the assertion of right authority. He continues: 'The intellectual, and especially the moral, situation of the age raises with ever-growing force what I have called the central question of religion, and therefore of everything – the question as to *authority*.'[4]

That, of course, is one of the many places in *The Principle of Authority* where the words of eighty years ago could have been written today. But the background to Forsyth's treatment of the relation between authority and liberty is provided not only by the modern predicament. It is also to be found in two other features of the tradition he received: the treatment of freedom in the Augustinian and Calvinist tradition against which the modern world is in such wholesale rebellion, to its manifest impoverishment or worse;

[4]*Authority*, 2nd ed., 17.

and the reaction to it in the liberalism that he found finally so unsatisfactory. So far as the former is concerned, although he clearly belongs in the tradition of Augustine and Calvin, Forsyth is interestingly aware of the weakness of what he had inherited. For example, twice in that book he prefers the notion of helpless guilt to that of total depravity.[5] And, with respect to the latter, there is a number of respects in which, as Ralph Wood has shown, he remains true to the liberal tradition in which he began his theological life.[6] The ways in which he deals with these two aspects of his past provide the keys to his own alternative, and in many ways, superior treatment.

The tradition of Augustine and Calvin does present a real problem, and its chief flaws could be said to be part of the cause of the widespread belief that authority and freedom are alternatives. The weakness is that isolated by John Oman in *Grace and Personality*, however unsatisfactory the solution he there essayed. The tradition's flaw is to be found in its tendency to impersonality, to the mechanizing or naturalizing of grace. Any notion of irresistible grace, such as appears to operate in parts of the systems of both Augustine and Calvin, overrides the autonomy of the agent, and generates a form of authoritarianism – of *absolute* dependence – which appears therefore to be hostile to any notion of freedom.[7] Yet Forsyth's solution is different from that essayed by Oman, who tends to make autonomy axiomatic and then rather lamely seek to find a place for grace. Oman's is essentially a modernist solution, while for Forsyth, any notion of freedom which does not conceive it as arising from divine action, and as therefore dependent upon a prior authority, is finally the denial of the gospel of justification by divine grace. Indeed he is a theologian of election, albeit not in the form associated with traditional Calvinism. In this paper, then, we shall be concerned with the consistency both of authority and freedom in general and with Forsyth's treatment of them in particu-

---

[5] He speaks, for example, of 'that moral helplessness through sin and guilt which used to be misunderstood as total corruption' *Authority*, 298.

[6] Ralph Wood, 'Christ on Parnassus: P. T. Forsyth Among the Liberals'. I am not convinced by all the aspects of this thesis, for Forsyth seems to me in some areas of his thought to have emancipated himself more successfully from his liberal past than Wood argues.

[7] John Oman, *Grace and Personality* (London: Collins, 1960; 1st ed., 1917).

lar. Is there, to use Alec Whitehouse's fine expression, an authority which is the authority of grace?[8] Forsyth certainly believed so.

2. Freedom as Limitation and Concentration

A rather obvious way of putting the question of freedom is to understand it in relation to Kant's philosophy of moral autonomy. This is broadly speaking the view that freedom is a kind of empty space in which the moral agent, to be autonomous, must be determined by nothing except the moral law which is at once discovered and imposed, or rather discovered by being imposed, by practical reason alone, apart from any *exterior* determination. Like Jonathan Edwards before him, Forsyth is rightly dismissive of any notion of freedom from determination, the freedom of empty space. Here his analysis is both subtle and wide-ranging. First, he gives reasons for showing that there is no *thought* that is free from determination. To imagine otherwise is to succumb unaware to forces that both determine and imprison in a slavery to immaturity. His first argument depends upon a distinction between the individual and the person. Individuals are those who not only believe that they are naturally free, but also succumb to the very homogenizing forces that deprive of true personality:

> It is often to be remarked how the tendency to a ready assertion of the natural self destroys personality.... Personal values are overwhelmed by the fashion of the time and place.... The man who does not rise to be a person becomes an item.... He does not live; only some gregarious force lives through him.... He is the slave of his heredity, his environment, his disposition, his mates.[9]

Second, he argues that freedom of thought is something that has to be attained. It is a freedom of maturity, the freedom of a formed person in distinction from the rootlessness of the individual:

[8]W. A. Whitehouse, *The Authority of Grace. Essays in Response to Karl Barth* (Edinburgh: T&T Clark, 1981).

[9]*Authority*, 285–6.

Freedom of thought is a hard-won power and glory.... It does not come like flight to a bird, or love to a boy. It is not its emancipation from the past, nor its escape from tutors and governors. But it is thought emancipated from the prejudices and passions of the common natural man, or from that 'collective suggestion', which makes a man the victim of his most ordinary environment.... . Thought truly free is an accomplishment and privilege of maturity.[10]

Although Forsyth is interested in the matter of education, and stresses its need in this very context – making youthful judgement a major symbol of a false notion of the freedom of thought – the freedom of intellectual maturity, is as with everything else, the fruit of redemption. We shall hope to glance at his hierarchy of values later.

The second area, that of moral freedom is, scarcely surprisingly, of more interest to Forsyth than intellectual freedom, although, because he refuses to divide up the person into faculties, its treatment is of a piece with that of the latter. In the tradition of Edwards, though it is Burke that he interestingly cites,[11] he holds that freedom derives from limitation. There are various ways in which freedom is given by being limited, but chief among them is that it is something that has to be given, from without. Above all, it must be given by God, and that means by 'the Christ of the Apostolic Redemption:[12]

So that if freedom must always be limited to remain free, and if it must be limited at last only by the principle that creates it, then the redemption of Christ must be the last regulative principle in the freedom of a Church, and finally of the world.[13]

Notice that Forsyth is not here playing a freedom of redemption against a freedom of creation. It is rather that freedom is the gift of the creator, but that, given that things are as they are, it can now

---

[10]*Authority*, 287–8; cf. 291 for an attack on modern 'anti-traditionalism'.
[11]"'Liberty,'" says Burke, "must always be limited in order to be possessed"' *Authority*, 235.
[12]*Authority*, 251.
[13]*Authority*, 250.

come only through salvation from sin that is slavery. That is the voice of Paul, John, Augustine, Luther, Calvin and Edwards. Freedom is not an empty space, but consists in service to the truth, to what is really there, to the personal authority that is God's.

But because it is service to the real, the limitation of freedom is at the same time its concentration, a word Forsyth uses in connection with the universal significance of the cross of Christ.[14] His primary interest is in the freedom deriving from the cross, that historic source of all creative authority, so that he is therefore able to play a variation on a central Augustinian theme, that freedom is to be understood as obedience.[15] 'Such limitation of freedom is really its concentration, and therefore its power.'[16] Limited freedom is not freedom destroyed, but freedom empowered. The more obedient the agent is to the heavenly vision, the more power is released. '*Absolute* obedience is the condition of *entire* freedom.'[17] That is not as authoritarian as it sounds, for, as we shall see, obedience to true authority is the way by which the self is established in its true integrity, and, indeed, rationality:

> When an active element begins to enter our obedience it becomes rational. We not only *feel* the force of our authority, we *see* the force of it. We see reason for it. . . . We have the kind of degree of freedom that goes with rational perception.[18]

The way is now open for us to show why it is that for Forsyth, far from being contraries, authority and freedom are mutually involving.

3. Redemptive Authority

The choice that all must make is not between autonomy and authority but between different forms of authority, between true

---

[14]Compare a similar use of the word 'condensation' in *Society*, 10.
[15]*Authority*, 211, 235.
[16]*Authority*, 259.
[17]*Authority*, 272.
[18]*Authority*, 307–8. Readers of his following sentences will see that for Forsyth this is a partial account only, but his general point remains.

and false authority.[19] Forsyth argues that autonomy as it is conceived in modern thought is not autonomy at all. Anticipating MacIntyre and Hauerwas, he claims in one characteristic judgement that 'it is a fatal fallacy of all such autonomy that it must regard virtue not as the principle of action but only as its result'.[20] And yet, again showing great subtlety of analysis, he presents alternatives in the way in which this is understood which are often absent from discussions of the topic. His arguments in support of his view that modernism is simply mistaken in its notion of authority include the following. First, he asserts that there is a sense in which all authority is external to the agent. To evade that is to fly in the face of reality. The necessary externality of authority provides a constant refrain in his argument. It is clearly one of its defining characteristics: 'An authority must be external, in some real sense, or it is none. It must be external to us. It must be something not ourselves, descending on us in a grand paradox.'[21] This is particularly the case with the divine authority with which he is ultimately, but by no means exclusively, concerned. 'All absolute authority must reveal itself in a way of miracle. It does not arise out of human nature by any development, but descends upon it with an intervention, a revelation, a redemption.'[22]

But, second, he shows that there are different forms of externality, those which are, we might say, heteronomous because they are foreign to the being of the person and those which in some sense or other reflect, or, better, constitute personal reality. 'External authority is only mischievous, not when it comes to us from without (for all authority must), but when it represents a kind of pressure which cannot evoke and nourish our moral soul.'[23] True authority 'is not foreign, but it is other'.[24] The distinction between what is alien and what is other is crucial, and highlights another dimension of the poverty of a modernity which in almost every respect treats the two as identical. In this connection, it is worth pointing out that Forsyth understands well that the rejection of tradition is a rejection of the other, and therefore an impoverishment of the present.

[19]'Liberty is illicit which renounces its own creative principle' *Authority*, 251.
[20]*Authority*, 311.
[21]*Authority*, 271.
[22]*Authority*, 299.
[23]*Authority*, 290.
[24]*Authority*, 300.

Third, the distinction between the alien and the other is established by developing a conception of inwardness which corresponds and answers to the external shape of authority. The language of pietism – or perhaps of Schleiermacher, if that is different – is drawn upon, so much indeed that there are times, and a sense in which, Forsyth appears to suggest that the only true authority is an inward authority. 'This authority does not indeed impinge upon the soul's surface, it wells up within the soul's centre.'[25] 'The cure for individualism … is some real authority interior but superior to the Ego itself.'[26] 'In the interior of the soul authority and freedom go hand in hand. For here it is soul that acts richly on soul… . Moral influence is entirely a matter of personal authority':[27]

> True authority, final authority, is personal. As it acts on wills, it must be a will. It must have moral quality. It must be good. It must be the one good thing in the world – a good will. At last it must be the will absolutely good – the Holy. We yield to the holy man; and to the absolutely Holy One … we should yield nothing less than our whole selves.[28]

Thus it is that the Kantian language of moral reason is transmuted, overturned, into the language of grace.

It follows, fourth, that the only absolute authority is that of God, and that God's authority is absolutely self-grounded:

> It is a deep remark of Höffding that if there be an absolute authority He can only express Himself in miracle. If He is absolute He can be founded on nothing outside Himself. He is His own norm. He can be proved by nothing… . His supreme revelation must be the supreme miracle… . The absolute is in history… . only by a miracle. That is what we worship as the miracle (and not simply the marvel) of the person of Jesus Christ.[29]

It is in this context that Forsyth engages in polemic, rather similar

---

[25] *Authority*, 301.
[26] *Authority*, 270.
[27] *Authority*, 285.
[28] *Authority*, 308–9.
[29] *Authority*, 309–10.

to that of T. F. Torrance in a recent article,[30] against the kind of external, and therefore, he rightly believes, ultimately self-grounded and subjective, authority exercised by the Church of Rome.[31] In contrast, 'the authority of the Church is but the weight of its experienced Gospel in a vast plexus and long series of regenerate and corporate souls'. It is, therefore, a derived but inward authority, flowing from 'God in His salvation renewing the soul'.[32] While Rome's authority may also be seen as a derived authority, Forsyth is clear about the difference. True authority can in no way be legal, but can only be exercised as personal authority continually renewed from the source. it is only as such that the church has authority in society, and Forsyth's vision is a classical dissenting one, reaffirmed most vigorously in recent times by Yoder and Hauerwas. 'The only moral authority that can save society is one that thus asserts itself in the individual conscience by its saved experience of a universal Redeemer.'[33]

It is in his stress on the inward and personal locus of authority that Forsyth most shows the marks of the modern. His relations with Kant provide an illustration of his dialogue with modernity. On the one hand, Kant was for him, as he was for Coleridge, something of a liberator from the more abstract forms of Enlightenment rationalism. He provided a way of moving from the priority of the mechanical to that of the personal, from nature to the will. Not only does he teach that the ethical is the real, but also appears to provide Forsyth with the 'clear distinction between natural life process, however rarefied or spiritual, and the action of the moral consciousness'.[34] As we have already seen, there are references to, and echoes of, Kant elsewhere, as we would expect in a pupil of Ritschl. Yet there is also a clear disagreement:

> But conscience is not a legislator, it is a judge. It does not give
> the laws either for action or belief, it receives them; it

---

[30]T. F. Torrance, *Church Times*, 21 May 1993.

[31]*Authority*, 317.

[32]*Authority*, 290–1. Eastern Orthodox theologians like to contrast their conception of authority with that of both Rome and the Reformation. The former is, they say, external and legal, the latter individualist and experiential. Forsyth, along with Calvin and much of the mainstream Reformed traditions, is not individualist.

[33]*Authority*, 298–9.

[34]*Authority*, 201.

recognizes the authority of laws from another source, and administers them to the occasions which arise.'[35]

The locus and weight of the various sources of inner and outer authority have been subtly but significantly changed.

How does Forsyth believe that in this way he can have his cake and eat it? Here he attempts an answer to a question which Barth tended to dismiss as improper, thus giving his own theology a sometimes rather authoritarian air. Although there is a sense in which for Forsyth authority is irrational and miraculous, there is also one in which it is rational, and that is its method of operation, which corresponds to the nature of that over which it is an authority: 'it emerges only amid psychological conditions'.[36] Corresponding to the form of authoritative divine action there is a form of human experience. We must avoid, he argues, 'spatial metaphors of extension and mutual exclusion' when we are speaking of 'spiritual action and inter-penetration'.[37] The conversion that is necessary to the process of redemption 'wears the garb and speaks the tongue of our spiritual and conscious experience'.[38]

Forsyth's chief difference from Barth in this respect is that he does not eschew the concept of experience and the use of categories drawn from psychology.[39] His difference from Schleiermacher, however, is that he is far more careful to develop an *a posteriori* concept of experience, one whose shape is constrained by that which is experienced:

> The first content of my religious experience is not myself as feeling so or so – *e.g.* dependent (Schleiermacher) – not myself in a certain frame, but God in a certain act, as giving, as giving Himself, as thus grasping, saving, new creating me.[40]

[35] *Authority*, 240.

[36] *Authority*, 300. Forsyth shows a sometimes touching hope in the future progress of Christian psychology. But we cannot expect him to have been right about everything.

[37] *Authority*, 300.

[38] *Authority*, 300.

[39] To read the work of this man, even one mercifully free from the modern compulsion to justify everything with a footnote reference, is to become aware of the catholicity of his reading.

[40] *Authority*, 372, cf. 142.

Experience is a medium, not a matrix, or, as he puts it, ground.[41] 'Our very response to it is created in us before it is confessed by us.... . It is something miraculously created in us by the Bible to respond to divine power acting as grace.'[42] We appropriate rather than verify.[43] Forsyth sets his face strongly against experientialism, and, while feeling free to draw upon William James, accuses him of neglecting the very determinant of experience that makes it what it is.[44] 'A Gospel mainly experiential and subjective ... is bound to have its obverse in a greater uncertainty and a freer challenge by contemporary society'.[45] Rather, the authority 'speaks in the midst of our most intimate experience ...; but its decisive word is not drawn from our experience'.[46] Experience is an ambiguous term: 'Sometimes it means the action on us of an objective fact which emerges *in* experience but is not *of* it.'[47]

Thus experience, although important, is not the main focus of Forsyth's account, which is the historic cross. For those incapacitated both intellectually and morally by sin and guilt there is no other way to freedom than through authority, and authority of a specific kind, that operating through redemption. It is, therefore, the nature of the cross and the God there revealed which finally shapes Forsyth's conception of authority and the locus of its action. The notion of the holy is the creative and dominating centre, rather as the notion of love in freedom is the centre of Barth's theology:

> The gospel of Christ's Cross is therefore the final centre of all Authority, because there alone the Holiness of God – the absolute sublimity, transcendence, and victory of the God of the Conscience – establishes itself for ever in the destruction of both guilt and sin.[48]

---

[41] *Authority*, 331.
[42] *Authority*, 333–4 – a rather Barthian note there.
[43] *Authority*, 333–4.
[44] *Authority*, 301.
[45] *Authority*, 348. 'In various ways religious uncertainty dogs the steps of an excessive subjectivity, such as marks an age that has just discovered the value of experience and can think of nothing else.'
[46] *Authority*, 301.
[47] *Authority*, 329.
[48] *Authority*, 364–5.

The contrast with Barth is here instructive. While both theologians frequently link revelation and salvation – the cross being the focus of both – there is a tendency in Barth to stress the noetic, while Forsyth stresses the moral. The freedom of God is a notion closely linked in Barth with revelation; the stress in Forsyth is on the moral quality of holiness.

4. The Principle of Authority

It is at this place that there arises a series of questions to Forsyth's theology which takes us to the heart of its unique character, as well as of its treatment of authority. All in some way concern the relation between creation and redemption. We can approach it with reference to Daniel Hardy's criticism of Forsyth's ecclesiology, a topic closely related to that of authority. According to Hardy, Forsyth's concentration on the church as the fruit of redemption makes it difficult for him to have a conception of what he calls 'created sociality'. That is to say, Forsyth has a conception of being in community in the church, but not an adequate conception of an underlying universal human sociality which might provide a basis for ecclesiology:

> One effect of these views … is to eliminate what one could call 'general sociality' or created sociality present in the human condition; there can be no such thing as the social transcendental present in human society as an element of nature, because its place is always taken by the specific gift of God in Christ.[49]

Although there may be good Forsythian reasons for questioning that diagnosis, the point for our purposes is that it raises the question of the relation, particularly as it has taken shape in the Western tradition, between reason and revelation. The Enlightenment can from one point of view be understood as the reassertion of the rationality of the created order, both natural and human, against their subservience to the imposed authority of a religion of revealed redemption. It asserted nature against grace, created, as against

[49]Daniel W. Hardy, 'Created and Redeemed Sociality', 40.

redeemed, reason, as we might put it. Forsyth is in strong reaction against this, and rightly so. The words of the title of this paper, 'the real as the redemptive', adapted from the title of chapter 10 of *The Principle of Authority* makes this very clear. Forsyth is writing in conscious opposition to either Hegel or a disciple making use of the master's principle that 'the rational is the real'. His concern was not so much to celebrate the authority of God over against that of thought, but nonetheless to oppose the rationalism that makes truth the immanent possession of the knower:

> We think of God, we entertain the idea of God, as we think anything else that is reasonable. But what everything turns on for the truth of the notion is the discovery of a right and a claim on us. It thinks us, it does not merely think itself in us.[50]

The overturning of Hegel's immanent rationality in favour of a more transcendent construal goes hand in hand with Forsyth's shift from the centrality of the rational to that of the moral. Rationality has its place, but it is secondary to the moral. He has, to be sure, a far from moralistic understanding of what he means by the moral realities of the gospel, as we shall see. Indeed, the title of the colloquium 'From a Lover of Love to an Object of Grace' suggests that the Aberdonian, after the much discussed conversion, moved from a moralism, or at least a religious stance suggesting that the onus of the faith was on the free agency of the believer, to the passive stance of one for whom to receive was, in view of moral helplessness, the prior requirement. Like Luther, he had come to elevate the passive righteousness of God who justifies by grace over the active righteousness of those who must make their own salvation.[51] That is true, but it is not the whole truth. It was not only redemption that was of grace for Forsyth, even though the order of creation does receive rather inadequate treatment. The citation at the head of this paper and many of his arguments suggest that he was aware of the fact that the question was one of ontology just as much as soteriology, and that is the case even when he is dealing with soteriology. His is

---

[50] *Authority*, 102.

[51] He does, however, prefer receptivity to passivity (*Authority*, 103–4). 'The process of thinking ... involves an act of will (that is of obedience).' Here he is classically Calvinist: '*Omnis recta cognitio Dei ab obedientia nascitur*', John Calvin, *Institutes* 1.6.2.

far more than a moralism of the pious soul, for it is a moralism which bases the moral agent in what is a theology of reality. In that sense, the created order is important for him as more than simply a backcloth to redemption.

What then is the relation of creation and redemption? 'The real as the redemptive'. The message shouted to the rooftops in our title is that Forsyth is revealing himself as a characteristically Western theologian, though a distinctive one, for I can think of no other theologian before him who would use words quite like that. Augustine? Too Platonist; for him the real is, when it comes to the crunch, that world ontologically closest to the creator, the eternal world of forms, first born of the Trinity's creative work.[52] Aquinas? Too Aristotelian; reality for him is that which is shaped by the creator's all-determining causality. Luther or Calvin? Well, there is a problem, for either of them could be found saying similar things, though none perhaps quite so apparently one-sided. Calvin certainly would suspect something of a lack of balance, perhaps; Book II of the *Institute* at the expense of Book I. Luther perhaps is in some respects nearer; but it is the reality claim that marks Forsyth's dictum as being of particular interest. Luther, as is sometimes claimed, was too interested in the existential relevance of the gospel to be much interested in what we call questions of ontology. It is rather in his engagement with specifically modern questions that Forsyth shows himself to be particularly himself, though, as I have suggested, also particularly Western.

What does that mean? In the first place, that it would be an odd theologian indeed of the Eastern traditions who could be heard saying anything remotely suggesting the priority of the redemptive in the way that Forsyth was urging. Of all things Western, it is the doctrine of the atonement with which Eastern theologians claim to be most uneasy. They are rightly suspicious of the Western tendency to elevate the doctrine of salvation at the expense of the doctrines of creation and what Barth called redemption: the beginning in Christ

[52]I am assuming that serious theologians would place God at the head of their account of what it is to be real. The question at issue here is how that divine reality bears upon and so shapes the reality that is not God. That may appear to disqualify a number of recent proponents of the art who deny, or affect to deny, the objective reality of God. This is in part a matter of definition, but it seems to me part of the definition of the word theology, proper, that is the *logos* of the one we call God.

and the Spirit from which all things derive, and the end to which in Christ and the Spirit they move. Does not Forsyth suggest that atonement is in some way either prior, on the scheme of things, to creation and eschatology, and does that not make him a typical Western exponent of salvation theology? Yes, but he is one who attempts, however inadequately, to shape a theology of nature in the light of redemption. In *Christ on Parnassus,* he makes the claim that in Christendom, as a fusion of the Hebrew and the Greek, 'the ground plan of Nature was now Redemption. The sphere of nature, which the Greek had leavened with his thought, received now a consecration from God's will and purpose'.[53] Forsyth has a doctrine of creation, but it is of creation understood in the light of redemption, and indeed reconstituted by it.

I would contend, therefore, that there is to be found in our theologian something more than a playing of soteriology against other doctrinal loci, even though for him redemption is the centre of systematic theology. One point worth noting is that he contends that salvation is redemption in, and with, the created order, not out of it, as the Western tradition is so often accused of doing. He could be, and probably is, attacking Ritschl when he says:

> For the whole creation groans for the Redemption, and is included in the process which works to the manifestation of the Sons of God. And the miracles of Christ show that His work is not simply to empower the soul to rise over an inferior creation and beat down Nature under its feet, but that it is also to involve Nature in the grand co-operation of all things in the everlasting kingdom.[54]

As he shows in another great book, the justification of God is at the same time the justification of the whole world.[55] And could it be that he has the weaknesses of the Western tradition in mind when he says that 'the curse of orthodoxy ... has been to sever the Cross from the whole moral fabric and movement of the universe and make it a theologian's affair'?[56] These remarks, however fragmentary, are

---

[53] *Parnassus,* 85.
[54] *Authority,* 206.
[55] *Justification,* 1st ed., 192
[56] *Justification,* 192.

further indications of Forsyth's systematic perceptiveness and comprehensiveness.

They also serve to focus our enquiry about authority. Has our theologian a view of authority so dominated by sin and salvation that he has nothing much to say on the general question of authority, on what we can call created authority? It is clear that in the order of knowing – perhaps we should say, in the case of this theologian, the order of experience – the only way to a theology of authority can be through the strait and narrow gate of the cross. In a human situation characterized by helpless guilt, and therefore moral impotence, the only true authority that can be exercised is the authority through which redemption is achieved.[57] Given the human situation, the real can only be the redemptive, so that Forsyth's ontology is an ontology of the holy as a doctrine of God. The balance of the matter is expressed thus: 'If there is any authority over the natural man, it must be that of its Creator; and, if the New Humanity has any authority above it, that authority must be found in the act of *its* creation, which act is the Cross of Christ.'[58]

It is further true that a theology of what can be called created authority follows from the basis given in redemption. The God of the cross is the one who is the power of all things. This means that the theology of the holy generates a universal ontology according to which the authority of God is not merely for the church, but for the whole of society: 'the harmonised judgement and grace of the Cross, at once critical and creative of the whole of society'.[59] Here the title of the book, not merely of a chapter, is significant: not *Christian* or *Ecclesiastical Authority*, but *The Principle of Authority*. Forsyth is writing for the whole world. This is clear from the one definition of authority which he essays: 'What we usually mean by authority is this. It is another's certainty taken as the *sufficient and final* reason for some certainty of ours, in thought or action.'[60] From the fact that authority is a *principle*, something of universal bearing, it follows that, 'the principle of authority is the foundation of education and

---

[57]*Authority*, 260: 'Human nature is great and wonderful; it is human will that has the blight and the doom.'

[58]*Authority*, 58.

[59]*Authority*, 405.

[60]*Authority*, 313.

of religion. And no ethic is possible without it'.[61] 'The sphere of authority is not in religion alone (though its final source is there). In all the affairs of life it has its action.'[62]

There is then to be found in Forsyth a theology of authority in general. Here two points can be made:

1. Not only does divine authority make a claim on society as well as on church, it is also true that without this authority, society flounders. 'The present decay in the matter of public liberty and its vigilance is more than concurrent with the decay of sure faith in a divine authority.'[63] Forsyth believes that the loss of the authority of the gospel in Western society is the cause of a deep loss of direction, and he is surely right. His description of the modern West as 'an outworn age trying to narcotise with mere energies its moral fatigue'[64] could scarcely be bettered.

2. There is to be seen operating in Forsyth's work a kind of hierarchy of authorities, for from time to time he recognizes that there is a general authority upon which redemptive authority supervenes, so to speak. He begins by recognizing that human beings as a matter of fact live by some authority or other, though he is not entirely convinced that such a natural theology gives adequate guidance to its exponents:

> Most people live under what they hold to be the authority of *all*. They do, or seek to do, what everybody else does. They are most secure in those things which are the universal fashion, in the primal unities, customs or instincts of society, in immemorial convention.[65]
>
> Some again are satisfied with the authority of *most*. They live as politicians do – by majorities … Their ideal is the popular.
>
> Others again follow the authority of the *few*. It may be a majority of experts, as in the case of science.[66]

---

[61] *Authority*, 307.
[62] *Authority*, 313.
[63] *Authority*, 409.
[64] *Authority*, 393.
[65] He adds, 'In the religious sphere we are familiar with the principle as "*Quod semper, quod ubique, quod ab omnibus*", or "*Securus iudicat orbis terrarum*", or the "*fides implicita*".' *Authority*, 313–14.
[66] *Authority*, 313–14.

It is here that Forsyth begins his acknowledgement of natural patterns of authority. In many things, we quite properly accept the authority of others, in varying relationships. Among the quite proper authorities are the expert and the educator. Indeed, democracy is lost without them.[67] But, and this is the key, they must be recognized for what they are, relative authorities. 'True faith releases us by passing us upward from one authority to another.'[68] Without the recognition of the authority of the holy God of the gospel, not only the church but also human society is lost.

5. Conclusion

I share with the writers of some of the other papers in this collection an awareness of the weaknesses of aspects of Forsyth's thought. Despite his affirmation of authority as a principle, it is there in little more than outline, and both that and the account of the relation of created and redeemed authority are fragmentary and at times indistinct. Moreover, despite the admirable moves through the development of a theology of experience to counter the impression of a sheer dialectic of freedom and obedience, there is a neglect of the pneumatological dimensions which are indispensable in any account of the relation between divine action and human response. Nevertheless, there is an overall coherence, impressive in its grasp, albeit sometimes a rather intuitive grasp, of the different dimensions, theological, hamartiological, anthropological, cultural and social which must be taken into account in a truly systematic treatment.

That said, the paper will conclude with a discussion of two of the general points of interest for today in what Forsyth has to say.

1. It becomes evident towards the end of the book that Forsyth's theology is a theology of power.[69] Many of its expressions are offensive, I suspect, because they are salutary, if exaggerated for the

---

[67]'It is the principle of authority, in whatever shape, that must save democracy from becoming easy, casual and corrupt, from mean, grey and gritty mediocrity.' *Authority*, 307.

[68]*Authority*, 324.

[69]'Faith is not faith in truths, but in powers.' *Authority*, 259.

sake of rhetorical effect. 'We are His property much more than His brethren.'[70] However, the link between a high doctrine of divine transcendence and human freedom is well-made:

> What was it that made the tremendous strength of Calvinism? What makes some form of Calvinism indispensable and immortal? It was this, that it cared more to secure the freedom of God than of man. That is what it found in the Cross. That is why it has been the greatest contribution to public liberty ever made.... Seek first the freedom of God, and all other freedom shall be added to you. The Calvinistic doctrine of predestination was the foundation of modern public liberty; and, deeply, because it was an awful attempt to secure God's freedom in Grace at any cost.[71]

There lies its contribution to contemporary debate, and in the face of two contemporary approaches to theology against both of which Forsyth is in healthy rebellion. One is the theology of signs and wonders associated with the American evangelist John Wimber, whose theology, according to one recent critique, could be summed up in the slogan, power without the cross: that is, the power of success, a finally anthropocentric theology justifying Christianity by its works. The second is the recent spate of theologies of the cross, whose assumption appears to be that some form of suffering God, or at least one whose primary concern would sometimes appear to be the equality of the sexes or the economic development and/or ecological salvation of the world.[72]

Let us examine the second of these before moving to the first. Against all forms of anthropocentrism, Forsyth's theology is contemptuous; the deity in whom he believes is glorious in his transcendent self-sufficiency. This God holds all merely human schemes in derision (Ps 2.4). Here is a splendid antidote for the utilitarian deity of so much recent theology:

---

[70] *Authority*, 253.

[71] *Authority*, 255. That the historical claim of the last sentence may be questionable does not detract from the general theological point being made. Forsyth's strength is to see precisely where the root of the modern predicament is to be found.

[72] That is not to suggest that these matters are unimportant, but rather to accept Forsyth's polemic against the anthropocentrism and opportunist pragmatism of much modern theology.

The supreme value ... felt in God is not His utility. If He slew
us we should praise His holy name. It is a question not of His
utility to us but of ours to Him, not of His service to us but His
right and glory over us ... His greatest mercy is not in sparing
us but in seeking and accepting our praise and service. His last
word to the soul is not only [note well] 'I save' but 'I claim'.[73]

That God has no need of the creation is not to say that he has no
concern for it; quite the reverse. Yet the need of the creation is not
for self-justification so much as for redemption by holy love.
Moreover, and here we come to the other comparison, the same
theology holds against a theology of signs and wonders. In one place
Forsyth specifically says that it is 'God the All-holy rather than the
Almighty' whom we meet in his chosen form of action.[74] 'All the
holiness of God bears down on my soul. Not His power, His
influence, but His holiness.'[75] It is Forsyth's theocentrism that is so
salutary for an era of deities made in the image of man or woman.

Interestingly, where modern theology of the cross, with its
patripassionist overtones, tends to transfer the qualities of the Son,
or perhaps we should say of the human Christ, to the Father, Forsyth
operates in a reverse direction. 'What is true of God is also true of
Christ. He is not only Saviour but Lord.... Through the Bible, God
with all His power and claim, comes in Christ.'[76] The focus is not
the suffering of God in Christ, the weight of whose human act
would thus be lost, but the efficacious action of God in the suffering
of Christ, though not only in that. He who has seen Christ truly has
seen the Father, for Christ is he who, above all, does the work of the
one who sends him. Do we not, or should we not, hear Forsyth
speaking directly to the condition of the modern church when he
resists the idea of God as an indulgent father – whether we take the
old Lear or the modern Lear – Père Goriot' – with the words, 'A
Cross which is nothing but a revelation of divine sacrifice and service
to us is an indulgent and demoralising Cross. It is a piece of
indiscriminate charity.'[77] The theology of power defined by love is

[73] Authority, 387.
[74] Authority, 54.
[75] Authority, 40.
[76] Authority, 373.
[77] Authority, 379.

nowhere better expressed than in the following powerful piece of
rhetoric:

> God is only God as absolute, eternal, holy love; His love
> conquers; it is the absolute power over us, and the final power
> over our world. All things work together for good to them
> that love God *in His universal, royal, holy, and final purpose*....
> Such is the God of the Bible. He reveals Himself, but it is of
> His absolutely free and royal choice for His own holy end....
> And God ceases to be God when He ceases to be such a God
> – the absolute, miraculous, personal, holy, and effective King
> and Lord of us and our world. To curtail His power is to
> infect Him with weakness; that is to say, it is to make Him
> a mixture of power and weakness – which again is to make
> Him part of the world, and destroy Him altogether as God.[78]

2. The second thing to say is that Forsyth's is a profoundly moral
vision, as I have already suggested, interestingly sharing Coleridge's
affinity for some aspects of Kant's thought. And the moral vision is
closely linked to the vision of power, because Forsyth is concerned
finally that God's will be done on earth as it is in heaven. The
concern with praxis would satisfy many a liberationist, if the praxis
took the approved form. But while Kant's morality finally becomes
a rational and paradoxically anthropocentric system, everything
requiring assessment at the bar of human reason, Forsyth submits
everything to the judgement of the God made known on the cross
of Christ. The vision is moral rather than moralistic, and from time
to time he clearly differentiates between the two. There are a
number of aspects to this vision, some less convincing than others.

His main enemy, slightly misconceived, is what he supposes to be
the naturalizing of salvation in the patristic era. Here he shares the
belief, perhaps associated most prominently with Harnack, in a
supposedly 'physical' theory of salvation, and with better reason
attributes to Anselm the beginnings of an emphasis on personal
reconciliation as being the heart of the matter. The most creative
contribution he has to make in this regard is his ontology of the holy.

---

[78]*Authority*, 371–2. 'We experience Christ as Brother, or as ideal, or as Master,
but we do not experience Him as Saviour; or if as Saviour, then not from perdition,
not as absolute Owner, King and Lord.' *Authority*, 367.

It is sometimes complained that his conception of the holy is unclear, but it seems not to be in its general outlines. The holy has some claim to be a fundamental notion, one we cannot do without if we are to understand who God is and we are – what Coleridge would call an idea, whose meaning is made clear in the contexts in which it is used. Its function is to express the divine love in judgement and forgiveness that is at the centre of things.

One does see here, perhaps, a salutary correction of the Western tendency, from Augustine through Anselm to Hegel and even, at times, Barth, to stress the divine rationality as being at the centre of things. It could be said that in his theology, Forsyth plays goodness against the other transcendentals of truth and beauty, for he sees truth primarily in the moral transformation made real by the historic cross of Christ. And perhaps that is as it should be. It is the human creation which is made in the image of God, the human creation through whose sin the remainder of the created order is subjected to futility and whose redemption it awaits, the human creation that is called to be conformed to the image of Christ. We are the problem, and through Christ alone, the locus of the solution. In that sense, the moral is the focus of the truth of reality, and Forsyth is right, as he is about so much. 'The saved conscience is integrated into the justice of the universe.'[79] But that is so by virtue of God's authority and the way it is realized in the world:

> Faith is such a delivering power because it has within it such a gracious authority. Everything else, Church or Bible, is authoritative for us in the proportion in which it is sacramental of this final and absolute authority, of the Creator as Redeemer, the authority not merely of God but of a God of grace. Authority reflects a dying King.[80]

The last word is thus of the authority of grace, the grace of redemption through the cross of Christ.

[79] *Authority*, 268.
[80] *Authority*, 299.

Chapter 4

DOMINATED BY HIS OWN ILLUSTRATIONS? P. T. FORSYTH ON THE LORD'S SUPPER

Iain R. Torrance

P. T. Forsyth's writings are paradoxical and elusive. Often disjointed, and more than occasionally obscure, they sparkle with metaphors and illustrations. *The Church and the Sacraments*, written in 1917, was Forsyth's penultimate book. He died in 1921. The aim of this short paper is to examine his understanding of the Lord's Supper in that book, and look hard and critically at his metaphors and illustrations, asking whether, ultimately, they illuminate or dominate his argument. My anxiety is that if you argue by aphorism and metaphor, at a certain stage you risk being led astray by your own rhetoric.

First, then, what is Forsyth attacking? The Supper is Christ's 'last parable', but it is 'more than that'.[1] So the supper is not simply illustrative. Nor is the church's supper 'mainly commemoration'.[2] It is not a 'tableau',[3] not simply the exposition of Christian ideas, but 'the conveyance of the Act of Christian grace'.[4] He claims that it was not an essence but an action which was symbolized, 'therefore it was an act which symbolized it, and conveyed it, not the elements'.[5]

---

[1] *Sacraments*, 2nd ed., 228. Subsequent references to this volume are to the page number only.

[2] 228.

[3] 233.

[4] 234.

[5] 235.

Christ was not setting up 'a contemplative religion'.[6] The elements are not the symbols: 'They are only materials to enable the symbolic act to be carried out.'[7] All of this is quite sharply polemical and expressed with passion. For Forsyth, this ends 'worship of the elements'.[8] The gift of Christ's death conveyed in the supper is 'not vision but life'.[9] Christ is present 'not to bless a religious coterie, but as having suffered and conquered in history for a sinful people, to whom his Passion brings the saving gift of forgiveness and regeneration'.[10] Christ conveys not merely a 'consoling presence', but 'a new moral order of things'.[11] It is not a case of 'friendly communion' but 'of a decisive Act' ... offered to us by Him anew'.[12]

Forsyth has a particular animus against what he calls 'theosophic' understandings of the supper. These draw up semiphysical understandings of presence. The metaphors fly thick and fast. The supper is not an occasion for 'a mystic union of transfusion';[13] it is 'not a benediction, not a large grant in aid',[14] but 'a moral transubstantiation'.[15] We need 'much more than just recharging';[16] it is 'the pagan residue' in Romanism which makes grace 'an emanative power' ... going out like a fine force'.[17] Forsyth's underlying dread, of course, is any idea of sanctification by contagion which might bypass a new moral relation, and this spurs him into a fine polemic against what he calls 'fasting communion':

> 'To be morally and mystically in Christ by the sacrament of His word must be worlds more than to have Christ in us by eating a piece of matter so substantial (whatever its consecration) that it could be tainted by contact with the previous contents of the stomach.'[18]

[6]236.
[7]236.
[8]237.
[9]249.
[10]253.
[11]253–4.
[12]254.
[13]264.
[14]264.
[15]265.
[16]262.
[17]262.
[18]289–90 and cf. 265 and 295.

In opposition to all of this, what is Forsyth's own constructive understanding of the Lord's Supper? If it is not a parable, not a tableau, not an exposition, not merely commemorative, what is it? Forsyth has one consistent answer. The supper is 'the conveyance of the Act of Christian grace'.[19] With a striking choice of phrase, he tells us: 'The Supper was an under-agent of the Cross – not the great Act to God but the transfer of it to believers.'[20] He continues: 'The occasion is an act of consignment, making over ... His great impending act.'[21] 'In the Supper we have not merely a symbol of His sacrifice to God but the actual consignment of it to them, as being *for them* and not simply for some (say cosmic) purpose of God to which they could contribute but which they could never share.'[22] 'The Supper was the gift to us of that gift of Himself to God. The Supper was the act, the gift, as anthropocentric, the Cross was the same act and gift as theocentric.'[23] 'The essential thing,' Forsyth insists – and this is the heart of his thesis – 'is the *bestowal*. In the supper, Christ 'was presenting to man that offering to God. It is the *consignment* of a blessing'.[24] The act was more than symbol, parable or emblem: it 'was donative'.[25] So here we have quite a tight cluster of images. Forsyth is concerned with a transfer, and borrows the vocabulary of a legal transaction. The supper was a conveyance, a consignment, a gift, a bestowal, an under-agent of the cross.

What then did Forsyth understand as being effected through the supper? What did the bestowal bring about? The church's celebration of communion is, Forsyth tells us, 'a[n] ... act on our part ... created by the indwelling presence of Christ... . We are under-agents of His great action on that evening... . We perpetuate it antiphonally'.[26] He presses a musical analogy: 'The sacraments ... are useless without the reverberation of that foregone and incessant Act of Christ.'[27] 'We help to make it one long act, like one great note

[19]234.
[20]236.
[21]240.
[22]241.
[23]242.
[24]247.
[25]248.
[26]242–3.
[27]231.

on many instruments, with endless reverberation.'[28] It was the bestowal of 'an Eternal Act vibrating in their observance'.[29] This takes us closer to Forsyth's vision of the role of communion in the church, and even of what it is to be a Christian. Communion, for Forsyth, is not a passive event: 'We are not quiescent. We do not *listen* as a congregation; we take part and *do* as a Church in a receptivity which is action in response.'[30] For the early community, and so for us, 'the repeated rite became the stated and pointed expression of what life must now be for them – the appropriation of Christ's heavenly, and eternal, and regenerating personality in a new creation'.[31] This in turn led to an understanding of the church. 'The new thing was not the fraternity, but its cohesion in His ever-present lordship through the Cross.'[32] It follows that the church is different from a mere brotherhood, and Forsyth tries to express its distinctive cohesiveness: 'Christ gives Himself as their food and future, the blood and bond of a new created life.'[33] He had hinted at this earlier in relation to communion: 'A mere religious association cannot do this act…. It can be done only by the society which He created by His act, which lives in the faith of it.'[34] Forsyth's overall, and famous, conclusion then follows: 'The Lord's Supper is the most complete and plenary of all the cultic ways of confessing the work of reconciliation, where the sin of humanity is conquered by the grace of God in a holy Kingdom. It is *therefore the real centre of the Church's common and social life.*'[35]

This shows us where Forsyth got to, and gives a flavour of his style. Looking at his work now more critically, how did he reach this conclusion? I want to suggest that he has a central and controlling insight that salvation and sanctification are not by contagion but through being enrolled into a moral community. It is not a large grant in aid, but a moral transubstantiation. The whole argument then moves backwards from this solution. Thus, Forsyth invests in

[28]243.
[29]264.
[30]242.
[31]249.
[32]257.
[33]258.
[34]243.
[35]260.

a particular theory about symbolism. He summons up what he calls an 'older sense' in which the symbol contains and conveys the significate.[36] He illustrates this with his example of a conquering general being given the keys of a vanquished city.[37] The symbolism conveys an act of surrender. A sacrament is more than a symbol and a symbol is more than a memorial. This allows him to divert attention from the elements and to focus on Christ's act. The supper then is a donation, the bestowal of a blessing. To back this up, he invokes a range of transfer metaphors.

This is an enormously imaginative and bold account. But is it entirely satisfactory? It is certainly elusive. So let us take a hard look at one of his illustrations. As part of his argument against concentration on the elements, Forsyth says: 'In music we repeat the performance often by means of the score (the elements); but the composer's finished work stands there ideally, eternally, functioning in many generations. So Christ's redeeming Act functioned in the Supper, conveying itself to its beneficiaries, and it goes on doing so in the Church. We repeat the ordinance often, and Christ acts as often in our midst.'[38]

This is revealing. On this analogy, the composer's finished work stands for the cross. The score stands for the supper. Repeated performances stand for repeated celebrations. That much is obvious. But in his choice of analogy, is Forsyth actually going further and implying that the supper stands to the cross as the score stands to the musical idea? If that is what he is saying, then as the score is the exclusive articulation of the idea, so the supper is the exclusive bestowal, or hinge, of the cross. The implication would be that if the supper were not there, the cross would not be bestowed.

That may seem a forced interpretation, but why else did Forsyth choose this analogy? The interpretation may be supported from elsewhere. Forsyth tells us that in the supper we have not merely a symbol of Christ's sacrifice to God but 'the actual consignment of it to [the disciples], as being *for them* and not simply for some ... purpose of God.'[39] Here again, Forsyth seems to be saying that Christ's death was not intrinsically vicarious, but only became

[36] 229.
[37] 234.
[38] 236.
[39] 241.

vicarious when it was bestowed, and that this bestowal took place exclusively in the supper.

A further indication that this is what Forsyth means is given by his statement that *with his death* Christ entered a new covenant with God, the value of which he *made over* to his own.[40] Once again, Forsyth is far more concerned to explain the benefit of the bestowal of Christ's death than inclusion into his life.

If this interpretation is correct, it leads to an understanding of the supper as the exclusive means of the transfer of the benefit of Christ's death. As we have seen, Forsyth develops a cluster of transfer terms. He needs this vocabulary because, underplaying as he does the incarnational unity of Christ with all people, he needs some means of expressing the communicability of Christ's work. For him, the transfer terms are vital.

But this in turn, I suggest, leads to a very particular, and I think over-narrow understanding of what it is to be a Christian. And here I want to turn to one of Forsyth's vivid and possibly idiosyncratic *words*. Forsyth twice uses the word 'under-agent': 'The Supper was an under-agent of the Cross',[41] and 'we are under-agents of His great action on that evening.... We perpetuate it antiphonally'.[42] 'Under-agent' is hardly a usual term, but again one must believe that Forsyth's choice of it is not haphazard. What on earth can he have meant by using it? There is an ordination charge of 1733 which runs: 'You [*sc.* clergymen] are made Ministers of Christ and, as I may say, his Under-agents'.[43] In 1805, Wordsworth in *The Prelude* XIII, 273, writes: 'Words are but under agents in their souls.' This is sufficiently close to Forsyth in another passage for one to wonder if Wordsworth was indeed his source. But, amusingly, and perhaps most helpfully, the *Manchester Guardian* for the 15 October 1883 tells us: 'The Earl of Dalhousie was driving near Carnoustie with his under agent.' Forsyth was looking for a word to express the relationship of the member of the eucharistic community to Christ. He wanted to avoid ideas of being merely inspired or enthused. He tells us: 'It is but a youth's Christ ... when He is but Hero, Leader, and Friend'.[44] Equally, he wants to avoid the idea of being under

[40] Cf. 247.
[41] 242–3.
[43] See the *Oxford English Dictionary*, under-, for citation of these instances.
[44] 253.

orders, and so of acting blindly, or, more importantly, not morally. My suggestion is that he opts deliberately for a word which implies 'being in the confidence of', 'being in the employment of'. The Scottish word for the Earl of Dalhousie's 'under agent' would be the Earl's *factor*, the one he trusts to manage his estate. I suggest that Forsyth's use is far from haphazard, and we have here a careful way of describing a close moral relationship which at the same time avoids the vocabulary of *being included into Christ* of which Forsyth is so suspicious. Where the supper is seen as the exclusive means of the bestowal of Christ's act, the Christian is seen as an under-agent, with the supper being virtually the terms of employment.

Few would dispute that this is too limited an understanding of both the supper and the Christian, so where did the narrowing come in? Forsyth is right to see that the work of Christ must be applied, or, as he puts it, *communicated*. However, he has such a passionate concern that Christianity should be *moral*, and is then so caught up with the transfer terms which this brings in its wake, that he is blinded to the flexibility and moral possibility of the language of grace and inclusion. I suspect this affects the way he reads the New Testament, which has a far richer range of images than Forsyth implies. The supper is only one of several ways in which the work of Christ is applied or persons are confronted with it.

For example, there is baptism, which surely illustrates terms of inclusion. There is the footwashing: 'If I do not wash you, you have no part in me',[45] there are the conversations with Nicodemus and the Samaritan woman at the well. There are the Synoptic 'hard sayings' and the Johannine 'I am' sayings which compel acceptance or rejection.

I would suggest that Forsyth rightly picks up the *urgency* in the narrative of the supper. But he reads this urgency as *exclusiveness*. The supper is then moralized to become the *hinge* of conveyance or bestowal. Against Forsyth, I would suggest that the urgency in the gospel tradition is wider. Indeed, compared to the supper, at the footwashing, Jesus is positively menacing. The issue is not the exclusiveness of one delivery point, but the absolute costliness of the gift and the unthinkableness of refusing it.

Forsyth lacks a notion of costly as opposed to cheap grace, and so tends to fight shy of grace altogether. This is where he is dominated

45John 13.8.

by his own rhetoric. He is so caught in the current of the transfer terms that he neglects the inclusive categories almost entirely.[46]

---

[46]My father, T. F. Torrance, on reading this paper, told me that H. R. Mackintosh had made very similar criticisms of James Denney.

Chapter 5

FORSYTH ON PRAYER

Gordon S. Wakefield

Forsyth's understanding of prayer could be summarized in the title of this colloquium 'From a Lover of Love to an Object of Grace'. He teaches prayer not as 'a lover of love' but as 'an object of grace'. In Heiler's famous distinction, later, of course, than Forsyth, his is the prayer of faith, or prophetic faith, not mystical prayer.[1] It is encounter with God in petition, importunity, wresting. It is co-operation with the divine will, but often after a striving which may in some sense change it. Prayer is this rather than meditation or contemplation, or even communion. Thus Forsyth would seem to be counter to the modern fashion, which has rebelled against the 'tyranny of request-response' and turned to techniques of meditation often derived from Eastern religions rather than from the Bible or the teaching of Jesus. This makes prayer 'a sustained introspective awareness that leads to perception of "the Self in the self" (*Bhagvadgita* 6.20), rather than "an inter-personal" conversation with God'.[2] Not so, Forsyth. For him, prayer is theology, *thelogia crucis*, not psychology. He would give short shrift to the modern vogue of Jung and Myers-Briggs, rehabilitations of an outdated psychology, and be profoundly suspicious of creation spirituality. We must not, how-

---

[1] Friedrich Heiler, *Prayer: A Study in the History and Psychology of Religion*, trans. and ed. Samuel McComb (London: Oxford University Press, 1932). This is, unfortunately, an abridged English translation of *Das Gebet* (Munich: Reinhardt, 1923).

[2] George M. Soares-Prabhu, 'Speaking to Abba: Prayer as Petition and Thanksgiving in the Teaching of Jesus', in *Asking and Thanking*, an edition of *Concilium* (1990), no. 3, 33.

ever, generalize thoughtlessly, or make dichotomies too sharp. He would not have been against the practice of retreats, as such. In the preface to *The Soul of Prayer*, Forsyth testifies that prayer is retreat and rest, 'an eyrie ... of large vision and humane'. Unless otherwise specified, citations in this paper are from this brief but instructive volume.

The Soul of Prayer was published in 1916 and takes some account of the raging War. It is a collection of occasional papers, which had appeared previously. The two which concern me most are on incessant and insistent prayer. They were first published in 1910 in a Hodder & Stoughton 'Little Book on Religion', edited by W. Robertson Nicoll, and are prefaced by an essay by Dora Greenwell, a much neglected and underrated devotional writer. She died in 1882, so Forsyth added his contribution to hers after almost twenty years.

Let me summarize what he says with some running comments. In the chapter on 'Prayer as Incessant',[3] he begins with a short section on 'the moral freedom involved and achieved in prayer'. Prayer 'is the effective work of a religion which hangs upon the living God, of a soul surer of God than of itself, and living not its own life, but the life of the Son of God', though in prayer 'we do not so much work as cooperate. We are fellow workers with God'. And since God is the freest being in existence, prayer is the freest thing that human beings can do. 'To pray in faith is to answer God's freedom in its own great note. It is to be taken up into the fundamental movement of the world. It is to realise that for which the whole world, the world as a whole, was made ... "the manifestation of the sons of God", the realisation of complete sonship and its confidences.' Prayer integrates us in advance into the final Christ, for whom, and to whom, the whole creation moves. But it must draw from the cross, 'which is the central act of our emancipation as well as the central revelation of God's own freedom in grace'.

Forsyth proceeds to an exposition of what it means to pray without ceasing. This is the essential extravagance of Christianity, the extravagance of life from the cross and by the cross. It is paradox. 'I live who die daily. I live another's life.' To pray without ceasing is not to pray

---

[3]Chapter 2 (pp. 55–92) in *The Power of Prayer*. This material was only slightly revised for *The Soul of Prayer*, chapter 5.

without a break. The sanctus of the company of heaven is not the iteration of a doxology, the repeated glorias of an office. 'It is deep calling unto deep, eternity greeting eternity.' Nor is he taking inspiration from the thought that 'o'er each continent and island ... the voice of prayer is never silent' as in Ellerton's much-loved evening hymn. Though Forsyth, assertively Protestant, is being pejorative about 'the continuous murmur of the mass following the sun round the world, incessant relays of adoring priests, and functions going on day and night'. I suppose he would deplore a mantra-like rhythm and a ritual fussiness, the correct performance of an outward act made more important than the motions of the heart.

Incessant prayer means 'the constant drift and bent of the soul', to be 'in Christ'. It is not identical with the occasional act of praying. 'Like the act of faith, it is a whole life.'

In some sense this is true of every human life, for ruling passions are prayer. 'Every life is a draft upon the unseen.' 'Every life that is not totally inert is praying either to God or God's adversary.' Forsyth makes one of his rare quotations from Kierkegaard, in some ways a kindred theologian, who incidentally, has kept so many in the 'Protestant' way, from W. H. Auden to Hans Urs von Balthasar.[4] It is from *Entweder-Oder*, a letter in which the seduced writes to the seducer, who has him inextricably in his power, in spite of his desire to escape the thrall. For worse not for better they possess one another, 'I call you mine and I am thine – thy curse for ever.' To say 'My God!' may be our doom. 'Prayer is the nature of our hell as well as our heaven.'

Forsyth gives some practical advice. 'To cultivate the ceaseless spirit of prayer, use more frequent acts of prayer. You may have to compel yourself, as with a task you are reluctant to take up and yet will enjoy in half-an-hour of doing so, or with a social engagement for which you do not wish to turn out and yet you will be in your element in laughter and the love of friends. Compel yourself to pray.' If you think that it is futile to tell God what he already knows, remember that 'petition is not mere receptivity, nor is it mere pressure; it is filial reciprocity'. 'And what kills petition, kills praise'.

'Write prayers and burn them.' Pray specifically out of your own condition, do not be trapped by fine phrases or by seeking in prayer

[4]For W. H. Auden see *Forwards and Afterwords* (London: Faber 1973), 167–8. For Balthasar's own testimony see *The Analogy of Beauty: The Theology of Hans Urs von Balthasar*, ed. John Riches (Edinburgh: T&T Clark, 1986), 201.

to emulate the saints. 'Pray as yourself and not as some fancied saint.' Do not pray in court dress. This is Forsyth's equivalent of the maxims of Dom John Chapman after tortured years, 'Pray as you can, and don't try to pray as you can't'; and, 'The less you pray the worse it goes.'[5] It may be noted that Lancelot Andrewes, certainly not the 'average' man, could only pray from the words of Scripture and ancient liturgy. He did not pray as 'some fancied saint' but rather in the communion of saints and deliberately in the long tradition of the church. And George Herbert prayed as a courtier – witness his famous poem with which *The Temple* ends, 'Love III': 'Love bade me welcome, yet my soul drew back.' Even there he is well aware of the dangers and seductions of court life.

Forsyth goes on to forbid philosophizing in prayer. This may be necessary in discussion, but we should pray as Christ bids us and not with the hesitations and speculations of the savant. Make everything the subject of prayer except the absurdly frivolous, but remember prayer does not work by magic and stormy desire is not fervent, effectual prayer. 'Better prayers are stirred by the presence of the Deliverer than even by the need of deliverance.'

Before prayer can be answered, it must itself be an answer, our answer to God's prayer in the cross. Faith is the attitude of the child who is an adult. It is not simply dependence but intelligent committal.

Forsyth deplores the barrenness, the lack of romance and of progress in many religious people, who have no personal religion. 'They do not face themselves only what happens to them.' 'We need the prayer of self-judgment more than the prayer of fine insight.' (Psychology is not absent, after all.) Too often prayer leaves us with self-complacency like 'the breezy octogenarian all of whose yesterdays look backward with a cheery and exasperating smile'. (I cannot say that this is true to my own experience. My retrospect is mostly of folly and failure, though prayer does help to set it in the perspective of the divine mercy and grace.) Forsyth concludes that prayer is an art to be learned and practised.

The second chapter is on 'Prayer as Insistent'.[6] Forsyth seems to be concerned chiefly with the prayer of the minister. For him, in the

---

[5] Dom John Chapman, *Spiritual Letter* (Sheed and Ward, 1959), 25.

[6] Chapter 3 (pp. 95–149) of *The Power of Prayer*. Six years later in *The Soul of Prayer*, this was divided into two chapters: 'The Vicariousness of Prayer' (chapter 6), and 'The Insistency of Prayer' (chapter 7).

tradition of Baxter, the Puritans and George Herbert, ministry is the most awesome of vocations.[7] His doctrine is high, too much so to be congenial to many today in the churches of his own tradition, or indeed in all the churches where the *auctoritas* of the minister of word and sacraments is gradually being eroded and the very concept of priesthood surreptitiously revised. 'The more we grasp our gospel the more it abashes us.' Every time we present it, we 'are adding to the judgment of some as well as the salvation of others.' Here we share the agony of Christ:

> How solemn our place is! It is a sacramental place. We have not simply to state our case, we have to *convey* our Christ, and to convey Him effectually. We are sacramental elements, broken often, in the Lord's hands, as He dispenses His grace through us. We do not, of course, believe that orders are an ecclesiastical sacrament, as Rome does. But we are forced to realise the idea underlying that dogma – the sacramental nature of our person, work, and vocation for the gospel. We are not saviours. There is only one Saviour. But we are His sacraments. We do not believe in an ecclesiastical priesthood; but we are made to feel how we stand between God and the people as none of our flock do. We bring Christ to them, and them to Christ, in a sacrificial action, in a way far more moral, inward, and taxing than official priesthood can do. As ministers we lead the sacerdotal function of the whole Church in the world – its holy confession and sacrifice for the world in Christ.

This is a dangerous industry. 'We have to tend a consuming fire. We have to reed our life where all the tragedy of life is gathered to an infinite crisis in Christ. We are not the fire, but we live where it burns.' 'But ... our doom is our blessing. Our Judge is on our side. ... We win a confidence in self-despair' (an echo of Charles Wesley on wrestling Jacob). Prayer is as wings on which we mount to the throne of God and a shield to protect our face from the all-consuming blaze when we get there. 'We are one with the Christ not only on His cross but in His resurrection.' 'And even the unclean lips

[7]See Richard Baxter, *The Reformed Pastor* and George Herbert, *A Priest to the Temple*, or *The Country Parson* various editions from 1656 and 1652 respectively.

then put a new thrill into our sympathy and a new tremor into our praise.'

George Herbert, whom Forsyth does not quote, called prayer 'engine against the Almighty'. Forsyth uses the same image, but says that it is the engine for the recovery of faith. He would have liked to illustrate his page with Dürer's praying hands and Milton's line, 'the great two-handed engine at *our* door'.

He then speaks of the minister's task of public prayer and is not against the use of notes, of which the Lord's Prayer is an example. He says in an earlier chapter of *The Soul of Prayer*, 'Public prayer should be in the main liturgical with room for free prayer.' This prayer must not be affectional, or chatty. It is 'the soul returning to the God that gave it ... the sinner coming to the Saviour ... the ransomed of the Lord returning to Zion ... the sanctified with the Sanctifier ... not primarily the child talking to the Father'. He would have welcomed James Barr's insistence that, contrary to some Puritans, Joachim Jeremias and many modern sermons, 'Abba' does not mean 'Daddy'.[8]

Public prayer can spring only from private prayer. Supremely the minister is intercessor whenever he prays which is the best corrective of the critical spirit. Forsyth is not thinking here primarily of the discipline of the historical criticism of the Scriptures, but of attitudes to other people, jealous carping, reductionism, dislike. 'Prayer is the spring of personality.'

'Prayer is for the religious life what original research is for the scientist.' It must have theology in it, the scale of the whole gospel, the range of searching faith. So much religious life, so much spirituality is trivial. We need prayer 'with the profound Bible as its book of devotion, and a true theology of faith for half of its power'.

It must be prayer with concentration, with will in it and the energy of Christ, though the minister must remember with relief that he is but Christ's curate. It demands patience, for the answer will not come all at once. It is in Christ's name, which is not simply like 'per carter Patterson' on a parcel in the old days or Parcel Force today. It means that it must be prayer for Christ's object – the

---

[8]See James Barr, 'Abba isn't "Daddy"', *Journal of Theological Studies* 39 (April 1988): 28–47, and Barr, '"Abba Father" and the Familiarity of Jesus' Speech', *Theology* 91 (May 1988): 173–9.

kingdom of God. The true amen is when the prayer expires in its
own spiritual fullness. It should end itself in heaven. It should yield
up its spirit like Christ on the cross, saying 'It is finished'.
This is very daring. It reminds one of a hymn in Charles Wesley's
collection *Hymns for the Use of Families* (1767), excluded from the
1983 *Hymns and Psalms*, which makes the life and ministry of Christ
our pattern:

> Till we on the sacred tree,
> Bow the head and die like thee.

For Forsyth, this cannot be the imitation or miming of Christ, but
the Lutheran total identity through imputation. And it is prayer
which utters the *tetelestai*, not our natural selves but the Holy Spirit
within.

Forsyth then comes to deal with importunity in prayer. This gives
prayer power and saves it from introspection or spiritual egoism.
Prayer may change the will of God, or resist it. 'Resisting His will
may be doing His will.' Prayer is an encounter of wills, not 'the
laying of the head on a divine bosom in trust and surrender'. It is not,
as with Schleiermacher, absolute dependence. 'It is a cause acting on
the course of God's world' (cf. Pascal). 'Thy will be done' is not
passive resignation but passionate cooperation. And God is 'an
infinite opportunist. His ways are flexible. His *intentions* are ame-
nable to us if His *will* is changeless'. 'We cannot change the will of
God, which is grace, and which even Christ never changed but only
revealed; but we can change the intention of God, which is a manner
of treatment, in the interest of grace, according to the situation of
the hour.'

Christ set more value on importunity than submission. This is
true throughout Scripture and in Christ's own experience. Prayer 'is
a wrestle on the greatest scale' and the result is not always peace.
Prayer is wrestling with God, a resistance that God loves, quite
foreign to a godless, self-willed resistance. It is the resistance of love,
not of hostility. Lovers achieve total oneness through yielding to one
another totally, body and soul. Forsyth does not even touch
delicately on the sexual aspect of this as a modern writer could hardly
avoid doing. He contrasts it with yielding to a foreign force and
there follows a Ritschlian passage:

> So when God yields to prayer in the name of Christ, to the

prayer of faith and love, He yields to Himself who inspired
it. Christian prayer is the Spirit praying in us. It is prayer in
the solidarity of the Kingdom. It is a continuation of Christ's
prayer, which in Gethsemane was a wrestle, an *agonia* with
the Father. But if so, it is God pleading with God, God
dealing with God – as the true atonement must be. And when
God yields it is not to an outside influence He yields, but to
Himself.

The prayer which resists God's dealings may be part of his will
and its fulfilment. Forsyth instances a boy born into a poor home
struggling to better himself – this has been scorned by some radicals
in our time, often from fairly prosperous homes themselves; also the
fighting of disease and death, the latter pertinent in Victorian times
when pious people not only expected early death, but longed for it;
also the need to restrain our natural instincts and passions. Obedience is not mere submission, mere resignation. It is not mere
acquiescence. It certainly was not with Christ. This is very important in a century in which the worst crimes may well have been
committed through obedience to orders, a selfish non-resistance.

Lose the importunity of prayer and you degrade it to 'a mere
walking with God in friendly talk; and, precious as that is, yet you
tend to lose the reality of prayer at last... . For you lose the *power* of
the cross and so of the soul'. 'Cast yourself into [God's] arms not to
be caressed but to wrestle with Him.... He may be too many for you
and lift you from your feet. But it will be to lift you from earth and
set you in the heavenly places which are theirs who fight the good
fight and lay hold of God as their eternal life.'

As a corollary, I would note the relation, in Forsyth, between
prayer and preaching. He wrote toward the end of the great age of
nonconformist preaching, when the Free Churches were at the
zenith of their influence and men outnumbered women in the
congregations for perhaps the only time in church history. It was, of
course, the time of 'muscular Christianity', which may partly
account for Forsyth's plea for the masculine in prayer and his
warning against piety being 'only feminine'. It is easy to deplore this
as sexist, until we remember that it is now recognized that masculine
and feminine are constituents of each of us in different proportions.

For Forsyth, preaching and prayer were part of the same priestly
activity, as they were for George Herbert, who thought a preacher

should often apostrophize God in his sermons. Forsyth, I am sure, would have insisted that the people's prayers should be led by the preacher, contrary to much modern practice, which in many places is anxious to diminish the preacher's distinctive role in the interests sometimes of what is thought to be a truer expression of the priesthood of all believers, sometimes as a supposedly better means of communication with the people if not with God.

Forsyth may be thought to have played down meditation in his direct teaching on prayer. But this passage, shorn of its homiletic eloquence, could almost be an Ignatian meditation on the healing of the ruler's son:

> Or, I read the story of the father who beseeches Christ to heal his son. I hear the answer of the Lord, 'I will come down and heal him.' 'Him!' That means me. The words are life to my distempered soul. I care little for them (when I need them most) as a historic incident of the long past, an element in the discussion of miracles. They do not serve their divinest purpose till they come to me as they came to that father. They come with a promise here and now. I see the heavens open and the Redeemer at the Right Hand of God. I hear a great voice from heaven and these are the words of the Saviour Himself to me, 'I will come down and heal him.' And upon them He rises from His eternal throne. He takes His way through a ready lane of angels, archangels, the high heavenly host and the glorious fellowship of the saints. They part at His coming, for they know where He would go. These congenial souls do not keep Him, and these native scenes do not detain Him. But on the wings of that word He moves from the midst of complete obedience, spiritual love, holy intelligence, ceaseless worship and perfect praise. He is restless amid all that in search of me – me sick, falling, lost, despicable, desperate. He comes, He finds, He heals me on the wings of these words.[9]

Much modern prayer, as it has been from Dionysius the Areopagite onwards, is a synthesis of the prophetic and the mystical, the prayer

[9]Quoted by Edward Shillito, 'The Preaching of the Word', in *Christian Worship: Studies in its History and Meaning*, ed. Nathaniel Micklem (Oxford: Clarendon, 1936), 220–1.

of faith and the prayer of love. Forsyth recalls us to the prayer of Christ and his cross, in which the union is not of passive absorption in the infinite but of active will. Petition is not relegated to the lowest level; importunity, passionate pleading, even strife with God are the marks of the prayers of the saints and of Christ himself. They demand an intensity of faith in a living God, which is no 'high state', but the prayer of those who know that the grace of God is ever prevenient and we dare to believe that he loved us before the foundation of the world. This in no sense excludes our love, which cannot be kept out of true prayer. Forsyth even hints at the analogy of sexual union, in which individual identity is not obliterated. The oneness and the joy are the result of personal encounter, sometimes resistance, which ends in a mutual yielding, the more absolute in self-giving than mere contemplation. Prayer is dynamic, it is energy. It is above all, not sentimental, what John Wesley eschewed as the 'namby-pambical'. Mind and will are not abandoned as in some contemplatives. There is certain detachment as well as affection and affectiveness. It is certainly not a matter, as in A. N. Whitehead's strictures, of 'paying metaphysical compliments to God'. It ends in heaven, but only after the union is consummated not simply in rapturous joy, but by being crucified with Christ. It is Protestant, yet not counter, so much as complement and part-corrective, to the long Catholic tradition.

Chapter 6

TRAGEDY IN THE THEOLOGY OF P. T. FORSYTH

George Hall

This paper examines P. T. Forsyth's understanding and use of the notion of tragedy, not only in his much admired work on theodicy, *The Justification of God*, where it is most prominent, but elsewhere in his major writings. It is clear that the concept of tragedy is a conspicuous feature of his theology and while often acknowledged, has not, so far as I am aware, received the close attention it deserves considering the weight he gives it. Of course, it is sometimes difficult to measure the force Forsyth actually gives an idea or concept given the earnest rhetoric and vigorous polemic that characterizes much of his writing but, rhetoric and polemics aside, I suggest that his use of tragedy is crucial for an adequate understanding of certain of his most important teachings. At the least, the frequency and character of his reference to tragedy begs careful examination.

The major part of this paper consists in a review of his use of tragedy in order to show that tragedy is a significant element in his larger theological project and while not developed in a systematic fashion, it was introduced neither in a casual manner nor merely for heightened effect. The importance of the tragic for Forsyth is apparent in his claim that 'in life's daily affairs it may be wisdom not to take things tragically. But they have to be taken tragically somewhere if we are to have moral realism at all.... . The world as a world has to be tragically taken.'[1] The mainstream of Christian

[1] *Preaching*, 3rd ed., 234.

77

thought has long been fed by a small and irregular spring from which there trickles, often unnoticed or, if noticed, resisted, various attempts to connect tragedy and Christian faith. Recently this flow has increased in strength, but there continues to be understandable anxiety that the dark impenetrability of genuine tragedy may pollute the substance of faith if even an attenuated form of it seeps in. For most, 'taking the world tragically' stands in sharp and indissoluble contradiction to the Christian view of human life and history. This may account, in part at least, for the fact that given the continuing interest in the theology of Forsyth, little serious account has been taken of the centrality accorded tragedy in his thought.

This neglect, however, becomes difficult to countenance when Forsyth asserts that 'the most tragic, the most portentous occurrence of all man's aching, bloody, and tragic history is the death of Christ'.[2] The tragic situation of humanity stems from a tragic collision between a sinful and guilty humanity and the holy God; a collision which is overcome only when God destroys sin through a 'new creation' tragically achieved. The very vehicle of eternal redemption is the supreme tragedy of the cross of Christ. Of course, it might be argued that at this very point Forsyth relinquishes tragedy since here it converts to and is encompassed by a *divina commedia*. But, says Forsyth, this provides no licence for neglect of the tragic – 'If it is our wisdom not to be tragic it is only the wisdom of faith, which does not ignore the tragedy, but is able to cast it on *One who did take things tragically*, and who underwent and overcame at the moral centre of men and things.'[3] To ignore or to dismiss as a rhetorical flourish the element of tragedy in Forsyth's theology is to eviscerate it not only of his understanding of the human condition, but of the atonement as well. It may be that his entanglement with tragedy counts against his theology or that its substance can be made independent of it, but this needs to be established by critical engagement with his scattered comments on tragedy. To ignore or hastily dismiss Forsyth's thoughts on tragedy in the light of his final commitment to 'the Divine *Commedia* on the scale of all existence'[4] is, within the context of his theology, analogous to allowing the joy

---

[2] *Justification*, 2nd ed., 149.
[3] *Preaching*, 234. My emphasis.
[4] *Justification*, 76.

of Easter not only to eclipse, but to eliminate, the agony of Good Friday.

I

Forsyth deliberately directed his Lyman Beecher lectures, published as *Positive Preaching and the Modern Mind*,[5] to the students among his audience, urging them to turn to the great dramatists in their search for an understanding of the world to which they would address their preaching of the gospel. He advised them that the tragic drama of the Greeks, Shakespeare, and Ibsen offered insights into the moral realities of the human situation of far greater value than the abstract philosophical and theological analyses of learned academics. They pierce to the very root of the pretence, shallowness, evil and guilt of 'a world whose history streams with so much blood, ruin, and misery'.[6] They mercilessly expose and challenge the hollowness of 'sunny piety, pseudo-liberalism and humanism' by which we seek to blunt the sharp, sometimes unbearable, edge of those calamities and evils that threaten or deliver inconsolable despair and final dissolution. Such 'shams' may offer hope and comfort but only until we are brought 'face to face with the utmost, the most devilish, forms of suffering and wickedness'.[7]

Forsyth cites Ibsen as a dramatist who lays bare life's moral realities and he heaped lavish praise upon him as he counselled his audience to read 'this great prophet'.[8] His commendation of Ibsen is worth quoting at length since he concludes by saying, 'Preach to Ibsen's world, and there are few you will miss.'[9] What is it that finds a fitting representation in the drama of Ibsen such that Forsyth can recommend that he not only be read but be read again?

> Mark and learn his unsparing ethical realism. Could that remorseless insight of his through the shams and clothes of ordinary society miss the grim dull ache of guilt? For him, as

[5] *Preaching*, 103–5.
[6] *Justification*, 42.
[7] *Justification*, 135.
[8] *Preaching*, 103.
[9] *Preaching*, 105.

for all the rest of the tragic poets, guilt is the centre of tragedy. 'Guilt remains guilt,' he says. 'You cannot bully God into such blessing as turns guilt to merit, or penalty to reward.' No, God can be neither bullied nor blandished into that. Yet the blessing is there. The one thing needful is there – not the merit but the mercy. The forgiveness is there, and there from God, there of His own free gift, at His proper cost. And to realise how awful that cost is use such as Ibsen. To save your soul from sunny or silly piety, to realize the deadly inveteracy of evil, its dereliction by God, its sordid paralysis of all redeeming, self-recuperative power in man, its incurable fatal effect upon the moral order of society, read Ibsen. Yea to realize how it thereby imports the element of death even into the natural order of the universe read Ibsen. It inflicts death on whatever power you call God. Unless, indeed, that power have the secret (unknown to this great prophet) of transforming the death which it cannot evade. Within the moral order there may reside (Christ says there does reside), a mortal power to make itself effective, not only in spite of the wound to it, but by means of that wound.[10]

It is important to notice that Forsyth's admiration of the dramatist is not without qualification. While preaching should be directed to Ibsen's world, it should not contain his '*word*'. Although he 'reads one book with uncanny penetration, the Book of Man, Church, and Society, he has never turned the same piercing eye on the other book, the New Testament, and never taken Christ as seriously as he takes man. He is grimly, ghastly interpretive but not redemptive – like his analytic age.'[11]

The insights of the great dramatists illuminate the fundamental moral realities of human life but they never, unless informed by faith, discover a solution to the problem of life. For life is not a riddle to be solved by human wit but 'a tragic battle for existence, for power, for eternal life'.[12] There is indeed a 'solution' to the problem, but tackled merely with our own devices of intellect and moral effort it proves insoluble. Rather the solution is given to us, it is practical

---

[10] *Preaching*, 103.
[11] *Preaching*, 104.
[12] *Justification*, 209.

not theoretical, and it is already done in God's revelation of grace in the cross of Christ – 'Life begins as a problem, but when it ends well it ends as a faith.'[13] The Ibsens of this world can help because they are finely tuned to the underlying realities of ordinary life and it is ordinary life that sets the problem. But they cannot proceed to identify the solution unless, unlike Ibsen himself, they have achieved the standpoint of faith which provides our only existential security and the only valid, though still clouded, view of the relation of the tragic human condition to the divine *commedia.*

Ibsen, at least in a substantial body of his literary production, was concerned with the obdurate moral predicament which confronted individuals in their personal struggle for wholeness and unity within a sick society. He ruthlessly unmasked the hypocrisy, self-deception, and sham with which contemporary society clothed itself. In his exposure of the inward dimension of the individual's struggle to realize his or her ideals, hopes, and dreams in a corrupt and fragmented society, Ibsen brutally traced the corruption and dissolution of the emotional and intellectual resources of his characters as they battled to the end only to be defeated and broken by the burdens and limitations imposed not only by the necessity to adjust to the sickness that gnawed at the heart of society, but through the slow recognition that this sickness was resident within themselves as well.

Forsyth found in Ibsen's dramas many of the themes which characterize his own thought: an emphasis upon the will, moral realism, the troubled conscience, the ubiquity of guilt, the destructive power of egoism, the intricate and often conflicting relationships binding the individual and society, the ultimate inadequacy of humanity's self-recuperative powers to effect genuine reconciliation – and this does not exhaust the list. If one had nothing more to go on than Forsyth's high regard not only for Ibsen but for any dramatist who plumbed the depths of moral reality through the medium of tragic art, it would suffice to say that he, like most of us, admired the art of the great tragedians for its insights into the moral conflicts and predicaments of humankind. But Forsyth's interest in tragic drama goes well beyond the deployment of these insights in an otherwise non-tragic discourse. Tragedy, he insists, can be overcome only through tragedy.

[13] *Justification*, 208.

II

The task of tracing the use of tragedy in the writings of Forsyth is made hazardous by the lack of any systematic treatment of the concept anywhere in his published works. He often refers to specific tragic dramatists and their plays but he rarely draws directly upon particular dramas to illustrate his understanding of what he takes to be the nature of tragedy or tragic art. We can, however, piece together a fairly clear and generally consistent pattern of use through an ordering of his scattered comments on tragedy and its significance for Christian theology.

For Forsyth, the 'great mirror of life – the stage', provides an apt illustration of the nature of history. 'History is a grand drama, it is not a mere process.' All dramas, he continues, are either comedies or tragedies:

> If life were a great comedy, the grand solution and reconcilement would come in its palpable close. All would be gathered up and finished off there. Life would be rounded, after some jars, with a heavenly smile. We should have but the story with the happy ending, all in one volume. But life is too large, and it moves in curves too great, to be trimmed down and rounded off in our brief first volume. There are two volumes at least. The powers at war in it (if I change the figure) are too vast to settle the eternal issue in a campaign too short.[14]

Hence, the drama of history is best represented as tragedy. Forsyth agrees with Wellhausen that the effect of history on the individual is a tragedy which as such always has an unhappy end. But in the case of the prophets, history carries their vision beyond the world. He buttresses this suggestion of something 'beyond' by quoting Darrell Figgis on Shakespeare, "'The play, with Shakespeare, is not all. It but shapes for something beyond. And so we take our stand according to the judgement of the Divinity beyond. We believe what we cannot see, and so we are exalted and purged in our outlook on life."[15] The tragic moral struggle of humanity indicates something beyond – the 'second volume'. This is all set within the context of

---

[14] *Justification*, 12.
[15] *Justification*, 214.

his earlier remark that 'all great drama, Greek or Shakespearean, has a divinity over it for its providence'.[16] Reconciliation comes from beyond the confines of world history, a Beyond which is implicated in that history although it cannot be discerned from within it:

> The key is the Beyond; though not necessarily beyond death, but beyond the world of the obvious, and palpable, and common-sensible... . The solution of all is indicated as outside all. But it is indicated. The unhappy endings do so indicate to the seer's eye. Failure is not yet destruction nor final defeat. Such closes are both prayers and prophecies. They mean that God alone may end things when they become as bad as they are great.[17]

The figure of the 'two volumes' provides a framework in which to structure Forsyth's understanding of the human drama where, though the story ends badly, it indicates a grand consummation and an eternal redemption from Beyond. History, though we command the whole course of it, cannot explain itself – the key lies beyond history, in 'the historic Christ who is above history and in command of it'.[18] Everything that Forsyth says about creation, sin, moral reality, reconciliation, and redemption can be structured in terms of the 'two volumes' – human and divine: the one is a tragedy, the other a divine *commedia*. And it is in and through, and not merely in spite of, the tragic irruption of the first that the tragic collision between God and a godless world is overcome by the merciful judgement of God.

We must speak, then, of two creations: the first is the arena of moral freedom, the second of spiritual, holy freedom – which is actually the goal of the moral freedom of the first, and thereby its key. The first creation was a divine experiment of fateful consequence since God trusted human beings with moral freedom; a freedom, which history has abundantly confirmed, they could all too easily abuse. But God would not have embarked upon so risky

---

[16] *Justification*, 212. Forsyth too readily assimilates the roles of the gods in Attic tragedy to the Christian of 'providence' with the result that he misses the ambiguous shadow of 'malevolent divinity' that stalks Attic drama.

[17] *Justification*, 213.

[18] *Justification*, 218.

an adventure without the power to redeem any misuse 'by a new creation more mighty, marvellous, and mysterious than the first'. The second creation is the first creation tragically 'arrived' and is a more creative act since to redeem the first creation is the final thing omnipotence can do – 'What is omnipotence but the costly and inevitable action of holiness in establishing itself everywhere for ever.'[19]

The first creation does not evolve or develop dialectically into the second but arrives through 'a crisis of entirely new departure'.[20] It is the tragic action of a holy God who rescues humankind from the ruin of its own making, a ruin brought about by human sin – the 'wrongest thing with the world'.[21] Forsyth avoids talk of 'total corruption' but this in no way diminishes the power and gravity of sin. He is at great pains to distance himself from those conceptions of sin that assimilate it to a process of reconciliation through the mistaken belief that there is something in sin that can be incorporated within God's reconciliation. And while he acknowledges a tendency to self-recuperation in the order and process, we can discern apart from redemption, this does not deliver us from the 'world of sin, sin in dominion, sin solidary if not hereditary, yea from sin which integrates us into the Satanic Kingdom'.[22] He speaks of what might be called 'a racial egoism, a self-engrossment of mankind with itself, a naïve and tacit assumption that God were no God if He cared for anything more than He did for His creature'.[23] The state of civilisation reveals 'this superhuman wickedness' which lies beyond the scope of any individual to fathom or master – 'Only the absolutely holy can measure sin or judge it.'[24] Sin is a malignancy which must be destroyed and only 'a supermundane Christ can cope with such evil.'[25]

It would be difficult to exaggerate either Forsyth's negative estimate of the moral state of humanity or what he takes to be at stake in its collision with a holy God. Sin is an absolute contradic-

---

[19] *Justification*, 123.
[20] *Justification*, 124.
[21] *Justification*, 167.
[22] *Justification*, 31.
[23] *Justification*, 11.
[24] *Justification*, 31.
[25] *Justification*, 32.

tion of holiness, of what life is meant to be, and 'is the death of God'. The great crisis of human life and history is the collision of 'eternal sin' with 'eternal Saviour' in which the 'eternal holiness is in conflict for its life'.[26] All sin diminishes God and if it 'were not repelled by God's judgement it would extinguish God'.[27] Forsyth may stop short of 'total corruption' or 'total depravity', but sin is an affliction that penetrates to the moral heart of the individual and fatally contaminates the social fabric. It must be judged and destroyed – 'Die sin must or God'.[28] Our civilisation is egoist, godless, and condemned to public madness and death without the saving judgement of God.

This is a severely negative view of moral life apart from God and Forsyth eagerly commends Nietzsche, the apostle of negation, for the profundity and depth of his insight.

> Nietzsche felt as millions feel, that life culminated in its tragic experiences, and that whatsoever solved the tragedy of life solved all life. That is why I say his challenge of Christianity is greater, more incisive, more searching and taxing than that of Strauss, and therefore more promising and more sympathetic, for all his contempt. He was not a spectator but an actor in this tragedy, so much so that it unhinged his mind. To grasp the real, deep tragedy of life is enough to unhinge any mind which does not find God's solution of it in the central tragedy of the Cross and its redemption.[29]

Forsyth admires Nietzsche for his acute awareness of the desperate plight of the human being caught up in the tragedy of life. Life is a grave and painful battle which, without the gracious judgement and redemption of the holy God, would close with no hope of fulfilment. But the battle ends with an even more painful and costly victory, a tragic victory given to us rather than won by us.

The ground covered thus far raises at least two questions about Forsyth's linking of Christian faith with tragedy. Even if we were to grant that life is a continuing battle from which there is no lasting

[26] *Justification*, 147.
[27] *Justification*, 148.
[28] *Justification*, 147.
[29] *Justification*, 210.

respite, that human fulfilment is always partial and ever vulnerable to suffering and irretrievable loss, and that human life and history are devoid of any ultimate meaning – these alone would not warrant its characterization as tragic. Is Forsyth warranted in calling his portrayal of the human drama tragic? Secondly, the battle of life ends with a victory that transforms human existence onto another, higher plane – 'All's well that ends well." Does this not convert the tragedy into comedy or perhaps tragi-comedy? If so, what has been gained by speaking so freely of tragedy in a situation which apparently was never really tragic from the start? Forsyth is keen to assure us that the battle of life 'is not a sport of heaven' and that its 'tragedy is not God's jest'. But, if so, why were the battle lines so blurred and the victory, when it came, so enigmatic?

III

The clue to the answer to our first question is found in Forsyth's refusal to speak of the 'total corruption' of the human being. He endorsed what he called 'Butler's great saying'[30] to the effect that 'morality is the nature of things'; indicating, not the content and criteria of morality, but its status – 'For what is so insistent, inevitable, and dogmatic as the categorical imperative which is at the moral centre?'[31] When we think upon life and history, the moral is the real since the 'spiritual world is not the world of noetic process or cosmic force, but of holy, i.e. moral order, act and power'.[32] Accordingly, Forsyth's anthropology is centred in free will and conscience. The human being:

> is more than a consciousness, he is a conscience. He is not only aware of himself, he is critical of himself. There is in the soul a bar, a tribunal; our thoughts and actions are ranged before it; judgement is passed there upon what we have been and done. Everyone who believes in morality believes in the conscience as the power we have in passing moral judgement about ourselves.[33]

[30] *Person*, 256.
[31] *Person*, 218.
[32] *Person*, 223.
[33] *Cruciality*, 2nd edn 62.

Conscience is the engrained gift of the Creator and we have no power by which to cancel or still its voice even if it pronounces us guilty. Here, then, is the seedbed of the troubled conscience, of inner division. We are one but also two and the two do not agree. However turbulent the division, there is one side that cannot be cast off or silenced – 'Our enemy is of our essence, taken from under our very heart. We are one by being two.'[34] The basis of conscience is our sense of responsibility, our sense that we are not here merely for freedom but for responsibility – our freedom is a responsible freedom.

Our conscience is a judge, not a legislator, and though we may freely commit ourselves to values, norms and goals, this, according to Forsyth, is not a permission for us to exercise our freedom in just any way we are inclined. Humankind has a goal, a destiny. Human beings crave fulfilment, wholeness, and unity but the way is uncertain. Where is the goal? What is our destiny? According to Forsyth, the anguish of inner strife testifies to the unity of the soul and so the question is really whether 'the perfecting of that unity' is our destiny or shall our 'warfare at a stage dissolve into dust'? But the question concerns not only the instinct of the soul to go on, but whether 'the world has a unity and a destiny corresponding to the instinct of the soul and to its resentment of dissolution?'[35] God works by 'moral compulsion' and has granted us the moral freedom to choose who shall be lord of our conscience. With fateful and tragic consequences humankind chooses human law rather than holy law, the anthropocentric rather than the theocentric way, and so even our religion centres on ourselves and God's love comes to be regarded, when accorded regard, 'as the greatest asset of man instead of man's trustful obedience as the supreme worship and due of God'.[36]

The anthropocentric turn alienates us from the holy God and exposes us to the self-destructiveness of an autonomy in which the imperative is rooted in ourselves. The blasphemy of sin has set us adrift from the holy law, from our destiny, and condemned us not only to estrangement from God but to self-estrangement and social strife:

[34] *Cruciality*, 63.
[35] *Justification*, 45.
[36] *Justification*, 106.

Life has what has been called a dramatic character. Will is involved in it – choice, conscience, reason, and action. It is a movement, a crescendo, of moral action, and not of natural process. Nay, it is further said, and with poignant truth, that it is, in most cases, not dramatic simply but tragic. But it is tragic in a deeper than the outward, obvious, and impressive sense. It is not the tragedy of an external fate falling on the inner will. It is the tragedy of the inner will itself falling. It is the man's own fall, and not the fall of his fortunes. It is his moral tragedy, the fall not from happiness but from holiness – the tragedy not simply of gloom but of guilt. Behind all the tragedies of incident lies the tragedy of guilt.[37]

A 'godless', that is, a human-centred world, is condemned to divisiveness, suffering, and calamity. But Christians know of their proper destiny through their experience of the revelation in Jesus Christ – it is the spiritual, holy freedom of the new creation. And just as moral freedom is a gift of creation, the second is the gift of the new creation. Of course, those without faith are not conscious of their sin against the holy God and are confused and anxious about the goal of their moral freedom. Consequently, the world will appear to them as one in which, in the end, they are subject to an unjustifiable 'destiny' of arbitrary suffering, ultimate meaninglessness, and final defeat.

Those on whom the problem of life presses most acutely, those who are 'unhinged' by the deep tragedy of life, may be plunged into hopelessness and despair. It is in the midst of this crisis that they may encounter their genuine destiny since God is a 'God of crisis, who is God most chiefly in the chief tragedy of things, and from the nettle of perdition plucks the flower of salvation.'[38]

Our destiny is found in our tragedy and not in our idyll, not in our hour of triumph but in our depths of distress. If man is one *in* conscience, he is not one *by* conscience; for by itself it reveals guilt and division. The unity is a unity effected *by* God *in* conscience, in the tragedy of our conscience, and not simply its voice or law. It is His gift of release to conscience,

[37] *Justification*, 50.
[38] *Justification*, 30.

His reconstruction of it. It is not at last a matter of our conscience but of Christ in our conscience. It is a divine reconciliation, but a reconciliation of the conscience more even than of the affections (cp. 2 Cor. v. 19 with 21); it is a recall from guilt and not from mere coldness.[39]

This is not merely a rehabilitation of the conscience, it is its re-creation. It is not the redemption of sin but its destruction – the dawning of the 'second creation'.

The tragic flaw of humankind means that its own resources of self-recuperation are insufficient to effect redemption but bring instead only greater disquiet and anxiety, especially where our well-intentioned efforts to do good bring ill in their wake. In times of acute personal and social crisis, we find that our confidence in the continual advance of knowledge, goodness, and spirituality is shattered as we come to realize that we have blindly underestimated the range and depth of humankind's capacity to inflict suffering and to accomplish horrendous evil. We have tended to take comfort in the picture of a world and human beings 'unfolding their powers, achievements, and joys in a waxing process of beneficent triumph, spreading light, and broadening boon'. But now, and here we should recall the occasion precipitating Forsyth's meditation on theodicy, all have been plunged into a 'bloody, monstrous, and deadly dark' that calls into question the costliness of a progress 'that cannot forfend such misery'.[40] If the First World War turned the air as 'red as the rains of hell', what of its ghastly sequels of even more fiendish cruelty? We are 'at a loss' because 'we have drawn our faith from the order of the world instead of its crisis, from the integrity of the moral order rather than from the tragedy of its recovery in the Cross' and 'we have been more engrossed with the ill we are saved from than with Him who saves us, and the Kingdom for which we are saved'.[41]

According to Forsyth, the cataclysm of the War is 'an acute condensation of what has been going on in nature, human and other, for millenniums'.[42] Now if faith could survive all that, there

[39] *Justification*, 20–1.
[40] *Justification*, 159.
[41] *Justification*, 76–7.
[42] *Justification*, 129.

is no reason to think that it must succumb to the present crisis. But this means that we cannot take refuge in those shelters which crumble and collapse when buffeted by the storms of human conflict and catastrophe. When things are gravely out of joint only 'something deeper than the wrecked world can mend them, only a God of love and power infinite':[43]

> To our present conscience there is no solution of the awful things whereof we are compelled to be a part. Yet it is we who are at a loss, it is not God. We have no vision of a moral harmony that submerges misery and evil, and spreads to order all, but we trust One who has not vision only but command; and we have absolute ground for trusting Him in Jesus Christ the Agent, and not but the seer, of the world of reconciliation. Not only can God solve the world, He has solved it – by an act done, and not a proof led, nor a scheme shown.[44]

Our trust and hope are not in the order of the world but in the 'Beyond'. The world's convulsions and calamities need not destroy faith since 'it rose from the sharpest crisis, the greatest war, the deadliest death, and the deepest grave the world ever knew – in Christ's Cross'.[45] Only the holy God can accomplish the one needful thing but it comes at great and painful cost – a cost borne by God. Sin cannot be ignored, it cannot be taken up into an overruling reconciliation, rather it must be judged, condemned and destroyed. But we do not receive what strict justice demands, rather God's act of atonement transforms judgement into mercy.

The very vehicle of eternal redemption, the cross of Christ, is the supreme tragedy and 'outweighs in gravity and in wickedness all that men or nations have done or can do – were even the whole world without exception involved in suicidal war'.[46] The regeneration of the first creation into the second is a more serious matter than it was 'to organise chaos into the first'. The upheaval caused by the social chaos of its gestation is greater and more terrible than anything we

---

[43]*Justification*, 194.
[44]*Justification*, 154.
[45]*Justification*, 57.
[46]*Justification*, 149.

find on the level of the first since the 'collision of the Holy with the wickedness of man is more grave than the conflict of the Almighty with crude matter' for the one is passive opposition, the other active.[47] The regeneration of creation is tragic inasmuch as it is a matter of will against will, with all the power of freedom behind it. It is not the appalling catastrophes people suffer, however devastating, 'but the less striking, though more paralysing, tragedy of what they have done and become'.[48]

At the centre of human tragedy is guilt and its fear of judgement. We fear being exposed not, in the first instance, to the interrogation of God but to our fellow human beings – 'It is the judgment of being found out, whether by self or society.' Some suffer the torment of being found out by themselves and henceforth carry the burden of knowing that they are living fraudulent lives, of having become 'moral corpses'. What strikes home 'is the nemesis of guilt in the course of life, not in the judgment outside life'.[49] Guilt needs 'redemption, reconciliation, the reopening of communication, the dissipation of guilt's cloud which darkens for us the face of God'.[50]

The 'face of God's is revealed in the cross of Christ the Redeemer. The cross is a self-offering to God's holiness, a self-offering in which God is both the 'chief sufferer and sole Doer'.[51] In Christ, the world passed judgement on God and in the self-same event God passed judgement on the world – and Christ took both judgements. The cross is 'the crisis of the moral universe, … the theodicy of the whole God dealing with the whole God dealing with the whole soul of the whole world in holy love, righteous judgement, and redeeming grace'.[52] What makes the cross so monstrous is the fact that it was inflicted on the holiest – the one who was totally innocent, assumed the total guilt of humankind's rebellion against the holy God. The death of Christ condenses within itself the warring collision between sin, the absolute contradiction of holiness, and the holy God whose victory can only be assured by an 'absolute salvation'.

Only an extraordinary, a supernatural act, could rescue the world from sin:

[47] *Justification*, 68.
[48] *Justification*, 50.
[49] *Preaching*, 102–3.
[50] *Preaching*, 105.
[51] *Justification*, 123.

The meaning of the Incarnation is that God was capable, in His self-emptying in Christ, of a self-limitation, *i.e.* a self-mastery of holy surrender, whose moral effect was more than equal to the foreign invasion by sin. He died *unto* sin, as man dies *by* it. But of course death has not the same sense in each case. God carries death as a blessed sacrifice. Sin carries it as an entail of curse. Divine death is moral surrender to sin's conditions but not to its nature. It is an exercise of moral strength which increases life in losing it; whereas the only death at sin's command is decay and destruction. All sin aims at a destruction of God, which His eternal holy life repels; were it unrepelled by the reaction of judgment it would extinguish God. But the reaction and the judgment is that of loving holiness. It is saving judgment. His holiness so dies as to inflict on sin a death which it has not power to repel.[53]

Sin is the absolute antithesis of holiness and there is nothing in it that can be absorbed and given value by God, and so God 'commands His own negation – even when it pierces as deep within Himself as His Son'.[54] Sin and death are the very antithesis of God and yet God could so identify with them that both were abolished.

Through an act of self-emptying, of self-disposal, the holy God of perfect mercy was placed at the mercy of sinful humankind and was broken by it. Forsyth never permits his celebration of *Christus Victor* to be severed from *theologia crucis*. On the cross, God became wholly vulnerable to the way of the world while retaining the means for overcoming the whole sinful and tragic course of history. Redeemed and reconciled by the atoning cross of Christ, we have the assurance of God's continuing presence, compassionate mercy, and forgiveness, even in the face of those darker sequels to Calvary which cast their tragic shadows on the tragedy there enacted. The cross is the compresence of the judgement of outraged holiness stung to the core and of holy love unpierced at its centre reaching out in merciful compassion – a deed done.

Must a divine love not go far with us and for us as to enter the wrath of holiness? Even that was not beyond Christ's love. He

[52] *Justification*, 133.
[53] *Justification*, 148.
[54] *Justification*, 149.

was made sin. God did not punish Christ, but Christ entered the dark shadow of God's penalty on sin. We must press the results of God's holy love in completely identifying Himself with us. Holiness is not holiness till it go out in love, seek the sinner in grace, and react on his sin by judging it. But love is not divine identification with us till it become sacrifice. Nor is the identification with us complete till the sacrifice become judgment, till our Saviour share our self-condemnation, our fatal judgment of ourselves in God's name. The priest, in his grace, becomes the victim, and completes his confession of God's holiness by meeting its action as judgment. To forgive sin he must bear sin.[55]

The atoning cross is the completion of God's love embodied in the person of Christ, 'the consummation of the holy conscience of God in the eternal action of love which incessantly creates a moral universe', and 'the foundation of faith, the atmosphere of worship, and the principle of life'.[56] In his death Christ acted, suffered, and atoned.

Forsyth is not primarily concerned with tragedy in the world, though it is never to be neglected, but with the deeper tragedy of the world; a tragedy that can be overcome only from within – through the supreme tragedy of the cross of Christ. This is an important distinction that needs to be borne in mind if we are not to lose sight of what, for Forsyth, connects the world's tragedy with God's tragedy. Nor is Forsyth primarily interested in non-moral suffering. He draws a firm distinction between evil as suffering and evil as sin, and while all sin is an ill, not all ill is sin. Animals experienced pain and suffering before human beings entered the scene with the moral freedom which makes sin possible. Reason cannot search out why it is that there is suffering any more than it can justify God in a world like this, or God's treatment of Christ, or why in this hard world sin descends upon us. What we can say is that God can transcend and sanctify suffering but must abolish sin. Christ can bear suffering directly and on the cross he submerges it and makes it a means of

[55] *Preaching*, 248.
[56] *Preaching*, 107–8.

salvation. But sin can be borne by Christ only sympathetically because it has no place in him.

It has been the modest ambition of this section to exhibit the tragic form Forsyth gives his theology. Much has been neglected that would demand inclusion in an exhaustive account. Chief among these would be his theodicy which has received only the barest mention in order to indicate that the self-justification of God is Christ. his probing meditation on this topic is of the first importance but since its key is to be found in what Forsyth called 'the second volume', the *divina commedia*, it does not directly bear upon limited scope of this section. Perhaps enough has been said to indicate not only the importance of tragedy and the tragic in Forsyth's theology, but also its pattern. But before we can give a final answer to the question with which we began, we need to clarify a few issues that arise regarding his use of tragic categories.

IV

Genuine tragic drama is rare, remarkable, and given its acknowledged variety, defiant of any attempt to distil its essence – here Wittgenstein's notion of 'family resemblances' finds useful service. Forsyth's actualism and his commitment to a dramatic reading of human life and history led him to grant priority to tragedy as the most appropriate narrative form for representing both the human situation and the cross of Christ. But he writes not as a dramatist but as a theologian who reshapes the aesthetic form of tragic drama to the purposes of a mainly narrative theology (a different order of discourse) which recognizes a tragic dimension in lived experience.

The experience of evil, suffering, the intractable, and the radically negative has always prompted profound and searching reflection in art, philosophy, and theology. The ubiquity of suffering and evil represent a particularly acute challenge to Christian belief, menacing both its intellectual and moral credibility. The characteristic response has been the disciplined intellectual quest for a theodicy that will satisfactorily reconcile the co-existence of God and evil. Forsyth believed that all such intellectual endeavours were bound to fail because there can be no rational vindication of God. The questions asked by philosophical theodicy really concern practical and moral interests and any solution will be found in the practical realm of lived faith.[57] Behind this lies his conviction that moral good and evil are a mystery, a transcendent mystery. But the questions elicited by our experience of and reflection on the extremities of life are also explored in tragic art which gives performative form and voice to that which is peculiarly resistant to thought. Forsyth did not believe that tragic drama provided the solution, only that it contained theologically relevant insights into the human condition and, in many tragedies, intimated a Beyond in which the action of the play continued.

Impatient of theory, it is hardly surprising that Forsyth never gave systematic shape to his understanding of tragedy and the tragic. At the same time, it is clear that he not only read widely in the field of literature, he was also acquainted with much recent, especially Continental, philosophical reflection on tragedy. Care must be taken when tracing the main lines of philosophical influence on his thought since the evidence is largely circumstantial and indirect. Forsyth's distinctive treatment of the agonistic character of tragedy and, particularly, of regenerative strife, an emphasis that enjoyed wide favour at the time, means that his treatment is not readily identified with any one theory or school of thought. On balance, it is probably safe to say that the principal influence on his understanding of tragedy was Hegel from whom he learned much even as he rejected the main thrust of his philosophy. There are also traces of the influence of Kierkegaard, Nietzsche, and Schopenhauer. Hovering over and interpenetrating all these is Kant. It is an interesting feature of Forsyth's writing on tragedy that those who seem to exercise the greatest influence on him are often those with whom he fundamentally disagreed. He appears to exploit certain ideas associated with one or another theory only to break with it at a crucial point. For example, his unrelenting attack on those who conceive of tragic conflict and its resolution as an ongoing dialectical process contributory to the emergence of a greater more harmonious good, signals his commitment to an understanding of the tragic crisis of humankind as an either/or between which no dialectic is possible. And, yet, when he speaks of the regenerative action of God in the cross of Christ, he draws directly on Hegel's 'positivity of negation' – set now in a framework at odds with Hegel's own.

[57] *Justification*, 136–9.

There is throughout Forsyth's writings an often noted inconsist-ency in his use of concepts and a lack of systematization, rendering any attempt to schematize his chief tragic themes and categories difficult. He draws mainly on the categories of modern tragedy and theory – at least when compared to classical and neo-classical drama and theory which is generally innocent of the modern preoccupa-tion with the agonistic collision. He bends these categories to the service of his theological commitments while remaining broadly within the orbit of the tragic theory of his day. Firstly, the ideas of collision and conflict were at the centre of his understanding of tragedy and, as we shall see below, collision is a feature of reality from the beginning of creation. Secondly, tragedy is about freedom, justice, responsibility, and guilt; which Forsyth understood largely in terms of the emphasis in modern tragedy on personal account-ability for one's own acts, and on taking guilt upon oneself. All these feature in his theological 'story' of the tragic human condition in which both the individual and society are riven by division. As we have seen, the inner division of the individual, the troubled con-science, the resistance to the acceptance of guilt as one's own, and the understanding of the individual as a social being, are at the root of what Forsyth takes to be the deepest and gravest human tragedy. It remains, then, to clarify the place of these in his theological 'story', now more or less shorn of the rhetoric.

1. Forsyth begins with 'collision'. The fundamental collision is between sinful humanity and the holy God. But even before humankind appears on the scene, from the very beginning itself, God collides with crude matter which passively resists God's shaping of it. The emergence of plant and animal life is marked by collision and struggle. Collision, struggle, and conflict are present from the beginning and suggest, though Forsyth is silent on the matter, that they cannot be understood in terms of an alien intrusion that, through the disobedience of the first human beings, disturbed the natural harmony and peace of some mythic 'Garden of Eden'. The conditions for the possibility of sin and evil are established before humankind makes its entrance.

Forsyth affirms original sin and the fall but refuses any specula-tion regarding the manner of its entry into the world. His theology is refreshingly free of the tyranny of 'Garden' language and its absence, when taken with what he says about sin, is highly sugges-tive. From the moment of their appearance, human beings are engaged in a battle for existence that necessarily involves collision and conflict. To struggle for life is natural and he even suggests that we begin as 'warring atoms' and that it is as natural to destroy as it is to help. The picture here is one in which the natural conditions of human existence are, at the same time, conditions conducive to, but not the cause of, sin. The fundamental problem is not that of creaturely finitude but the more radical problem of human sin. At whatever point in history one cares to look, one finds finitude infected by sin. Human beings, in varying degrees, are enmeshed in the 'the malign and organised evil of a whole intricate and infected world'.[58] Even the development of moral personality is not an orderly and harmonious process which from time to time is disrupted by conflict, defects, and accidents. Rather, these are the normal world for the unity and wholeness we crave since it is a gift and not the result of some process. Somehow sin is bound up with the conditions of life itself but the key is to be found in the human will. For Forsyth, as we have seen, the deepest tragedy in life is the 'fall of the inner will'.

Original sin appears inevitable simply because of the basic conditions of human existence and humankind's natural response to those conditions, and any uneasiness in this regard is not assuaged by being told that we are born to be redeemed. It almost seems as though these conditions and forces are such that, given human free will, sin is irresistible. And, yet, God could not ordain sin, and since sin is primarily a matter of the will, we are wholly responsible for the infection that has time and again poisoned whatever progress humankind has made in the actualization of unity, harmony, and reconciliation. We are responsible because the alternative of not sinning is a possibility, if only in principle. Hence sin is inevitable, though not necessary. Freedom seems to be the point at which creation and fall coincide. This suggests that God is not blameworthy, though perhaps in some sense responsible. But why does the will turn from God?

Forsyth speaks of sin as 'solidary' or corporate but there is the other side, namely his non-natural understanding of morality in which there is always the possibility of *responding* to God or the holy. We are so constituted that the impulse or drive to unity, harmony,

---

[58] *Justification*, 31.

and wholeness is present from the beginning even if the spiritual
blindness consequent upon our immersion in sin and an egoist
civilization reinforces the misdirection of this impulse. The important thing to notice is that given the basic constitution of the world
and of human beings, original sin is freighted with possibilities,
including the possibility of eventual redemption. Even the characters in absolute tragedy must have some sense of possibility, of things
being different from the way they are, of themselves as in some sense
agents, even if it is the burden of the drama to expose this as nothing
more than a cruel self-defeating illusion. Forsyth, in observing the
ways of a sin-ridden world, was able to identify the possibilities
which through the failure of their fulfilment signalled to him the
tragic element in Christian faith.

Forsyth's reticence to speak of the origin of sin and his silence on
the myth of the Garden of Eden, taken together with what he says
about collision, struggle, and the fall of the will, is indicative not
only of the ambiguity of human freedom and the inevitability of sin,
but also, by implication only, the possibility that here we speak of
a surd element in things – wherever we look, sin and evil are already
there. While it is not said explicitly, the message seems to be that 'sin
posits itself' – Forsyth says nothing that would contradict it and
much that he does say implies it. If sin and evil are always 'already
there' this only reinforces Forsyth's conviction that the battle
between 'eternal sin' and 'eternal Saviour' is of such magnitude that
only God's tragic self-negation could gain the victory. Nothing else
could call forth such a sacrifice. The ambiguous play here of
freedom, contingency, inevitability, and God's role in the drama of
creation and life is the very stuff of tragedy.

Of course, this is to carry Forsyth's talk of sin and the fall beyond
what he expressly said; and while silence is just that, it must be said
that he helpfully provides the carriage. In everything Forsyth says,
it is clear that sin and evil and presupposed. Important here is the
fact that while he is aware of these complex problems to which there
seems to be no rational solution, he utters no protest against the
essential conditions of life which in large part give rise to them.
Forsyth maintains silence on the doctrinal issue and sees in tragic
drama an aesthetically shaped, near-mythic exposure of the character of sin and evil.

2. If Forsyth was reluctant to speculate on the whence of original
sin, he is very clear about the sin itself. The great judgement falls not

upon human works but upon our 'standing life-act which practically and eternally disposes of the person'.[59] The ultimate judgement is an adjustment between persons, between wills: God's and the human being's. Our works are merely the fruits of this 'life-act'. This is the 'act' of the whole person which establishes his or her fundamental stance. It is the act in which the whole of humanity chooses human law rather than holy law. It is the personal act which is a transgression, against the holy God, and a state of guilt – a guilt not to be confused with a guilty conscience. It is the act in which humankind rejects the love and purposes of the holy God and centres itself within itself. But humankind still stands in relation to God, although now it is a relationship of rebellion and active enmity. Henceforth, life is centred anthropocentrically rather than theocentrically and since sin blinds, humanity cannot even measure the damage and the loss.

At root, we are dealing with two planes of being: the one antagonistic to and estranged from God and the other is obedient communion with God. This can be seen in Forsyth's insistence that by faith the believer is placed in a 'new situation' that redemption is a 'new creation', and that the redeemed 'live in but not of the world'. The tragedy of an anthropocentric, and therefore godless, world is that life cannot fully divide itself, its unity is its goal and it is destined to advance to a higher, spiritually free, plane of being or, put theologically, the kingdom of God. We crave what it alone can give and yet all our efforts are for nothing through our slavery to sin. We battle only to be defeated in the end by a world which often appears cruel, unjust, and without ultimate meaning – our 'warfare' having turned to dust. This collision between sinful humanity and the holy God is the source of the tragic ambiguity of human existence.

3. Forsyth believed that the deepest truth about human moral life, both personal and social, was conflict and collision, divisiveness and enmity. Life is 'not an ordered process but a tragic collision and despair' rooted in sin's antagonism to holiness, to the holy God. Humankind is confronted with an either/or: either a holy God or no God in its affairs – without God there is no hope for humankind or the world. At bottom, it is a collision between holiness and nihilism.

[59] *Justification*, 181.

On the one side, there is redemption and the perfecting of spiritual freedom, of holiness. On the other, there is a life of constant strife, estrangement, division, and death-nothingness. Human beings, blinded by sin and therefore unaware of their actual situation, do not see that they still stand in a relationship to God, even if it is one of enmity. But they have cast themselves adrift and in their blindness experience themselves as aliens compelled to undergo unmerited, arbitrary, and meaningless suffering, ruin, and death.

Forsyth believed that there is a 'solution' to the 'problem of life' – a 'solution' from 'beyond'. But what is important here is its only alternative. If, *per impossible*, evil conquered it would be a victory for nihilism. A sinful and unrepentant humanity may see the tragedy of life, but for them it will be a tragedy that has nothing beyond it; a 'death of God' tragedy, so to speak. This, for Forsyth, is what is at stake in the life and death battle between sin and holiness. Nihilism is the only alternative to the costly sacrifice made by God in the transformation of the wrath of divine judgement into the merciful judgement of redemption. God rescues humanity from its servitude to an unmerciful nihilism.

4. It is not difficult to understand why Forsyth was sympathetic to the agonistic quality of modern tragedy with its characteristic emphasis on regenerative strife. But he was convinced that every finite resolution of conflict either fails to endure or is doomed to eventual failure or destruction. This is what happens even to those forms of resolution or reconciliation which undeniably contribute to the betterment of human life and spirituality. An apt example of this is his *Christ on Parnassus* where he argues that art can give aesthetic deliverance granting release, calm and joy; but always in an experience that cannot endure.[60] He also had a rare eye for 'negations of the negation' that lower than raise to a higher form. Hence, the only genuinely regenerative strife is the supreme tragedy in the cross of Christ in which the world is redeemed – for ever.

V

The 'first volume', the tragedy of the first creation, closes with the supreme tragedy of the broken figure of Christ upon the cross which

---

[60] *Parnassus*, esp. 264–8.

is, at the same time, the arrival of the 'second volume', a *divina commedia*, in the victory over sin and death on the selfsame cross. This paper has focused attention on tragedy in the theology of Forsyth, not the divine comedy, and so our first task is to draw together the threads of this survey. But we cannot close without at least a brief glance at the relationship between the divine comedy and the tragedy in order to give an answer to our second question of whether the second volume renders the first an ironic jest.

There can be little doubt that Forsyth has given a theological account of the tragic dimension in human life. It is important to be clear that his 'theological story' is grounded in his theology, a theology which resisted isolation from the public course of affairs and its moral realities. It was there that he observed irretrievable loss, waste, and calamity. He was aware of human vulnerability, of contingency in human affairs, of unforeseen and unintended consequences of actions undertaken in service to justice, of those who were cut down in their course toward holiness, of humanity's combined love and hate of sin, and of a Christianity that produces not only love toward God but also hate, that repels as well as attracts, that produces estrangement as well as communion. Life has a tragic dimension, a dimension resistant to rational thought.

Forsyth accepted the primacy of the practical and saw sin and evil as a reality that could effectively be confronted only by a practical solution. But while tragedy qualifies life and history, it is never total or absolute. Life has a tragic dimension, as does the gospel, but it is not final. Finality rested with one who did take things tragically, who on the cross took tragedy into himself. Our lives are sustained and finally redeemed by such a God. The 'story' Forsyth tells is not to be confused with a tragic drama, it is of a different order. He discerns a tragic dimension in human life and seeks to do justice to its reality without granting it finality. It would be an eccentric prejudice that insisted that tragedy is only tragic when it is absolute. The finality of tragedy is rare in tragic drama and even more so in those who are said to have a tragic sense of life. Of course, there will be those who point to the existence of a substantial body of modern work in which tragedy has been separated from religion, but this hardly precludes re-connecting them in a different context.

In addition, some might object to the transcending of tragedy through tragedy. But I can see no grounds for ruling this movement out of bounds from the start. There is historical and contemporary precedent for an ascent from the tragic to the comic and Forsyth represents the tragedy of the cross in Christ in precisely these terms. Moreover, the crucifixion of Christ and all that led up to it lends itself to, even calls out for, tragic representation. Some of the finest tragic dramas end badly but a bright horizon looms beyond their close.

Tragedy is of great importance in the theology of Forsyth but it never dominates his theology. At the same time, if the place of tragedy in his theology is to be replaced, its substitute would need to be equally capable of representing the magnitude of sin and evil in its collision with holiness in such a way that it too could do justice to the costliness of God's self-negation. Pull the tragic dimension out of Forsyth's theology and you pull the plug on much else as well. Of course, any appropriation of Forsyth today will be an exercise in reconstruction for there is much in his theology that cannot stand. I have argued only that tragedy is essential in his theology taken as a whole. But I would go on to suggest that reconstructions of theology for our day would do well to attend to the strengths and weaknesses of his impressive but hardly flawless struggle to do justice to the moral realities of life, culture, and history within the context of Christian faith.

When we turn to what he calls the 'second volume', little hangs on whether we speak of two volumes, one a tragedy and the other a comedy, or of a tragi-comedy in two volumes. In either case, the tragic remains tragic. What is important is the fact that Forsyth has given voice to the irreducible tragic element in Christian faith. It is to Forsyth's credit that he never suggests that the past is changed, adjusted, or repaired. The monstrous evils that have brought pain, suffering, and death to so many; the sheer loss and waste; the terrifying anguish, the brutal cost, remain in the past and even God cannot change what has been. In fact he does not flinch from saying, in accord with his moral teleology, that all of this was the judgement of God working itself out in an immanent dialectic by which evil disorganizes itself as evil. The cross of Christ creates in faith the assurance of God's whole providence with the universe, that the whole course of the world is a means for destroying sin and effecting union with God. There is still much that the Christian does not know, but even though we do not see the answer, 'we trust the Answerer'.[61]

<hr />

[61] *Justification*, 220–1.

Be still and know that I am a God, whose mercy is as His majesty, and His omnipotence is chiefly in forgiving, and redeeming, and settling all souls in worship in the temple of a new heaven and earth full of holiness. In that day the anguish will *be forgotten for joy* that a New Humanity is born into the world.[62]

Tragedy remains tragedy but *is forgotten for joy* by those who enter the kingdom of God. The past is not eliminated and the loss through tragedy remains loss, but through the divine grace of forgetfulness its ghosts may no longer haunt. This, I assume, is an eschatological 'forgetfulness' since the theology he commends to us is one in which we are not to ignore the tragic element. So long as the Christian lives in, but not of, the world, the forgetfulness of joy will be fleeting. Here, it would seem, much theological work requires to be done on the topic of joy in a world wracked by horrendous evils that threaten to turn the tears of joy into a bitter brew of desolation. Joy, as Forsyth saw, must arise the other side of the tragic, not through a denial of it.

In the midst of his lavish and sometimes excessive rhetoric, Forsyth shows admirable restraint and an appropriate agnosticism in the articulation of a theodicy in which tragedy is central but always under the command of theology. But there are places when he seems to relax this discipline. It may be a result of the pressure a preacher is under when proclaiming the good news, the urge to allay every anxiety and to answer every outstanding question. In any event, Forsyth comes perilously close to succumbing to the temptation to reveal more detail of the workings of divine providence than could possibly be vouchsafed by the revelation of God in the cross of Christ. When he speaks too easily of world history as a means for schooling the soul, of tragedy as merely a means, he runs the risk of making tragedy a utility – and this is to court trivialization, the avoidance of which is overall one of his greatest strengths and one of the important lessons he has to teach us.

There is much to criticize in Forsyth's use of tragedy, not in order to eliminate it but so as to make it available for our own attempts at theological reconstruction. But even as it stands, it probes deeply questions that cannot be avoided and represents a challenge to

---

[62] *Justification*, 165. My emphasis.

anyone who seriously reflects upon the problem of evil as it confronts the claims of Christian faith. He still has lessons to teach for which we all should be grateful. And it is worth noting, that his use of tragedy accords well with his equally challenging treatment of kenosis. Perhaps it is fitting to end this paper by quoting another Scot with close associations with Aberdeen, Donald MacKinnon, who, in a different way, also brings together tragic representation and kenosis and whose disciplined restraint and agnosticism is an appropriate corrective to those few occasions when Forsyth allowed his to relax:

> It is when one allows one's attention to fasten upon the sorts of exploration of the human reality that we have here reviewed that we come to recognise the paradox that, while in one way a proper respect for the irreducibility of the tragic inhibits ambitious metaphysical construction, in another the sort of commentary on human life which one finds in the tragedies here reviewed ... makes one discontented with any sort of naturalism. It is as if we are constrained in pondering the extremities of human life to acknowledge the transcendent as the only alternative to the kind of trivialisation which would empty of significance the sorts of experience with which we have been concerned.[63]

---

[63]D. M. MacKinnon, *The Problem of Metaphysics* (London: Cambridge University Press, 1974), 145.

Chapter 7

TELEOLOGY AND REDEMPTION

Donald M. MacKinnon†

It was in 1916 that Peter Taylor Forsyth offered the world his essay on theodicy – *The Justification of God*. In the context of his *oeuvre*, it undoubtedly belongs with his major treatises on Christ's life and work. Yet a brief glance at the book's bibliography shows the reader the extent of the author's reading and reflection. It is very much more than a footnote to Forsyth's writings on the atonement: this though the cross remains central to its argument.

In the final chapter there is a quotation from none other than Gustave Flaubert, which provides a text for the apologetic emphasis of the book. 'Real life is always misrepresented by those who wish to make it lead up to a conclusion. God alone may do that. The greatest geniuses have never concluded.'[1] Thus the theologian finds the grounds of his rejection of any sort of facile teleology, articulated by the author of *Madame Bovary*. It is a mark of the depth of his theological culture that Forsyth immediately grasps the penetration of the writer, finding in Flaubert's words clear statement both of the teleological vision he rejects, and of the grounds of that rejection.

Although Forsyth quotes Hegel's *Religionsphilosophie*, his temper is always more Kantian. There is little evidence that he was familiar with the opuscula of Kant's latter years, in which the philosopher sharply criticized the optimistic theodicy of the great rationalist Leibniz. But his bibliography shows his familiarity with Voltaire's *Candide*, surely the best known riposte to the claim that 'all is for the best in the best of all possible worlds' in the light of the Lisbon

---

[1] *Justification*, 1st ed., 223.

earthquake of 1 November 1755. Such events gave the lie to any facile argument for an overriding, beneficent design; they compelled agnosticism in the face of horror. But that same agnosticism, properly interpreted by means of a Kantian philosophical discipline, was the foundation for a theology of divine redemptive action. And it is in such a theology, defined by the reality of Christ's cross and passion, that Forsyth would seek, and hope to find, the only valid theodicy. 'The Cross of Christ is God's only self-justification.'[2]

Forsyth had certainly read and pondered *Candide*; but the central role of the cross in his theodicy led him to give greatest weight to the issues raised by the reality of moral evil (Böse). The physical ills (Übel) of which the Lisbon earthquake was a supreme example, are somewhat peripheral to his concentration. The reader of *The Justification of God* is never allowed to forget that its argument is born of attention to the evils of the First World War. Forsyth never conceals his conviction that its origin lies in the assumptions of German *Macht-politik*. Yet he is vividly aware that all the participants, however just their initial response to German action, are committed to courses of action involving them in moral guilt. 'The evil that men do lives after them.' This oft-quoted line from Antony's speech in Shakespeare's *Julius Caesar* might serve as a grim epitaph to very much incidental to human, collective action in time of war. 'The good is oft interred with their bones' (of the fallen). In language that gives sharp emphasis to much that is most permanently significant in evangelical theology of the cross, Forsyth speaks of 'a movement, a crescendo of moral action, and not of natural process'.[3] Again, he writes of the cross where judgement is changed into mercy, where indeed Christ became Saviour 'because He loved God more than man', where indeed a change was wrought more in God than in man.[4] It is in the depths of Christ's passion that judgement is transformed into mercy,[5] that by confession of God's unyielding holiness, mercy flows even to those who have chiefly outraged it.

Forsyth's language is apt to pass into a kind of loose rhetoric, and the reader craves a closer attention to the detail of the Gospel narratives. Such concentration would be entirely consonant with

[2] *Justification*, 34.
[3] *Justification*, 47.
[4] *Justification*, 4.
[5] *Justification*, 55.

Forsyth's fierce insistence on the primacy of action, especially if one remembers that action must be particular, even though one discerns within it that which is universal. Aristotle claimed superiority for the poet over against the historian on the ground that the latter was only concerned with the detail of what Alcibiades did and suffered; while the former probed the universal import of Oedipus' suffering. The Gospel writers (Mark and Luke as well as John) are in this respect nearer to Aristotle's poets than to his historians; they guess and hint a universal import in those events whose detail they chronicle, constrained to this effort by the mystery of the resurrection to which their often stumbling and contradictory conclusions bear witness. The authentic Anselmian theology of the atonement is ultimately continuous with the Evangelists' interpretation of the details they record.

At the very outset of his book, Forsyth insists that 'His Son spared not Himself in the hallowing of that name ... [He is Saviour] because He loved God more than man.'[6] The theocentrism is relentless; the affirmation of the Father's holiness and righteousness is without qualification. This interpretation of Christ's passion is grounded in the manner of its presentation in the Gospels, where (to repeat) the universal is manifested through the particular – the judgement of God through the particularities of human envy, and cruelty, through the grim actualities of Judas' greed, of Caiaphas' cold *raison d'état*, of Pilate's self-regarding capitulation. It is Jesus who tears away the masks from their faces, his witness to the truth the ordeal imposed upon him by his fidelity. Even the women of Jerusalem who lament his fate, are warned in almost harsh tones, of the disaster that awaits their city, oblivious of the summons to a new way offered them by Jesus. Human pretension is stripped bare, and the judgement of God accepted in an action profoundly tragic in its cost. 'And thou continuest holy, O thou worship of Israel.'

But how far does this theology of atonement comprise a complete theodicy? Forsyth includes Job in his bibliography, and rightly so. But how far does he succeed in joining the issues raised by that most nearly Aeschylean of the Old Testament corpus with the themes of Christ's passion? Certainly both the writer of Job, and the authors of the Gospels engage with the problem of the suffering of the innocent. But the death of Jesus is contrived by human malice; it

---

[6] *Justification*, 4.

does not belong with the ills to which the flesh is heir. Further the manner in which Christ protests his innocence, is very different from that in which Job insists that he is not being punished for some unacknowledged guilt. Christ's innocence is portrayed in John's Gospel in the setting of Pilate's interrogation; whereas in Luke it is the penitent thief who in words that are at once confession of Christ's dignity, and of his own guilt, affirms the innocence of his fellow-suffer. In the end (as Paul made plain in the agonized argument of his letter to the Romans), it is an innocence that tragically and terribly involves the suffering of those who refuse to confess it. In other words, it is an innocence whose affirmation plunges others into inescapable guilt. If the cross provides a theodicy in which there is no facile extrapolation of teleological schemata, it does so at the cost of a continuing tragedy. If the atonement shows God himself profoundly engaged with human evil, it is an engagement (even when its authenticity is affirmed by Jesus' resurrection) that leaves many questions unanswered.

And this most certainly Forsyth acknowledged through his insistence on the reality of the divine kenosis. Jesus enters on the climactic stage of his *via dolorosa*, suddenly and traumatically unsure that this is the way for him. If, unlike the Anglican kenoticists, who were his contemporaries, Forsyth in an indifference to metaphysics interprets the divine self-emptying in dramatic terms, at this point he rejoins those for whom the incarnate's limited human knowledge was a central theological concern. For the most part, his Kantian metaphysical agnosticism enabled him to avert from ontological exploration, and emphasize the cruciality of dramatic action. But the realities of Gethsemane refuse to allow him to neglect the extent to which the passion was suffused by a kind of terrible uncertainty. And here he might have found the temptations of Christ in the desert, whose Christological significance is too often ignored, illuminating. For in the Lukan version, Christ's ordeal ends only when he puts his comings and goings at his Father's disposal, disdaining the bloodless victory available through descent from the pinnacle of the temple, renewed by the suggestion of a descent from the cross.

Forsyth's emphasis is laid on what he has called a 'crescendo of moral action'. In an impressive contribution to the debate on religious education in the *Times* on 14 June 1993, Professor Stewart R. Sutherland finds the possibility of a 'non-sectarian' provision for the development of spirit in the wonder and awe induced in the individual by reflection upon the 'moral law within' and the 'starry heavens above'. He offers these words of Immanuel Kant as a 'short-hand for making central to education the task of self-understanding and the capacity to stand in awe and wonder at the world'. It would not be unjust to say that for Forsyth it is an emphasis on the transcendent significance of 'the moral law within' which occludes treatment of the cosmological dimension. His sense of the tragic, the weight he allows to fall on the atoning passion of Christ, his refusal to allow a place to historical teleology (even to the muted teleology discernible in the Acts of the Apostles) – all reflect his presupposition of the cruciality of the moral order. The bibliography in *The Justification of God* shows his awareness of the issues raised, for instance, by Voltaire's *Candide*. But his passionate hostility to the facile extrapolation of teleological conceptions does result in a neglect of the manifold issues raised by the surd element in the created universe.

It may be that he might have found a way forward if he had brought together the agnostic element in Kant's theory of knowledge with his awareness of the limitations of Christ's human knowledge. These limitations assume a nearly tragic quality on the threshold of the passion, when, as Forsyth profoundly recognizes, an element in the agony was uncertainty whether indeed this was the way in which as Christ, he had to *go*. All had to be received, as it were, step by step from the Father in the manner accepted (according to Luke's order) in the climax of his temptation in the desert. Christ entered upon the road into the unknown – a way that led to a place of disintegration, where the limitations of human knowledge were suffused by a sense of the ultimately impenetrable.

There are aspects of the theology of the incarnation that Forsyth's emphasis on the cruciality of the cross leads him to neglect, or to dismiss in too facile a manner as 'Chalcedonism' – a ballet dance of bloodless categories. It is a weakness of the New Testament that the cosmological dimension is neglected: it was an undoubted achievement of the age of conciliar orthodoxy that under the influence of Greek philosophy, this dimension was acknowledged. There was a cost in evangelical penetration; but the way was suggested (for instance in the work of the Cappadocian fathers) of a trinitarian theology which would provide, in the relation of Christ to the Father, the context in which in the reality of the incarnate life as it was lived, the salvific significance of its order may be more clearly perceived.

Chapter 8

P. T. FORSYTH AS UNSYSTEMATIC SYSTEMATICIAN

Alan P. F. Sell

If ever a theologian deserved to be treated under a paradoxical title, that theologian is P. T. Forsyth. His pages are peppered with paradoxes, enlivened by epigrams and they abound in antitheses. All of these devices assail the mind and challenge the heart. I shall be content if the paradox in my title stimulates thought on the themes of one whose message is, to a high degree, as fresh and as pertinent as when he uttered it, and whose theological method is systematically unconventional, and this to surprisingly good effect.

I set out from the verdict of H. F. Lovell Cocks who, until his death in 1983, was among the last surviving students of Forsyth.[1] Although Lovell Cocks held his teacher in the highest regard ('I shall never cease to regard it as a signal act of Divine Providence that it was to Dr Forsyth that I was led to be instructed'),[2] he nevertheless had to open his assessment of Forsyth's *The Person and Place of Jesus Christ* with the words, 'Peter Taylor Forsyth was far from being a systematic theologian.'[3] The emphasis upon the term 'systematic' is clear from the context. It is not being said that Forsyth was more the historical or the philosophical theologian; still less that he was not a theologian at all – how could that be suggested in the case of one

---

[1]For Lovell Cocks, see Alan P. F. Sell, 'Theology for all: The contribution of H. F. Lovell Cocks,' in Sell, *Commemorations: Studies in Christian Thought and History* (Calgary: University of Calgary Press, 1993), chapter 13.

[2]Cocks, 'Ordination Statement', in the Lovell Cocks papers at Dr Williams's Library, London.

[3]Cocks, review of *Person*, 195.

who believed that 'non-theological religion can do but a coasting trade'?[4] J. K. Mozley who, as much as any other Anglican of his generation saw Forsyth's point, some reservations notwithstanding, declared in a half-sentence redolent of understatement that 'Systematic is not a word that one would naturally apply to Dr Forsyth.'[5] What grounds have been offered in support of this widely-echoed judgement?

I

First, it has been said that Forsyth's writings are insufficiently scholarly. He is sparing with references, most of his works lack indices. Unlike Samuel Morton Savage (1721–91; D. D., Marischal College, Aberdeen, 1767),[6] Congregational tutor at the first Hoxton Academy, who 'was apt to take from the interest of his lectures by entering into learned minutiae',[7] Forsyth seldom deals in detailed biblical exegesis or takes special pains to provide full evidence for his often rapier-like and accurate assessments of Christian thought ancient and modern.

Where the Bible was concerned, some found Forsyth unbalanced in more than one way. To T. Hywel Hughes, Forsyth's God was too much of the Old Testament sort: 'The God of Forsyth seems to be more concerned with Himself, with His holiness, His judgement, His satisfaction, than with the sinner, whereas in the Gospel the supreme object of interest is not law, judgement, not even sin, but the sinner.'[8] Forsyth's younger colleague, A. E. Garvie, Principal of

---

[4] *Person*, 262.

[5] J. K. Mozley, *The Doctrine of the Atonement*, 182.

[6] The University of Aberdeen, for whose quincentenary this series of lectures is being prepared, has not been ungenerous to theologians of the Congregational Way. The centenary of the award of its degree of Doctor of Divinity to P. T. Forsyth will fall on 30 March 1995, and he is our main concern. However, in the course of my paper, I shall refer to other Congregationalists who have been similarly honoured.

[7] *Protestant Dissenter's Magazine* 3 (May 1796): 162.

[8] T. Hywell Hughes, 'Dr Forsyth's View of the Atonement' (1940): 37; cf. 36. Cf. his *The Atonement: Modern Theories of the Doctrine*, 38–46. Hughes was Principal of the Scottish Congregational College from 1922 until his death in 1936. He was succeeded by Lovell Cocks (1937–41), who in the latter year became Principal of Western College, Bristol, until his retirement in 1960.

New College, London, likewise lamented that Forsyth put more emphasis upon God's holiness than upon his love.[9] My own reading is that Forsyth, as few others, conjoined the terms 'holy love' and could scarcely think of the one without the other. And as for the 'Old Testament God' charge, it is interesting to observe that on another wicket and on an earlier occasion, the same Hughes contrasted Forsyth favourably with Barth-to-1934 in these terms: 'Barth is unwilling to apply the term "Father" to God.... We should speak of him as "Sovereign" or "Judge". To Forsyth, however, fatherhood is basal, and the result is that whereas Barth's God is much akin to the *Old Testament* conception, Forsyth's God is the God of Jesus.'[10]

More serious was the charge that Forsyth neglected, or gave inadequate place to, the ministry of Jesus. The context of the charge was the desire of some to flee what they regarded as grotesque doctrines of the atonement, and to turn instead to the quest of the historical Jesus. To them Jesus' words and deeds were crucial, even if some of his miracles caused them embarrassment. Thus, Joseph Warschauer, who transferred to the Congregational ministry from the Unitarian, and who was an implacable foe of Calvinism, objected to the way in which Forsyth opted for Paul's understanding of the fall and of total depravity. He pointed to the importance Jesus himself attached to 'these words of mine' (Mt 7.24–27). Nowhere, observed Warschauer, did the words of Jesus include references to the fall or to total depravity.[11] A weightier opinion was that of A. S. Peake, who would not go so far as to say that Forsyth dwelt too much upon Christ's death, but thought that he was 'in danger of concentrating on it too exclusively'.[12] In Garvie's view, Forsyth's 'absorption in the Cross made him insensitive and unresponsive to the truth and grace which [the ministry of Jesus] disclosed. He depreciated any attempt to understand the inner life of Jesus, especially His relation as Son to God as Father'.[13] Forsyth's antitheses, thought

---

[9]A. E. Garvie, 'A Cross-Centred Theology' (1944): 325.

[10]Hughes, 'A Barthian before Barth?' (1934): 311.

[11]J. Warschauer, '"Liberty, limited": A Rejoinder to Dr P. T. Forsyth' (1912): 834.

[12]A. S. Peake, *Recollections and Appreciations*, ed. W. Howard (London: Epworth, 1938), 193.

[13]A. E. Garvie, 'Placarding the Cross: The Theology of P. T. Forsyth', (1943): 352.

Garvie, were instruments too blunt for useful service in this field of enquiry. If we do not have data concerning the inner relations of Son and Father, how, asked Garvie, could Forsyth defend the antithesis, 'Jesus was more engrossed with the will of God than the needs of men in his last hours'?[14] Garvie did not deny that 'the relation to God must be primary, and to man secondary, yet His love for God need not be contrasted with His love for man'.[15]

Forsyth did not become more exegetical, but neither did he wilt under criticism levelled during his lifetime. He was content to assert his position positively. In so doing, he revealed himself to be a thoroughly biblical theologian – not in the sense of a systematic exegete, not in the sense of a seeker of the 'Jesus of history', not in the sense of a 'word-study' scholar of the 1950s, but in the sense of one saturated by what he took to be the Bible's fundamental message.

Forsyth's point is that the 'ethical, cosmic, eternal estimate of Christ cannot be based on his biography alone, or chiefly, but upon his cross, as we shall again find when we have surmounted the present fertile obsession by "the historical Jesus"'.[16] Indeed, as he elsewhere remarks, satisfaction concerning 'the historic evidence for every fact recorded in the New Testament' would not necessarily yield the certainty that we were 'amidst time, on the Rock Eternal'.[17] If he focuses much more on Paul than on the Gospels, it is not because of scepticism concerning the major details of the life of Jesus; it is not because the life of Jesus is unimportant; it is not because he was 'a latter-day Marcion distinguishing between an inspired Paul and a mistaken Twelve'.[19] After all, 'what Jesus preached was but part of the whole Gospel';[20] indeed, 'in the teaching of Christ nothing was done, in the strict sense of that

---

[14]Garvie, 'Placarding the Cross', 352, quotes Forsyth's annotations to Robert Mackintosh's paper of 1906, 'The Authority of the Cross' (1943): 216.

[15]Garvie, 'Placarding the Cross', 352. We should note Garvie's (and Hughes's) temperate interest in the then ascendant 'new psychology'. Moreover, Garvie had published a book in 1907 under the title, *Studies in the Inner Life of Jesus.*

[16]'The Insufficiency of Social Righteousness as a Moral Ideal' (1909): 611.

[17]'A Rallying Ground for the Free Churches: The Reality of Grace' (1906): 831.

[18]Mozley, *The Heart of the Gospel,* 80. Mozley did not, of course, think that Forsyth was a latter-day Marcion.

[19]*Theology,* 41.

[20]*Person,* 101.

word'.[21] Moreover, to concentrate exclusively upon Christ's precepts is to make him a legislator, 'a finer Moses'. All the precepts are to be read, and if necessary, to be revised, in the light of the cross.[22] What must carry weight with us is the view of Christ's place and person which pervades the New Testament.[23] Hence, for example, while it is true that 'the Cross was not central to Christ's teaching as the kingdom was, ... it was central to what is more than His teaching – to His healing, to His Person, work, and victory ... Christianity spread, not as a religion of truth, but of power, help, healing, resurrection, redemption'.[24] No doubt one less fond of antitheses would have paused at the realization that Christianity claims to be a word of truth as well as of redemption; but Forsyth's intention to deny that we have exhausted Christianity's meaning when we have gathered and presented its teachings is sound. As if echoing some of his critics, Forsyth could write, 'To preach only the atonement, the death apart from the life, or only the person of Christ, the life apart from the death, or only the teaching of Christ, His words apart from His life, may all be equally one-sided, and extreme to falsity.'[25] More bluntly still, he declares, 'You cannot sever the death of Christ from the life of Christ.'[26] But that the scales were weighted in the direction of the comprehensive 'fact of Christ' is undeniable. This is because

the real evidence that Christ is risen is something I can verify, who am little skilled in handling documents and assessing evidence. It is that I have had dealings with Him. It is like the evidence for the whole Bible. It is laymen's evidence, not scientific but moral. It is the witness of the evangelical conscience, and of Christian experience to a risen Redeemer. The essential thing is not historic belief in the Resurrection of Jesus (which devils might believe and tremble), but moral faith is a risen Saviour.[27]

[21] *War*, 52.
[22] 'A Holy Church the Moral Guide of Society' (1905), in *Society*, 16.
[23] *Person*, 181.
[24] *Missions*, 11.
[25] *Cruciality*, 2nd ed., 42.
[26] *Work*, 153.
[27] *Society*, 82. Cf. for example, 'The Evangelical Churches and the Higher Criticism' (1905): 578.

Summoning Paul as a witness, Forsyth avers, he 'would seem to have had something like a constitutional inability to respond to Christ the parablist or even the character till the Cross broke for him access to Christ's person. I cannot think Paul was ignorant of Christ's words or biography. But they did not *find* him'.[28] All of which reinforces Forsyth's conviction that 'in the Gospels Christ appears as acting, in the Epistles the same Christ interprets His own action'.[29] Again, and now more broadly still, 'It is the whole Biblical Christ that is the truly and deeply historic Christ.[30]

It is not without significance that despite his failure to provide systematic exegesis, and much as we should have wished to hear him at greater length on such important biblical concepts as covenant and creation,[31] Professor A. M. Hunter, sometime of this University, could nevertheless write an article entitled, 'P. T. Forsyth Neutestamentler', in which he showed that Forsyth was in advance of subsequent biblical scholars in his emphasis upon the historic, redemptive deed rather than upon truth as propositional; in his adumbration of the *kerygma*, in his anticipation of realized eschatology; and in his understanding of the one Church as being manifested in various places.[32] As the same writer elsewhere said, 'One of the supreme strengths of Forsyth's theology is that it is biblically based as few modern theologies are.'[33]

As with the Bible, so with his observations upon thought through the Christian ages: Forsyth does not trouble us with apparatus; indeed, he does not supply the grounds of his assertions as often as we should like. It is not surprising that a reviewer of *The Church and the Sacraments* should regret the absence of detailed discussion of the patristic witness on the matter – especially given Forsyth's determination to question certain aspects of it.[34] Forsyth's often unsupported summary judgements of persons and movements can sound

---

[28]Annotations to Mackintosh, 'The Authority of the Cross' (1943): 213.

[29]'The Evangelical Churches and the Higher Criticism', 584.

[30]*Person*, 169.

[31]John H. Rodgers regrets these omissions in his *The Theology of P. T. Forsyth*, 263. But for creation see 'Veracity, Reality and Regeneration' (1915): 208ff., where Forsyth relates creation to the new creation in Christ.

[32]See A. M. Hunter, 'P. T. Forsyth Neutestamentler'.

[33]Hunter, *P. T. Forsyth. Per Crucem ad Lucem*, 31. Cf. Mozley, preface to *Sacraments*, 2nd ed., vii.

[34]See Harold Hamilton, review of *Sacraments*, 93–4.

gnomic – for example, his rejection of 'a Monism which is rather the absolutising of the immanent than the incarnation of the transcendent'[35] – and to this extent he is a dangerous model to any who would 'sound off' in similar fashion, but without having done their homework. Theology is not free of such to this day: to refer to them pejoratively as 'theological journalists' is to slander a noble profession. Forsyth was not of their number. He declared that 'it really takes a great deal of theology to revolutionise theology'.[36] He knew of what he wrote in shorthand, and those who have themselves travelled the ground can see that this is so. They can see too that Forsyth seldom regurgitates, and that he generally qualifies the insights of those from whom he has learned most, recasting their contributions in his own terms. The words he used of others apply to himself: 'There is an amplitude and an atmosphere about the great dogmatists of theology which is absent from the dogmatists of research.'[37]

The indebtedness of Forsyth to others is considerable.[38] 'What have I that I have not received?' he asks in one place, immediately citing Rothe, Kähler, Seeberg, Grützmacher, Wernle, Schmiedeland Zahn as being among those from whom he has learned.[39] But, to repeat, he is no scissors-and-paste eclectic. Everything has been processed by a sharp, critical mind. If he leaves us with positive conclusions unsystematically bereft of the stages through which he has passed on the way to them, this only serves to underline his conviction that theology is a practical business of some urgency; and it is consistent with the fact that as with Paul so with Forsyth: the majority of his writings were occasional in nature.

Among easily detectable and personally acknowledged influences upon Forsyth is F. D. Maurice: 'I owe a great deal to Maurice; in some respects I owe him everything.'[40] The Anglican is approved for his view of church and sacraments, though not of ministry; and he

---

[35] *Freedom*, 342.

[36] *Person*, 264.

[37] *Person*, 263.

[38] On this matter, see further 'Ministerial Libraries: V. Principal Forsyth's Library at Hackney College' (1904); W. L. Bradley, *P. T. Forsyth: The Man and His Work*, chapter 3. I am grateful to Dr Leslie McCurdy for drawing the 'Ministerial Libraries' article to my attention.

[39] *Person*, vi–vii.

[40] Quoted in 'Ministerial Libraries', 268.

is an important stimulus towards Forsyth's view of the solidarity of the race and the consequent necessity of an atonement universal, and not merely individual, in scope – a position also advanced by R. W. Dale in his Congregational Lecture, *The Atonement* (1857). 'It was a race that Christ redeemed,' thunders Forsyth, 'and not a mere *bouquet* of believers.'[41] Forsyth was encouraged to read Hegel's *Logic* by A. M. Fairbairn,[42] and he later bore witness that 'no books have done more for my mind than Hegel's "Logic", or for my insight than his "Aesthetik"'.[43] But he remained unsatisfied by Hegel's system which he deemed more intellectualist than moral, and by Fairbairn's metaphysical rather than moral approach to kenotic theory.[44] While welcoming the emphasis of Kant and the Neo-Kantians (and of T. H. Green, who seems now more Kantian, now more Hegelian) upon the primacy of the will in the appropriation of reality, Forsyth found their understanding of history as the theatre of God's activity deficient. Learning of the primacy of faith from Pascal and Kierkegaard, valuing the life philosophers' view of reality as organic, he nevertheless objected to the way in which von Hartmann, for example, while seeing the need of redemption, placed humanity in an impersonal process rather than faced it with the grace and judgement of a personal, redemptive act. That revelation is supremely in a historic act Forsyth learned from Hermann, though while indebted to the Marburg scholar for theological and religious insight, he distanced himself from Hermann's philosophical position.[45] For this he gave no reasons – a fact the more surprising in view of Hermann's espousal of a Kantian voluntarism generally acceptable to Forsyth. If Forsyth followed Kähler in replacing the two-nature theory of Christ's person with his account of two personal movements within Christ's personality, he almost certainly derived his conviction that atonement theory must do something to satisfy

[41] *Sacraments*, 43.

[42] *Preaching*, 3rd ed., 195. Forsyth wrote a tribute to Fairbairn in *British Weekly* (1912).

[43] Quoted in 'Ministerial Libraries', 269.

[44] He could nevertheless say, 'After Ritschl I think I owe most to Dr Fairbairn', 'Ministerial Libraries', 269.

[45] 'Revelation and the Person of Christ' (1893): 97. This article is commonly regarded as marking Forsyth's final break from the liberal theology which he had espoused during the first part of his ministry.

God's holiness (and not simply do something for human beings) from the Puritan Thomas Goodwin, whom he called 'the apostle and high priest of our confession'.[46]

As might be expected in one who took his stand on morality, Forsyth regarded Schleiermacher's elevation of the conscience as a theological breakthrough of the greatest importance. He was generous in praise of his older contemporary, the Unitarian Martineau, for his fidelity to conscience. But he could not rest in Schleiermacher's experimentalism. The elevation of human experience could only detract from the significance of that which we experience – namely, God's grace revealed and active in history at the cross. Accordingly, 'Schleiermacher must be corrected by Ritschl'.[47] 'From the nettle danger in the Tübingen treatment of the historic Bible [Ritschl] plucked the flower of safety in a historic Gospel,'[48] he declared. In perceiving that faith is an act of judgement and of obedience, Ritschl did well; but he too stands in need of correction. Believing that justification was forgiveness, he was weak on the need of an atonement which could satisfy holy love. The juristic note was insufficiently sounded by Ritschl: 'The chief defect of the great revolution which began in Schleiermacher and ended in Ritschl has been that it allowed no place to that side of Christ's work.'[49] Correct in pointing to the pitfalls of pietism – self-engrossment, withdrawal from the world, the acquisition of 'more religious taste than weight'[50] – Ritschl wrongly depreciated the inward aspects of the kingdom. In embracing kenoticism, Forsyth stood at a considerable remove from his Göttingen teacher.

Much more could be said of the materials on which Forsyth went to work. I have not mentioned such literary persons as Carlyle, for example; but I have said enough to indicate that however unsystematic his writings from the point of view of demonstrated arguments from history, close textual criticism, and the provision of scholarly apparatus, Forsyth was a thoroughly biblical theologian who knew his history of thought and who, brooding on the whole territory

[46] *Freedom*, 118.

[47] 'The Place of Spiritual Experience in the Making of Theology' (1906) in *Revelation*, 68.

[48] *Revelation*, 74.

[49] *Work*, 228–9.

[50] *Sacraments*, 91.

with systematic intensity, emerged with something fresh and incisive to say.

II

Secondly, it has been suggested that Forsyth is unsystematic not only in his refusal to behave in scholarly fashion, but also in his willingness to leave loose ends in argumentation, and in his proneness to declaim rather than to dissect. I shall offer some random examples.

It cannot be denied that at times Forsyth's antithetical style trips him up. Edward Caird might almost have had him in mind when he wrote, 'While ... an antithetic writer ... is likely to bring out certain aspects of life and history with a vividness and force which could not be attained in any other way, he is likely at the same time to fall into an over-estimate of these aspects, and an under-estimate of other aspects, which by this method are necessarily thrown into the background.'[51] It would be tedious to record at length the many occasions on which Forsyth's antitheses prompt the responses, 'Why may we not "both ... and?"' or 'May it not be partly one and partly the other?' Thus, to take one example, he declares that 'the mighty thing in Christ is his grace and not His constitution'.[52] Are his grace and his constitution thus separable? As he is towards us, so he is in himself. Granted, Forsyth's context here is the primacy and facticity of the evangelical experience over intellectual construction and forms of thought. But the antithesis nevertheless hinders rather than helps.

On the substantive point concerning the person of Christ, Forsyth, though stimulating, leaves us with puzzles at certain points. Of course the final mystery can never be probed by us, and Forsyth rightly recognizes the place of a proper agnosticism: 'If we ask *how* Eternal Godhead could make the actual condition of human nature His own, we must answer, ... that we do not know.'[53] But this does

---

[51]Edward Caird, 'St Paul and the Idea of Evolution', *Hibbert Journal 2* (Oct 1903): 2.

[52]*Person*, 10.

[53]*Person*, 320.

not excuse human confusions. Thus, in a number of writings he conducts a running battle against the Chalcedonian formula. In the formula, he declares, the two natures of Christ are united miraculously, not morally: 'The person was the resultant of the two natures rather than the agent of their union.'[54] His complaint is that the underlying thought is metaphysical rather than ethical, and the terms employed were material rather than personal and ethical.[55] More generally, he contends that 'the Roman or the Chalcedonian type of doctrine begins with the Incarnation, beyond experience but believed on authority, and then it descends on the Atonement; instead of beginning with the Atonement, in a moral departure, and going on from that experience to the Incarnation, since God only could atone'.[56]

Forsyth does recognize the service performed by the formula in blocking the exit routes into a variety of heresies, but I feel he might have been more generous in his appreciation than he is. No doubt the early theologians used terms which lay to hand – what else could they do? But their intention was undoubtedly to maintain the unity of Christ's person, and to be as agnostic as to the 'how' of it as was Forsyth himself. When he elsewhere avers that 'Chalcedonism means the substitution for experience of truth, and metaphysical truth, on the external authority of a Church over the intelligence',[57] we may suspect that he is attempting truth by definition. Moreover, Forsyth's suggested replacement-theory is not without its difficulties. He recommends that we think in terms of two modes of being in Christ: 'it might be better to describe the union of God and man in Christ as the mutual involution of two personal movements raised to the whole scale of the human soul and divine'.[58] But when he proceeds to indicate what this means in terms of our salvation, he comes perilously close to an antithesis which threatens the mutuality he has just advocated: 'Our Redeemer must save us by his difference from us, however the salvation get home to us by his parity with us. He saves because he is God and not man.'[59] The

[54] Person, 223.
[55] Person, 331.
[56] Sacraments, 197.
[57] Justification, 2nd ed., 94.
[58] Person, 333; cf. 307.
[59] Person, 342.

matter is further complicated by Forsyth's reiterated view that the offering of the cross is made by God and to God. Thus when Forsyth observes that 'when we find God actually reconciling us in [Christ] we cannot help inferring some more substantial unity between him and God than between God and ourselves', it is possible to divine his meaning, though I think the term 'substantial' is problematic. But when he immediately adds, 'The inner life of Jesus could not really reveal to man the inner life of God if at his centre he was not more God than man, and doing the redeeming thing which God alone can do',[60] it is impossible not to see the chasm of docetism opening up before us as Forsyth by implication resists synergism. No doubt God alone can save, but he does it through the Son who is fully human. Another mode of Forsythian expression is that on the cross, Jesus obediently says 'Amen' on behalf of humanity to God's holy judgement upon sin.[61] It is not that the Saviour was punished, 'but He took the penalty of sin, the chastisement of our peace'.[62] Many have felt that the ground of Forsyth's claim that the sinless one (and he is insistent that Christ was sinless) could both bear the penalty and not be punished is presented in a manner which is less than fully clear.

Christ's atonement is for the race: Forsyth insists upon this. More than one friendly critic has noted the impersonal, metaphysical ring to the concept of racial solidarity.[63] This would seem to be born out by Forsyth's claim that 'the first charge upon Christ and His Cross was the reconciliation of the race, and of its individuals by implication'.[64] In so far as Forsyth wished to counter the individualistic – even atomistic – understanding of salvation which was current in some circles in his day, he was in the right; but at times his language is problematic. The problem arises because of Forsyth's use of the term 'cross'. He is frequently, according to taste, comprehensive or slippery. 'Cross' characteristically functions as shorthand for a constellation of ideas including the actual cross of Calvary, the cross eternally in the heart of God, the lamb slain from the foundation of

[60]'Faith, Metaphysic and Incarnation' (1915): 718–19.
[61]See, for example, *Cruciality*, 102.
[62]*Cruciality*, 103.
[63]For example, Bradley, *P. T. Forsyth: The Man and His Work*, 272.
[64]*Work*, 199; cf. *Missions*, 340–1.

the world, the Son's voluntary, obedient, juristic, victorious work. In this way, numerous soteriological strands are entwined in Forsyth's language. It is not that they are improper in themselves; the difficulty is that it is not always easy to determine which he has in mind in a given instance. Furthermore, when Forsyth claims that 'it is Christ that works out His own redemption and reconciliation, from God's right hand, throughout the course of history' – and this with reference to 'His whole celestial life from the beginning',[65] the question of the relation of the eternal cross to Calvary's cross is raised but not fully resolved. Given the intellectual climate of Forsyth's day, and with reference to the eternal cross motif, there are times when I am tempted to think that there is in operation what might be called a post-Hegelian-idealistic drag, momentarily tempting him in the direction of the idealized cross remote from the historic cross, the importance of which had so strongly been impressed upon him by Ritschl.

On the question of our appropriation of God's redemption, Forsyth is ambiguous. On the one hand, the Christian experience of salvation is given; but, on the other hand, when considering the accusation that Christians, in adverting to their experience, are guilty of psychologism, Forsyth replies that what we have in Christ is not an impression but a life-change which places us within a community of experience, the church; and this experience is the product of a 'venture of faith' which believers make. The relation between God's gracious immediately received gift and the Christian community's venturing is far from clear.[66]

Forsyth's antitheses are frequently inspired by the horrors he wishes to avoid. So concerned is he, for example, to avoid any suggestion that grace is a mysterious, manually-communicable substance conferring *potestas* upon members of the priestly caste that his doctrine of ordination is not as 'high' as the rest of his churchmanship seems to require. He writes, 'The grace conferred at ordination is but the formal and corporate *opportunity* provided by the Church to minister [the] Gospel; it is not a new spiritual gift belonging to an order and its canonical entry.... Our ordinations

---

[65] *Work*, 154, 153.

[66] For further discussion along these lines, see Arthur Boutwood's review of *Person*, 686–90.

are acts of denominational order and worship. If they do not convey grace they do impart public authority, corporate responsibility, and representative opportunity.'[67] The first puzzle here is that within thirty pages, Forsyth declares that ordination does and does not confer or convey grace. The second puzzle is that the last sentence quoted may be taken as implying that God's grace is operative everywhere except in ordination. Surely those of Forsyth's tradition may deny what they deem to be untoward notions of priestly caste whilst at the same time maintaining that ordination is more than the formal and corporate bestowal of an opportunity of representative service. May they not believe that God hears the ordination prayer and bestows the grace sought in it? As to grace itself, in one memorable phrase, Forsyth announces that 'it is not mercy to our failure, or pity for our pain, but it is pardon for our sins!'[68] As a protest against sentimental understandings of the divine Father-hood this may have some point; but as a definition of grace it is needlessly disjunctive, for while we ought certainly to place the pardon of sinners (and what has been done to secure it) at the heart of our understanding of grace, we surely cannot exclude from it the Father's mercy and pity. A similar comment seems to be called for in relation to the Lord's Supper. Forsyth asserts, 'In the Supper Christ is present not to bless a religious coterie, but as having suffered and conquered in history for a sinful people, to whom His Passion brings the saving gift of forgiveness and regeneration.'[69] He is right in what he affirms, and (passing over the tendentious term 'religious coterie') wrong in what he denies. If Christ is present the people are blessed: we may not appear to divide the presence of Christ from his benefits.

III

I turn from my random and by no means exhaustive list of Forsythian loose ends – many of them linguistically inspired – to two areas where his failure to follow through both exemplifies his unsystematic ways and bequeathes us tasks of the greatest importance.

[67] *Reunion*, 32, 59.
[68] 'The Churches' One Foundation' (1906): 197.
[69] *Sacraments*, 253.

I refer first to Forsyth on the Trinity. There is no question but that Forsyth was a convinced trinitarian, or that 'Unitarian' was on his lips something akin to a term of abuse. His Congregational forebear Thomas Ridgley (1667?–1734; D. D., King's College, Aberdeen, 1738), would have agreed with Forsyth that 'the triune God ... is what makes Christianity Christian',[70] though, because of Forsyth's conviction that 'where you fix a creed you flatten faith,'[71] I cannot imagine that he would have joined Ridgley among the subscribers at the Salters' Hall in 1719.[72] But while his writings are replete with trinitarian references, Forsyth takes no special pains to anchor his major theological concerns in a fully-fledged doctrine of the Trinity. I do not say he is culpable here – I am not so insubordinate! An unsystematic theologian may write on whatsoever he pleases; and it is understandable that one who sets such store by the order of Christian experience should have written as he did – how many *begin* their Christian pilgrimages from a fully-fledged articulation of the doctrine of the Trinity? It is the last thing we come to – and this is reflected in the Christian year. As he said, 'any belief in either a Trinity or an Incarnation can only flow from a final experience of grace by the sinful soul'.[73] Or again, 'Paul in Romans, when he wants to condense Christian doctrine into a compendium, does he philosophise about the mysteries of the Trinity, or the method of incarnation, or an active and a passive creation? He does nothing of the kind. He speaks of law, sin and grace; of conscience, guilt and salvation.'[74] On the other hand, Forsyth recognizes that 'The Father who *spoke* by his prophets must *come* to save in the Son and must *occupy* in the Spirit.'[75] In other words, redemption is the work of the triune Godhead.[76] Accordingly, however it may be in

---

[70] *Freedom*, 263.

[71] *Preaching*, 141.

[72] It will be recalled that at the Salters' Hall the question of subscription was paramount, though the Trinity was ostensibly the point at issue. The non-subscribers denied that they were Arian, and declared that 'we ... sincerely believe the Doctrine of the Blessed Trinity'. See *An Authentick Account of Several Things Done and agreed upon by the Dissenting Ministers Lately assembled at Salters-Hall* (1917), 15; Sell, *Dissenting Thought and the Life of the Churches* (Lewiston, N.Y.: Edwin Mellen Press, 1990), 137–8.

[73] *Person*, 325.

[74] *Person*, 221.

[75] *Person*, 327.

[76] *Work*, 152; *Cruciality*, 101.

the order of our experience, for *theology* the activity of the triune God is both the base and the context of reflection. As he puts it:

> All the metaphysic of the Trinity ... is at bottom but the church's effort to express in thought the incomparable reality and absolute glory of the Saviour whom faith saw sitting by the Father as man's redeeming and eternal Lord, to engage the whole and present God directly in our salvation, and found the soul in Christ on the eternal Rock.... A doctrine of the Trinity may be, so far as the crude individual goes, a piece of theological science, but for the church it is part of its essential faith.[77]

In view of this, I respectfully suggest that some who embrace Forsyth's fundamental concerns for an objective atonement provided by the God of holy love should show more clearly than he did how (and not merely declare that) the entire Godhead is implicated in the work and reception of redemption.

With Forsyth's observation that 'it is impossible with due reverence to speak in any but the most careful and tentative way of the relations in the Godhead'[78] none may reasonably quarrel. But here as elsewhere he is sometimes more opaque than is strictly necessary. He strongly asserts that 'the idea of an Eternal Father is unthinkable without an Eternal Son of equal personal reality and finality',[79] but when writing of the subordination of wives to husbands he refers to the Son's obedience and declares that 'obedience is not conceivable without some form of subordination. Yet in His very obedience the Son was co-equal with the Father.... Therefore, in the very nature of God, subordination implies no inferiority'.[80] It is difficult not to believe that we have here a mauling of concepts which is prompted by something other than a proper agnosticism before mystery.

Again, Forsyth does not hesitate to couch the motivating force of Christian mission in trinitarian terms: 'The first missionary was God the Father, who sent forth His Son in the likeness of sinful flesh.'[81] The second missionary was the Son, and the third was the

[77]'Faith, Metaphysic, and Incarnation', 707.
[78]*Person*, 283.
[79]*Person*, 116.
[80]*Marriage*, 70.
[81]*Missions*, 270.

Spirit, sent forth by the Saviour into all the earth. But then we are told that the fourth missionary is the church. Is not this different in kind from the others – especially given Forsyth's insistence that the church is not and cannot be the extension, or continuation, of the incarnation, for 'that which owes itself to a rebirth cannot be a prolongation of the ever sinless'?[82] Again, what is the precise meaning, and what happens to the Trinity when we are told that the Holy Spirit is inseparable from the work of Christ?[83] Yet again, what are we to make of the claim that 'detached from the Word [meaning here, the Bible] the supernatural action of the Holy Spirit becomes gradually the natural evolution of the human spirit'?[84] Forsyth rightly protests against those who claim a mystic 'hot-line' to God which bypasses, claims to supplement, or even contradicts, the Bible. But does he really mean to say that the third person is ineffectual apart from the sixty-six books of the Bible? There is much more to be said concerning Forsyth and the Trinity, but I trust that the evidence supplied will suffice to justify my conviction that Forsyth's treatment of this foundational doctrine is not rigorously systematic.

IV

The second territory in which activity is called for is that of apologetics. On the one hand, Forsyth is by no means as hostile to traditional apologetics as were some who came after him. He accords a place to natural theology, although he does not produce a systematic apologetic himself. As with the Trinity, so here: we need not fault a theologian for failing to do what he did not set out to do. But on the other hand, some of Forsyth's utterances seem to preclude apologetics. There is thus an ambivalence in his corpus on this matter which needs to be exposed. When this is done I think he emerges as more in favour of apologetics than not, and this I find enormously encouraging given the present situation in many mainline Western churches which are losing and not replacing minds at an alarming rate, and which here and there are displaying signs of a

---

[83] *Freedom*, 13.
[84] *Freedom*, 95.

most disturbing anti-intellectualism – sometimes in the name of what are alleged to be pastoral practicalities.

Forsyth's attitude towards apologetics, natural theology, general revelation, was shaped by his struggle against what he took to be the question of the hour: liberalism within the church. 'The greatest issue for the moment,' he writes, 'is within the Christian pale; it is not between Christianity and the world. It is the issue between theological liberalism (which is practically unitarian) and a free but positive theology, which is essentially evangelical.'[85] He insists that

> Christianity does not peddle ideas; it does things.... What cries to be done is to make the spiritual world a moral reality. To do that we must present it as an atoning Gospel adjusted to our peculiar moral extremity. We shall never get what we want by coquetting with the higher physics, nor by physical research, nor by theosophic religion, nor by undiluted Hegel, nor by mystical, fanciful, sermonic, and unhistoric treatment of the Bible. We can get it only by the moral power and effect of a historic Gospel, one that draws us from the belly of hell.[86]

It is well known that Forsyth had himself imbibed liberalism in his early days; and we have it on his own testimony that he was 'turned from a Christian to a believer, from a lover of love to an object of grace'.[87] The change was radical – it even took sartorial effect, so that he came to rebuke preachers who wore tweeds and bright ties, as he himself had once done. But no more than Newman utterly shook off the evangelical piety in which he was reared did Forsyth completely break free of liberalism. 'The service rendered to Christianity by the great critical movement is almost beyond words,' he declared.[88] He was no 'conservative' obscurantist, tied to revelation-in-propositions, and he regretted the way in which the Bible had, following the Reformation, become regarded as the infallible source of pure doctrine which yielded a quasi-Aristotelian

[85] *Person*, 84.

[86] 'The Grace of the Gospel as the Moral Authority in the Church' (1905), in *Society*, 95, 97.

[87] *Preaching*, 193. Cf. Robert McAfee Brown, 'The "Conversion" of P. T. Forsyth'.

[88] *Person*, viii.

system grounded in medieval logic.[89] To him revelation was God's supreme redemptive *act* in Christ. Furthermore, since 'humanity ... is an organism, with a history', God's treatment of us must be by a historic redemption: 'its compass is cosmic; its sphere is human history, actual history'.[90] None of which, of course, was intended as denigrating the Bible. On the contrary, 'I do not believe in verbal inspiration. I am with the critics in principle. But the true minister ought to find the words and phrases of the Bible so full of spiritual food and felicity that he has some difficulty in not believing in verbal inspiration.'[91] 'Revelation is not a statement,' he declared, 'but it must be capable of statement.'[92] The fact remains that 'the Gospel of God's historic act of grace is the infallible power and authority over both Church and Bible'.[93]

Forsyth's fundamental objection to what he calls liberalism is methodological. I suggest that because of his desire to shun this method he is dissuaded from pursuing the apologetic path, the legitimacy of which in principle he admits. He believes that in liberal circles of the philosophical kind scholasticism is the order of the day, and while Hegel, or another, takes the place of Aristotle, everything which the Christian wishes to say has to be articulated under the favoured, albeit extraneous, systematic rubric.[94] In fact the gospel of moral redemption by a historic act cannot be thus contained or constricted. When the attempt is made we reach an intellectualism which is either mystical or aesthetic in tone.[95] Hence, for example, Forsyth's strong opposition to R. J. Campbell and the so-called New Theology, whose proponents 'become as much the doctrinaire victims of a speculative theology as our forefathers were the victims of an orthodox theology'.[96]

Alternatively, everything, as with Harnack, must be made to conform to modern historical method, so that if the miracles are by this criterion awkward, they must be dispensed with. In either case, the gospel is pared down to suit prevailing intellectual fashions, and

---

[89] *Sacraments*, 305. Cf. *Authority*, 2nd ed., 53. See further, Garvie, 'Placarding the Cross', 343–6.

[90] 'Revelation and Bible' (1911): 241.

[91] *Preaching*, 26.

[92] *Freedom*, 239.

[93] 'The Evangelical Churches and the Higher Criticism', 574.

[94] *Preaching*, 143.

[95] See *Freedom*, 99.

[96] 'The Distinctive Thing in Christian Experience' (1908): 485.

this with a view to persuading modern human beings that the gospel was only what they had always thought. 'Reduce the burden of belief we must,' says Forsyth, for 'the old orthodoxy laid on men's believing power more than it could carry.'[97] Not for him any reversion to Calvinistic scholasticism. But the problem now was that 'too many are occupied in throwing over precious cargo; they are lightening the ship even of its fuel'.[98] He would thus have the immanentist evolutionists learn that 'any theology that places us in a spiritual *process*, or native movement between the finite and the infinite, depreciates the value of spiritual *act*, and thus makes us independent of the grace of God'.[99] He would have the historians understand that the exemplar Christ, Christ the first Christian – these were Christs who, on Forsyth's reckoning, were almost worse than no Christ at all, for 'with the person of Jesus comes a new religion, of which he is the object, and not simply the subject as its saint or sage'.[100] The underlying problem was that 'the liberal theology finds Christ's centre of gravity in what He has in common with us, a positive theology in that wherein He differs'.[101] His general affirmation, made with reference to pointedly-chosen names is that 'there is no greater division within religion than that between Emerson and Kierkegaard, between a religion that but consecrates the optimism of clean youth, and that which hallows the tragic note, and deals with a world sick unto death. We choose the latter'.[102] Neither the heart nor the reason can stand in judgement over God's redemptive revelation.[103] Indeed 'if we had theology brought entirely up to date in regard to current thought, we should not then have the great condition for the Kingdom of God. It is the wills of men, and not their views, that are the great obstacle to the Gospel, and the things most intractable'.[104] This is why truths as such will not save, but only God's redeeming act.[105]

---

[97] *Preaching*, 84.

[98] *Authority*, 261. Cf. *Theology*, 25: 'We must not empty the Gospel in order quickly to fill the Church.'

[99] *Preaching*, 146.

[100] *Person*, 114.

[101] *Person*, 163.

[102] *Authority*, 203.

[103] 'Revelation and the Person of Christ', 107, 109.

[104] *Preaching*, 197.

[105] 'Revelation and the Person of Christ', 102.

As we have seen, a large part of Forsyth's work is in the form of an inner-ecclesial apologetic. He is out to confront Christians with the gospel they have denied or overlooked, and to expose counterfeits of the gospel. He believed the crucial battle of the moment to be within the church and not between it and the world. He wished to hammer the gospel home to those who should have known it all along: hence his crusade against that then current variety of religion which 'seeks rather to commend the Gospel to the natural man than to set the natural man in the searchlight of the Gospel'.[106] While I think it true to say that Forsyth was not of the patiently-argumentative kind, and that he was temperamentally disinclined to the apologetic enterprise in its more technical form, he does not altogether shun the apologetic task of defending the faith against its cultured despisers from without. He does somewhat more than indicate the lines along which such an apologetic might travel. At its heart is natural man's conscience which affirms human culpability. Conscience is the bar before which we all stand. It is the Word of God within us, and we cannot flout it with impunity.[107] As he elsewhere says, 'At the heart of man you will find divine symptoms, but not a divine salvation.'[108] Expecting the answer 'Yes,' he asks, 'Is not all illumination revelation – the light of nature, of reason, of the heart? Is there no revelation in earth's daily splendour around us, in heaven's mighty glory above us, in the heart's tender or tragic voice within us?' True, they reveal what he calls 'a borrowed light' which comes from the Saviour, but they do reveal it.[109] Forsyth can thus commend the Quakers for holding to 'the light that lighteth *every man*'.[110] Thus, while 'nature cannot of itself culminate in grace, at least it was not put there without regard to grace'.[111] Indeed, 'nature, if not the mother, is the matrix of Grace'.[112] Nowhere does Forsyth concede so much to general revelation as in his aesthetics: 'The great Christian truths are not truths of a church or of a book, but of the human spirit in its very nature and constitution. They are the

---

[106]'Lay Religion' (1915): 779.
[107]*Cruciality*, 62–5.
[108]*Society*, 112.
[109]'Revelation, Old and New' (1911), in *Revelation*, 14–15.
[110]*Sacraments*, 91.
[111]*Life*, 2nd ed., 69.
[112]*War*, 171.

exposition of that Reason which constitutes the unity of God, man, and nature. They are truths which are at the foundation of Science, Religion, Art.'[113] No doubt these sentiments must be set against such an assertion as this: 'The sole content of Revelation ... is the love, will, presence and purpose of God for our redemption';[114] and it is this sentence and others like it which mislead John Rodgers into thinking that 'Forsyth has rejected all natural theology'.[115] Rather, here is the ambivalence of which I warned.

On the one hand Forsyth, the undeserving recipient of God's gracious revelation, can protest, 'We do not review God's claims and then admit Him as we are satisfied.'[116] That is, we are in no position to judge the Word of the holy God by the use of our reason. Nor, with 'the religion of Monism', can we posit a God-humanity rational continuity whereby 'to be glorified we have but to be amplified'.[117] On the other hand 'we must own the justice of that demand for some *a priori* in the soul to which the revelation comes, and on which it strikes its proper note'.[118] But this *a priori* is 'not in the region of the reason but of the will. Its function is not criticism but obedience ... We do not accept [Christ] on His credentials; we fall down dead before Him'.[119] Once again the antithesis is unhelpful. Forsyth is no irrationalist, and he knows that there can be no legitimate, non-idolatrous 'falling down' before one whose credentials have not in some sense been judged by us: why, otherwise, would he repeat the scriptural injunction that 'we must prove the spirits whether they are of God'.[120] No doubt religious faith is not simply rational assent to propositions: it is a life-commitment. But propositions are never far away, as Forsyth realized when he insisted that 'God's own act of redeeming is not completed without its self-

[113]*Art*, 2nd ed. (1901), 147.

[114]'Revelation and the Person of Christ', 102.

[115]Rodgers, *The Theology of P. T. Forsyth*, 253. Similarly, Bradley is 'inclined to question' Hughes's assertion that 'in Forsyth there is not "the radical dualism between truth from revelation and truth by man's unaided reason".' See Bradley, *P. T. Forsyth: The Man and His Work*, 168; Hughes, 'A Barthian before Barth?' 314–15.

[116]*Authority*, 146.

[117]*Authority*, 170.

[118]*Authority*, 168.

[119]*Authority*, 168, 173.

[120]*Authority*, 39.

interpretation. That is *His Word*.[121] His entire approach is that of one whose faith seeks understanding – an understanding which can be commended to others on the basis of the shared common ground of reason and conscience: 'A philosophy can bring us to no security of a revelation; but a revelation develops a philosophy, or a view of the world.'[122] In developing a Christian view of the world, Forsyth is supremely concerned to preserve the revealed *fact* inviolate. Hence his complaint that 'rationalism, whether orthodox or heterodox, consists in measuring Revelation by something outside itself'.[123] A similarly grave mistake is made along affective lines, for 'to make the heart the judge of Revelation is to raise sentiment and individualism to the control of Revelation, and so to make them the real Revelation'.[124]

To repeat: Forsyth is no irrationalist, and he does not deny the existence of epistemological and moral common ground as between Christians and others. Hence his protest against the empiricist reductionists that 'you are doing to religion what you fiercely resent that religion should do to art or science. You are limiting its freedom by a foreign dogma'.[125] He contends against historicism, the dissolution of the objective of faith into a handful of facts, and psychologism, the resolution of religion into subjective processes or symbols, insisting that 'for a religion the first requisite is an objective reality ... which we either reach or receive. According as we receive it we have it as revelation and by the way of living faith; according as we reach it we have it by way of discovery, of thought, of metaphysic'.[126] If historicism and psychologism successfully vanquish metaphysic then, he is convinced, 'the sense of a real and objective God fails; the note of reality goes out of such religion as we have left, and with that in due course all fails'.[127] Lacking metaphysical anchorage, religion would survive for a time only because suspended by traditionalism, constitutionalism and nationalism.[128]

---

[121]'Revelation and Bible', 243.
[122]*Preaching*, 170. The gospel, he argues, has to be distilled from the Bible; *Preaching* 251.
[123]'Revelation and the Person of Christ', 109.
[124]'Revelation and the Person of Christ', 107.
[125]'Theological Liberalism v. Liberal Theology' (1910): 557.
[126]'Faith, Metaphysic, and Incarnation', 697.
[127]'Faith, Metaphysic, and Incarnation', 697.
[128]'Faith, Metaphysic, and Incarnation, 698.

Again, running through Forsyth's work is his quoted concurrence with Butler, confirmed by Kant,[129] that 'morality is the nature of things'.[130] Such a conviction cannot be annexed by any one religion, nor would Forsyth wish it otherwise. The sphere, though not the source, of morality is human consciousness.[131] It is true that in Forsyth's hands the moral is construed as personal, active, holy love, its task being that of redeeming a sinful race; but this is because metaphysic, by which he means the ordered articulation of what one has perceived, cannot but reflect upon what has been given in experience.[132] 'Our theological capital,' he declares, 'is not ideas we arrive at but experience we go through.... . The theologian is not a syllogist but an experient, an observer.'[133] Paul, indeed, had 'to coin a new metaphysic' in order to convert, rather than to develop an intellectual heritage which gave no place to 'the experienced redemption of a ruined world'.[134] Similarly, 'what we have to ask about Christ then, is this, what account of him is demanded by that work, that new creation of us, that real bringing of us to God, not simply in nearness but in likeness?'[135] No doubt 'it is by no metaphysic that we come to the faith of Christ's Godhead; but, having come there, some metaphysic is inevitable wherever religion does not mean mental poverty, the loss of spiritual majesty, and a decayed sense of the price of the soul and the cost of sin'.[136] The upshot is that 'it is not to metaphysic that we need ever object, but to archaic metaphysic made final and compulsory'.[137] Furthermore, 'since Kant opened the new age must it not be a metaphysic or ethic?'[138]

But once again comes the warning that 'notions' will not suffice (compare the Quakers once more): 'We cannot start with a view of

---

[129] *Authority*, 4.

[130] Cf. 'Veracity, Reality, and Regeneration' (1915): 206.

[131] *Authority*, 75.

[132] See *Preaching*, 255. Cf. 170; *Authority*, 6, 8, 44.

[133] *Authority*, 93. Presumably 'theologian' here needs to be qualified by 'constructive'.

[134] *Authority*, 80. Cf. *Society*, 80–1.

[135] *Person*, 346.

[136] 'Faith, Metaphysic, and Incarnation', 708.

[137] 'Faith, Metaphysic, and Incarnation', 701.

[138] 'Faith, Metaphysic, and Incarnation', 702.

God reached on speculative or other similar grounds, and then use Christ as a mere means for confirming it or giving it practical effect.'[139] 'It takes a sound education to get rid of that notional religion' which thinks 'that faith rests finally on any truth or synthesis of truths.'[140] Indeed, 'in a strict use of words, there is no such thing as saving truth'.[141] The ultimate choice is between 'a rational Christianity and a redemptive'[142] – an antithesis which on Forsyth's own terms seems to be too strong: he is not for irrationalism or anti-rationalism. We can, however, sympathize with a bluntness which probably derives in part from experiences which called forth this remark: 'The bulk of the questions with which the amateur critic poses faith, and the illiterate heretic delights the public, are as unanswerable as if it were asked – what is the difference between London Bridge and four o'clock?'[143] There could hardly be a greater contrast than that between such trivializing and Forsyth's understanding of prayer according to which 'all the meditation of Nature and of things sinks here to the rear, and we are left with God in Christ as His own Mediator and His own Revealer'.[144]

V

I hope that I may have persuaded you that Forsyth is not a systematic exegete or historian of thought – though he has done all of the required homework in those fields; he does not systematically ground arguments or pursue them wheresoever they lead; and there are loose ends in his work, some of them inspired by his fondness for antithesis. In particular, he bequeaths to those who follow him the tasks of attending to trinitarian foundations and to apologetics (which he does not rule out).

But I have not so far mentioned the most blatantly obvious way in which Forsyth is unsystematic. He simply does not set out from the doctrine of God or, like the Westminster Confession, for

---

[139] Authority, 353.
[140] Theology, 203.
[141] 'Authority and Theology' (1905): 69.
[142] Person, 96.
[143] Person, 312.
[144] Prayer, 2nd ed., 30.

example, from the doctrine of Scripture, and take us step by step through the so-called 'departments' of theology in sequence. In this, he contrasts dramatically with his Dissenting forebear Thomas Ridgley, whose two-volume *Body of Divinity* comprises a thorough-going progression through the Westminster Larger Catechism. Or consider Forsyth's colleague, A. E. Garvie, a master of thorough exegesis and patient exposition, whose major works are replete with numbered sections, ample references, and copious indices.

However, to say that Forsyth is unsystematic in all the ways described is, in the end, to say one of the less important things about him, and to express a judgement which would probably not have disturbed him in the slightest. It may even be said that his formally unsystematic approach highlights his ever-reverberating themes and makes him appear less dated than might otherwise have been the case. There is, after all, something to be said for a theologian of his generation who is not consumed by the felt need to engage in incessant blow-by-blow refutations of Herbert Spencer, or by an insatiable desire to pulverize repeatedly the higher critics, or by the conviction that theological salvation is to be found in a marriage with absolute idealism. To what is most important about Forsyth, I now turn.

At the outset I quoted his pupil, Lovell Cocks, as declaring that Forsyth was not a systematic theologian, and in support I summoned half a sentence of the Anglican, J. K. Mozley. But the second half of Mozley's sentence is of great importance, and I now quote him in full: 'Systematic is not a word that one would naturally apply to Dr Forsyth; yet I know of no theologian of the day who has fewer loose ends to his thought.'[145] I claim to have shown that there are loose ends, but Mozley clarifies his point by further remarking that 'at every point which he reaches in the gradual development of a position, or by some bold *coup de main*, one knows that there is a straight line back, as from any point on the circle's circumference to its centre, to that which is the moral and therefore the only possible centre of the world – the Cross of Christ'.[146] Here we approach the heart of the matter, provided that we understand 'cross' as encompassing a cluster of convictions: God's fatherly love as holy and

---

[145]Mozley, *The Doctrine of the Atonement*, 182.
[146]Mozley, *The Doctrine of the Atonement*, 182.

victorious; grace as judgement; Christ as having wrought once and for all at Calvary an atonement for the race, by virtue of which penitent sinners receive new life in the Spirit, are engrafted into the church, and are in fellowship with God and the communion of saints eternally. For all of this, at least, 'cross' is shorthand in Forsyth. Sustained reflection having brought him to this point, these themes become refrains which permeate all his post-1893 writings. We know that no matter what the ostensible subject of a discourse, these themes will underlie it and reverberate through it. Here is a highly sytematic – in the sense of sustained and consistent – application of central convictions to the whole range of human concerns. Forsyth's complex of fundamental convictions are his controlling passion; they dictate his method and motivate his testimony. What he coveted for the whole church he manifested in his own work: 'The faith of the evangelized Church must suffuse its mind.... . The Church's experience of its revelation must not only be stated but it must be organized by its own principle in the manifold wisdom of God and riches of Christ.'[147]

To underscore points which have already emerged: Forsyth centres in the cross, which is the place where, once and for all, something is not merely shown, but done, by God: 'The cross does not in the New Testament exhibit God as accepting sacrifice so much as making it.'[148] Indeed, God being supremely holy and just, he alone could move in love to redeem. The testimony to Christ's divinity flows from the realization that 'no half-God could redeem the soul which it took the whole God to create';[149] hence the claim that 'a Christ that differs from the rest of men only in saintly degree and not in redeeming kind is not the Christ of the New Testament nor of a Gospel Church'.[150] The 'holy God could be satisfied by neither pain nor death, but by holiness alone. The atoning thing is not obedient suffering but suffering obedience'.[151] 'It was [Christ's] holiness, with which the Holy Father was perfectly pleased and satisfied.'[152] Hence, 'Christ is more precious to us by what distin-

---

[147] *Theology*, 47.
[148] *Cruciality*, 92; cf. *Work*, 24, 92, 93, 99.
[149] *Person*, 86; cf. 'Faith, Metaphysic, and Incarnation', 703.
[150] *Society*, 99.
[151] *Work*, 205.
[152] *Person*, 235.

guishes Him from us than by what identifies Him with us.'[153] Not surprisingly, Forsyth insisted that 'only the Atonement gives the Incarnation its base and value in any moral and religious sense. Without it, it is but a philosophic theme';[154] but he had no time for atonement theories which he deemed immoral: 'The atonement did not procure grace, it flowed from grace.... We must renounce the idea that [Christ[was punished by the God who was ever well pleased with His beloved Son.'[155]

Inspired and motivated by this constellation of convictions, Forsyth treats themes as various as theodicy, socialism, pacifism and ecclesiology. I can only briefly indicate his procedure by way of illustration.

Thus, the cross judges the then (and in some quarters still) popular religion of humanity for its failure to reconcile ethic and religion in the supreme moral idea of holiness, and its contentment with the worship of our better slaves.[156] Neither will sophisticated versions of monism suffice. For here 'the fundamental relation is one of identity. To be glorified we have but to be amplified.'[157] While conceding that 'we are all Monists in the sense of striving to introduce unity of conception into our view of life and things ... we do not all think that the principle of the world is wholly within the world.... Beware of a juggle, however honest, by which a homogeneous and singular identity is slipped in to meet our need for a manifold and solidary universal.'[158] Revelation requires a dualism of giver and receiver; a God conceived on monistic and immanentist lines could not reveal himself for he would have no other; hence God must be regarded as for ever distinct from the world.[159] What is required is 'a Dualism with a unity of Reconciliation, and not a

[153]'The Distinctive Thing in Christian Experience', 486.

[154]*Society*, 120. Forsyth had considerable grounds for this judgement in view of the widely-prevalent post-Hegelian idealism of his day, and that variety of Anglican incarnational theology, exemplifed in *Lux Mundi*, which came near to regarding incarnation as evolution 'Christologized'. Cf. *Cruciality*, 50; *Preaching*, 216; *Missions*, 68.

[155]*Cruciality*, 41.

[156]*Authority*, 66.

[157]*Authority*, 170.

[158]'Monism' (1909): 14, 15.

[159]'Monism', 7, 8, 9.

Monism with a unity of Identity as real in the sin as in the Saviour.'[160]

Forsyth speaks not on the authority of the Bible or the church, but of the redeeming gospel which called forth both. Those regenerated by the Spirit and called by grace under the proclamation of the gospel comprise the church. With reference to the cross he declares, 'It is that thing *done* that makes a Church at last, and gives dynamic both to preaching and hearing.'[161] The church is 'a new creation of God in the Holy Spirit'.[162] Moreover, the church is inescapable, for while 'salvation is personal ... it is not individual ... it is personal in its appropriation but collective in its nature'.[163] To be a believer is to be of the gathering of saints.

It follows from Forsyth's understanding of the cross that true liberty is not freedom from, but for and under the gospel.[164] It is not the liberty of individualists – and the doctrine of the unlimited right of private judgement derives more from the Renaissance than the Reformation;[165] it is the liberty of those who stand under 'the authoritative Word of an evangelical Church'.[166] Hence his determined opposition to those of his own Congregational family who, in those theologically free-wheeling days, behaved as if Christian liberty conferred the right to believe and do as one pleased. On the contrary, 'there must surely be in every positive religion some point where it may so change as to lose its identity and become another religion'.[167] Christianity can never legitimately slip its anchorage in redemption by holy love. As he repeatedly insists, the freedom of Congregationalists is a 'founded freedom'[168] – it is freedom created and founded and reared by an authority which cannot be either evaded or shaken; and which creates our emancipation ... by the eternal redemption at the heart of all history in Christ's cross'.[169] In

[160]'Monism', 12.
[161]'Church, Ministry and Sacraments' (1916): 39.
[162]*Sacraments*, 34.
[163]*Work*, 119. Cf. *Sacraments*, 43; *Charter*, 41.
[164]*Authority*, 219; cf. *Freedom*, 216–17.
[165]*Authority*, 283.
[166]*Authority*, 224.
[167]*Authority*, 219.
[168]*Freedom*, 290, 293, 336, 347.
[169]*Freedom*, 347.

the interests of the Lordship of Christ over the church, and in opposition to the heresy that Free Church polity is democratic, he thunders, 'Between a Church and a democracy is this eternal gulf, that a democracy recognises no authority but what arises from itself, and a Church none but what is imposed on it from without. The one founds on self-help, the other on Redemption'.[170]

All of this, however, is more than Congregationalist, it is catholic; and on the basis of it Forsyth has a word for others – not least the Church of England. Since 'the Church stands on eternal certainty, the State on public security',[171] the church cannot be legitimated by, or regarded as co-terminus with, the state; for 'it is the adoption as sons that gives us the fellowship of brothers'.[172] Further, since Christ is the only Lord of the church, no monarch can assume that role. As he said, in the patient tones of one explaining things to uncomprehending infants, 'what we protest against is not the abuses but the existence, the principle, of a national Church'.[173] 'Christianity is not national in spirit,' he averred. 'Its conception is catholic and universal ... "elect from every nation, yet one o'er all the earth".'[174] We may surmise that Forsyth would have approved of the earlier Aberdeen graduate, Savage, who was urged by friends to enter the ministry of the national church, within which he would have the advantages of the patronage of a relative who was the Irish Primate. In the event, 'this scheme was dropt in deference to his own judgment, which determined him for nonconformity'.[175] None of which is to deny that church and state have mutual responsibilities the one towards the other, for the gospel is entrusted to the church for the whole of society. Forsyth sought a 'deepening of the real distinction between Church and State in the interests of the true function of each part, and its complementary service to the social whole. It is not a severance so much as a moving of the two far enough apart to give them room to act, and to grow, and to be themselves.'[176]

[170]*Authority*, 253.
[171] *Theology*, 211.
[172]*Reunion*, 47. Cf. *Missions*, 80.
[173]'The Evangelical Basis of Free Churchism' (1902): 693. Cf. *Charter*, 32.
[174] *Charter*, 49.
[175]Walter Wilson, *The History and Antiquities of Dissenting Churches and Meeting Houses* (London: 1808), 1: 321.
[176]'The Evangelical Basis of Free Churchism', 681.

If God's action in the cross is the supremely authoritative event, on the ground of which the church is called out by the Spirit, the grace revealed in the redemptive act, and not the ministry and the sacraments as such, is what constitutes the church and makes it one: 'In our view the unity of the Church is founded in the creative act of our moral redemption which creates our faith to-day and which created the Church at first; it is not in the traditional polity, creed or cultus we inherit. If unity is in polity Christ died in vain. Unity is in the Gospel, it is not in orders or sacraments, valuable as these are.'[177] Hence Forsyth's conviction that any doctrine of ministerial orders and any sacerdotal view of the sacraments is divisive and anti-catholic because it erects barriers between those who have been made one in Christ. To use his own word, it is 'monopolist': 'The correct name of the Church which limits the true Church to a particular community is not the Catholic, but the *Monopolist* Church. No Church has a right to name Catholic if it insists on unchurching all others which are not episcopal or established by the State.'[178] After all, 'what the Gospel created was not a crowd of Churches but the one Church in various places'.[179]

None of this is to depreciate either the ministry or the sacraments: on the contrary, Forsyth takes a 'high' view of both. But it is to understand both as authorized by, and as witnessing to, the gospel. Accordingly, the crucial question is not whether the church has a threefold ministry of bishops, priests and deacons; it is what is believed about such ministers – especially *vis à vis* the sacraments, and whether the doctrine is wielded in a monopolist, sectarian manner.

Positively, Forsyth affirms that 'the ministry is a prophetic and sacramental office; it is not a secretarial, it is not merely presidential. It is sacramental and not merely functional. It is the outwards and visible agent of the inward gospel Grace'.[180] How sad, then, that 'the pulpit has lost authority because it has lost intimacy with the Cross, immersion in the Cross. It has robbed Christ of Paul'.[181] He is

---

[177] *Reunion*, 21.

[178] *Charter*, 39; cf. *Sacraments*, 46.

[179] *Sacraments*, 68; cf. *Theology*, 124.

[180] *Sacraments*, 133.

[181] A. E. Garvie did not consider that the loss or the robbery were as complete as Forsyth supposed. See his 'Placarding the Cross', 345.

convinced that 'no pastoral, social, theological work will ever atone for defect in [preaching]. Nothing will atone for neglect or inability to feed the flock in the plentiful pasture of Scripture, or to speak to the world the word of God so that they shall either love or hate, trust or fear, and shall listen either unto their perdition or unto their life'.[182] But as well as speaking to the people in the name of God as a prophet, the minister must 'also speak to God as priest in the name of the people. He must pray as well as preach; and in private as in public he must carry his people into the presence of God'.[183] Concerning the sacraments, Forsyth is in no doubt that they 'are not emblems but symbols, and symbols not as mere channels, but in the active sense that something is done as well as conveyed'.[184] They are acts not of the ministers, but of the Church. In somewhat polemical tones inspired by his opposition to monopolism, he refers to the sacraments in his own communion, affirming that 'our Sacraments as acts of the Church, and of Christ's indwelling in the Church by His Spirit, there offering Himself crucified to us anew, are at least equal to any sacrament where the virtue is in the elements or in the canonical succession'.[185]

Forsyth's vision of the church's task is wide but, once again, it is grounded in the cross: 'we shall never worship right nor serve right till we are more engrossed with our God than even with our worship, with His reality than our piety, with His Cross than our service'.[186] The church's work is determined by Christ's work on the cross, which secured 'once for all the Kingdom of God in the real world unseen, by an ethical and spiritual victory'.[187] Accordingly, 'the prime duty of the Church is not to impress, or even to save, men, but to confess the Saviour, to confess in various forms the God, the Christ, the Cross that does save'.[188] Indeed, 'our missions will escape from chronic difficulties when our Church recovers the ruling note

[182]'The Ideal Ministry' (1906), in *Revelation*, 107.

[183]*Revelation*, 99. Forsyth was writing before the first woman, Constance Mary Coltman, was ordained into the Congregational ministry in 1917. Many have now become aware of good theological reasons for unease with the masculine pronouns he uses in this connection, and would nowadays cast such sentences in the plural.

[184]*Sacraments*, xv.

[185]'Church, Ministry and Sacraments', 52.

[186]*Sacraments*, 25.

[187]*Society*, 10.

[188]*Freedom*, 220.

of the redeeming Cross and the accent of the Holy Ghost ... A Church cold to missions is a Church dead to the Cross'.[189]

When we turn to the ethical obligation of the church towards society as a whole we find, once again, that the cross is central. 'The source of the new life must be also its norm'; and this is to be found 'neither in the affections nor the intuitions of the individual heart, but in Christ. And it is not in Christ's conviction and teaching, nor in His example, but in His great creative and crucial Act behind all His teaching and beneficence. It is in the Cross, where is the one all-comprehensive gift of a holy God, and the one constant source and principle of the new life.'[190] The Christian ethic is paralyzed by 'a demoralized Christian religion which is more concerned to conse-crate a natural ethic than to create a new ethic from the fountain of a New Humanity in the Cross'.[191] It follows that 'if we bring a Gospel whose first charge ... is not the honouring of God's holiness, then the moral demand must slowly slacken; whole tracts of life will be exempted from it; the soul's worth will decline with our concep-tion of God's requirement and the soul's price; and men will be more easily treated as tools in a great concern, or as pawns in a great game'.[192] What does this mean in practical terms? I give one example:

> Christian ethics cannot be satisfied with calling on ... people to glorify God in their station. It must go on to promote such a reorganization of industry as may give the worker freedom to live and hope as a man should, to keep a secure home and property, and become, in some sense, a responsible partner in the industry of which he is so great a part. This cannot be done simply by the goodwill of certain employers; it involves a gradual change of the whole system, under the ethical influences which it is the business of a Church that under-stands its business, its Gospel, and its world, to foster.[193]

In the last decade of his life, Forsyth wrestled as determinedly as most with the societal upheaval occasioned by the First World War.

---

[189] *Missions*, 12, 250.
[190] *War*, 136; cf. 133; *Society*, 24.
[191] 'Veracity, Reality, and Regeneration', 202.
[192] *Society*, 29.
[193] *Society*, 54.

The need of a theodicy was clamant, and Forsyth produced one which was by no means to the liking of all of his contemporaries. The War showed that bland humanism would no longer suffice: its roots were shallow and its remedies ineffectual. The prevailing mentality 'is not used to first-class crisis. And in its shock it can find no theodicy in the course of history, no conduct of things by God worthy of a God – worthy of its kind of God, whose Cross was but a kindly boon to crippled men, and not chiefly an honour done to the Holy Name, and the foundation of the Holy Realm'.[194] When many were asking, 'How can there be a love of God if all of this destruction is permitted?' it took a particular kind of courage to declare that in view of God's righteous, holy love 'the scandal and the stumbling block would have been if such judgments did not come'.[195] His consolation is that since 'our faith did not arise from the order of the world; the world's convulsion, therefore, need not destroy it'.[196] Our faith arose from the once-for-all victory of Christ's cross. The last enemy is destroyed; the final victory won: 'The thing is done, it is not to do. "Be of good cheer, I *have* overcome the world".… . The evil world will not win at last, because it failed to win at the only time it ever could. It is a vanquished world where men play their devilries. Christ has overcome it. It can make tribulation, but desolution it can never make.'[197] In that confidence believers continue their pilgrimage, remembering that 'the Christian idea is not happiness and it is not power, but it is perfection – which is the growth of God's image and glory as our destiny'.[198]

VI

The inscription on the tomb of Thomas Goodwin, Forsyth's Puritan hero, includes words, translated from the Latin by another of Aberdeen's Congregational D. D.'s, Thomas Gibbons (1720–85; D. D., King's College, 1764), which may, perhaps with a slight

---

[194] *Justification*, 36.
[195] *Justification*, 119.
[196] *Justification*, 57.
[197] *Justification*, 166–7, 223. Cf. *Work*, 160.
[198] *Life*, 87.

hesitation over the word 'clearly', be applied to Forsyth himself,

> None ever entered deeper
> Into the mysteries of the gospel,
> Or more clearly unfolded them
> For the benefit of others.[199]

Of Goodwin another wrote words which most certainly describe Forsyth: 'He appears to have been specially raised up for great purposes.'[200] By announcing the gospel of victorious holy love, Forsyth served such purposes then, and he continues to serve them now.

As I have shown, Forsyth was unsystematic in a variety of ways. If by 'systematic theologian' is meant one whose biblical foundations are displayed with exegetical thoroughness, whose judgements on thinkers and movements are supported by copious apparatus, whose linguistic challenges and argumentative loose ends are few, and whose method is to take us stage by stage through the several Christian doctrines with more or less equal thoroughness, then Forsyth fits the description less than adequately. Accordingly, he cannot be our *intellectual* refuge. However, that is not our greatest need. Forsyth proclaims an eternal refuge, in the victory of whose holy love we may trust. What he said of Independency characterizes his own founded, systematic, reflection: 'Its note has not been theological system but theological footing, not an ordered knowledge of divine procedure but an experienced certainty of divine redemption.'[201] In proclaiming the holiness and victory of God's love (at Calvary something is done for God and for us, not merely shown); in insisting upon the authority of grace and upon the

---

[199]Quoted by Walter Wilson, *The History and Antiquities of Dissenting Churches and Meeting Houses*, 3: 431. The third line here may give some pause: much has been written concerning Forsyth's alleged obscurity. It must be granted that this style and urgency can cause him to tumble along to the puzzlement of most readers at times; on the other hand, there are none so deaf as those who will not hear. For Forsyth's own remarks on the matter see *Preaching*, 23–4. See also Thomas D. Meadley, 'The "Obscurity" of P. T. Forsyth' (1946): 308–17.

[200]An unnamed 'late eminent minister', quoted in J. A. Jones, ed., *Bunhill Memorials: Sacred Reminiscences of Three Hundred Ministers and Other Persons of Note who are Buried in Bunhill Fields* (London: 1849), 67.

[201]*Freedom*, 139.

inescapability and catholicity of the church; and, above all, in making the umbrella term 'cross' central and determinative for Christology and all else, Forsyth sounded notes which must never be absent from the score of Christian theology. Indeed, apart from these notes there would be no score at all. Because he realized this, and because he viewed everything from the vantage-point of the cross in a sustained, passionate, urgent, practical, and (to a high degree) consistent manner, he may be deemed a systematic theologian *par excellence*. Small wonder that the Scottish Congregationalist Charles Duthie (1911–81; D. D., Aberdeen, 1952), who was the last in Garvie's line as Principal of New College, London, testified, 'One page of Forsyth can do more to stir the conscience and inflame the heart than a dozen pages of some thinkers of quite high repute.'[202] Not surprisingly, on the occasion of the closing of New College, London, in 1977, Lovell Cocks bore witness: 'During my lifetime I have learned much from many teachers but it is to Peter Forsyth that I owe my theological soul and my footing in the Gospel.'[203]

Students who had the good fortune to sit under both Garvie and Forsyth were inclined to say that while Garvie got them through their B. D. examinations, Forsyth gave them a gospel to preach. Be that as it may, both Principals would without question have joined in the words of Aberdeen's most widely-sung Congregational D. D., Philip Doddridge (1702–51; D. D., Marischal College, 1736; King's College, 1737):

> Grace, 'tis a charming sound,
> Harmonious to my ear;
> Heaven with the echo shall resound,
> And all the earth shall hear.

---

[202]Charles S. Duthie, 'Fireworks in a Fog?', 'The Faith of P. T. Forsyth' (1964): 9. Duthie, who also held the M.A. and B.D. of the University of Aberdeen, trained at the Scottish Congregational College, and was Principal of it from 1944–64. He was Principal of New College, London, from 1964 to 1977, when the College closed.

[203]Cocks, 'New College', manuscript address delivered on 16 June 1977; in the Lovell Cocks papers, Dr Williams's Library, London. I should like to add my testimony that nobody has aided my understanding of the gospel more than Forsyth and, with the passage of the years, my sense of gratitude to him grows.

Chapter 9

P. T. FORSYTH: A POLITICAL
THEOLOGIAN?

Keith W. Clements

In one sense the answer is quite simple. P. T. Forsyth was most
certainly a theologian, and also had clear and oft-stated political and
social sympathies. Those commitments were clearly manifest in his
twenty-five years of local church ministry when his practical concern for the poor and his sympathies with working-class and trades
union movements were outstanding features of his pastoral work.
Moreover, one could say that with his humble social background
and upbringing in Aberdeen, such solidarity with the poorer side of
society was natural, a commitment he was literally born into, not
one he had to contrive or adopt in adult life. Perhaps that concern
is best summed up in the anecdote, which I am assured is not
apocryphal, of his student at Hackney College who one Sunday was
sent to preach in a comfortable suburban chapel, and whose route
on the omnibus took him through one of the worst slums in
London. The sight of barefoot children in sordid alleyways, and all
the other signs of deprivation, incensed him to an anger which he
could not contain as he faced his furred and feathered congregation
from the pulpit. Waxing eloquent on social justice he recalled to his
hearers what he had seen, and being met with a sea of complacent
faces he blurted out: 'You don't care, do you? Damn you!' Next
morning, he found himself on the carpet in Principal Forsyth's
study. Forsyth was holding in his hand a letter of complaint from the
church officers, and for several minutes the student was subjected to
a stern lecture on proper pulpit behaviour. Eventually dismissed, the
hapless young prophet was just going through the door when

Forsyth called out to him: 'Oh, just one word more, Mr —. They never will care, you know – damn them!'

However, a theologian who has strong political and social commitments is not necessarily a 'political theologian' in the sense which that term has acquired in the last twenty years or so. The question is, first, of the direct bearing of the theology and the political concerns on each other, their being integral to each other, not just their co-existence in the same person's life and thought. In current discussion, by a political theologian is meant one whose very theology is political, for whom political implications spring directly and centrally from the theology he or she creates, and moreover, for whom the political context is itself a vital starting ingredient in the making of theology. Liberation and feminist theologies are the best-known contemporary examples of political theology in this sense. In very broad terms, a political theology rejects the 'privatization' of Christian belief, that is, its restriction to essentially individual matters of belief and behaviour, and insists on its application to the totality of public life. It sees this application as primarily devoted to establishing justice and peace through the 'preferential option for the poor'. Moreover, it ascribes a special role for the poor or disempowered themselves in setting the agenda for theology and social action. And it is much occupied with identifying and analysing what it sees as the misuses of theology and religion generally by social and political interests serving the causes of power and privilege.

It is in this light that I ask, was P. T. Forsyth a political theologian? My approach to an answer is in three stages. First, I will sketch what appear to me to be the main lines of Forsyth's mature thinking on the relation of Christian belief and theology to public life. Second, and more briefly, I will point out some features whereby Forsyth's thinking on these matters was particularly distinctive in his own time and context. Third, I will suggest certain possibilities for Forsyth's continuing relevance for our contemporary debates on political theology.

1. Forsyth's Theology for Society: An Outline

Forsyth said and wrote much on the social bearing of Christianity, but simply for the purposes of trying to answer the question, I will confine myself to two main sources: the long lecture he delivered in 1905 as Chairman of the Congregational Union, *A Holy Church the Moral Guide of Society*,[1] and the chapter entitled 'The Failure of the Church as an International Authority' in his wartime book on theodicy *The Justification of God*, written a decade later.[2]

Forsyth begins *A Holy Church the Moral Guide of Society* with an assertion that the church is called to be just that. The church as the trustee of the moral principle of Christ's redemption is not just to apply that principle to certain practices in society, but 'to infuse it into the very structure of society as its organizing principle'.[3] He then works out what this means both in principle and in practice.

The supreme social crisis, states Forsyth, is the moral one, and contemporary Christianity is failing in its calling to meet this crisis because it has debased its own understanding of Christian love to mere sympathy and heart-felt affection. If that love meant but philanthropy, turning on precepts of brotherly kindness or non-resistance, 'then love would not give us a basis for political action on the large scale'.[4] It cannot be based simply on the parables or even precepts of Christ, but on the great principle of moral holiness in the atonement itself. Thus it was for Calvin, who seized on the public and social aspects of the gospel in a way the German reformers never did. 'Sympathy is not adequate to redeem. God's love is all sympathy, and more. It is sanctity. It means the moral principle of holiness which in the cross is in standing conflict with the egoism which rules the world.'[5] In a striking phrase Forsyth goes on to describe it as 'the frame of holy mind which is engrossed with the righteous weal of others'. It is real social and political principle, moving us both to private concern for souls and general concern for the state and the race:

> Politics ceases, then, to be a partial system of doles, and legislation a mere series of passing reliefs. This holy love enlarges charity to the dimensions of justice, and confirms

[1] Republished as the first part of *Society*. Future references to the lecture therefore give page numbers in the edition under this title.
[2] *Justification*, chapter 6.
[3] *Society*, 3.
[4] *Society*, 5.
[5] *Society*, 8.

mercy with the assurance of righteousness and peace. It finds in progressive law and order one of the great charities of God to human need. And upon that gift it puts a grace. It sets up a kingdom rooted in the infinite moral holiness of a redeeming God. God's love has given us a settled and political society. Then surely both the care and conversion of that social order is a true service of God, and a true work of the love which is holy, and not merely kind. Christian holy love may take the form of benevolence on the one hand, or of conciliation on the other, but it must also for public purposes take the form of righteousness.[6]

What this holy love is opposed to, is the egoism to which all constitutions and polities in the world are prey. And the only power which can adequately counter such forces is a morality rooted in the holy work of Christ. That work was the securing of the kingdom of God by the ethical and spiritual victory of the cross, and the scope of this work was the whole of society. Christ was not an individual saintly soul, but the Son who adequately answered the Father's holiness – 'Hallowed be thy name' precedes 'Thy kingdom come'. The kingdom already exists outside of us because Christ has established it in the cross. 'What we have to do is not produce it but introduce it.'[7] The fact that it is a kingdom already established by God through the cross is both the unshakeable authority and the inexhaustible inspiration for the cause of social righteousness. That cross, which is the final judgement on evil, sets up God's rule for the whole public realm, not just an individual pietist holiness. Christianity is both supernational and – interesting choice of words – ultramondane.

As contemporary answers to their divine vocation, Forsyth notes first the activism of the British churches, of which he is critical insofar as it exhibits a typical English restlessness rather than genuine Christian energy. Second, and more sympathetically, he remarks on the increasing concern among the churches for the wider social malaise and the bearing of the gospel upon it. But he still doubts whether the churches as yet have any word which authentically challenges and renews the ethical condition of the time. The

[6] *Society*, 8–9.
[7] *Society*, 12.

basic need, he asserts, is to measure 'the old cross and the crisis of today'.[8] Only in the cross, wherein is established the triumph of God's holiness in humanity through Christ's atonement, lies the authority and the energy for the establishment of holiness in society.

Forsyth recognizes that all along he is presupposing the significance of religious ideas in shaping social life. Indeed, he asserts this unequivocally. The other ideals competing for allegiance, such as humanism and positivism, cannot hope to counter the egoist tendencies in comparison with Christian morality focused on and shaped by the triumph of holiness in the cross, which is the final safeguard against ethical trivialization. The Reformation, for example, crucially shaped the emergence of the modern state – a witness to the work of Christ having a total, public scope.

Forsyth then moves to the practical application of these theological principles, though not before expounding a certain theory of the history of social morality. The two main elements of the life of society, he states, are the economic and the moral, and the *determining* ideas in the social life in any historical period are the moral. Each historical age has produced its own blend of material and egoist power, which in turn has been captured by a higher stage of civilization imbued with a greater morality: from primitive tribalism and serfdom through monastic ideals to those of the Reformation, and eventually the present day philosophy of individual liberties and natural rights. But this individualism, says Forsyth, has simply bred egoism on an even larger scale. The freedom of all results only in the freedom of some. Hence the result of the industrial age in producing, by reaction, socialism. The tyranny of accumulative capitalism has had to be met by the protest of organized labour. Indeed, from trusts to trades unions, the temper of the age is increasingly collectivist in every direction – but 'we are not yet morally ready for a power so new as Collectivism'.[9] This is the challenge facing Christianity, for human action becomes moral when sacrifices are made for the sake of the future; and the greater the future, the greater the morality. The Christian future is the great eternity, which carries time and is the root of the ethical. And our eternal is Christ, the image and action of holy God.

[8] *Society*, 17.
[9] *Society*, 39.

Christianity, Forsyth argues, has in the main taken an anti-capitalist stance, from the prophets who stood for the poor to Christ (who was more impressed with the moral dangers of wealth than with the Christian possibilities of its use), through early monasticism and the concern of Luther against the massive inrush of wealth from the Americas. But now high finance rules everywhere. The need of the hour is for an ethic to counter its particular brand of egoism, and Christianity must face up to this challenge. 'If the Church do not save the situation, directly or indirectly, it cannot be saved. But it must be done by the moral influence of the Church's Gospel, not by the prestige of the Church as an institution. The Gospel is the only moral force which has power on a scale to subdue inordinate egoism.'[10] The churches should therefore be producing people not only captured by this gospel but also of deep knowledge and insight into the social and economic facts, an 'ethic of information'. 'We have enough of ideal ethic, and of the cheap ethic of indignation.'[11] There must be authoritative voices speaking out of the fullness of their holy faith to the strength, not the weakness, of the busy world. 'They should be experts on the moral problems created by the economic life.'[12] This, generally, is in fact how Forsyth conceives the proper influence of the church on society, through the informed actions of its members.

The facts of economic life, Forsyth argues, render inadequate for today such essentially individualistic concepts as vocation in daily work – a central theme of the Reformation indeed, and still beloved of preachers waxing eloquent on glorifying God in one's everyday life. Through industry and international finance, we now inhabit a totally different economic world from that of the Reformers. Theirs was a world of consumption, ours is a world of productivity for its own sake, and of ruthless financial competition. It is easy for the ignorant and blatant to take lofty rhetorical ground on the wickedness of such a life as money-making is. But people are trapped and enmeshed in it, not always by their choice, and the church is not yet in a position to give such people plain guidance. The same is true for many people whose secular employment demands that they work

---

[10] *Society*, 48.
[11] *Society*, 48.
[12] *Society*, 49.

amidst pressures which require compromises with private virtue –
from the politician who has to make compromises in order to stay
in power (and unless he does so he cannot achieve anything good),
to newspaper editors, cabmen and innkeepers. To tell such people
that what they do is always to God's glory is banal; equally, to advise
them to leave such security as their work offers, and go out like
Abraham not knowing where they are to go, is irresponsible.

Christian ethics, says Forsyth, must rather go on to promote such
a reorganization of industry as may give the worker freedom to live
and hope, with secure home and property, and become in some
sense 'a responsible partner in the industry of which he is so great a
part'.[13] This requires more than the goodwill of individual employ-
ers: it involves a gradual change of the whole system under the
ethical influence which it is the business of a church which understands its gospel, to foster. This will mean new relations between
employer and employed, new mutual respect and dignity, but it will
mean more than sentiment: economics, not just philanthropy.
Forsyth drums home the message again and again that 'it is the
whole social system that is involved in the crisis',[14] and therefore
such palliatives as helping the unemployed each winter will not do,
for unemployment is but the symptom of the disease. Equally, he
reiterates that the only hope for a regeneration of society is that
gospel of holy love entrusted to the church. 'The millennium for the
worker rests on the moral principle which is the holy soul of the
Church and the power of the Gospel.'[15]

This is the substance of the 1905 lecture. Before passing on to
what he wrote a decade later during the First World War, a
comment is in order on two aspects of his thought revealed thus far.
First, it is evident that Forsyth is no socialist in the sense of taking
up the side of labour as against capitalism, as did Bishop Gore and
the Christian Socialists of the time. Certainly, his sympathies are
with the economically disadvantaged and exploited. But it is a
capitalism modified and controlled for the good of the whole of
society, not a capitalism abolished, to which he aspires. He has
rejected the individualistic liberalism of the radicals, to embrace a

---

[13] *Society*, 4.
[14] *Society*, 56.
[15] *Society*, 63.

wider corporateness. But it is a Maurician corporateness transcending the partial and opposed claims both of capital and labour. Forsyth, in effect, welcomed the advent of socialism without becoming a socialist himself. But in *The Charter of the Church* of 1896, and *The Church, Socialism and the Poor* of 1908 we find him warning against the church adopting socialism as a new creed, and against allowing socialism to co-opt the church for its own ends.

Second, and not unrelated to this first point, it is not at all clear from this lecture whether Forsyth has read Karl Marx, above all Marx's contention that economics and the class-relations involved in production are the determinants of moral and religious ideas, not vice versa. At any rate, whether in blithe ignorance or conscious choice, he affirms the diametrically opposed view: 'It is religion that shapes even economics at last. "Two people," says Ribot, "who do not worship the same God, do not till the soil alike".'[16] Marx, of course, would have said something to the effect that two people who till the soil differently will worship different gods. What is interesting, however, is that Forsyth expounds what is an almost Marxist, or at any rate quasi-Hegelian, view of social history. The successive stages of social organization succeed one another, and as each rises to the height of its potential for productivity, it produces the seeds of its own decline, and is followed by the next and higher stage. I am not sure if Forsyth understood this as a strictly dialectical process, but he certainly seems to perceive an immanent righteousness at work in the historical process. Therewith, of course, he faces the same problem as does the Marxist who believes in a determinism within history in the direction of social progress, yet also calls for a moral protest against the status quo. Forsyth, however, believed that the main energy moving this progress was that of the church's moral influence in each and every age. That commits him, of course, to be able to demonstrate historically that the church did so influence the course of history.

This is the appropriate point to move to 1915, 'The Failure of the Church as an International Authority' might have been expected to deal quite concretely with the churches' need to develop an international structure of their own to counter the nationalism which had eventually erupted in August 1914. In fact Forsyth, throughout this

[16] *Society*, 37.

chapter, is scathing about all the pulpit and platform talk of the churches needing to become a restraining influence on war and to influence the course of reconstruction afterwards – 'meeting the Atlantic with a mop' he called it. It is not as though the churches have after all been inactive, says Forsyth:

> They have been active even to bustle, not to say fuss. Is there something wrong or inept in the rear of their activity, in the matter of it, in their mental purview, spiritual message, and moral power? And is it more than fumbling with the subject to indulge in platform platitudes about 'wielding a universal influence over the actions not only of individuals but of the whole community of nations'? This kind of speech does something to depreciate the value of language, and to lighten the moral coinage.[17]

If the churches could not prevent the War, asks Forsyth, how can they imagine they will be any better placed to help afterwards? The churches have their own impotence to repair as their first duty. That can only be done from the resources of the gospel which will enable it to 'acquire from its own neglected resources the moral dignity and judgement, bold, serene, and august, which would save it from the busybodies and tittlebats to become the conscience of the world'.[18] The church's failure as an international moral authority among the nations was therefore not organizational or structural – in a revealing comment, Forsyth says that the Roman Catholic Church in view of its claims to universality might have been expected to provide such a counter-influence to nationalism and militarism and that if it had done so we could forgive it its Romishness (cf. his remark in the 1905 lecture, above, that Christianity is by nature supernational and ultramondane). But that church like every other had failed there. The real failure was in the church's inadequate perception of its gospel in relation to the moral crisis which the War had brutally brought out into the full light of day.

For Forsyth, the War was the culmination of that egoism which was infecting every sector of human existence. In a starkly unsenti-

[17] *Justification*, 1st ed., 100–1.
[18] *Justification*, 102.

mental way, he rejects as misplaced the question of how a merciful God could allow such a horror to be visited upon Europe. The real question was how a holy God could allow egoism to continue without precipitating a judgement of this order. 'A visitation of this royal Lord was well due.'[19] And the supreme manifestation of such egoism was to be found in the kind of religion which was masquerading as Christianity: anthropocentric religion in which God's Fatherhood had replaced the atonement as centre of belief, in which sentimental or mystical piety had displaced faith and righteousness, in which God's love had been regarded as a supreme human asset instead of the awesome claim upon human life, demanding and creating holiness. In fact, Forsyth takes a sharp knife to the concept of 'religion' itself, and here above all Forsyth was certainly in tune, and in time, with what the young Swiss pastor of Safenwil, Karl Barth, was saying at just that time.

That egoism, Forsyth saw clearly, was also well seen in the way God had been co-opted by the respective nations as their chief ally. But, and this is the point I would finally draw from this essay, Forsyth does not allow his perception of a fundamental and universal malaise in the contemporary human condition to reduce or elevate all moral misdemeanours to the same level. As is well known, Forsyth was not a pacifist. Nor on the other hand was he swept by the anti-German hysteria which engulfed much of Britain during the early part of the War. He himself owed too much to Germany for that, the Germany in which he had studied and whose culture he had deeply inbibed. The man whose favourite composer was Wagner, and one of whose happiest experiences was to have attended the first performance of *Parsifal* in Bayreuth in 1882, was hardly likely to have been a convert to the belief that everything German was satanic to the core. But he did believe that Germany was more in the wrong than her enemies, that while Britain's record internationally was not unstained she was now on the side of justice in this struggle, and that international order needed to be restored so that the nations could once more be given an opportunity of becoming the vassals of the kingdom of God. *That* was the overriding moral imperative of the hour.

That meant, Forsyth implied, recognition of a kind of hierarchy of moral values and duties. Not all public sins are of equal weight in

[19] *Justification*, 107.

a particular situation. The fact that a degree of violence had been entering British political struggles, from those of the Ulstermen to the suffragettes, did not mean that condemnation of German 'frightfulness' was sheer hypocrisy. He inveighs against what he sees as one of the most insidious forms of religious egoism, a pharisaism he calls it, which adopts a lofty, elitist tone of moral superiority over against the wicked world. For Forsyth, remarkably, a genuinely theocentric faith, focused on God's holiness as manifest in the atonement, meant not detachment but ever deeper engagement in and with the historical struggles of the hour. Only so could the strong delusion gripping the power-drunk people of the time be overcome:

> It is the absolute self-delusion which ends in moral madness, because it shrinks, beyond everything else, from a habitual self-reference to the Cross as the judgment-seat of Christ, and a constant correction there. Christ's servants, and not his comrades, we are.... A religion whose ethic is not founded in its forgiveness, which is not a daily repentance but a constant self-satisfaction, and which only abets by sanction the passion for power of unredeemed man, is a daily invitation of judgment. And we are now learning what judgment is. We have descended into hell.[20]

In summary, Forsyth was deeply convinced that the gospel of God's holy love in Christ bore upon the whole public, political realm and was not confined to the individual and inward dimensions of life; that contemporary politics and religion were alike infected with human egoism; that it was the basic structures of social and economic life that needed to be changed; and that right relations between classes and nations could only be restored by a moral regeneration centred upon the judgement and forgiveness of the cross in which God's righteousness was acknowledged. By that cross God's kingdom of righteous relations was already established. Into that kingdom all human social relations were to be brought, and in that task lay the church's divine calling.

---

[20] *Justification*, 120f.

2. The Distinctives of Forsyth's Social Theology in His Context

A good deal of the outstanding features of Forsyth's social theology will already be apparent thanks to the polemical thrust of his arguments and his choice of targets to be opposed in contemporary religious thought. But it is important to draw the distinctive contours in a little more detail, both in relation to his Free Church contemporaries, and also in comparison with the Christian Socialism of Anglicans such as Charles Gore.

Forsyth never disowned his Free Church tradition with its emphasis on 'a Free Church in a free state', and its political alliance with Liberalism. But this alliance was not for him an unqualified value. 'The only kind of religion which can work Liberalism to its true issues for Society,' he said in his 1905 lecture, 'is the Christianity of the Free Churches.'[21] That is, Liberalism needs the theological direction of the Free Churches – and, he significantly adds, it needs Labour also. But his question was whether the Free Churches in their present state of theological amnesia were themselves in a condition to supply that direction. They themselves were in danger of losing hold on the moral centre of Christianity, the holiness of God. They had been 'gaining more in public attention than in public weight',[22] were becoming forces rather than guides. They had of late been political enough (he was writing in the immediate aftermath of the great education controversy of 1902 and during the continuing campaign of passive resistance), but not truly *national* in their ideas of a universal Christianity. That is, they were still ingrained with the sectarian attitude of a persecuted minority rather than providing a social ethic for the whole body politic. They were interested in gaining influence through numbers and direct hold on the levers of political power, and their contemporary optimism was based largely on what – till very recently at least – had been their steady numerical growth and apparent political advancement. 'It is unfortunate,' Forsyth observes, 'that the numerical growth of the Free Churches coincided with their decay of interest or certainty as to the nature of Christ's work.'[23] If the gospel preached is one not

[21] *Society*, 62.
[22] *Society*, 6.
[23] *Society*, 29.

first of all centred on the honouring of God's holiness, and the restoration of right moral relations achieved by God in the atonement, then the depth and scope of the moral demand will slacken. There is a perfect consistency between what Forsyth says here in 1905, and his castigation of egoistic, anthropocentric religion and piety a decade later in *The Justification of God*. I have written elsewhere[24] on the parallel between Forsyth's critique of the theological vacuum at the heart of Edwardian nonconformity, and the critique offered a generation later of the Christianity of the United States by Dietrich Bonhoeffer, a 'Protestantism without Reformation' as he called it.[25] Both theologians were targeting an ideology of undefined 'freedom', a liberty not intrinsically anchored in obedience to the Word of God. In 1905 Forsyth, for his part, identified symptoms of this condition in the indulgence by many of his Free Church contemporaries in a perpetual moral indignation untempered by recognition of the actual responsibilities which political power brings with it, a condition fostered by a whole generation of political Liberalism spent in opposition. Continual vociferous protest uninformed by the actualities of political and economic life, indignation rather than judgement, was, he argued, alienating more thoughtful political thinkers and activists. He was, of course, speaking just before the Liberal landslide of 1906.

There was more theology at the heart of Anglo-Catholic Christian Socialism, as was to be revealed when the most effective theological riposte to the 'New Theology' of R. J. Campbell, himself a meteoric convert to socialism, was offered by Bishop Charles Gore.[26] But the theological centre of Christian Socialism was the incarnation rather than the atonement whereas, in Forsyth's own words, the atonement was 'the very nature, focus and function, of the Incarnation', instead of being treated, as in his view it was wont to be, as 'a theological arrangement in sequel to the Incarnation'.[27]

---

[24]'The Freedom of the Church: Bonhoeffer and the Free Church Tradition', chapter 6 in K. W. Clements, *What Freedom? The Persistent Challenge of Dietrich Bonhoeffer* (Bristol: Bristol Baptist College, 1990).

[25]D. Bonhoeffer, 'Protestantism Without Reformation', in *No Rusty Swords: Letters, Lectures and Notes 1928–1936* (London: Collins, 1965).

[26]C. Gore, *The New Theology and the Old Religion* (London: John Murray, 1970).

[27]*Justification*, 108.

A Christianity centred on the incarnation rather than on the holiness revealed in the atonement, argued Forsyth, tended to the metaphysical, mystical and sentimental rather than the moral. 'And it is why it is socially so sterile; it is ethically too inert and aesthetic.'[28] That inertia was all too clearly revealed in the War and the responses to it. The soul requires to be judged and morally energized, not simply spiritually soothed and comforted.

3. P. T. Forsyth and Today

P. T. Forsyth confidently asserted that the only moral force with power and authority adequate to renew European society in the twentieth century would be that which arose in the first and which will be secured in eternity: the acknowledgment and proclamation of the holiness manifested in the atonement. Nearing the end of the century whose opening Forsyth experienced, Christian theology is now engaged in an even more intensive debate on the relationship between the gospel and politics, between the City of God and the city of this world. Any answer to the question of how significant Forsyth may be for our contemporary debates can be on two levels. On a relatively superficial level, we might be struck by the apparent and immediate relevance of some of his explicit statements, or equally dismiss some of them as too distanced from our current concerns and perspectives, educated as we have been by so much intervening history and theological thought.

Thus for example, many of us engaged in the witness of the churches in public affairs will be reassured to find Forsyth inveighing against what he calls 'ethical vulgarism' – 'the mental condition ... which tells the best of the clergy to mind their own business when they press the moral aspects of economic questions. That is just what they are doing. It is their business to apply a holy faith to the public conduct. To sever the economic question from the moral is to ruin both in the long run. A man is one, and has but one conscience'.[29] Ethical vulgarism is still alive and well, as we all know. Or we may take as remarkably prescient his observation that commercial and

---

[28] *Justification*, 110.
[29] *Society*, 33.

military war are twin aspects of the capitalist age.[30] Then, reading
Jürgen Moltmann and others on the social significance of the tri-
unity of God, can convey a sense of déjà vu in the light of Forsyth's
insight that 'whatever is the unity of a moral God must be the moral
unity of Society. The unity of a tri-personal God is the foundation
of unity for a society of persons'.[31] And much of what Forsyth called
for in a Christianity informed by social, economic and political
realities as well as prophetic passion, was in fact taken up by the
succeeding generation of thinkers such as J. H. Oldham, George
Bell, William Temple and more recent thinkers such as Barbara
Ward, Alan Booth and Ronald Preston, and of course in much
ecumenical discussion on the worldwide scale. It still needs saying.

On the other hand, when Forsyth states for example that 'men are
naturally gregarious, but they are not naturally collective' on account of their egoism,[32] he seems to be on the far side of all that such
figures as Reinhold Niebuhr have taught us. We almost take it for
granted that human collectivities of classes, economic interests and
nations are natural and inevitable products of human social organization and, far from contradicting egoism, these manifest egoism on
an even greater and more intractable scale, such that the demonic
tendencies of collective power can only be counteracted by the
resistance of other collectivities.[33]

However, any continuing relevance of Forsyth can and should be
sought in a more profound way than simply awarding particular
statements with ticks or crosses. The heart of his theology, and the
place where he himself located the social significance of Christianity, was the atoning cross of Christ and its proclamation. The most
important question regarding Forsyth's contemporary significance,
therefore, is whether this cardinal point in his theology, and his own
perception of its social import, still offer us a challenge and resource
in the debate about political theology today. 'The Gospel does not
get its political dimension from one or another particular option,
but from the very nucleus of its message,' writes Gustavo Gutierrez,
perhaps the most well-known of contemporary liberation theolo-

[30] *Society*, 33.
[31] *Society*, 20.
[32] *Society*, 34.
[33] Reinhold Niebuhr, *Moral Man and Immoral Society* (London: SCM Press
Ltd., 1963).

gians,[34] and with him Forsyth would profoundly agree. I believe that Forsyth would also substantially agree with Gutierrez's inclusive description of the saving work of Christ and its scope for all levels of human existence:

> The Christian life is a passover, a transition from sin to grace, from death to life, from injustice to justice, from the subhuman to the human. Christ introduces us by the gift of his Spirit into communion with God and with all men. More precisely, it is *because* he introduces us into this communion, into a continuous search for its fullness, that he conquers sin – which is the negation of love – and all its consequences.[35]

As we have seen, Forsyth insisted that the claims of the gospel were inclusive and had to be worked out in terms of justice as well as personal charity. Also like liberation theologians such as Gutierrez, Forsyth saw the need to relate very carefully and positively the kingdom of God on the one hand, and all progress in social justice on the other. Unlike R. J. Campbell who virtually identified socialism and the kingdom of God, and unlike those pietist contemporaries who either banished the kingdom from this world altogether or who limited it only to the growth of the evangelical Free Churches (and who were therefore becoming increasingly worried after the turn of the century), Forsyth saw history as determined by and presaging eternity. I hear Gutierrez ringing some Forsythian bells when he states:

> The life and preaching of Jesus postulate the unceasing search for a new kind of man in a qualitatively different society. Although the Kingdom must not be confused with the establishment of a just society, this does not mean that it is indifferent to this society. Nor does it mean that this just society constitutes a 'necessary condition' for the arrival of the Kingdom nor that they are closely linked, nor that they converge. More profoundly, the announcement of the Kingdom reveals to society itself the aspiration for a just society

[34]G. Gutierrez, *A Theology of Liberation* (London: SCM Press Ltd., 1974), 231.
[35]*Justification*, 176.

and leads it to discover unsuspected dimensions and unex-
plored paths. The Kingdom is realized in a society of brotherhood and justice; and, in turn, this realization opens up the
promise and hope of complete communion of all men with
God. The political is granted into the eternal.[36]

With such an emphasis on justice, manifest in a new communion
of humankind, and on justice having a history of fulfilment neither
wholly identified with, nor detached from, the coming of God's
kingdom, Forsyth, in view of what we have heard from him earlier,
would certainly agree. The reasons for such affinity between the
Scottish Congregationalist and the Peruvian Roman Catholic liberation theologian, far from being incidental, may well lie very deep
within their respective traditions. A good deal of interest is being
shown in the parallels between, on the one hand, Calvin's understanding of the kingdom of God and public responsibility, and on
the other hand, more recent Roman Catholic thinking on the
relationship between nature and grace in human history, and I
would particularly mention the study made by the South African
theologian John de Gruchy, *Liberating Reformed Theology*.[37] But
throughout, Forsyth, as we have seen, would wish to stress the
establishment of the kingdom already and specifically in the cross of
Christ, nor just in the preaching and life of Jesus nor even his gift of
the Spirit, and the atoning cross as itself the ground, inspiration and
authority for that moral regeneration required for the just society:

> We need for the moral purposes of Society a Christ who
> redeems because He atones, and atones because He is holy,
> and who is holy because He is God. Christ's redemption is as
> wide as His God-head. He secures social goodness because
> He incarnates and secures God's holiness. He satisfies and
> commands the evil conscience of mankind because of the
> satisfaction His holiness was to the holy conscience of God.
> The Holy God found Himself in the holiness of the cross,
> and in the same act established His kingdom.[38]

[36]Gutierrez, 231.

[37]John W. de Gruchy, *Liberating Reformed Theology: A South African Contribution to an Ecumenical Debate* (Grand Rapids, Michigan: Eerdmans and David
Philip, 1991). De Gruchy has three references to Forsyth's ecclesiology.

[38]*Society*, 30.

For Forsyth, it is specifically in the cross that the true communion, true at-one-ment, between God and humankind, and among
humankind, is established. There is a tendency in some forms of
contemporary liberation theology to see the cross primarily as a sign
of negation, of the evil of the world and the political powers which
crucified Jesus, or at the most as a sign of God's love for the world
through Jesus' identifying with its misery and godlessness: Jesus as
victim, or as identifying with the victims. These are important
elements in a *theologia crucis*, but left to themselves they, in fact, tend
to evacuate from the cross all political significance by making Jesus'
death an absolutization of powerlessness in this world. And absolute
powerlessness, like absolute power, can corrupt absolutely. It provides the excuse for non-responsibility, or total irresponsibility. It is
often the stage immediately preceding terrorism. A piety of total
rejection of the present order results.

Jürgen Moltmann, for his part, does not make Jesus a purely
helpless victim. Not only is Jesus delivered up by the Father, but he
surrenders himself.[39] There is thus a paradox of unbroken communion between the Father who gives up his Son, and the Son who gives
himself up among the godless and is thus godforsaken, community
in separation and separation in community. The political ethic that
results from Moltmann's trinitarian theology of the cross is still
primarily a *critical* one, subverting all absolute rule within this
world, though also a *hopeful* one: 'Christians will seek to anticipate
the future of Christ according to the measure of the possibilities
available to them, by breaking down lordship and building up the
political liveliness of each individual.'[40] But Forsyth, I would argue,
is in fact better placed than Moltmann to relate the cross directly to
the human, historical, political scene, because from the beginning
Forsyth stresses that it is both with and on behalf of the whole race
that Jesus the obedient Son confesses the Father's holiness and thus
establishes the just society. In his death Jesus actually does something. The cross, therefore, is not just a sign to flaunt over the world
either in judgement or encouragement. It is itself the point at which
the new world begins in the midst of the old, the kingdom which has
not to be produced so much as introduced, the kingdom of just –

[39]J. Moltmann, *The Crucified God* (London: SCM Press Ltd., 1974), 243, etc.
[40]Moltmann, 329.

that is, morally right – relations between humankind and God, and among humankind.

Forsyth, I would therefore suggest, offers us an unusually direct route from the heart of the gospel in the cross itself, to public, political responsibility. The cross is where political egoism, like all human egoism, is judged and shown to be the evil that it is; it is also the place where the new, God-given community of justice, which is holiness, is set up. It is that which inspires 'the frame of holy mind which is engrossed with the righteous weal of others', that is, genuine public responsibility. At first, it might have seemed that such a focus upon the atonement would have inhibited a theology of political and social commitment – we might expect a theology centred on creation, or sanctification, or the kingdom of God itself, to do more in this direction. But as Forsyth saw, that is simply because the atonement has become entrapped in pietistic, individualistic and juridical understandings which offer the individual a safe passage from this world to eternity, rather than the means by which eternity embraces this world and the whole race in order to make it holy.

In concluding this section, and to illustrate just how politically significant a proper understanding of atonement, as sought by Forsyth, may prove to be, consider the controversy generated by the South African *Kairos Document* of 1985.[41] One of the most outspoken examples of political and contextual theology in practice, this called for a fundamental shift by the South African churches from accommodation (however 'critical') to apartheid, to radical confrontation with the regime still promoting it. Not the least controversy fastened on the document's contention that 'no reconciliation is possible in South Africa *without justice*; and that 'no forgiveness and no negotiations are possible *without repentance*'.[42] Peace and unity, stated the writers and signatories, must not be preserved at all costs. Rather, disciples of Jesus should 'promote truth and justice and life at all costs, even at the cost of creating conflict, disunity and dissension along the way'.[43] There can be no reconciliation with sin and the devil.

---

[41] *The Kairos Document: Challenge to the Church* (London: Catholic Institute for International Relations and British Council of Churches, 1985).

[42] *Kairos Document*, 12.

[43] *Kairos Document*, 13.

To some of its critics, the document seemed to be denying the gospel itself, which is that of reconciliation and peace, and the love of God which is offered to us prior to our repentance. Justice seemed to have been promoted higher than love, and higher even than God's grace. Such critics might equally, however, have been offended by Forsyth's statement in his wartime essay of 1915, that the gospel is 'not primarily and offhand a message of peace among men, but of peace among men of goodwill'.[44] I have a feeling that Forsyth would have enjoyed the stark clarity of the *Kairos Document* as compared with much of what he dismissed as sentimental *blague* about peaceful Christian influences upon the world:

> If the amateur advisers of the Church will realise that its first work, which carries all else with it, is not to lubricate friction but to create among men that goodwill, to revise and brace the belief which has failed to do it, to think less of uniting the Church and more of piercing to a deep Gospel that will; if they will distrust the bustling forms of activity, the harder beating of the old drums, the provision of ever more buns and beverages; if they will court more the silent, searching, hateful regenerations that transform conduct, private and public, by a transformation of the faith that breeds Christian love and saves it from mere fraternity and comradeship – then they will be doing more than all the press, platforms, societies, or crusades can to aid the Church to acquire the moral influence it has confessedly lost.[45]

Like the *Kairos* authors, Forsyth knew in his own time and place, and in his own way, that the role of genuine theology is to uncover the truth, which must include the uncomfortable truth of the forms and masks worn by egoism in society. But he was also able to handle with great precision the biblical vocabulary associated with the atonement. Justice *or* reconciliation? Repentance *or* forgiveness? Conflict *or* peace? Forsyth did not set such terms off against each other, or fasten on one to the detriment of the others. Because he was able to discriminate between the terms, he was also able to give them due weight in turn. The act of the holy God in creating holiness

---

[44] *Justification*, 101.
[45] *Justification*, 101.

among humankind through the holy self-offering of his Son, was, Forsyth knew, an act which required a whole spread of terminology which must be handled with some care. The *end* of Christ's work is reconciliation, the *means* is atonement, with all which that implies about the acknowledgment of God's holiness[46] and therefore his justice. We stand much in need of that kind of precision in our present debates on political theology. Karl Barth is often quoted as saying that Christian social responsibility means reading the Bible in one hand with the newspaper in the other. Forsyth would, we can be sure, agree but also insist that the reading of the Bible be very, very careful precisely for the sake of a proper reading of the political world.

4. Conclusion: A Political Theologian?

Was, then, P. T. Forsyth a political theologian? There is always something contrived and ultimately unhelpful in trying to make anyone from the past a prototype for later or contemporary figures and movements. But it will already have become clear that Forsyth meets at least some of the general criteria for a 'political theologian' which were listed at the beginning. His theology, centred on the atonement, and his social thinking were indeed integrally related. He powerfully rejected a privatized religion and vigorously advanced a Christianity with a gospel for the whole social order. *Structures* of economic and political life, not just individuals, were to be transformed. He recognized the bias of the biblical faith towards the poor, and called for the re-organization of the social and economic system to provide *justice* instead of charitable palliatives. Although in 1905 he seemed relatively innocent of the Marxist critique of religion as a socially determined human project, by the time of the First World War he had clearly identified the ambiguity of 'religion', especially in its anthropocentric tendencies whereby God was co-opted as a human asset rather than worshipped for his own holiness' sake, as became clear above in all nationalistic piety. In these senses, yes indeed, P. T. Forsyth was a very political theologian. He was not, however, a political theologian if by such

---

[46]Cf. A. M. Hunter, *P. T. Forsyth: Per Crucem ad Lucem*, 60.

a term is meant one who specifically advocates a programme such as socialism, or who identifies one section of society, such as the poor, as the main agents of the gospel. Some will want to ask *why* he was not a socialist. The answer may be in sociological terms. Perhaps by the early 1900s he was yet another middle-aged, middle-class academic. But perhaps the answer lies deeper, in his having a theology centred on a cross which *ipso facto* prevented him from giving an equal weight to any ideology or 'ism'.

The other question, however, is whether current political theology has anything to learn from P. T. Forsyth. Again, it is to be hoped, at least one possibility has emerged in this brief exploration, in particular the positive and substantive connection between the cross and social justice. This also has a bearing on the style of political theology. A problem with all theology, and perhaps especially political theology, is how it can empower without becoming triumphalistic. In the case of political theology, it is the problem of how to inspire the struggle for justice and peace without handing over faith and hope to a crusading ideology which, like all ideologies when absolutized, ultimately oppresses and destroys if it has not itself already been destroyed in disillusion. Hence the debate now going on about the place of liberation theology in a world where socialism seems, politically, in almost universal retreat.[47] Forsyth's cross-centred theology offers inspiration for commitment to justice, since it is at the cross that a just community is already established in the holiness of God. At the same time, such a theology recognizes that it can only be inspired as it is itself also continually brought to repentance against self-satisfaction, in that 'habitual self-reference to the Cross as the judgment-seat of Christ, and a constant correction there'. It is a theology which, like all real theology, begins and ends in prayer, and therefore we can fittingly make our own the prayer with which Forsyth concludes his 1905 lecture: 'Holy Father! So increase our faith that by Thy Holy Church we may come into Thy holier Kingdom through the grace of Christ, who is the Holiest of all. Amen.'

---

[47]Cf. the essays on liberation theology after the Cold War in *Religion, State and Society* 21, no. 1 (Keston Research, Oxford: 1993).

Chapter 10

P. T. FORSYTH AS CONGREGATIONAL MINISTER

Clyde Binfield

What marks a minister? Such a one, for example, as this, formed within Scottish Congregationalism but formative for and proved by English Congregationalism. Born 1848, died 1921. Born under Russell, died under Lloyd George. Or, from almost Peel and almost Disraeli to almost Balfour and quite Bonar Law, though not quite Baldwin. Or, from Palmerston to Asquith with Gladstone as the longest fact of political life. Born Aberdeen, died Hampstead. Born a postman's son, died a college principal, lived a theologian. Formed educationally by Aberdeen, London and Göttingen and indirectly by Manchester and Cambridge. Culturally Pre-Raphaelite, a man for Rossetti and Holman Hunt and also G. F. Watts, for Ruskin and Giotto, for Wagner as for Hegel. Peter Taylor Forsyth, set apart by ordination in 1876; twenty-eight years, therefore, in preparation for ministry, twenty-five years in congregational ministry, twenty years in training Congregational ministers.

The spoken word dies with the memory of its last hearer. Forsyth's word lives chiefly through what he wrote in that last twenty years and since ministerial training was then more academic than practical, a matter therefore of words and Word for the wordy, he is remembered accordingly, a mass of contrary evidence notwithstanding: remote and mannered, grandly, unforgettably different on both counts.

Such a man must first be seen in denominational perspective. Forsyth has best been seen as the preacher's theologian, a phrase describing as much his medium as his message.[1] However 'academic' the training, the Congregational college principal trained preachers. That 'difficult' style of Forsyth's was to be communicated in a pulpit or at a lecturer's desk. It was best not read and it was never found difficult by his students.[2] Again, the Congregational college principal had a role in his denomination which was quite different from any role played in the established church by that much newer animal, the Anglican college principal. He was a representative figure, almost uniquely so, a bishop indeed, a key man at ordinations, called frequently to arbitrate in congregational disputes, preaching at the solider special occasions. He was a minister of and for ministers. His was ministry writ large.

But what was such ministry? In the half-century after Forsyth's death, the phrase 'Ministry of Word and Sacraments' became a Congregational cliché. The Congregational minister broke the Word as he broke the bread. He poured the wine as he sprinkled the water. He re-*presented* the ordinances for God's people consciously gathered in responsive obedience. There was nothing chance or haphazard about this relationship of stated ministry to duly constituted church. It was brought about by a call, with the church – as gathered in that place – as intermediary, at once caller and sharer in call. The mutuality of minister and people validated that call, subject only to the constraints (but also, therefore, the generosities) of the voluntary principle. That is all. There was no parson's freehold. There were seldom any endowments. Given human nature, it was hard for such a minister truly to be a *pastor*, though that word was in vogue. He might easily be a slave. He was most naturally a managing director for God's entrepreneurs, staving off hell's bankruptcy, leader yet servant in a relationship built ideally on trust, frankness, honesty, manliness but formed inevitably by the limitations of personality and the facts of social and economic life. Moreover, though founded on call this relationship apparently owed as much to skills in calling: to the vocal more than to vocation.

Forsyth as minister expressed all this. 'You have called and I have answered gladly,' he told the church at Cheetham Hill, Manchester,

---

[1] Browne Barr, in Miller, Barr, and Paul, *P. T. Forsyth – The Man, The Preacher's Theologian, Prophet for the Twentieth Century: A Contemporary Assessment.*

[2] Thus his pupil, H. F. Lovell Cocks's review of *Person*, 195; and in Miller, Barr, and Paul, 71–2.

in his induction sermon in 1885. 'But it is not your call that has made me a minister. I was a minister before any congregation called me. My election is of God.' And he went on to stress the sacraments: communion and baptism – and the Word, that 'distinctly Protestant Sacrament'.[3]

The Forsythian elements are all there, as they were throughout his ministry, though their emphasis changed: the Congregational dynamic of call and response; the perfect freedom in service; the Calvinistic resonance ('My election is of God'); the disciplined churchmanship; the high role of ministry, which was the consequence of such things. Above all, there is the sense of time captured in that vital act for each Christian – election, that point at which eternity meets time.

Forsyth's sense of time sprang from his apprehension of the revelation of God in history. That revelation was recorded in the Bible. It was experienced by each Christian. The record was preserved and the experience communicated through the church. There was thus for Congregationalists an equipoise between a critical investment in the Bible, the authority vested in personal faith, and churchmanship – a concept which must find room for tradition and doctrine and order.[4] Forsyth most keenly celebrated that equipoise. That it was seldom other than an ideal, seldom even to be approximated, is as beside the point as the fact that Forsyth has been presented as a man out of joint with his age, a conservative smothered by liberals, so persistently ignored that he has needed constant rediscovery.[5] Forsyth was no more out of joint with his times than he was then or thereafter ignored or forgotten. As minister, trainer of ministers and writer for ministers, he criticized keenest what almost enthralled him, those criticisms and grand enthusiasms mediated like his turns of phrase through the manse studies of two decades of pupils and into their pulpits to rest in who know whose pews.

But Forsyth's foundation was that particular discipline imposed by responsible congregational ministry. That discipline was as

---

[3]Quoted in W. L. Bradley, *P. T. Forsyth: The Man and his Work*, 38.

[4]Willis B. Glover, *Evangelical Nonconformists and Higher Criticism in the Nineteenth Century*, 22–3, 138, 273ff.

[5]Miller, Barr, and Paul, passim.

consistent in its elements as it was also consistent in its antitheses. Here, as with all the Victorian prophets, was a balancing of the boxes.

The consistence in antithesis can be observed most easily in the incidental of Forsyth's calling. This latter-day proponent of ministerial authority stood nonetheless in his days of London suburban ministry in his pulpit 'wearing a short black coat, shepherd's-plaid trousers, turndown collar and a brilliant tie'. He took to preaching gown only to hide a sling after he had broken his collar-bone when figure skating on the Serpentine.[6] This apparently casual pulpiteer, more widely known in his earlier prime for his skills in lecture, debate and after-dinner speech, where culture must be worn lightly and with wit (precisely those rare skills which are soonest forgotten when not most suspect), nevertheless concentrated his emotional energies in his words of life in the time-honoured manner of preachers. He left his pulpit drenched and limp with perspiration (what was his metabolism? He was preternaturally sensitive to the draughts which infested every chapel), as drained as he had left his preparation: 'at these times he was wrestling with thoughts almost beyond human expression; and he wrote with a physical and nervous intensity which shook the desk, and which after an hour or two left him utterly spent, stretched out white and still upon his study couch, until the spirit drove him back to pen and paper'.[7] These antitheses – those of a man who in his prime seemed tall and handsome when really he was neither – can be demonstrated in three quite separate consistencies: his appeal to the young; his drawing on art and the social conscience – that is to say, the culture of the race; and his sense of that race, of society as organism. Each issued from his experience of the Congregational dynamic.

Forsyth's appeal to the young long survived his reputation as a denominational Young Turk. His first book was for children and his Sunday ministry regularly included children's services and addresses.[8] In July 1878, at Shipley, his first pastorate, he preached one of his first published sermons.[9] It was to schoolgirls. he began with

---

[6]Jessie Forsyth Andrews, 'Memoir', in Forsyth, *Work*, 2nd ed., xiv.

[7]Andrews, 'Memoir', xxvi.

[8]Parables (1886).

[9]*'Maid Arise': A Sermon to School Girls*, preached in Shipley Congregational Church, 28 July 1878.

a picture which hung 'in the dining-room of one of my tasteful friends'. It was of a flaxen-haired girl, paddling. Inevitably Forsyth quoted George MacDonald, the brother-in-law of his unorthodox theological college tutor, J. H. Goodwin.[10] In his own Aberdeen student days, MacDonald had lodged in the house where Forsyth's mother was keeper.[11] But the MacDonald whom Forsyth now quoted was not here in story telling vein. This was a sermon to schoolgirls, daughters of the Yorkshire middle-classes who, should trade take a down-turn, would have to work for a living as well as for their own good. 'I wish every woman like every man were brought up to the view that work of some real and earnest kind was to be a necessity for them.'[12] And the Forsyth who was newly married to a clever London governess, whom he had met in Brixton and married in Notting Hill, could not resist an almost epigram: 'A clever woman's real conversation is one of the best delights and highest stimuli I know.'[13]

Children were men and women in preparation moving, God willing, into the church. Proportion fascinated Forsyth for whom life, which made sense only in relation to eternity, was best grasped as shape, with due proportion. 'The soul of man,' he told Shipley's Congregational girlhood, 'cannot expand and leave the soul of woman behind. Both sides of the sphere must expand symmetrically. God himself is more than a man. The Divine is part womanly. Hence the divine call, "Maid arise".'[14]

But Forsyth's admiration for clever women sharpened his mounting suspicion of the effeminate in contemporary religion. The effeminate was unwomanly, the more so for its verbal association with woman. Similarly, Forsyth's concern for children was a box which needed balancing. In 1900, towards the end of his Cambridge ministry, he addressed a Sunday School Union meeting and deplored the shapelessness which passed for Sunday School Teaching:

> The Sunday School is too much left to well-meaning and hard-working people, who, with all their earnestness, have no

---

[10]John H. Godwin (1809–89): *CYB* (1890), 143–5.
[11]Andrews, 'Memoir', 12.
[13]'*Maid Arise*', 10.
[14]'*Maid Arise*', 5.

experience of controlling others, and no sense or power of discipline. The teachers are ... gentle and fear to hurt feelings; or they are too tender about ejecting black sheep... . They have young ideas about what Christian love means. They are too anxious to be loved and not enough concerned to be obeyed... . I am afraid that many teachers have more interest in the affections of their scholars than in their souls.[15]

That Cambridge Forsyth was entirely consistent with the Shipley Forsyth of twenty-two years back, and that was so because of the realities of Congregational ministry. Between 1878 and 1900 Forsyth had undergone a deepening of religious experience, almost an overturning, even a further conversion. His own health had collapsed temporarily at the point of the most critical of his moves from one pastorate to another and his wife's had collapsed totally at the same point. Her death left him with an adolescent daughter, his only child. But these things, though unique to each sufferer, are unique to no ministry. Even in his Shipley days, thirty years young, just ordained, newly married and careless of convention, Forsyth sounded the depths which every minister must sound. His sermon to those girls, 'Maid Arise', was grounded on the story of Jairus's daughter (Lk 8.52–6). It was based on a story of family tragedy, a fact to be faced even by school leavers. It was completed by a prayer which is not to be dismissed as a young liberal's natural meliorism, for all the hostages to fortune which it offers up to latter day historians of patriarchy or social control or separated spherism. This prayer conveys that young minister's *pastoral* power. It is mannered indeed, conventional in form. It is also a true leading in prayer, congregational yet individualizing each member of that congregation, properly extempore therefore, yet above all things shapely – or at least striving after such shape as schoolgirls, whose reach must exceed their grasp:

> Almighty Father, who dost school us by life and try us by pain and reward us by death, we give Thee thanks for Thy kind discipline of patience and Thy rich gifts of grace. We gather in Thy house to forget ourselves and remember Thee, to lay

---

[15]'The School at the End of the Century' (1900): 850.

by our rivalry and take up our prayer, to lose our fears and feel Thy comfortable thoughts. Put out the noisy world from the chamber where we meet with Thee. We are not dead utterly to things divine. Our souls do but sleep, and the crowd of soulless comforters would mock Thy power to rouse and save. Bid us arise and eat heavenly food, restore us to simple life and homely love, and give us back to faith and our Father again. Clothe us in all the charities that minister and bless. Consecrate duty and sanctify grief. For sin give penitence, from passion give us rest, and for ambition and vanity teach us divinely to serve, through the cross of Jesus Christ our Lord. Amen.[16]

Forsyth the exponent of religion in art is better known than Forsyth the pastor for women or children. Here too, however, is a similarly sustained consistency in antithesis. In part this is the reflection of an educated, yet arguably self-cultivated, Scotsman's temperament, in part the reflection of the enlarging subculture which formed him. It is also, and this is what shaped it, a reaction to the culture to which he ministered. There is a clue in 'Maid arise': the gentle irony which enjoyed, even valued, without displacing that picture in the dining-room of one of his tasteful friends. There is more than a clue in the genesis of his first considerable work, *Religion in Recent Art*.[17] These lectures, published during his Leicester ministry (with Forsyth eventually drafted onto the Museum and Art Gallery Committee), were delivered in the wake of that most significant English provincial cultural explosions, the Manchester Art Treasures Exhibition of 1887. That was the prime cultural event of his Manchester pastorate.

In each of his pastorates, Forsyth encountered church members who were educated in art and architecture, especially their technicalities. In his Sunday morning pews and at dinner parties, he met the moral purpose of mental art men whose interests were the next logical extension from the restlessly inquisitive concerns of Shipley wool and worsted men or Cheetham Hill cottontots. And he mediated their moral purpose to the Sunday evening gallery pews of

---

[16] *'Maid Arise'*, 3.
[17] *Art* (1889).

the mutual improvement, university extension, institute and settlement age, to young men at several removes from Shipley or Hackney
dinner parties. So his lectures on recent art were to Charles Rowley's
Ancoats Brotherhood. They were masterpieces in moral story telling
with Wagner as climax.

There are still few more suggestive overtures to *Parsifal* than
Forsyth's exposition of 1889, fresh as he had experienced it at
Bayreuth with a rich Hackney friend seven years before. Here was
redemption music. Here, perhaps with the exception of *The Messiah*
(and how pedagogically impeccable to annex to *The Messiah*, which
all knew in their sleep, *Parsifal*, which none would probably ever
know save in their dreams); 'we have ... the greatest Redemption
music in the world.... It is long since a work of first-class art took
its stand upon the almost extinct sense of sin, and made its central
motive the idea of Redemption'. Forsyth was almost bowled over,
but not quite. Even here there were boxes to be balanced, for this was
only one side of Redemption music: 'It is not so much a message
from the delivering God as a representation of deliverance in man's
soul. It is the soul singing its own deadly sins, its own mortal agony,
and its own regenerate beauty. Wagner sang one side of the truth.
"Work out your own salvation." ...' And he sang from this side of
it, this 'most gifted and passionate expositor of that semi-religious
philosophy and semi-Christian atheism'; he sang from the manward
side, inevitably pessimistic: 'There is one principle in Christianity
which separates it by an impassable gulf from every form of
Pessimism.... We can never know things at their worst till we stand
where they are at their best.'[18] The Cross was that standpoint.

Forsyth was a Germanophile, like so many educated Dissenting
ministers; and the increasingly perceived formlessness of German
culture was growing agony to him. We are back to shape.

There was nothing formless about Forsyth's grasp of Christianity. Election forbade that. So did the Trinity. Here too we begin in
Manchester for consistency in antithesis with a Forsyth who is
assumed not to have lasted the course: Forsyth the socialist, whose
first political pamphlet was called *Socialism and Christianity in Some
of their Deeper Aspects (1886)*, bold with its reference to 'the greatest
Socialist thinkers, like Marx'. It must be doubted whether the

---

[18]*Art*, 287, 292, 287, 237, 280.

socialistic Forsyth ever voted other than Liberal. W. L. Bradley, whose biographical study remains the best guide to Forsyth, is clear that what drew him was less socialism than 'that aspect of Christianity which makes a social ethic essential', and that aspect lay at the heart of evangelical orthodoxy: God as Trinity, the society of persons in the Trinity, sign and seal of the organic solidarity of society and arguably 'the religious base of a Socialism as far from Egoism on the one hand as from Communism on the other'.[19]

But if the Trinity is ultimate form, matters cannot be left at that. Forsyth ministered successively to five independent aggregations of atoms. Where was their place in the form of things? How might the solitary soul be set within the church congregational and the church Congregational be set within the Church catholic? Forsyth's answer is an organ note from his own experience set in a passage which reads as a hymn of the Evangelical Revival, delivered from the Chair of the Congregational Union when he was at last, though only for the time being, recognized as its representative figure: 'I have found my rock, my reality, my eternal life in my historic Redemption. And what is moral rock, real existence, and spiritual mastery for me is also the authority and charter for the Church, the living power in all history, the moral foundation of society, and the moral warrant of an infinite future for the race.'[20] That sense of church and soul is breathtaking:

> All history exists for the Church, but for a Church of living souls as the distillation of history ... Apart from these souls the Church is an abstraction ... Truly election contemplates a vast totality of souls as the direct object of God's choice and work, but the election ... is apprehended by individual faith, sure that the believing soul is thus in the eternal thought of God. There alone have we due ground for realising the unspeakable value of a soul.'[21]

But what was to shape this relationship? Authority was. And sacrament. And ministry. In 'every true Church the note of author-

---

[19]Bradley, 63, 67–9, quoting *Socialism and Christianity in Some of their Deeper Aspects* (1886), 3.

[20]*Society*, 127.

[21]*Authority*, 1st ed., 354, quoted in Bradley, 217.

ity must be uppermost. To put liberty, which is a secondary matter, before authority, which is primary and fontal even for liberty itself, is to confess a sect and not a Church'.[22] Those were bold words for Congregationalists, and there were bolder: 'The Sacraments are the acted Word – variants of the preached Word. They are signs, but they are more than signs. They are the Word, the Gospel itself, visible, as in preaching the Word is audible. But in either case it is an act. It is Christ in a real presence giving us anew His Redemption.'[23] And it was the minister who mediated that Word, that *act*, to the church, commissioned by God thus, and thus alone, to recreate the souls of his people. And Forsyth was such a minister. All his writings have in common with his Shipley prayer that elusive, exasperating, but most comforting quality of breathing life, unexpected and often outrageous, into traditional language. The resonances are always impeccable. This quality was forged and tempered by his years as a Congregational minister.

Forsyth ministered in Shipley (Springwood), London (St Thomas's Square, Hackney), Manchester (Cheetham Hill), Leicester (Clarendon Park) and Cambridge (Emmanuel). Each church save the last was suburban. Forsyth once reflected that each save the last was a call to a forlorn hope.[24] That was exaggeration. Certainly St Thomas's Square and Cheetham Hill were on the inner-suburban slide and Springwood died out, but Clarendon Park could not have been better placed for Congregational ministry. Each demonstrates consistency in antithesis. The Shipley church was new and frail, excluded from the Yorkshire Congregational Union which later so affronted Forsyth's churchmanship. Forsyth's Shipley call came about through the denomination's liberal network and his explains his subsequent calls. His predecessor at Hackney was the 'heretic' J. A. Picton.[25] At Cheetham Hill Picton had been Forsyth's predecessor but two. When Forsyth reached Leicester, Picton was the constituency's Radical M.P., and he had earlier ministered at a church whose membership furnished some of Forsyth's founder

---

[22] *Freedom*, 290, quoted in Bradley, 218.
[23] *Sacraments*, 1st ed., 176, quoted in Bradley, 240.
[24] 31 October 1894, Church Minute Book, 1892–1922, in possession of Emmanuel United Reformed Church, Cambridge.
[25] James Allanson Picton (1832–1910): *DNB*.

members. Indeed, when preaching there 'with a view' (to use the current jargon), Forsyth stayed with the family of a Picton sister-in-law. Only the call to Cambridge issued from the denominational mainstream – and then it was given and taken more as a call to a national than to a local church.

Yet each of these churches was, in fact, in the denominational mainstream. Shipley was in the most Congregational part of the West Riding; Hackney was London's most Congregational suburb; Cheetham Hill was set firm in Manchester's immensely prosperous Congregational confederacy; and Emmanuel, Cambridge was still more of an East Anglian county town's leading Congregational church than it was anything else. The pulse of each church was a denominational pulse and successful ministry in each would depend on fidelity to the denominational culture. And Forsyth's were successful ministries. At Hackney and Cheetham Hill he discovered Wagner, corresponded with G. F. Watts, communicated with working men and refined his power over words. At Shipley, Hackney and Cheetham Hill, moreover, he moved within the orbit of the Congregational theological colleges. A. M. Fairbairn of Airedale stood firm when Forsyth was isolated by Yorkshire's official Congregationalism.[26] In Manchester, there was Lancashire Independent College, sootily emparked in Whalley Range. St Thomas's Square was the nearest chapel to Hackney College, the most evangelistic of the denominational colleges.

An examination of three of the churches, Shipley, Leicester and Cambridge, will make the point. Springwood, Shipley, had grown from a Sunday school in 1870. Its order was pragmatic.[27] There was no 'church'. Instead all members of the congregation elected a management committee. Forsyth was its second minister. He was heard in April 1876. He settled in July. He left in December 1879. His stipend was £200. The church minute book's references to him are brief but suggestive. Thus, within four months of his settlement: 'Litany introduced for first time in Morning Service, and the

---

[26]W. B. Selbie, *The Life of Andrew Martin Fairbairn* (London: Hodder & Stoughton, 1914), 29–80, 95; Forsyth, 'Tributes to Principal Fairbairn', *British Weekly* (1912); Bradley, 32, 92.

[27]This section relies chiefly on Shipley Congregational Church Minute Book, 1870–92, Bradford City Archives.

Beatitudes in Evening Service.' This was to an order prepared by Forsyth who took care to preach on it first. Again, shortly before his removal, Forsyth preached on baptism. The occasion was the baptism of his daughter, Jessie. That family sacrament was followed by a more representative occasion, the farewell sermons preached to large audiences 'who were much impressed with the ernestness [sic] and scholarly attainments of the preacher. His morning sermon on "Jesus Christ the same yesterday, today and for ever" was a discourse which no hearer can ever forget.' The spell had begun of those scholarly attainments, so distancing yet so gratifying, remarked upon at each subsequent farewell, and of that earnestness, as yet more for Christ than his cross, the prayer for 'Maid arise' notwithstanding.

A pastorate means people. Two men might be picked out from Forsyth's Shipley years to suggest both the genesis of consistency in antithesis and the denominational pulsebeat even in the heat of a radical youth.

Although Springwood failed to draw its expected clout of Bradford woolmen it attracted one whose family name was firmly in the Congregational mainstream: Stephen Philip Unwin of Hall Royd.[28] Unwin belonged to that tentacular family of Unwins who farmed and traded in Norfolk and Essex, printed in Surrey and published in London. An uncle was the first principal of Homerton College in its Normal School days.[29] Theirs was traditionary Congregationalism: 'I knew the old divines. I often sat on Mr Binney's knee when he came to my father's and grandfather's houses.'[30]

Stephen Unwin's immediate background was Colchester woolbroking sensibly diverted by removal to the West Riding. By 1876, he lived in Shipley. His sister married William Pollard Byles, a distant family connection whose father was founder-proprietor of the *Bradford Observer*.[31] S. P. Unwin and W. P. Byles were birds of

---

[28]Stephen Philip Unwin (1836–1919): [F. G. Byles], *William Byles by His Youngest Son* (Weymouth: privately printed, 1932), 73–4.

[29]William Jordan Unwin (1811–77): *CYB* (1878), 355–7.

[30]S. P. Unwin reminiscing in 1902. *Greenfield Congregational Church Bradford, 1852–1902: A 'Souvenir' of the Jubilee Celebration Services* (1902), 56.

[31]Sir William Pollard Byles (1839–1917): M. Stenton and S. Lees, eds, *Who's Who of British Members of Parliament: A Biographical Dictionary of the House of Commons*, vol. 2, 1886–1918 (Sussex: Harvester, 1978), 53.

a feather, politically radical (Byles as a future MP and Unwin as future president of Bradford's Liberal Association), hanging loosely to their inherited Congregationalism ('I have a special interest in those days, although, like many others, I have, without fear, departed from them').[32] Unwin's sympathies moved swiftly along the liberal lines of 'new theology'. Forsyth would have no truck with that sort of thing but in the 1870s theirs were the same chapel, social and civic circles.

In 1877, the High Schools were inaugurated in Saltaire, the famous industrial community which bordered Shipley. Their first governors included Unwin, his sister Sarah Byles, and Alice Glyde whose father, William Evans Glyde of Moorhead, was the partner in Salt's with the most active interest in the works and its welfare.[33] The Glydes's Congregationalism was as tentacular as the Unwins's, its source the south-west rather than the east. Glyde's pastor, J. A. Hamilton, was Forsyth's closest local ministerial friend and literary collaborator and when Glyde died and Hamilton's commemorative sermons were published they were accompanied by a poem of Forsyth's *in memoriam*.[34] Its words are not memorable. Like many with a poet's sense of words, Forsyth wrote bad poetry. But four stanzas to 'our dear, grave Puritan's' memory bear repetition. Here is civic gospel, chapel's walled garden extroverted into collectivism. Here too, is *shape*:

> ... Vision flows
> Of men that shall be, when the City of God
> Rises through earth, like forests from the sod,
> And public minds shall public things dispose.
>
> When social men shall make the social hour
> At last not trivial but imperial,
> When personal concerns at last shall fall
> In modest tribute to the general power.
>
> When once again our civic life shall be

---

[32] *Greenfield Congregational Church: A 'Souvenir'*, 56.
[33] J. Waddington-Feather, *A Century of Model-Village Schooling: The Salt Grammar School, 1868–1968*.
[34] 'In Memoriam W. E. Glyde' (1884).

A liturgy; and altars smoke unseen
To no unknown god, where hot hearts have been
In streets and lanes, to cleanse, and heal, and free.

Thou hadst the earnest in thy saved soul
Of the salvation of the social whole.

That was in August 1884 and Forsyth was now in Hackney. That December a building committee was convened for a new cause in Leicester.[35]

Theological colouring and suburban expectations apart, Clarendon Park was to be a very different enterprise from Springwood. Four thousand people already lived in its ecclesiastical parish. Barely sixty of them could get into the sole Dissenting chapel.[36] The need seemed patent and with four aldermen on the building committee as well as the man who ran the *Leicester Mercury*, a brother of Stead of the *Pall Mall Gazette*, and a kinsman of William Baines the Church Rate proto-martyr, here was bound to be such a Congregational church as could only turn civic life into a liturgy.

The church was formed in January 1886, with twenty-seven members. Its buildings were opened in March. It was a grand and free guildhall of a place created by the leading local chapel architect,[37] facing a major road, seating seven hundred, its hinterland roomy with aldermanic houses. Denominational grandees opened it and some preached at it, but from the first, its line of preachers showed how liberally the land lay: two of S. P. Unwin's ministerial Byles connections, Thomas Gascoigne of Northampton, John Hunter of Glasgow, Garrett Horder of Wood Green, J. T. Stannard of Huddersfield, Joseph Halsey of Anerley, not a safe name among them.[38] There was one old war-horse, Edward White the proponent

[35]This section relies chiefly on Clarendon Park Congregational Church, Leicester, Church Meeting Minute Book, 1886–1907, and Deacons' Meeting Minute Books, 1886–90, 1890–97, in the possession of Clarendon Park Congregational Church, Leicester.

[36]Building Committee Brochure in Minute Book, 1886–1907. See also Norah Waddington, *The First Ninety Years: Clarendon Park Congregational Church, Leicester*, 1.

[37]James Tait, fl. 1870s–80s.

[38]Gascoigne (1833–1913): *CYB* (1914), 173; Hunter (1849–1917): *CYB* (1918), 135–7; Horder (1841–1922): *CYB* (1924), 98; Stanndard (1844–89): *CYB* (1890), 137; Halsey (1842–1919): *CYB* (1920), 99–100.

of conditional immortality from Camden Town, but most were young or youngish men of light and learning with a significant sprinkling of college tutors – Armitage of Rotherham, Paton of Nottingham, Duff of Airedale.[39] A few had a future in the making: George MacDonald's nephew, E. P. Powell, who became one of the first Congregational moderators; and two young men from the new Mansfield College, Oxford, W. B. Selbie and C. S. Horne.[40] Horne came three times. Such names are explanation enough of the deacons' unanimous decision to cut out of the church minute book the printed 'Declaration of Faith and Church Order' which such books habitually contained. Its twenty 'Principles of Religion' and its thirteen 'Principles of Church Order and Discipline' were at once too much and too inadequate.

Forsyth, now moved from Hackney to Cheetham Hill, was not the first to 'preach with a view' at Clarendon Park. He was at least the fifth; but a call was issued unanimously in April 1888 (stipend £400) and he accepted in May. He set his terms in two characteristic letters written a month to the day after Clarendon Park's deacons had agreed to recommend the call to church meeting. The first was to one of those deacons, Alexander Baines, an advanced business man with wide denominational links and just such a practical interest in provincial culture as would most appeal to Forsyth.[41] To Baines, Forsyth wrote authoritatively yet in such a way as to draw this young church into the excitement of the whole church:

> I have some time got past the mere love of novelty but I always shall see and say some things individually and strongly. And if I cannot preach freely, I cannot preach the *truth* – not, that is, with any of the *power* which is the essence of preaching as distinct from writing. And I am more the wishful the whole Church should understand this point because of the agitation going on and the conflicts which may be impending in our religions world.

[39]White (1819–98): *CYB*(1899), 205–6; Armitage (1844–1929); *CYB*(1931), 222; Paton (1830–1911): *CYB* (1912), 161; Duff (1845–1934): *CYB* (1935), 272–4.

[40]Powell (1866–1933): *CYB*(1934), 272–3; Selbie (1862–1944); *CYB*(1945), 441; Horne (1865–1914): *CYB* (1915), 154–6.

[41]Baines (1848–1907), nephew of William Baines the church rate martyr; lived in an Ernest Gimson house; W. Scarff and W. T. Pike, eds, *Leicestershire and Rutland at the Opening of the Twentieth Century* (Brighton: 1902), 161.

To that church at large, Forsyth certainly wrote individually and strongly. It was in its detail a most old-fashioned letter though entirely free from the honest cant conventional for such occasions. Every word told as the minister-elect built up his case from unimpeachable foundations to a job description which would have spelt disaster for most pastorates. But Forsyth knew and liked his Baineses, Hewitts, Staffords and Chamberses of Clarendon Park. 'I have the honour of your Christian call,' he began with Scotch correctness: 'I am your servant in Jesus Christ, if, when you hear the whole of this letter, you still will have it so. And let us trust that our interpretation of the Lord's will is right, and that we unite because *He* will have it so.' There were four stages to what followed. First, the ground of evangelical ministry: 'I come, not in the main, to make a certain congregation a prosperous concern, but, as a minister of Christ and of the Church Universal, to declare and apply the Gospel of the Cross. I believe in the Incarnation of the Eternal Son of God in the sinless person of Jesus Christ; in the Redemption of Mankind through His death; and in His risen life as the unseen personal power which guides both the world and the Church to fulfil the Kingdom of God – especially through personal union with the Saviour.' Then came liberty: 'I view these great truths not as a mere seal of orthodoxy, not as confining the action of the human mind, not as hedging it up, so to speak, against mistakes. But I view them as a *Gospel*, as the charter and impulse of the soul's liberty, and the guide to heights and ranges of freedom, both in heart and head, which without Christ's gospel we should never have won.' As to his own place in that gospel liberty, Forsyth requested 'the completest freedom ... both to the specific ways of applying these truths to modern conditions and to my own personal style of phrase and speech. I always feel that my freedom is a responsibility[,] that the feelings of others are entitled to respect, and that it is cowardly to use the privilege of the pulpit to the disadvantage of those who have both to listen and perhaps to differ.' This was take-it-or-leave-it language and few churches can have been written to so strong-mindedly by the man whom they had just called. It was not cavalier. Forsyth wrote as one busy professional man to other busy professional men. They too were civic-minded, with a constitutional sense and recognized standards to keep. He was called by them to declare and apply a gospel which was 'the charter and impulse of the soul's liberty'. Hence the balanced firmness of what followed: 'I may further add that I have neither time nor energy to waste in such contentions as sometimes arise in Churches on doctrinal points,' but should this church find his ministry unacceptable, 'an ordinary vote of the Church with a decided majority to that effect will be quite sufficient'. Meanwhile, 'I am yours for Jesus Christ'. Divine call was thus shaped into act by human contract. And it worked. Long after he left Clarendon Park, Forsyth still returned to marry or baptize new generations of its people, or to preach on the arrival of two of his successors. Immediately after he left, Minna Forsyth died and her husband wrote to John Stafford of how Clarendon Park's sympathy 'came to me like a warm air from the circle of those who knew her ... And it came from those who had often been witnesses and partners of my anxiety on previous occasions in the long conflict with illness and imminent death. Still more it came from those with whom I have so often shared the deep sweet things of the Saviour's death.' And to Alex Baines he sent a poem, 'The Healing of the Paralytic', which he had printed in the *British Weekly*.

The Forsyth who was soon to write so memorably of the soul's darkest night had now experienced his own. He had shared them with the people to whom he had been contracted and, thus sharing, he had moved with them further into the sacramental life, almost beyond the bounds of time. Here was pastoral experience at its most intense, in a straightforward, prosperous, suburban congregation.

That side of things flowered too. The infant church which heard J. A. Picton lecture on 'The Character of Cromwell' was more than ready for October 1888 when the mayor and fourteen councillors attended evening worship and Forsyth preached to them on 'Civic Christianity'. With Forsyth, came monthly Sunday morning children's services and weekly Sunday evening lectures to young men and women. There also came music and liturgy: a sermon, for instance, on 'The Song of Miriam' followed by a performance of Schubert's work; or a lecture on Handel; or services built upon Sullivan's 'Prodigal Son' or Miss Downing's 'The Ten Virgins'. There were sung responses to start the service and there was 'the singing of the Lord's Prayer to a musical note' on Sunday evenings. That was discontinued, though the responses were retained and indeed extended, with the congregation standing to sing them and to listen to the opening sentences. Membership rose more steadily than dramatically. It reached eighty in 1893. That was small for a building which seated seven hundred and very small for a stipend of

£400, but it is clear that congregations promised well. The only stresses lay with the persistent ill health of the minister and his wife. Then came the call to Cambridge.

It was almost unique in Congregational ministry. The Leicester press swiftly spelt out its possibilities. Indeed their leaking of the news precipitated Forsyth's decision. As the *Evening Mercury* put it, Emmanuel Church was 'the chief if not practically the only Congregational church in Cambridge'; more Nonconformist students graduated at Cambridge than Oxford; and 'the principal Nonconformist training college for teachers [Homerton, where S. P. Unwin's uncle had been principal] has been removed to Cambridge, and thus from that town large numbers of young students and teachers are continually going out over the whole country'. That was hyperbole on all three counts but the scope of the call was underlined by the eight nationally known ministers who urged on Forsyth that here was 'a case where the field was measured rather by the university and the opportunities it supplied than the city and its boundaries'.

That was the new fact in an old situation. Emmanuel Church was unusually conscious of its past.[42] Its minute books were headed by the succession of ministers, their names incorrectly transcribed, from Joseph Hussey who had settled in 1691.[43] The church had suffered, and at times, enjoyed, every tension natural to an urban congregation but it had sustained its order more clear-headedly than most. It was not yet Cambridge's leading Nonconformist church, although it was the oldest, and in Forsyth's time it was not the town's largest Congregational church, though its membership was solid and its deacons were the sort whose businesses dignified Market Hill. What was new was the opening up of the university as a source of intellectual stimulus and evangelical mission rather than commercial opportunity for keen-eyed tradesmen. Emmanuel's building witnessed to that novelty. Its sturdy, dominating, fourteenth-century Victorian gothic thrust through the carapace of Peterhouse, Pembroke and the Pitt Press.

---

[42]This section relies chiefly on Emmanuel Congregational Church, Cambridge, Church Meeting Minute Book, 1892–1922, in the possession of Emmanuel United Reformed Church, Cambridge.

[43]Joseph Hussey (1660–1726), minister at Cambridge, 1691–1719: G. F. Nuttall, 'Cambridge Nonconformity from Holcroft to Hussey', *Journal United Reformed Church History Society* 1 (April 1977): 241–58.

That building was twelve years older than Clarendon Park. It too held seven hundred. Forsyth was the third to minister to it. One of his predecessors still lived in Cambridge as a philosophy don at Trinity.[44] His ministry had been terrible for him. So it was at first for Forsyth, plunged into the abyss of personal despair and physical prostration. He emerged. He remarried. He grew fond of the people who had sustained his collapse. His church's membership reached two hundred for the first time in its history and his stipend reached £500. And his ministry was uttered on a deeper note. The whole denomination heard it when he preached his assembly sermon, 'God the Holy Father', and in one memorable passage cuttingly outlined such styles of ministry as had so closely engaged his own recent energies:

> He might take the genial cultured way of natural goodness with philanthropy for repentance, an easy optimism, a beautiful Fatherhood, tasteful piety, social refinement, varied interest, ethical sympathies, aesthetic charm, and a conscience more enlightened than saved. Or he might take the pietist's way. And then is the risk fanciful of his sinking, perhaps, in the ill-educated cases, though a fluent religionist into a flimsy saint, lapped in soft airs, taking a clique for the Kingdom, and sold to the religious nothings of the hour with all their stupefying power; with no deepness of earth, no pilgrim's progress, no passion of sacred blood, no grasp on real life, no grim wrestling, no power with God, no mastery of the soul, no insight, no measure of it, no real power to retain for himself or for others, to compel a belief in the soul, its reality or its Redeemer.[45]

Emmanuel's regulatory arrangements were not too different from Clarendon Park's, though there was more liturgical conservatism. At his first Emmanuel church meeting, Forsyth worried over 'the lack of response to the Amen at the close of the prayers during service, he trusted that it would be more general, failing which he would have to suggest a remedy'. Emmanuel was not to be steam-

---

[44]James Ward (1843–1925), first Professor of Mental Philosophy and Logic, 1897: *DNB*.
[45]*Father*, 14–15.

rollered. It was much the same with the serving of communion. At Emmanuel, the deacons were served with the bread and wine after they had served the communicants seated in the body of the church. Forsyth preferred it the other way round. He said that it was more usual; but he would, of course, 'follow the custom of the Church till the church members themselves express a contrary desire'. It was an easier matter to introduce another Leicester practice, which was to link monthly church meetings with weekly worship, as when he gave a 'short address dwelling upon the hymn of Luther which had been sung at the Sunday morning service'.

Forsyth's church meetings at Emmanuel were carefully educational. Thus the meeting so concerned with the ordering of communion also included words on the diaconate, 'bidding them remember that the office only differed from that of the Pastor in degree the Pastor himself really being the chief Deacon'. Two meetings later his fellow deacons presented their chief deacon with the robes of his Aberdeen D. D. A question-and-answer session followed the presentation: 'Several present asked questions relevant to the sermon preached last Sunday morning by the Pastor, bearing upon "the limitations of Christ's knowledge". A further question was asked whether it was thought that the spiritual life of the present generation was as full and deep as that had been of the older people.'

Such a question presupposed a negative answer, so the core of the next meeting was to be conversation, introduced by a deacon, on the Christian experience of the present time. Its quality defied the minute secretary's descriptive powers: 'It is not possible in the minutes of a large meeting to express how interesting and helpful to spiritual life this conversation proved to be.'

So the rhythm flowed of conversation, education, self-questioning, encouragement. That December Forsyth regretted 'that so few male members were present, but took heart at a "most interesting letter which he had received from a Norwegian seaman, the Keeper of a lighthouse on the North west coast of that country who had been moved to correspond by reason of the interest he had in the subject of the recent sermons preached in Emmanuel Church by the Pastor on "The Religious Grounds of Nonconformity"'.

In June 1897, the pastor's concerns were for the church as sacramental community. First, church meeting discussed the Sunday service. Forsyth had preached on baptism (shades of Shipley, 1879) and then he had baptized seven infants, '*Most of the congre-*

gation staying and taking part in an exceptional unique and edifying service which will be long remembered'.[46] Then with wounded *amour propre*, he referred to the lack of Church *esprit de corps*, as evinced by the smallness of the congregation, in his absence, on the previous Sunday evening and pointed out that it was 'apt to give strangers an erroneous impression of the condition of the Church'. How could he ask country ministers to take his pulpit in such circumstances?

The mundane and the divine jostled naturally at church meetings. In March 1899, after they discussed the church's ventilation, Forsyth 'gave a most helpful and interesting address on the Power of the Holy Ghost'. In May, two deacons pledged themselves not to buy any publications issued by the owners of the new 'Sunday daily papers' and church meeting was to tell the owners of the *Daily Mail* and the *Daily Telegraph* so.

By January 1900, it was perhaps clear that Forsyth's Cambridge days were numbered. The church noted 'the growing recognition within and beyond the Church of his worth, and his conception of the power and dignity of the Pulpit'. In March, as if to demonstrate the point, Forsyth read out a soldier's letter from the South African front. It was about Forsyth's address to the International Congregational Council in Boston, Massachusetts. At the same meeting, a minister from Nova Scotia prayed and Forsyth spoke on 'the offerings made by the Wise Men from the East'. By now Emmanuel's conservatism was almost mellowing. Though a sung amen after each prayer was too much to take, worship now closed with a 'Musical Amen' and it opened (as at Clarendon Park) with the worshippers standing in readiness, as they now stood at church meetings when new members were received.

Forsyth left Emmanuel in the summer of 1901 to take over the college which had been so close to his former church in Hackney, though it was now bright and beautiful in Hampstead.[47] Emmanuel did not, could not, longer detain him. His last church meeting as a minister in congregational charge was thankful for such harmonious and faithful ministry: 'The Doctor replied ... it was his hope and

---

[46]My emphasis.
[47]C. Binfield, 'Hackneyed in Hampstead: The Growth of a College Building', *Journal United Reformed Church History Society* 4 (October 1987): 58–68.

desire to do for the men whom he expected to train for the ministry at Hackney College what he had tried to do for this Church – strike a deeper note and expound the teaching of the Gospel, that nothing good could come but by sacrifice, for it was true of all that without shedding of blood there was no forgiveness of sins.' And Mr Almond, the church secretary, suitably noted: 'With singing and prayer the church meetings of a unique and memorable ministry was [sic] brought to a close.' Memories of that ministry were long-lived; the depth of sympathy which Forsyth brought to the bereaved – even his ability to convey it on a postcard; his sparkle among friends; the difficulty of his sermons. That was a memory which grew in retrospect. Perhaps the sparse evening congregations testified to it. Certainly the piling of paradox upon antithesis, so marked in his books, fed on memory's impression of the instinctive debater never quite tamed, that style so cruelly seized by a fellow minister as 'fireworks in a fog'.[48] That was never again to be Emmanuel's style, as it had never really been the Cambridge style. Forsyth's successors were masters of unadorned prose. Nearly seventy years after Forsyth's departure one of his flock, whose family had moved up from Southampton in 1897, recalled: 'I must admit that I chiefly remember P. T. F.'s sermons as the moment when I took off my hat, put my head against my mother's shoulder and went to sleep! – but from the grown up conversation later I knew there had been something *they* thought well worth listening to – and before he left I began to listen to him and to feel the power behind his speech.'[49]

A chapel's secular life culminated in the bazaar. Emmanuel's great bazaar was to promote its Sunday school extensions, though it seized on this opportunity to celebrate two centuries of church life held joyously in a programme with the proportions of a book.[50] It was called the Past and Present Bazaar. Forsyth's contribution to the souvenir programme was an essay on the theology of the bazaar, a divine sledgehammer to crack a jolly nut. He called it 'Gain and Godliness'. Here was the very essence of Forsythery: grandeur,

---

[48]Thus J. G. Stevenson: T. Rhondda Williams, *How I Found My Faith* (London: Cassell, 1938), 94.

[49]Miss F. Bunten to A. A. Smith, 31 March 1967. I am grateful to Mr A. A. Smith for this reference.

[50]*Past and Present, 1691–1895* (Cambridge: 1895).

paradox, common sense, the debater's original sin pointing up the better way. There were fine turns of phrase (reverence in worship is 'spiritual manners, the good breeding of the soul'). There was condemnation ('such things as raffles, lotteries, and prices and importunities which are only impertinent'). If the title hinted at Carlyle, the text quoted Goethe, and declared that 'movements of Church Reform are the church's self-criticism. To rise higher, they are the actions of the Holy Spirit in the church on the church.' Churchmanship was brought into play (he spoke of narrowing the 'mind of Christ to a kind of unworldliness which is only sectarian after all' and he deplored such 'a subtle kind of protestant monasticism'). There was common sense ('We must take it as we find it to mend it'). And there was a debating point to please the Market Hill side of his people: 'If the methods of business may not be used for the service of the church, has the church any right to accept of contributions from men who have made money in the way of business?'[51]

There were three further points to his essay. One was in liberalism's mainstream: the exclusion of business from the religious meant unchurching 'more than half of life and the people who live in it'. The second was reaffirmation of civic liturgy: 'Our Sunday schools are not sectarian nurseries... . We seek to service the neighbourhood, the town, the public.'[52] The third marked a political retrenchment: 'An idea is current among some eager spirits that no form of business is really Christian except some plane of socialism. This is too large a question to enter in here. It may only be said that as competition has a necessary place in moral developments it has therefore its place, however subordinate, in historical Christianity.'[53] The debate was over. Historic Emmanuel's Past and Present Bazaar was justified. Its minister could end as he had refused to begin, with a text: 'Good Luck in the Name of the Lord'.[54]

The bazaar book was a splendidly academic production. The future Downing professor of the Laws of England wrote on Emmanuel's earlier history.[55] A Fellow of Trinity hall contributed

---

[51]'Gain and Godliness' (1895): 5–7.
[52]'Gain and Godliness', 7.
[53]'Gain and Godliness', 8.
[54]'Gain and Godliness', 8.
[55]Courtney Kenny (1847–1930): *DNB*.

two poems.[56] A recent Fellow of King's contributed a string of verses.[57] A Caius man described the rigours of Elizabethan university life and a Peterhouse man outlined the evolution of the bazaar.[58] This was the side of Emmanuel which had clinched Forsyth's acceptance of the call.

There had never been a time when undergraduates had not sometimes worshipped in Emmanuel's predecessors. From the 1850s an undergraduate presence, continuous yet transient, was a chapel fact of life. From the 1870s, it was a church fact of life and it was not just an undergraduate presence. Senior members of the university from Nonconformist families joined the church. Some worshipped there in their gowns. This was the prayed-for consequence of the relaxation of university tests. Emmanuel Church was built to celebrate that relaxation and to institutionalize its consequence.

It is tempting to see Forsyth as minister to two Emmanuels, town and gown. Town was prominent enough: Mathers and Munsey the jewellers, Almond the outfitter, Thrussell the bootmaker, Macintosh the ironmonger, Wright the physician, Few the solicitor, Bond the grocer, men whose solidarity was never in doubt. But this town became gown or married gown: Flora Mathers was at Newnham, Henry Bond at Trinity Hall; Mary Munsey and Beatrice Macintosh married young men whose apprenticeship was as undergraduates. By Forsyth's time, there was a resident nucleus of university families: the Neville Keyneses of Pembroke, the Courtney Kennys of Downing (the most devoted attender never to become a member, for he was a Unitarian), the A. S. Ramseys of Magdalene (who were none too fond of Forsyth's paradoxes), the A. J. Wyatts of Christ's.[59] The

[56](Sir) A. W. W. Dale (1855–1921), Fellow of Trinity Hall, 1880–99: J. A. Venn, *Alumni Cantabrigienses,* part 2, 2:213.

[57]Arthur Reed Ropes (1859–1933), Fellow of King's, 1885–90; subsequently known to theatre-goers as 'Adrian Ross'; deacon at Emmanuel, 1889–96: Venn, 5:355.

[58]G. E. Green (1863–1931) and F. J. C. Hearnshaw (1869–1946): Venn, 3: 128, 311.

[59]Mrs Neville Keynes, her sister and mother-in-law, were members; her husband was an attender. Her daughter, Mrs A. V. Hill, was married at Emmanuel in June 1913. A. S. Ramsey was a member, and became a deacon and church secretary. His wife was an attender. A. J. Wyatt was an Anglo-Saxon scholar and university coach.

young Baptist T. R. Glover was an associate member.[60] A. W. W.
Dale of Trinity Hall was on the diaconate.[61] That was the key. Dale,
Glover and Ramsey were sons of the manse. Keynes was a manse
son-in-law. Where it did not repel (and the social and cultural
presuppositions of Cambridge life made it a powerful repellent), the
manse cousinhood made Emmanuel a natural home, especially for
that first generation of married dons. For such households
Emmanuel's was an inclusive fellowship. Thus, of the four deacons
elected during Forsyth's ministry, one was town, two were gown
(Joseph Reynolds Green F.R.S., of Downing, and German Sims
Woodhead, the professor of pathology)[62] and one was neither town
nor gown, since as a lecturer at Homerton he belonged to higher
education's intermediate rung.

As for the transients, the undergraduates, the stream was steady,
most as sermon-tasters but a core as associate members, from at least
a dozen colleges and most strikingly from the two women's colleges.
Some were exotic, like the two Russian Lutherans from Emmanuel
College, but most were children of the manse and the diaconate. A
few came from grander backgrounds, held by traditionary loyalties.
At Forsyth's first meeting John Evan Spicer of Trinity, from the
papermaking family, was received as an occasional member recom-
mended by his minister A. A. Ramsey, whose son was at Magdalene.

Their concerns were felt at church meetings. When Forsyth
mooted the idea of a Sunday morning communion two views were
expressed. One was that the Sunday school teachers would find it
inconvenient. The other was that 'the lady students of Homerton
would be glad to avail themselves of such an opportunity, being
forbidden by the rules of the College to be out in the Evening'.
Homerton won.

The essence of the relationship was distilled at Forsyth's welcome
social when Lewis Gaunt of Clare 'was called to express the opinion
of the undergraduates: this he did not hesitate to do saying he envied

---

[60]Glover (1869–1943), Fellow of St John's 1892–98, 1901–43, became a
leading Baptist layman and a pillar of St Andrew's Street Baptist Church. In
September 1892, however, he became an associate member of Emmanuel, which
remained his Cambridge church for the rest of the decade.

[61]Deacon, 1886–1900.

[62]Green (1848–1914), F. R. S., 1895: Venn, 3: 130; Woodhead (1855–1921):
Who Was Who, 1916–28.

the very freshest of the freshmen by reason of the lengthened opportunity they would have to sit under Mr Forsyth's teaching: he further raised considerable enthusiasm by saying that his experiences were such that though called to speak for the undergraduates he had no hesitation in saying that his interest was first with Emmanuel and secondly with the university members'. That, for most of the regular University members, was Emmanuel's attraction. Forsyth made his position clear to them: 'The pulpit must necessarily be the test of his work: it was natural to him and the power of preaching a faithful Gospel was to be felt still, particularly in Cambridge where he hesitated not to say that his desire was to influence for good the members of Nonconformist families who were here for a time and thence departed to make their influence felt.'

In Cambridge, these young men and women were Trinity, Jesus, Christ's, St John's, Newnham, Girton. At Emmanuel, they were also Dulwich, Highgate, Stoke Newington, Islington, Kensington, Tollington Park as well as Cheetham Hill or Edgbaston, Sunderland, Lincoln, Bradford, Birkenhead, Colchester, even Belfast or Cape Town, congregating still in family pews, experiencing Forsyth's twin aims: beautiful worship and church meetings to reflect 'the highest ideals of family life'.

At Forsyth's church meetings women regularly spoke: Homerton's Miss Farren on behalf of her students; Mrs Neville Keynes about her mothers' meeting or Dr Barrett's Congregational Union Lecture on worship. At the annual church meetings, it became the custom for young gown to play a formal part. In 1898, W. H. Austin, the Senior Wrangler, moved the adoption of the church reports, and F. H. Pyman, of the Hartlepool shipping family, seconded him. That June, Pyman wrote to express his sadness at leaving Cambridge and sent £10. In December, he repeated the gift.

Emmanuel was thus Forsyth's greatest opportunity as it was certainly his grandest frustration. Never before had he been so much the outsider looking in. At last Emmanuel had a minister whose intellect filled the building and the purpose; and he was excluded, save by courtesy, from the community of Christian scholarship to which that intellect entitled him. That frustration met Forsyth's fidelity to his call. The result was sermons and lectures hammering out for him and his people why they stood as they did: 'If I am asked why I do not belong to the Established Church, I reply that my chief reason is, because I am such a Churchman – a High Churchman – with such a high ideal of the Church.'[63] That paradox became a commonplace for Congregationalists. He announced it in the first of two published lecture series, delivered from Emmanuel: *The Charter of the Church* and *Rome, Reform and Reaction.*[64]

At one level, these works are in the exasperated tradition of anti-catholic polemic. Forsyth overboils as a latter-day Edward Miall, surveying Anglicanism, that 'great, godly, and unfortunate Church'; seeing in its monopoly 'a relic of Protection … [bringing] in its train the torpor, neglect, and corruption of monopoly'; doubting 'whether all of us have really measured … and with a stateman's eye, the depth, intimacy, and passion with which the Established Church interpenetrates, happily or unhappily, our social system and our national life'.[65] There is Miallite sarcasm at Anglicanism's yearning for the Greeks and Latins who discounted it rather than for the Reformed who would value it: 'For the rich madame, who will not recognise people in business because she is set on being recognised by the old aristocracy who snub and ignore her, is not only amusing, but, when she parades her religion as the reason, she is – let us say – pathetic.'[66] Forsyth's history was forcefully Whiggish made gloomier by fear of 'the awful Armageddon which awaits Europe sooner or later'.[67] Anglicanism was demoralizing. Romanism was the antithesis of all that had made Britain. Were it ever to return, Rome 'would in course of time reduce it from the most free, adventurous, powerful and righteous nation on the earth to the timid, vainglorious, petulant, cruel, pleasure-loving and bankrupt race which it has made Spain'.[68] He turned to the empire:

> It is not the English Parliament nor the English Constitution that is felt in the English proconsul on the skirts of the Himalayas, but the English *man*… . An empire like ours could not hang together for a century ruled simply as a magnificent and compact organisation, and worked like a

[63] *Charter*, 7.
[64] *Rome* (1899).
[65] *Charter*, 58, 59, 60.
[66] *Charter*, 55.
[67] *Rome*, 167.
[68] *Rome*, 159.

gigantic post office. But what does that mean? It means that our power is in its nature and genius Protestant and not Catholic, that its salvation is the development of individual resource and responsibility; that its doom would be to settle down into mere officialism ... and to regard the ideal Englishman more as a machine to obey orders than as a living moral centre of freedom, confidence, and power. Make our religion Catholic, and above all things institutional, and in due time you reduce English enterprise to something in the nature of a Jesuit mission.[69]

Cambridge could take that sort of thing in its stride, save that Forsyth admired what he excoriated and appropriated its language because it was his mother tongue: 'The whole history of the Church up to the Reformation at least is as much ours as theirs'; 'we recognise that the nation is a unity. It is a moral unity. It has a sanctity. It cannot dispense with a religion'; 'the living Christ is only realisable on an historic scale by His action through the living and historic community of the church ... the moving area of the Cross'.[70]

Here is Forsyth, protestant for the church catholic: 'This Church where I preach is a priest much more than I am, more than any member of it is, more than any clergyman. The great visible priest on earth is the Church in its various sections.'[71] As for that preaching, it was 'spiritual struggle, the Lord's controversy. He has been wrestling with men – at grips with their soul, their fugitive, reluctant, recalcitrant soul.'[72] Who dare preach when a sermon has been so defined? Or sup, when 'in that act the Church identifies itself ... in a ceremonial way with Christ in His sacrificial act. It offers Christ, the one eternal sacrifice to God. And Christ dwelling in His Church body offers Himself, preaches Himself to the world as crucified Redeemer'.[73]

This was not, after all, the usual vein of Dissenting polemic. It came naturally from a minister forced to relate his present position

---

[69] *Rome*, 168–9.
[70] *Charter*, 9, 10, 61.
[71] *Rome*, 212.
[72] *Rome*, 217.
[73] *Rome*, 219.

to the cumulative weight of all the Christian centuries since that act of the cross, for whom nonetheless the Reformation must remain their crucible for modern man. Here, consequently, was a Free Churchman who would accept dogma as the church's footing, doctrine as its grasp, theology as its reach.[74] For the church, not the individual, 'is the correlate of Christian truth. The great music needs orchestra and chorus round the conductor and round a theme'.[75] For this minister, Emmanuel Church and Clarendon Park and Cheetham Hill and St Thomas's Square and Springwood too, all provided orchestra and chorus; and he was now just within sound of the great music.

[74] *Theology*, 13, quoted in J. W. Grant, *Free Churchmanship in England, 1870–1940*, 232.
[75] *Theology*, xviii, quoted in Grant, 236.

Chapter 11

THE AMBIVALENT RAINBOW: FORSYTH, ART AND CREATION

Jeremy Begbie

What is this life if, full of care,
we have no time to stand and stare?[1]

W. H. Davies' plea for unhurried attention is especially apt for any theologian who ventures into the terrain of artistic endeavour. Amid the eagerness that theology engage at depth with the arts, the danger of doing violence to the integrity of individual works of art is immense. A Rembrandt self-portrait, for example, or a Duke Ellington song, can be hastily swept up into some grand metaphysical scheme and stifled under the smothering embrace of premature theological closure. Forsyth was not immune to this tendency, as we shall see. But one of the many merits of his approach to the arts is his obvious and very strong desire to take time to stand and stare at (and listen to) specific pieces of art.

1. *The Scapegoat*

Nowhere is that more evident than in his first major book of 1889, *Religion in Recent Art*, where he invites us to stand and stare at paintings by leading Pre-Raphaelites. One picture which elicits a striking eulogy is Holman Hunt's *The Scapegoat* of 1855 [Plate 1], painted on the shores of the Dead Sea to satisfy (at least to some

---

[1]W. H. Davies, 'Leisure', in *The Golden Book of Modern English Poetry*, ed. T. Caldwell (London: Dent, 1935), 222.

William Holman Hunt, "The Scapegoat" © Manchester City Art Galleries.

degree) what some have regarded as a misplaced quest for historical accuracy. Faced with this painting, Forsyth draws on his most sonorous powers of prose and acute theological insight to produce what the art-critic Peter Fuller called 'a *tour de force* of twentieth century art criticism'.[2] In the glowing mountain range and the sky above, Forsyth tells us, we see nature's beauty and promise.[3] But more obviously, the picture speaks of a curse on creation: there is 'the accursed lake and dismal swamp'; the 'vegetation has become contaminated with curse … mark the slimy surface of the water … mark how the blessed promise of the rising moon is marred and turned into ghastly mockery in this cursed land by placing the bleached skull of a goat long perished right in the disc of the moon's reflection upon the damp shore… . Here there is no life, but total curse'.[4] Nevertheless, in the midst of the desolation there is atonement. In Forsyth's words, 'Another life than the mere glow of nature must redeem the mysterious curse upon nature.'[5] The staggering, faltering goat is the scapegoat of the Day of Atonement ritual, driven into the wilderness, bearing the accumulated weight of the sins of Israel. So Christ bears the sorrow of a world in travail. Hunt makes 'the groaning of the innocent creature … an *organic part* of the great and guiltless sorrow which bears and removes the curse of the world'.[6] Forsyth concludes his account of the painting by drawing our attention to another decisive feature: the rainbow, signifying the 'redemption from the curse into a heavenly glory and promise above all telling'.[7] It 'is the symbol of the Encircling Father, the triumph of inclusive bliss, beautiful above all the curse, with its blessed arms sanctifying the very agony from which its cherishing presence is hidden, and *full of promise for a new heaven and a new earth*, wherein dwelleth righteousness and there is curse no more'.[8]

One of the intriguing aspects of Forsyth's commentary on *The Scapegoat* is that he seems to be familiar only with the earlier (and smaller) Manchester version. In the final and well-known painting,

---

[2]Peter Fuller, *Theoria: Art, and the Absence of Grace*, 145.
[3]*Art*, 3rd ed. (1905), 183–4.
[4]*Art*, 185.
[5]*Art*, 185.
[6]*Art*, 181–2.
[7]*Art*, 183.
[8]*Art*, 188–9. My italics.

now in Liverpool, the rainbow is omitted [Plate 2]. For Hunt, it would appear, the rainbow was not crucial since his main interest was in the redemption of human sin, not creation at large. Certainly, on his first visit to the Dead Sea he witnessed 'a magnificent rainbow' spanning the whole landscape,[9] and in Victorian painting, the presence of a rainbow did often reflect theological convictions about the created world.[10] But there is little in Hunt's copious account of this painting to suggest that any kind of divine pledge to the whole creation was fundamental or necessary to his conception.[11] His principal concern was with the typology of human redemption, in line with the increasing popularity of typological preaching in his day.[12] The omission of the rainbow would have presented no significant problem. (The most likely explanation for the rainbow's erasure was that when Hunt decided to use a white goat instead of a black one, the extra light and colour of a rainbow was rendered superfluous.)[13] For Forsyth, on the other hand, much depends on the rainbow because it acts as a sign of hope for the re-creation of the entire cosmos. His comments, as we have already seen, make it quite clear that he is casting his mind over a far wider realm than the human alone. Whether or not he knew the other version, this is the one which excites his passion, and a large part of that excitement is due to what he sees as its cosmic import.

[9]Draft of a letter from Hunt to Morland Agnew, as cited in Judith Bronkhurst's entry on the Manchester version of the picture. Bronkhurst, 'The Scapegoat', in *Pre-Raphaelite Papers*, ed. Leslie Parris (London: Tate Gallery, 1984), 44–5.

[10]Cf. George P. Landow, 'The Rainbow: A Problematic Image', in G. B. Tennyson and U. C. Knoepflmacher, *Nature and the Victorian Imagination* (Berkeley: University of California Press, 1977), 341–69.

[11]Cf. W. Holman Hunt, *Pre-Raphaelitism and the Pre-Raphaelites*, 2 vols. (London: Macmillan, 1905).

[12]Landow, *William Holman Hunt and Typological Symbolism* (New Haven: Yale university Press, 1979). Indirect support for this comes from Fuller, *Theoria: Art, and the Absence of Grace*, 218–33, 83ff. Fuller notes that John Ruskin's criticisms of Hunt's picture, unlike many of Hunt's contemporary detractors, do not focus on its intense naturalism. (Landow, *William Holman Hunt*, 111, adopts basically the traditional complaint: 'Hunt's naturalism has distracted us from his deeper meaning, rather than led us to it.') For Ruskin, Hunt was too interested in typology and not interested enough in the typical beauty of natural forms; it was in the latter that Ruskin came to find the deepest 'spiritual' significance.

[13]Cf. Landow, *William Holman Hunt*, 112. All that Hunt tells us is that he decided to use a white goat instead of black and then felt it best to omit the rainbow. Bronkhurst, 'The Scapegoat', 44.

From this we might well surmise that Forsyth was operating with a full and robust doctrine of creation and a philosophy of art to match. However, on closer inspection an ambivalence can be detected here, and it is one on which we can usefully dwell. In what follows, I shall argue that, in his writings on art at least, the promise of Forsyth's exposition of *The Scapegoat* is not entirely fulfilled. Despite his patent conviction that the scope of salvation extends beyond humanity, he displays a hesitancy in speaking of the material realm as meaningful and theologically significant in its very materiality, and this, I shall contend, has substantial ramifications for the way he views the nature and purpose of the arts.[14]

2. Religion in Recent Art

To explore this hesitancy further, and in order to set it against the background of the considerable strengths of Forsyth's aesthetics, let me trace some of the leading features of his argument in *Religion in Recent Art*. Written while a minister at Cheetham Hill, the book grew out of a series of talks on an exhibition of paintings in Manchester. He deals not only with works by Hunt but also by Rossetti, Burne-Jones and G. F. Watts – and two chapters are added on Wagner. Forsyth is anxious about what he sees as a gulf between secular art and religious institutions in late nineteenth-century Europe, against the background of what Ruskin called 'the storm-cloud of the nineteenth century' – humanity's alienation from nature and the disintegration of culture. Forsyth believes that the time is ripe for a renewal of religious art which will take due account of the lessons to be learned from contemporary secular art. 'Religion,' he asserts, 'can revive and regenerate Art.'[15] And it is from the Pre-Raphaelites that we can learn most if we are to encourage and promote such a renewal.

Forsyth believes that artistic renovation is possible only if certain conditions are met. Here I draw attention to two which emerge

---

[14]Ironically, this brings him quite close to some of his non-Christian contemporaries who in their art were questioning the inherent goodness and order of creation and seeing only the naked shingles left by the ebbing sea of faith. On this, cf. Fuller, *Theoria: Art, and the Absence of Grace*, 146ff.

[15]*Art*, 3.

prominently in *Religion and Recent Art*. First, he urges, with substantial courage and penetrating discernment, that we embrace the relative truth of the kind of pessimism which finds philosophical articulation in Schopenhauer and artistic expression in Pre-Raphaelite painting. Such pessimism reveals aspects of the human situation which are an essential part of 'the great dialectical movement which is to bring all things into union with God'.[16] In the paintings of Rossetti, Forsyth detects a 'sultry, tropical feeling', a melancholic world-sorrow, the sorrow of his race and age.[17] There are signs of hope but only a 'broken-hearted hope'. In the picture entitled *Found* – where a man meets the woman he had once married but who has since fallen into ruin – Rossetti has gone to the roots of our 'festering' culture.[18] In G. F. Watts' painting *Hope*, the soul of the age is depicted as having conquered the world. Now she strains to hear just one string of hope, yet her face is turned away from heaven's star. She cannot look beyond the world and see what will give her peace, nor can she bear to look at the world itself, having found merely earthly hopes ephemeral. Certainly, there is more than despair here – for the viewer is given to see that there can be authentic supernatural hope – yet there is no evasion of the plight of our times.[20] Forsyth makes parallel observations about Holman Hunt's work, as evinced in his interpretation of *The Scapegoat*.

The main point to underline is that in Forsyth's eyes, any rejuvenation of religious art cannot ignore the pessimistic tone which imbues these paintings, for Christian faith speaks of a love which 'is made perfect by suffering and enriched by all loss'.[21] His final chapters on Wagner show similar emphases: in these monumental music-dramas – *Parsifal* is singled out for special attention – we hear the depths of the world's cries for forgiveness and redemption. Wagner may not have been a Christian theologian but

---

[16]George Pattison, *Art, Modernity and Faith: Restoring the Image*, 87.

[17]*Art*, 9.

[18]*Art*, 27.

[19]*Art*, 58ff.

[20]*Art*, 107–11. Forsyth's daughter tells us that the writing of *Religion in Recent Art* brought Forsyth into personal friendship with Watts 'who discussed the meaning of his own pictures with [Forsyth], and came to regard him as his best interpreter'. Andrews, 'Memoir', in Forsyth, *Work*, 2nd ed., xiv.

[21]*Art*, 38.

he has every right to be called a Christian anthropologist.[22] So it is that in painting and music which some others were (and are) happy to dismiss as morbidly decadent, Forsyth bids us look and listen harder so that we can discern the addition of a 'deeper note to the great chord of the Cross, and a new chastening to the glory of its close'.[23] (Comparisons with the writings of Paul Tillich are almost inevitable at this point; Tillich was probably the only other major Protestant theologian of modern times to be so bold in his attempt to voice the existential and theological significance of contemporary art.)[24]

Second, the renewal of religious art can only come about through a fresh apprehension of 'Nature' animated by divine Spirit. Disentangling the ontology from the rhetoric here is a demanding task, but 'Nature' in this context appears to refer to the entire material order which in art finds a measure of redemption. The artist does not simply imitate or copy nature; rather nature is interpreted through the artist's soul, through the conscious intentionality of human spirit.[25] This human spirit becomes in art a medium of the divine Spirit, which is the Spirit or soul of Christ ever active within nature. So it emerges that art 'is the interpretation of Nature by Spirit'.[26] It 'is the process of Nature prolonged, turned back, and applied to Nature herself'.[27] And hence through art we are given to see nature in a new way, as permeated by infinite Spirit.

Despite the opaqueness of the argument, some such broad scheme provides the backdrop to Forsyth's declaration of the Pre-

[22]*Art*, 209–316. Generally more sympathetic to Wagner than to Schopenhauer, because – among other things – of the former's realization that love conquers death, Forsyth believes that 'no artist of any kind … has ever realised as Wagner did in his own way the moral depth and sting of [our] need for redemption, in the sense of a total conversion of the soul and deliverance of the race from the universal burden and unspeakable curse'. *Art*, 235. Forsyth's daughter recounts how a rich friend enabled him to attend the first performance of *Parsifal* in 1882; 'henceforth it always seemed to my father a sacrament rather than an opera'. Andrews, 'Memoir', xiii.

[23]*Art*, 251. For a radically different and negative Christian verdict on the Pre-Raphaelites, cf. H. R. Rookmaaker, *Modern Art and the Death of a Culture* (London: Inter Varsity, 1970), 75.

[24]Cf. Jeremy S. Begbie, *Voicing Creation's Praise* (Edinburgh T&T Clark, 1991), part 1.

[25]*Art*, 89ff.

[26]*Art*, 147.

[27]*Art*, 90.

Raphaelites. Through Rossetti, Burne-Jones, Watts and Hunt, he charts a progressive intensification of the Christian truth that ultimately reality is not earthly beauty nor earthly sorrow but divine Spirit. Holman Hunt's work stands at the climax of this development: he, supremely, is able to paint according to what Forsyth terms the 'spirit of the resurrection', that is, in a way which demonstrates that God is 'self-buried' in the natural world and ascending continually 'from the Holy Sepulchre of Nature'.[28] The following quotation will serve to give an indication of the direction of his thesis:

> The effect of the doctrine of the Resurrection is to consecrate the truth and reality of Nature, to make us realise that we live in a world wholly redeemed and continually rising, that the visible world is full of divine suggestion, full in every vein of the ceaseless striving after a crown of spiritual perfection, straining in universal evolution after a fuller expression of itself than its own material sphere allows, and waiting in strenuous patience for the relief of utterance in the manifestation of the Sons of God. It is such a manifestation, in one sense, when the artist comes to give Nature an organ for self-expression, and the spirit in Nature a vehicle of self-revelation.... . Nature, in her wonderful veracity, her fixity of law, her fluidity of process, her swell of evolution, is rising with Christ; and so rising that she is fit to express the enhanced powers of the Spirit of Europe, as Christ ascends through its growing insight and its enforced obedience to the divine law.[29]

Of course, we are still in 1889. However, notwithstanding the massive theological gear-changes to come, a number of important features of the argument in *Religion in Recent Art* were retained and carried forward into Forsyth's later aesthetic reflections. Two in particular are worth highlighting for our purposes. First – and this relates to our earlier discussion of the rainbow – there is virtually no recognition of the physical aspects of art and artistic activity as being significant in their own right. So eager is Forsyth to hurry our

[28] *Art*, 159.
[29] *Art*, 158.

perception on to the non-material realm, very little attention is given to the intensely sensuous and physical character of most artistic creation – mixing pigment, twanging strings, chipping stone – and, we might add, to the physical character of our encounter with most art. Second, supporting this at a deeper level, we find very little to suggest that Forsyth is keen to affirm the material world as meaningful *in its very materiality*. Forsyth does indeed argue that all art must cease if we believe nature is fundamentally cursed.[30] And, it should be acknowledged, arguments from silence are invariably perilous. But this is more than an argument from silence. As we have observed, there are more than a few signs that the physical realm is consistently being treated as something to be looked *through* in such a way that insufficient status is being given to it in its own distinctive, created modes of being. As George Pattison acutely asks of Forsyth's view of *The Scapegoat*, 'is nature really being taken in its own terms or is it simply being used by the artist as a "means" to a strictly non-natural "end"?'[31] As I have just suggested, a parallel critical question could be asked of Forsyth's account of art itself.

3. Christ on Parnassus

Those familiar with Hegel's aesthetics will have noticed already the Hegelian overtones in Forsyth's early work, and they are even more audible when we come to Forsyth's second major study of art, *Christ on Parnassus* of 1911. With the memory of his dispute with the Idealist R. J. Campbell still fresh in his mind, he turns, of all people, to Hegel for inspiration. He declares at the outset: 'I am preaching Hegel, not, I hope, without judgement, but certainly as the text I expound.'[32] Needless to say, he offers us baptized Hegel, even if not by full immersion. Rather than try to outline the similarities and

---

[30]*Art*, 144.

[31]Pattison, *Art, Modernity and Faith*, 95.

[32]He is referring to Hegel's lectures in aesthetics, gathered and first published after his death in 1835; cf. G. W. F. Hegel, *Aesthetics* (London: Oxford University Press, 1975). Forsyth's dependency on Hegel may go a large part of the way in explaining why *Christ on Parnassus* receives so little attention from commentators on Forsyth. Cf. Ralph C. Wood, 'Christ on Parnassus', 85. One participant at the Aberdeen conference described the book to me as an 'aberrant work'.

differences,[33] my main concern here will be to show something of the manner in which the two strands I have traced in *Religion in Recent Art* are drawn out and elaborated.

In this compelling and often puzzling work, Forsyth's stated aim is to show that Christianity has transforming power over the whole of human culture: 'a Gospel which saves society must also save culture' he proclaims.[34] In that context an overview is offered of the relation between Christianity and art, concentrating on the on-going struggle between human spirit and the natural order. Like Hegel, his account is both historical, in that he follows lines of development through different historical epochs, and relational, in that he attempts to delineate the structural interrelationships of the arts one to another.

In Greek religion, according to Forsyth, an equilibrium or harmony was thought to exist between humanity and nature which gave a powerful impetus to the arts. In Indo-European civilizations, the human spirit was dominated by nature's vastness; in Egyptian culture, the human spirit began to assert itself, symbolized by the sphinx – a human form struggling free from its animal embodiment. In Greece, however, 'man found his own eternal laws imprinted, reflected in Nature, and by a pre-established harmony she became his friend, his ally, his consort'.[35] The material is thought equal to the task of expressing spiritual content, for there is an immanence of God in nature – matter and spirit are in complete accord – and in this setting art is enabled to flourish. The great failing of the Greeks was their fixation with natural harmony and their conse-quent inclination to conflate the ethical and the aesthetic. They had little sense of the inadequacy of nature as a vehicle of spirit, and lacked a conception of an infinite divine love plunging into the depths of the human condition and forging a more abiding *moral* reconciliation between God and humanity.[36]

In Hebrew religion, the primary axis is not that between the human and natural, but the relation of human and divine spirit. This is the most important reason for the virtual absence of art in

[33]Cf. Dr Russell's essay in this volume.
[34]*Parnassus*, viii.
[35]*Parnassus*, 11.
[36]*Parnassus*, 1–42.

Hebrew culture. God's shrine is in the human soul, not in nature, nor in art. Forsyth quips that 'a lecture on Hebrew Art is like the chapter on lions in Norway'.[37] God is a moral Self who is known and symbolized through moral relations, which are inward, invisible, unrepresentable. If the Greeks idealized nature, the Hebrews spiritualized it and passed beyond it.[38] Hence the Jews' attraction to the least sensuous of the arts, namely poetry.[39] Despite producing little art, however, because of their refusal to idolize nature, the Hebrews did bequeath to later generations a new confidence that nature need not be thought of as an enemy but could be approached confidently in the interests of serving the one true God.

And so to the climax. Following Hegel, we move from Greek through Hebrew to 'Romantic' or Christian art. If Hellenism represents the principle of divine immanence and Hebraism the principle of divine transcendence, then Christianity manifests the immanence of the transcendent, the divine loving infinity amongst us. Here Hebrew inwardness is combined with Greek outwardness.[40] Jewish confidence in spiritual reality is allowed to express itself freely in the external beauty of nature and art. The material creation is found to be a friend though certainly not to be worshipped. Forsyth writes: 'To the Greek the world was his familiar home, to the Jew only his inn.'[41] Forsyth wants to combine both and speak of nature as the proper environment for which we were made, as showing forth God's power, character and intent, and as being in intimate relation with God. Yet at the same time, Forsyth's sense of the finitude and impermanence of creation leads to his eschewing any variety of monism, pantheism and the notion of creation as God's body.[42] Our principal orientation in art, as in any part of culture, should be towards the Creator. It is in this connection that

[37] *Parnassus*, 45.

[38] *Parnassus*, 62.

[39] *Parnassus*, 60. There is a surface inconsistency in Forsyth in this respect, for he is also capable of calling music the most spiritual of the arts (*Parnassus*, 195; 'Music And Worship' [1955], 342). However, it is clear from the argument of *Christ on Parnassus* as a whole that his overriding conviction – along with Hegel – is that poetry is to be accorded pride of place in this respect.

[40] *Parnassus*, 82.

[41] *Parnassus*, 84.

[42] *Parnassus*, 80ff.

Pre-Raphaelite art makes its only appearance in the book: as exemplifying the Christian conviction that 'the wealth of Nature's beauty is but the reflection of the immanent beauty of the Infinite Spirit, who moves and lives and has His Being in it all'.[43]

Christian art itself, Forsyth continues, follows a distinct course of development. Again taking his cue from Hegel, Forsyth discerns a movement from painting through music to poetry, and interprets this as a procession of increasing spiritualization, a 'progressive attenuation of the material' which displays the impact of a religion which hinges chiefly on a spiritual, moral reconciliation between humanity and God. The metaphysical context of this is provided by the notion that divine Spirit – which Forsyth is also content to call the 'Idea' – is 'entombed within material Nature' and comes to self-realization through the artist.[44]

With limited space, I shall have to confine myself to only a few remarks on Forsyth's treatment of the three Christian art-forms: painting, music, poetry. Painting is praised as an advance over architecture and sculpture because its materiality – merely a flat surface – need not obscure the dynamics of spiritual life, nor obtrude between artist and spectator. Forsyth comments on the way in which painting works through illusion and takes this to correspond 'with the inwardness and spirituality of Christianity – which teaches us that the outward and sensuous is but a reflection of spiritual reality, not reality itself, which is in the soul'.[45] The following sentences are particularly revealing:

> Christianity ... repaired the discord of the world in terms, not of matter, but of spirit.... . It was inward, spiritual, and free. The art, therefore, which would reflect it should tend to this inwardness, this spirituality, this moral freedom. It should direct our attention away from material things, ... passing away into the spiritual world. It must use, as its organ or medium, a form of matter so fine as to be just on the borderland where sense ceases and soul begins. A solid substance like marble does not satisfy this condition. An

[43] *Parnassus*, 80.
[44] *Parnassus*, 259–60.
[45] *Parnassus*, 123.

ethereal substance like light or colour does; sculpture therefore is not spiritual, painting is.[46]

In music, the material all but vanishes.[47] Now there is no surface,
only time and tone. We listen to a Beethoven symphony in
performance, but it never, as it were, coagulates to form a thing. It
lives on only in its audience. Properly speaking, it only exists in the
human soul (and the soul of God). Instead of speaking of the
external world, music plunges 'us into our own soul's depths,
explores with us the winging ways of passion, and wakes us to the
knowledge of a whole vibrant world within'.[48] In other words, music
is primarily concerned with the expression of our emotional life,[49]
although, as such, it can gather up particular and private human
responses into the pulse of the eternal life which sweeps through
creation.[50] The distinctive drawback of music is its indefiniteness, its
ambiguity, which can quickly lead to an undisciplined flight from
truth and goodness: music can encourage us 'to dwell ... in a vague
world of formless impulse, lawless emotion, vacant yearning, and
impossible dreams'.[51]

This is why, with Hegel, Forsyth believes that music must be
dialectically transcended by poetry, under which heading he includes all imaginative literature. Poetry combines the spirituality of
music (which painting lacks) with the definiteness of painting
(which music lacks). 'The Art which crowns the edifice of Art,' he
says, 'must have the fine spirituality of music, but also the faithful
drawing and colouring of painting, and both on another plane.'[52]
Poetry paints pictures, not in colour on canvas but in ideas on the
mind. It also uses sound but only as a medium for the expression of
non-material ideas.[53] Hence, in poetry we have the spiritualization
of art taken to its peak: poetry is the 'most perfect of all the single
arts'.[54] And, precisely because of its spirituality it is the art which is

---

[46] *Parnassus*, 106.
[47] It is 'the most sacramental' of all the arts, *Parnassus*, 199.
[48] *Parnassus*, 192.
[49] *Parnassus*, 203–4, 229.
[50] *Parnassus*, 214–15.
[51] *Parnassus*, 208.
[52] *Parnassus*, 231–2.
[53] *Parnassus*, 235–6.
[54] *Parnassus*, 236.

the most supple and flexible in the service of Christian religion. Through its narrative it can represent all the subtleties of divine spiritual process and yet simultaneously be quite specific.[55]

A telling illustration of his view of the relation between poetry and music can be found in an article on 'Music and Worship' of 1914. Forsyth reiterates his views on the spirituality of music – the 'sense medium is almost refined away' – and goes on to comment on the need which 'the great musicians' have felt to crown music with 'intelligible world'. The classic case, he believes, is Beethoven's ninth symphony, where with the entrance of the choir in the last movement 'poetry comes to the rescue of music' in order 'to save it from inadequacy and collapse'.[56]

In the preface to *Christ on Parnassus*, Forsyth makes it clear that he sees himself as less dependent on Hegel in the final part of the book. And indeed it is here, as he develops what Ralph Wood calls an 'evangelical critique of the arts',[57] that we find the major theological shifts of the previous two decades most evident. Now deliberately distancing himself from the Idealist tradition, Forsyth insists that in Christ we encounter an irreducibly new act from beyond, outwith the immanent capabilities of creation, which finds its culmination in the definitive moral reconciliation achieved on the cross. Art may be able to construct a new world within the old but it cannot atone or reconcile us to the Creator.[58] To believe otherwise is to fall into idolatry, to accord ultimacy to something finite and sensuous. Art provides proximal, but not final, truth. In the opening pages of the book, we should bear in mind, Forsyth had declared that he was aiming to convince the reader that art is the 'servant and representative, though not the vassal of Faith, to be surrounded with all the state and honour due to the ambassador of a mighty king, but no more to be placed in supreme control of life than an angel is to be put in supreme charge of home or State'.[59] *Christ* must reign on Parnassus in order to redeem the failure of even the greatest artistic achievements. Only in this way may art be used as a faithful servant of religion in the transformation of culture.

[55]Poetry 'comes nearer than any art to that spirit of infinite and redeeming love which is the soul of religion', *Parnassus*, 238.

[56]'Music and Worship', 342ff.

[57]Ralph C. Wood, 91.

[58]*Parnassus*, 260–97.

[59]*Parnassus*, 4.

We are, then, presented with a very marked concrete Christological focus in the last chapters. Nevertheless, questions can legitimately be asked about the extent to which this was allowed to shape Forsyth's theological outlook on creation as a whole, and, linked to this, the way he conceives the distinctive nature of the arts as such. Interestingly, in *Christ on Parnassus* the characteristic Forsythian theme of the uniqueness and decisiveness of the historical Christ assumes a mainly critical function, serving to eradicate any claims for the ultimacy of art. In short, it is put to work in the refutation of idolatry. What it does not do is play a major role in the construction of a positive theology of art in the earlier parts of the book. With this in mind, it is instructive to draw attention to the ways in which the two strands I spoke of in his earlier work have been extended and developed. The first was an inclination to abstract art and aesthetic experience from its physical embeddedness. The fact that the sensory matrix of an artwork and its physical presence are integral to its being and to its perceived value, and the fact that when we inscribe marks on paper, pile stone on stone or whatever, 'we are dealing with things which bear to us the most intimate of relation'[60] – such matters receive scant attention in *Christ on Parnassus*. To be sure, in one place he speaks of the material element in art being inseparably related to the idea communicated but very quickly proceeds to downgrade the material in comparison with the unseen world to which he believes art should be constantly directing our gaze.[61] The overall thrust of his argument is better represented by passages such as the following:

> We must have some sensuous element in all Art, else it ceases to be art; but the object in artistic development is to transcend, rarefy, and throw down that element as much as possible, consistently with exalting in a real way the ideal and spiritual element. The competition among the arts, so to speak, is like a tea race between China clippers. It is to combine the maximum of spiritual cargo with the minimum of material tonnage.[62]

[60]Nicholas Wolterstorff, *Art in Action* (Grand Rapids, Michigan: Eerdmans, 1988), 70–1.

[61]*Parnassus*, 258.

[62]*Parnassus*, 235.

In propounding such views, Forsyth is hardly alone in Western aesthetics. He has many predecessors and successors.[63] (One way of reading some of the more vaporous examples of post-modern art is as extreme instances of a long-term and pervasive Western suspicion about the inherent rationality of matter.) But whatever its history and antecedents, it is an outlook which has met with a considerable force of criticism in recent years from a myriad of theologians and philosophers – for example, John Dixon, Nicholas Wolterstorff, John Dillenberger, Aidan Nichols, George Pattison.[64] Despite their differences, these scholars generally operate with somewhat stronger ontologies of creation than we find in Forsyth – they are less anxious about 'material tonnage' impeding the movement of 'spiritual cargo'.

This brings us to the second strand in Forsyth noted earlier, concerning the inherent meaningfulness of matter. To be sure, Forsyth does not oppose matter to form as if it were intrinsically chaotic or distorted. Unlike Hegel, he clearly holds that nature is imbued with meaning apart from human spirit. Moreover, he can show a strong wish to do justice to the particularities, details and contingencies of creation. Even his very brief observations on the Pre-Raphaelites in *Christ on Parnassus* bear this out.[65] And he can even speak of the artist wooing Nature in love.[66] Nevertheless, there is an identifiable and somewhat stronger momentum in a rather different direction which renders his attitude to the finite physical order, and to specific conformations of matter within it, decidedly uneasy. His account of Old Testament religion drastically overplays God's freedom from creation at the expense of his relation to it. In writing of the incarnation, Forsyth seems to have large hesitations,

---

[63]Cf. Colin Gunton, 'Creation and Re-Creation: An Exploration of Some Themes in Aesthetics and Theology', *Modern Theology* 2 (1985): 1–19; and Gunton, 'Particularity and the Transcendentality of the One: Toward a Recovery of the Doctrine of Substance', unpublished paper delivered at the Society for the Study of Theology, 29 March 1993, at the University of Cardiff.

[64]John Dixon, *Nature and Grace in Art* (Chapel Hill: University of North Carolina Press, 1964); Wolterstorff, *Art in Action*; John Dillenberger, *A Theology of Artistic Sensibilities* (London: SCM Press Ltd., 1987); Aidan Nichols, *The Art of God Incarnate* (London: Darton, Longman & Todd, 1980); Pattison, *Art, Modernity and Faith*.

[65]*Parnassus*, 80.

[66]*Parnassus*, 269f.

not about God's presence to the world in Christ, but about the created materiality of that presence, the full penetration and engagement of the incarnate Son in the network of limited (and fallen) creation. In a recent article on *Christ on Parnassus*, Ralph Wood remarks that 'Forsyth's concern with the soul's pure inwardness makes him embarrassed at its naked outward embodiment'.[67] A less sympathetic commentator writes that 'Dr Forsyth did not very much like the sort of flesh the Word became'.[68] However unfair that jibe may be, the link between the Son's incarnation and the renewal of the whole created order is conspicuous by its absence in Forsyth's writings on art. Little is made of the possibility that the material world's innate meaningfulness might in some way be affirmed by the enfleshment of the one through whom all things took shape, and that here the arts might find a profound theological grounding. Just as telling is the failure to make any link between the cross and the redemption of the whole creation, as in Colossians 1.20 (cp. Eph 1.7–10). The theme of the moral reconciliation of divine and human spirit seems to have largely eclipsed the wider, cosmic implications of Calvary (and Easter)[69] and consequently the possibility of relating art to God's redemption of the entire created order.

Other essays in this volume allude to this area of weakness in Forsyth's theology.[70] The extent to which it can be traced to his

---

[67]Wood, 88.

[68]Gilbert Cope, review of *Parnassus*, 388. It should be noted that here Cope has in mind principally Forsyth's wariness of emotion, but the phrase can still serve to pinpoint a serious weakness in Forsyth. It may be that there are connections here with Forsyth's sceptical attitude to certain schools of biblical criticism which over-concerned themselves with detailed verisimilitude. Forsyth is ready to praise Hunt's love of particularity and veracity. (Hunt fiercely rejected what he saw as the sceptical historical criticism of people like Renan and D. F. Strauss, believing that a concern for historical accuracy can go hand in hand with a living faith.) Indeed, Forsyth attacks those who would ignore the concrete history of Jesus of Nazareth. But consistently the thrust of his argument is that we should look *beyond* and *through* historical forms to apprehend the dynamic of divine Spirit. Cf. e.g. *Art*, 155ff., 163ff.

[69]The virtual absence of any mention of the resurrection of Christ is another notable feature of *Christ on Parnassus*.

[70]J. H. Rodgers writes: 'One wonders whether Forsyth really does justice to the significance of the physical realm, to creation. He treats it teleologically, under the rubric of history, but does he really reflect the Biblical appreciation and joy in the earthly blessings of the Lord? perhaps he has remained too much under the influence of Ritschl at this point. It is good to be a redeemed person, but redeemed in the body.' Rodgers, *The Theology of P. T. Forsyth*, 264.

indebtedness to Hegel is a complex issue and one taken up more fully in Dr Russell's chapter.[71] My focus here is on what Forsyth has to say at the interface of theology and the arts, and the chief question I am left asking is whether or not the Christian affirmation of the distinctive rationality of the contingent creation, established, judged and renewed in Christ, has been allowed to mould adequately his reflections on art. The rainbow, so to speak, never quite seems to touch the ground. Very tentatively, it might be said that we require a more central place to be given to the agency of Christ as creator, in whose incarnate humanity the integrity of the finite world is restored; a greater stress on the distinctive and particular agency of the Holy Spirit as the one who promotes creation to be genuinely itself and renews it in the image of Christ; and a more pointed accent on *creatio ex nihilo* and thus on the liberty of the creation in its contingent otherness.[72]

4. The 'Spirituality' of Music?

It would be a serious error to forget Forsyth's major purpose in *Christ on Parnassus* – to demonstrate that Christianity has, and can still have, a transformative impact on culture through the arts. That we have registered some reservations about the theology and aesthetics which Forsyth employs need not weaken our support of this overarching concern. However, in an effort to promote that concern while avoiding some of the more dubious features of Forsyth's own approach, perhaps we might be allowed to engage with Forsyth on his own ground with regard to just one of the arts, namely music.

[71]For a clear discussion of this issue with respect to the arts, see Pattison, *Art, Modernity and Faith*, 95ff. Where I find myself disagreeing with Pattison is in connection with his claim that Forsyth's tendency to treat art as an allegory is not an immediate or obvious consequence of his system but only of the way he applies it (Pattison, 98). As will be obvious by now, I believe there are good reasons to suppose the tendency derives chiefly from significant weaknesses in Forsyth's theology, especially in his doctrine of creation.

[72]Elsewhere, I have tried to outline what a theological aesthetics which proceeds along these lines might look like. Cf. Begbie, *Voicing Creation's Praise*. For a particularly astute treatment of the doctrine of creation in relation to Christology and pneumatology, cf. Gunton, *Christ and Creation* (Carlisle: Paternoster, 1992).

We recall that Forsyth regards music as the least material of the arts, except for poetry. Like so many before him, he is struck by its impermanence and insubstantiality – where is the symphony once the last chord has sounded?, its inwardness – it primarily arises from, and is directed towards our emotional life, and its indefiniteness – wherein resides its greatest weakness. Linking these is the basic belief that music is essentially concerned with releasing us from the bonds and limits of the finite and material order. Theologically, this makes it superior to painting, sculpture and architecture, where materiality and spatiality are present in the finished artwork.

In contrast, it can be contended – and here I follow, among others, the Austrian musicologist Victor Zuckerkandl – that music functions chiefly not by liberating us from the temporal and spatial but by opening up and deepening our engagement with time and space, and with concrete finite being. Zuckerkandl points to what he calls the 'the dynamic quality of tones': music is the product not merely of individual notes but also of their interrelationships one to another. These relations are intrinsic to the particular notes themselves; they are not imposed by us, nor incidental. The constituent sounds of a piece of music thus demonstrate a way of being in relation which, though short-lived and evanescent, is nevertheless substantial. Moreover, Zuckerkandl seeks to demonstrate that the relationships between the successive notes of a piece of music are irreducible to strictly acoustical or indeed psychological analysis – it is *time* which reveals itself to the ear as a function of the relationship between concrete notes. Similar arguments can be advanced with respect to music and space. Far from drawing us ineluctably away from spatiality, music can afford – even through a simple chord, for instance – the experience of a relational kind of space which involves distinction but not exclusive juxtaposition, an apprehension of space as an irreducible dimension of concrete entities.[73] It is perhaps no surprise to find physicists such as Capek, and more recently biologist Arthur Peacocke, suggesting that musical models of space be explored and employed much more extensively.[74]

[73]V. Zuckerkandl, *Sound and Symbol* (London: Routledge and Kegan Paul, 1956); and Zuckerkandl, *Man the Musician* (Princeton: Princeton University Press, 1973).
[74]M. Capek, *The Philosophical Impact of Contemporary Physics* (Princeton: Van Nostrand, 1961), 371ff.; Arthur Peacocke, *Theology for a Scientific Age* (Oxford: Blackwell, 1980), 173–7.

Reflection on the activity of making music suggests similar conclusions. Especially instructive in this regard is the practice of improvisation, which many musicologists would view as revealing fundamental practices at the root of all musical activity. Without written music, the relation between performer and instrument is seen to be especially close. You are directly aware of the instrument you are playing, its limitations and possibilities. You become acutely conscious of the sounds themselves: in so far as making music is a thought process, it is not so much imposing a grid of pure thought on acoustic phenomena, it is rather thinking in notes and rhythms; not thinking on to them or through them but thinking *in* physical sound. You indwell these physical realities, showing them respect and courtesy. It has been said that an improviser helps a theme along, provides the dynamic field within which the music may take place. One is aware too of one's embodiedness in particularly intense ways. Étienne Gilson, in *Painting and Reality*, argues that the painter's hand is not a mere tool subservient to the mind or imagination; the hand is usually integral to the conception of the work. Gilson comments: 'One of the main reasons painters find it so hard to make themselves understood ... is that their hearers listen with their minds only, not with their hands.'[75] In his compelling book, *Ways of the Hand*, David Sudnow describes in exhaustive detail the process of learning to improvise jazz on the piano, repeatedly stressing that it is essentially 'embodied conduct', entailing profound trust in the momentum of one's hands.[76] These and other aspects of improvisation, it has been urged, rather than representing a distortion of what music-making is all about, serve to bring to the fore basic aspects of all musical activity, whether explicitly acknowledged as 'improvisatory' or not.

If such arguments have any substantial weight – and we acknowledge that they would require a good deal more justification and elaboration than is possible here – Forsyth's assumption that the essence of music is to abstract us from what is finite and limited is seen to be distinctly problematic. Music would seem to offer us particularly intense engagements with physical, material realities

[75]As cited in Zuckerkandl, *Sound and Symbol*, 276.
[76]David Sudnow, *Ways of the Hand: The Organisation of Improvised Conduct* (London: Routledge & Kegan Paul, 1978).

and with time and space as intrinsic dimensions of created existence. Moreover, his belief that music works chiefly through emotional evocation and stimulation is also thrown into question. (Indeed, all purely subjectivist theories of music – where the meaning of music is said to lie solely in the responses or projections of the hearer or composer – are undermined by the contentions of those such as Zuckerkandl.) Music is undeniably often ambiguous – certainly one of the most ambiguous of all the arts – but we need not follow Forsyth in his propensity to run together ambiguity, infinity, spirituality and inwardness. Significantly, whereas Forsyth insists that music does not speak of the external world, Zuckerkandl subtitles his first book 'Music and the External World'.[77]

The positive upshot of this brief musical conversation with Forsyth, however, is that the phenomenon of music might usefully be considered as a field of enormous potential assistance in articulating a doctrine of creation less prone to the weaknesses we find in Forsyth, one in which configurations of matter are allowed intrinsic significance, and one which encourages us to believe that we can entrust ourselves more fully to the physical world we inhabit and find in it a rich texture of meaning and value. Music, far from strengthening Forsyth's own case about the spiritualization of the arts, will I believe severely weaken it, but in the process, something might arise which can better advance Forsyth's laudable desire to see the arts as vehicles for the renewal of culture.

5. The Rainbow Revisited

This brings me, finally, back to the rainbow. Earlier, we mentioned in passing the work of Peter Fuller. Though an avowed atheist, in his last book, *Theoria*, he found much to praise in Forsyth, above all the theologian's resistance to any form of reductionism. In Fuller's own quest for contemporary painting which offers a non-reductionist, non-atomistic depiction of nature in its depth and beauty, he speaks warmly of a number of recent Australian landscape artists. Australia, of course, largely a desert land, littered (like Hunt's wilderness) with skulls and carcasses, a giant *memento mori*. Yet these painters, some

---

[77]Zuckerkandl, *Sound and Symbol.*

of them deliberately echoing Hunt, have sought to find what Fuller calls 'living values' in the intractable barrenness.[78] It may be that here we glimpse some examples of a more convincing promise of creation's deliverance from decay than in Forsyth (or Hunt) without any evasion of its fallenness and dissolution. To cite just one example, Arthur Boyd in his *Nebuchadnezzar* series offers a striking depiction of the Old Testament king driven away from his people and at the mercy of natural forces (Dan 4.33ff.) – a lion and screaming crows become symbolic of the ferocity and menace of the natural world. In one painting, however, 'Lion's Head in a Cave with Rainbow', we are presented with an arching rainbow, and the renewal of the earth of which it speaks has already begun to take effect – shown, among other ways, in the lion's head being transfigured in silver light. Here, in pigment, shape and colour, creation has begun to lose what Hegel called its 'inflexible foreignness'.[79]

In *The Waste Land*, T. S. Eliot wrote: 'Come in under the shadow of this red rock/And I will show you something different.' If I may be so bold as to adapt these words, we would say that we have been made to stand and stare by Forsyth under the red rock of Hunt's painting but that we have chosen to see something rather different from Forsyth in the created world depicted therein. That we have been pressed to do *both* witnesses to the extraordinary power of this man's theological determination to take art seriously. We sorely need others of his stature who, even if full of care, will make time to stand and stare.

[78]Fuller, *Theoria: Art, and the Absence of Grace*, 218–33.
[79]Hegel, *Aesthetics*, 31.

Chapter 12

SPOILING THE EGYPTIANS:[1] P. T. FORSYTH AND HEGEL

Stanley Russell

In what is probably the most personal of his works, *Positive Preaching and the Modern Mind*, Forsyth, who is generally very reticent on such matters, gives us a brief but telling sketch of his intellectual development. Speaking of the early influence of Maurice and Ritschl, he then goes on: 'I immersed myself in the Logic of Hegel, and corrected it by the theology of Paul, and its continuity in the Reformation.'[2] Over Forsyth's Paulinism there can be no question, though it would be interesting to trace his particular selection of the various motifs within the apostle's theology. It is the reference to Hegel which comes as the great surprise, and the aim of this paper is to show his ability in wrestling with, and utilizing, a great thinker about whose overall position he had very serious reservations. This engagement is not altogether easy to trace, for though Forsyth did not on occasion disdain the footnote, he hardly provides anything in the way of thorough documentation for the source of the ideas which he uses. It was not his fortune, or misfortune, to have had to produce a Ph.D thesis as part of his academic development.

We note, first of all, his reference to the 'Logic' of Hegel, but this word needs to be taken in a very loose sense indeed, for very little of Forsyth's argumentation falls into the dialectical mode reminiscent

---

[1] This phrase seems to have entered Christian theology with Origen's Letter to Gregory Thaumaturgus.
[2] *Preaching*, 3rd ed., 195.

of the great master. In fact, when he does develop his case in such a manner, he goes out of his way to tell us what he is doing, as for example at the beginning of chapter 6 of *The Person and Place of Jesus Christ*, where he is discussing the nature of revelation he says: 'So that we have three things – first the incarnate fact, then, the word or interpretation of it by apostles, and, thereby, the fact again, but enshrined in the soul of the believing Church. To use philosophical terms, we have the thesis, planting itself out in an antithesis, and, then reclaiming, recovering itself in a synthesis.'[3] That, however, is a rarity, though it is significant to note that the one work which he produced in the field of the theological interpretation of history falls into just such a pattern. So, in *Faith, Freedom and the Future*, the conflict between the Calvinist and Anabaptist tendencies is depicted as producing the genius of English Congregationalism. Though this one work is too little to go on, it may suggest that Forsyth would put on Hegelian spectacles when it came to trying to discern patterns within history.

There is certainly no doubt that Forsyth had the highest intellectual regard for Hegel; for him he was 'the greatest philosopher the world ever saw'.[4] Yet beyond this acknowledgment, Forsyth had the deepest reservations concerning his achievement and its consequences for Christian theology. Primarily, as he saw it, Hegel had made the fundamental mistake of considering human spiritual development in terms of a process rather than as arising out of moral action:

> Any theology that places us in a spiritual *process*, or native movement between the finite and the infinite, depreciates the value of spiritual *act*, and thus makes us independent of the grace of God. Its movement is processional, spectacular, aesthetic, it is not historic, dramatic, tragic or ethical. If it speaks of the grace of God it does not take it with moral seriousness. It understands by God's grace no more than the Idea moving to transcend our error, or love acting in generosity, or in pity. It reduces mercy to a form of pity by abolishing the claim of holiness, the gravity of sin, and the action of an Atonement.[5]

[3] *Person*, 159.
[4] *Work*, 60.
[5] *Preaching*, 146; see also 229; *Work*, 67; *Person*, 95; and *Justification*, 2nd ed., 56–7.

As Forsyth saw it, the real distinction between liberal and positive theology was that the former was concerned with God's involvement in the world process, whilst the latter concentrated upon his moral action.[6] From this fundamental cleavage in outlook certain other things followed: to conceive of the world primarily in terms of process did not do justice to individuals, who were the real makers of history, not some immanent cunning of *Geist*:[7] 'Could a personal soul be judged by a mere historic process?'[8] It meant, therefore, that judgement was essentially transcendent to history, not just worked out in the ongoing development. On the other hand, the result of the Hegelian tendency is that 'it drops us to a moving series of integrations and eliminations with no law but causation, no values but those that are relative, and no standard to measure whether movement is progress, or evolution is development to any end'.[9] Furthermore, it moves the centre of the faith from Christ and his historic, personal accomplishment to Christianity in its ongoing development; 'the spinal cord has the same value as the brain it prolongs.'[10] Inevitably, such an attitude has certain consequences in our basic moral assessment of the world in that it undermines any significant recognition of the holiness of God, which for Forsyth was the primal category in our acknowledgment of the divine.[11] When it comes to dealing with the problem of evil, it only provides us with an anodyne solution, in presuming that the evil which surrounds us is but the necessary preliminary to the furtherance of a greater good, and that if we could rise to the height of a more universal contemplation we should be satisfied.[12] In what Forsyth says about Hegelianism and its consequences, we can detect all the main charges directed against this position by Kierkegaard, a writer with whom he was acquainted, though in this particular matter hardly dependent upon for his assessment of the issues.[13] Also like

---

[6] *Preaching*, 165.

[7] *Justification*, 51.

[8] *Cruciality*, 2nd ed., 83.

[9] See whole passage; *Justification*, 201–2.

[10] *Preaching*, 154.

[11] *Preaching*, 161–2.

[12] *Justification*, 141–2.

[13] Forsyth was one of the few people in Britain in the first decade of the century who had some acquaintance with the Dane's thought. He calls him the 'Pascal of the North' (*Authority*, 2nd ed., 71), and says that he and Emerson represent the two

the Dane, Forsyth is aware that Hegelianism had effected a transmutation and dilution of classical Christian terminology.[14]

There were other consequences implicit in Hegel's position of which Forsyth was deeply aware. It tended to undermine the objectivity of God, who became rather a projection of our own consciousness, and who eventually might be dispensed with altogether: 'Even in the great idealisms like Hegel's we are asked so to view the whole procession of being as the expansion of our rational selves that a real visitation from an objective God is but a way of putting things.'[15] God becomes the name we give to the imposition of our own subjectivity upon the cosmos.[16] Though Forsyth gives no overt recognition of the path taken by Feuerbach and the left-wing Hegelians, he is well aware of what was implicit within the overall position.

Moreover, Forsyth saw Hegelianism as being reactionary in the sense that the emphasis upon morality and personal faith gained by the Reformation was likely to be lost in a new scholasticizing of doctrine. What initially seemed to offer so much in construing the centrality of Christ for faith would only degenerate into a new form of intellectualism, which ignored his work of moral redemption. Salvation was falsely conceived of in terms of knowledge rather than renewal by the Holy. 'Knowledge is for life not life for knowledge.'[17] Once reconciliation is thought of in such terms, a complete change in spiritual attitude is bound to occur, the dominant note no longer being that of communion but rather resignation.

> But this Christian idea of reconciliation, this idea of communion with the living and holy God, is replaced in philosophic theology by another idea, that, namely, of adjustment

poles of modern religion (*Authority*, 203). How many of Kierkegaard's writings Forsyth actually knew is difficult to ascertain as he would almost certainly be dependent on the translations and selection provided by Barthold in German. However, Forsyth refers to Kierkegaard's profound grasp of the psychology of sin (*Authority*, 71) which would suggest he knew something of the argument in *Sickness unto Death* and *The Concept of Dread*. Explicit reference is made to *Either/Or* (in *Prayer*, 2nd ed., 61), while a passage in *Preaching* (36–7) seems reminiscent of a part of the argument in *Philosophical Fragments*. Beyond this there is little to go on.

[14] *Work*, 60.

[15] *Authority*, 194; cf. 179.

[16] *Justification*, 73–4.

[17] *Authority*, 179; see also *Person*, 218–19 and *Freedom*, 99.

to a rational Godhead, our adjustment to that mighty idea,
that mighty rational process, which is moving on throughout
the world. Sometimes the Godhead is conceived as personal,
sometimes as impersonal; but in any case reconciliation
would be a resigned adjustment to this great and overwhelm-
ing idea, which, having issued everything, is perpetually
recalling, or exalting, everything into fusion with itself.[18]

If knowledge is the ultimate, salvation could only mean the enerva-
tion rather than the liberation of will.

From this short summary, it can be seen that Forsyth was well-
acquainted with all the points that a positive Reformation theology
would wish to make about Hegelianism. Doubtless all of these could
be gathered from those middle and late nineteenth century German
theologians with whom he was so familiar, for they were certainly
not blind to the shortcomings of their illustrious predecessors at the
beginning of the modern period. yet when this is acknowledged, it
is doubtful whether any of them had such a systematic grasp of what
was at stake in dealing with the Hegelian system. Generally they
made their protest when there was a clash with their own immediate
predilections; only Kierkegaard pursued the antitheses over a com-
parable range. In his handling of Hegel, Forsyth was fully aware of
the implicit challenge to be met with everywhere in the material, and
yet as we shall now see, he was not afraid to use it even in expounding
what to him was the central point of his understanding of the gospel.

All would agree that the atoning death of Christ was at the very
heart of Forsyth's theological position; the '*per crucem ad lucem*' of
his memorial tablet puts it in the most succinct of forms. Moreover,
it was not just the bare apostolic statement, 'Christ died for our sins',
which was foundational for him, but rather it was a very definite
interpretation of that happening which held together his entire
doctrinal enterprise. Remove this and his overall position just
disintegrates. Yet it is here, I wish to argue, that Forsyth takes over
from Hegel the basic material from which his rationale of the
atonement is constructed.

Let me here very briefly outline Forsyth's understanding of the
nature of Christ's atoning work, the position which is outlined in

---

[18] *Work*, 68–9; see also 70ff., and *Justification*, 70–1.

chapters 4–7 of *The Work of Christ* and perhaps most passionately in the concluding chapter of *Positive Preaching and the Modern Mind.* The fundamental and all-inclusive quality of God is his holiness, a term which for Forsyth meant 'absolute moral Reality',[19] and which is determinative for our understanding of all his actions. It is on this quality that the world as a moral order is founded, and it must prevail under all circumstances. Holiness cannot permit itself to be trifled with or set at nought, but if this occurs God's moral aseity must be vindicated at all costs. As a result, where evil occurs God's holiness needs to assert itself by judgement which at the same time exposes the offence for what it is and negates it. Only in such a fashion can God be said to justify himself. Human beings, because of their sinfulness, have violated this order of the holy, and as such judgement for what they are and have done is inevitable. Moreover, as they had sinned by deed, so must the reaction of the holy be. Is there then any way in which the offenders might be reintegrated into the order of the holy? According to Forsyth there is but one possibility, which is, however, precluded from sinful human beings, and that is by a 'due and understanding acknowledgment, of the holiness offended.[20] This, however, is no matter of mere verbal and emotional acknowledgment, for 'if we sin by deed we must so confess'.[21] The specific work of Christ was to accept that judgement on the cross as a member of the human race, and it was only he, because of the holiness of his divine human nature, who could make that proper acknowledgment which was required. Because of this act which consummated the whole significance of Christ's life, it could be said that in the first place God has justified himself; the order of the holy has not been undermined, as an adequate confession of that holiness in judgement has been made by an inclusive representative of the human race. Secondly, because that confession has been made by such a representative, humanity as a whole has been put in the right before God. In this sense, we all belong to a reconciled race. What Forsyth does not really develop to an equivalent extent is how this reconciliation is subjectively appropriated,

[19] *Authority,* 4.
[20] *Work,* 189.
[21] *Work,* 153.

though he does argue that Christ's acknowledgment of the holiness of the Father is the root of all human penitence.[22]

It might be said that what we have here is but a repristinated Anselmic interpretation of the atonement, the great difference being in that satisfaction is offered not to God's honour but to his holiness. Moreover, the disjunction in Anselm between *poena* and *satisfactio* has been overcome, in that Christ satisfies the Father through his entering into the state of penalty in which the judgement on the race is enacted. As Forsyth expressed it: 'He entered the penumbra of [our] judgment.'[23] Such an assessment would indeed place Forsyth's interpretation within the appropriate typology of atonement theories, but it does not account for its distinctive elements. From whence does he derive these notions of a moral order which needs to re-integrate itself through penal judgement inflicted upon the offender, and that the offender himself may be brought back within the order through a proper acknowledgment of the rightness of the penalty inflicted upon him? Whence did he derive the impetus for this significant twist in the tradition?

The solution to this, I believe, is to be found in Hegel's treatment of crime and punishment as delineated in sections 90–103, taken together with 220 in the *Philosophy of Right*. Forsyth never makes mention of this particular work as his source, but as we have seen earlier, he eschews comprehensive documentation of his intellectual sources. From his writings generally, we gain the impression that he was well-acquainted with Hegel at first hand, and in view of his ongoing interest in the political consequences of Christianity, it is unlikely that he would have neglected the *Philosophy of Right*. In any case, Hegel's views on the nature of punishment were certainly known in philosophical circles in Britain at that time, and it is just possible that Forsyth indirectly derived his knowledge of them from such sources.[24]

---

[22]In regard to this aspect of the matter, Forsyth's language tends to become exceptionally opaque: 'The answer is that our repentance was latent in that holiness of His which alone could and must create it, as the effect is really part of the cause – that part of the cause which is prolonged in a polar unity into the sequential conditions of time.' *Work*, 192.

[23] *Work*, 147.

[24]J. M. E. McTaggart, for example contributed an article on 'Hegel's Theory of Punishment' to the *International Journal of Ethics* in 1896.

The *Philosophy of Right* is not one of the writings of Hegel which has specifically theological overtones. For him, the state, justice and politics belonged to the realm of 'objective' rather than 'absolute' Spirit. Before human beings could realize adequately for themselves the truth about the world-process, it was necessary that they should belong to the appropriate social matrix in which reason had incarnated itself in institutional form. As he viewed it, human society was implicitly rational – at the lowest level in the family, then in 'civil society', the entrepreneurial sphere, and finally in the state. Specifically in the area of objective Spirit, rationality took the form of morality, and so this rather than the threefold realm of absolute Spirit, art, religion and philosophy was the appropriate domain of the ethical. The state, in fact, was to be thought of as a moral organism, whose task it was to maintain the right of its members to participate in Spirit as morality at the social level. Therefore, if the right of any one of its members was infringed, either by being deprived of property in which in a sense their subjective spirit inhered, or of their proper freedom, the state needed to act so that such a disruption was negated. If this was not done, the whole structure of morality would in a degree be undermined, and if the state neglected so to act, it would be denying its *raison d'être* as the bearer of Spirit. In other words, the negation of the negation was not an optional task as far as the political order was concerned, but bound up with its very essence. To redress the balance brought about by the infringement of right was an unavoidable obligation.

The more intricate question was how such an upset of moral balance was to be redressed. Hegel's answer was that this was the role of punishment, which was to be conceived of as inflicting some kind of deprivation on the offender to balance the earlier infringement of the moral order. Here, of course, Hegel like all retributionists had to face the Mikado's dilemma of how to make the punishment fit the crime. He rejected the necessity of any crude equivalences as that of the *lex talionis*, but insisted that there must be a certain proportionality between the offence and the retribution. In fact, he allowed that if the state's authority was being generally flouted, it may need to be harsher in the punishments it inflicted in order to maintain itself for what it truly was. To that extent it might be allowed that a certain element of deterrence tended to drift into Hegel's theory. On the other hand, his main thrust still stood: if the state is a moral organism, punishment becomes for it an objective necessity. Then there was the question of the relation of the criminal to the penalty inflicted. The perpetrator of the offence was also a rational being, and therefore had a right that he should be punished for his misdeed. If the moral order neglected to do this, it would be implicitly denying his rationality and foregoing its inherent responsibilities towards him. In other words, the offender should be informed by deed in no uncertain fashion as to his proper position in regard to the order. Presumably, insofar as he wholeheartedly accepted this judgement, his own re-integration with that order was made possible. Thus the maintenance by the state of its own moral authority through judgement made possible the rehabilitation of the offender as a rational member of that order.

Now what it appears Forsyth has done to lift this schema of the state as the moral order and transpose it to that of the Holy. God establishes his holiness by exposing and overthrowing evil through judgement, and yet by the vicarious endurance of this same judgement it is made possible for the offender to be reconciled to the Holy. There are, of course, certain qualifications as compared with the Hegelian scheme. First, both the citizen and the state participate in the same immanent rationality, and therefore it is a situation of mutual responsibility, the offender being owed proportional punishment. Thus judgement as an act of grace does not come into the equation. Second, in Hegel's integration of the political order, there is no question of rehabilitation through vicarious acceptance of judgement. Yet even when these differences are allowed for, it does appear that Forsyth has used Hegel's interpretation of the maintenance of moral order by the state as providing the groundwork of plausibility for his own rationale of the atonement. Now such use of contemporary political and legal plausibilities to give some sort of explanation of what lay behind the atoning death of Christ is by no means uncommon amongst theologians. One thinks of the use by Grotius of the notion of God as *rector* in order to rebut the arguments of the Socinians against the classical Reformed position. On the other hand, it appears to me that Forsyth has here behaved with much greater subtlety; it is not just the question of a direct, univocal transference of the notion of God as *rector* as in Grotius, but rather an example of the analogy of proportionality. Just as the political order maintains itself as moral through punishment, so does God the Holy One justify himself, and makes possible the reconciliation of the sinner through judgement. The Hegelian model has been taken from its original context and used to make plausible what was implied in Christ's self-offering on the cross. In no way is it a matter of philosophy providing the answers which theology is then obliged to follow. If a criticism is to be made, it is that Forsyth never fully faced how that model was to be systematically supplemented so as to give some equally plausible understanding of how the objective event of divine self-justification was also creative of the sinner's response. Thus we have here an example of the exploitation of a significant idea entailing no further philosophical indebtedness, and Hegel of all philosophers is the most generous in his largesse in such matters. What the borrowing does indicate, however, is Forsyth's acquaintance with the overall range of the philosopher's thought.

Christ on Parnassus is Forsyth's most overtly Hegelian work, and as such it raises the deepest problems concerning his dependence upon him, and paradoxically is the hardest to fit into his overall theological position. There can be no doubt that he is a faithful expositor of the philosopher as far as the main thrust of the argument goes, though what is offered has been digested in a certain evangelical fashion and reduced in overall extent. (Forsyth's work comes to a mere 297 pages as compared with the 1237 larger pages of T. M. Knox's translation of the *Aesthetic*.) What is surprising is that Forsyth more or less completely avoids mention of the basic philosophical position of Hegel, which avowedly underlies the work:

> For it is only the *whole* of philosophy which is knowledge of the universe as in itself that *one* organic totality which develops itself out of its own Concept and which, in its self-relating necessity, withdrawing into itself to form a whole, closes with itself to form *one* world of truth.[25]

Now many commentators would argue that Hegel's *Aesthetic* can be appreciated as a highly significant work of lasting value in regard to the metaphysical foundations of our appreciation of beauty, without in any way accepting the basic principles which underlie

---

[25]G. W. F. Hegel, *Aesthetics: Lectures in Fine Art*, trans. T. M. Knox (Oxford: Clarendon, 1975), 24.

it.[26] On the other hand, what generally seems to be meant by this is that Hegel often indicates interesting connections between the mental cast of a society and the art forms which it produces, and can be utilized in some other general understanding of what is implied in aesthetic appreciation. My own reading of Forsyth is that such an outlook does not represent his attitude in the matter; what Hegel says about the spirituality underlying art can be very largely lifted wholesale and transposed into a Christian context. If this is the case, it raises questions whether Hegel for Forsyth is more than the great storehouse from which useful ideas might be extracted to prove fruitful in other contexts.

It is, for example, surprising that Forsyth, who elsewhere had described Hegelianism as the aesthetic fallacy in our understanding of the relationship of God to the world just as deism reflected the scientific,[27] nowhere warns his readers about the underlying principles of the writing which he is retailing. Only occasionally do we find certain sentiments occurring which go beyond anything that Hegel would have penned, as, for example, when he speaks of the new recognition of infinity which Christianity brought, 'it was an infinitude of holy, redeeming love'.[28] Again one detects a different note when he discusses the interrelation of words and music in Christian worship:

> It is not on the element of artistic symmetry, intellectual grasp, and organic completeness that Christian worship dwells. It is the element of sympathy, of unity which is not so much symmetry as harmony, uniting God and man in love, and joining in one chord different orders of character and energy; it is the affinity and concourse of spirits reconciled and made kindred, amid all their variety by a common faith and love. The theme is a unity of thought; harmony is a unity of love. Therefore the worshipful element in music is the element of rich, deep, and varied harmony, not the severe control of a pervasive and developed melody.[29]

[26]As J. Kaminsky: 'Hegel's metaphysics is not a crucial element in his aesthetics, so that a rejection of the metaphysics does not entail a rejection of the aesthetics.' *Hegel on Art* (Albany N.Y.: State University of New York, 1962).

[27]*Authority*, 150–1.

[28]*Parnassus*, 76. Note also that Forsyth gives a more positive appreciation of Israel's faith, particularly the prophetic element, than did Hegel.

[29]*Parnassus*, 218–19.

As a result he emphasizes the necessity of fundamental unity of words and music, with the former predominating, a rather different attitude to the subordinate role which Hegel tends to assign to librettos.[30] Again, we note on occasion that when Forsyth seeks to amplify Hegel by bringing into purview certain artists subsequent to his time, he moves less surefootedly than his mentor in delineating the spiritual significance of their accomplishment, recognizing that such interpretations might be developed in more than one direction. For example, in discussing Turner, he contends that the blending of individual figures into the landscape is a sign that these need to limit and sacrifice their self-assertion, and that, therefore, 'it is not only, nor chiefly, in great altar-pieces of the Crucifixion that Art bears witness to the power of the Cross, just as it is not in the heroic moments and scenes of our own life that for the most part we have to show forth the Lord's death'. Immediately, however, he goes on to recognize that the significance of this feature of the landscapes might be something different: 'I would observe, in passing, that the seamy side of this tendency is the submersion of the soul in the cosmos, and that reign of monism which is in such paradoxical conjunction today with the worship of the superman.'[31] Here, Forsyth had inadvertently encountered the point made so often against Hegel's procedure: if you understand artistic productions to be dependent upon human apprehensions of the outworkings of Spirit, how do you discriminate between candidates for what might be said to underlie them? If Hegel provides only an heuristic principle all possibilities are open, but if only certain interpretations are to be deemed legitimate what criterion for discrimination have we but the system as a whole?

In spite of these occasional deviations from the general Hegelian position, the problem of *Christ on Parnassus* is that Forsyth gives every indication that he is willing to accept it, at least for the realm of art. Why does Hegel here appear so congenial to him, whilst, when it comes to the doctrine of redemption, he is the great opponent who is to be guarded against at every turn? Three factors might be suggested which would account for Forsyth's relaxed attitude in this matter.

---

[30]See Hegel's discussion in *Aesthetics*, 934–5.
[31]*Parnassus*, 120.

First, he seems to have been deeply imbued with the conviction that creation is essentially a form of divine self-expression, in the sense that in bringing the world into existence, God was actualizing what was latent within his own being. He did not like the doctrine of *creatio ex nihilo*:

> Nothing could be made out of nothing. The original nothing was not there. There was always and everywhere the Being of God Himself. Creation out of nothing is a phrase with no meaning. It is unthinkable. It is that meaninglessness that has driven many into Pantheism, and especially into the crude form of it, which says that everything is made of God.
>
> That view can become absurd enough when God is thought of as a substance. But if God be thought of as a subject and a soul it is not so absurd. We *are* His offspring, we hold of the Over-soul.[32]

Or again:

> Our deeper views of creation, and of the relation of the creature to the Creator, do not allow us to think of the universe as an external and mechanical product of His, which He could destroy and make another. The existence of the universe is too closely bound up with the being of God for that. Its life is the immanence of the Transcendent. It does not emerge into Eternity, which is not simply a beyond. The infinite is the content of a finite which holds of the Eternal. The world belongs to God in a deeper sense than being His property. The body is not but the property of the soul. The world holds of God.[33]

The sheer contingency of the created order affirmed by traditional Christianity seems to have been an offence to him, and this in itself would predispose him towards accepting what Hegel had to offer.

Second, and this is closely allied to what has just been considered, Forsyth throughout his intellectual career seems to have been gripped by the idea that nature was in itself a revelation of God, and that through our activity the divine Spirit returned to its transcend-

[32]*Authority*, 158.
[33]*Justification*, 75.

ent source. In his earliest theological work, he writes as follows:

> We are learning to think of Him as the constant ground and
> breath of Nature, its pervading presence, and its sustaining,
> quickening spirit. We are coming to think of Him as the
> living and true God – living, because through Him all life
> lives; and true because he is the truth of all things, and the very
> nature of Nature itself. That is the Christian, though not
> always the Scriptural conception of God. He is a God of
> whom nature is a constant Incarnation and living Revelation.
> The Jew certainly believed that God gave revelation, but he
> did not realise that God *was* revelation.[34]

and in *The Soul of Prayer*, one of his last writings, we find this:

> In our prayer God returns from his projection in Nature to
> speak with Himself. When we speak to God it is really the
> God who lives in us speaking through us to Himself. His
> Spirit returns to Him who gave it; and returns not void, but
> bearing our souls with Him. The dialogue of grace is really
> the monologue of the divine nature in self-communing love.
> In prayer, therefore, we do true and final justice to the world.
> We give Nature to itself. We make it say what it was charged
> to say. We make it find in thought and word its own soul.[35]

To use a rather slippery term, it does appear that Forsyth worked
generally with a panentheistic understanding of the relation of God
to the world, and this in turn would predispose him towards the
Hegelian viewpoint.

This conclusion is reinforced when we consider what on occasion
Forsyth wrote about the relationship of the divine and the human
spirit. In his preface to *Christ on Parnassus*, he avowed as his aim that
he wished his readers to 'realise how high, subtle, and manifold the
paths of the Spirit are on the way to its evolution as Holy Spirit'.[36]
Towards the end of the same work, he gives his credo on this matter
in no uncertain terms:

[34] *Art*, 1st ed., 156–7.
[35] *Prayer*, 2nd ed., 32.
[36] *Parnassus*, viii.

> I do believe that there is an essential unity between what is
> spirit in man and what is spirit in God, that the nature and
> constitution of man's spirit (I am not speaking of man's
> ruined moral will) reflects the constitution of the divine, and
> the movement of its process, and that the great ideas which
> rule the human spirit are either the reflection or the comple-
> ment of still vaster spiritual ideas reigning in the Divine
> Spirit. Spirit is one, our rational personal nature is one,
> however various be its conditions and manifestations, how-
> ever rent may be our harmony of will.[37]

In other words, as Forsyth saw it the Holy Spirit must primarily
be viewed in relation to the work of Spirit in nature, rather than in
the light of being the eschatological, sanctifying gift, who draws a
world back from its fallenness into completion. May it not be here
that we can see why Forsyth seems unable to balance the objective
work of reconciliation with an equally compelling doctrine of the
sanctification of human life? On occasion he does indeed echo the
emphases of Reformed orthodoxy in delineating how the Holy
Spirit brings home to us the historic act of Christ, but that is
somehow unconnected with his understanding of the wider work of
the Spirit.[38] His presupposition concerning the general role of the
Spirit is the inhibiting factor which prevents him exploring how the
new life in Christ is achieved and controlled through the trinitarian
action of God.

There is one other factor which may have attracted him to the
Hegelian interpretation of reality, and that is his deep concern,
probably learned from F. D. Maurice in the first place, with the
corporate nature of salvation. As he once expressed it in a sermon:

> It is a social salvation, and it is a final salvation. It was the
> world that lay on God's heart, and not only the rebels or
> unfortunates within it. He came to save the good as well as
> the bad. And the world was saved, redeemed, reconciled once
> for all when Christ died and rose. Its relation to God was
> changed as a whole. We are each one of us saved in Christ's

---

[37] *Parnassus*, 227.
[38] See e.g., *Authority*, 116–17.

Cross as members of a saved race, and not by private bargain with God on personal terms.[39]

For Forsyth, salvation was as much a social and corporate matter as it was personal, and Hegelianism was perhaps the most persuasive, available philosophy which through its emphases on 'objective spirit' could assist him in working it out in an intelligible manner. Yet, though he constantly insisted that it was to be viewed in such terms, he never spelled out in detail what it meant for one to live in a reconciled as opposed to an unreconciled world. He never gave more than hints of a politics or a sociology of redemption to compare with that outline of the work of the Spirit upon art which we find in *Christ on Parnassus*. His writings in these fields are too occasional, and also one suspects that often his rhetorical facility enabled him to escape from the concrete analysis of his phrases. To spell out what it meant to live in a reconciled world was doubtless always a part of his personal theological agenda, and because of that Hegel could never be removed from consideration. Yet he never got round to it: was this due to shortage of time, or perhaps because he felt an adequate answer was already at hand in the writings of the philosopher?

So how is the influence of the philosopher upon our theologian to be assessed? At the outset any charge that he capitulated to Hegel and allowed him to dictate the terms of his doctrinal enterprise must be rejected. When it came to delineating the saving core of the Christian faith, Hegelianism was the enemy, against which it was necessary to define oneself on every issue. If one concentrates on these aspects of his writings, it would be easy to portray him as a Kierkegaard *redivivus*. It is when he turns to the effects of the gospel on certain aspects of culture that the whole picture changes, and we almost sense that we are dealing with a right-wing Hegelian, somewhere in the progression between Marheineke and Hans Küng.

At the same time, even when it comes to the heart of the faith, he is not above using pieces of the philosopher's construction to make intelligible the nature of Christ's atoning work. Such utilization, however, is done in so neutral a fashion as not to reshape signifi-

---

[39]'The Church as the Corporate Missionary of the Gospel' (preached, but apparently not published, in 1909), in *Revelation*, 35.

cantly in Hegel's direction the overall doctrinal construction. His achievement in this respect is rather similar to the more extensive use made by L. S. Thornton of Whitehead's categories to explicate the person of Christ, without in any way capitulating to the basic direction of that metaphysic.[40] We cannot either compare Forsyth's handling of Hegel to the use made by Aquinas of Aristotle as 'the philosopher', seeking throughout to appropriate his conceptual tools as long as the revealed faith was in no way undermined. Rather, Hegel was for Forsyth the ongoing temptation with whom there was an intellectual affinity of spirit – did not our theologian always eschew the details and prefer to think in terms of broad tendencies? He recognized that the philosopher was strong in just those very areas where the faith had tended to become weak, and yet he must not be allowed a foothold within the citadel of salvation. It was neither a question of takeover or capitulation but rather of an ongoing dialectic in which the logic of Hegel was corrected by the theology of Paul and its continuity in the Reformation, sometimes proceeding sharply and yet in other areas with a considerable degree of slackness. The gospel in no way could be confined by the system, but Forsyth never abandoned the hope that the gospel could take over the system and make it serviceable to its needs. Whether this is an appropriate way of doing theology, or whether it founders because it blatantly contradicts that principle enunciated by Hegel, and upon which his own enterprise historically came to grief, that form and content are integral to each other, is bound to be a question of ongoing debate. For the credit we award to Forsyth as a theologian is according to how far in this ambiguous world, we believe the gospel is capable of being presented in a tidy, comprehensive form, and if not, where the right balance between central grasp and systematic scope is to be found.

---

[40]L. S. Thornton, *The Incarnate Lord* (London: Longmans, 1928).

Chapter 13

WAS FORSYTH REALLY A BARTHIAN
BEFORE BARTH?

John Thompson

The very first thing to say about this title[1] is that the allegation
contained in it would have been immediately rejected by Karl Barth
and, had he lived to hear it, almost certainly by P. T. Forsyth also.
The reason is that it implies a school of so called Barthians – a view
of which Barth thoroughly disapproved. For Barth, the main aim of
his work was 'Die Sache Gottes' – the being and action of God, who
he is and how he is known; but a school of disciples who possibly
slavishly and uncritically repeated Barth – no.[2] Having said this, it
is true that in many respects but by no means all, Forsyth did
anticipate much of Barth's approach. A brief general survey shows
parallels in their lives, experience and thought. Both were brought
up in, and for a time accepted, the liberal theology of the nineteenth
century and began their work as radicals in the active ministry of the
church. Both spent a considerable time as parish ministers and were
concerned with what and how to preach. As a result their theology
was no mere academic discipline but was carried out in and for the
church. Both had a fairly sudden change of direction in their lives

---

[1]The description of Forsyth as a 'Barthian before Barth' was apparently coined
by John McConnachie, foreword to F. W. Camfield, *Revelation and the Holy Spirit:
An Essay in Barthian Theology* (London: Elliot Stock, 1933), vii.

[2]Arthur C. Cochrane, who knew Barth well, writes, 'Barth never wanted to
found a "Barthian" school of theology, much less a new church bearing his name.
In 1963 he gave me a photograph of himself signed: "Karl Barth – kein Barthianer".'
'The Karl Barth I Knew', *Footnotes to Theology: The Karl Barth Colloquium of 1972*,
ed. Martin Rumscheidt; S. R. Supplements (N.pl.: Corporation for the Publication
of Academic Studies in Religion in Canada, 1974), 145

which coloured the whole of the rest of their thought and activity. Barth became disillusioned with his nineteenth-century teachers in Germany, who in a dark day in 1914 signed, as he called it, 'a terrible manifesto'[3] supporting the Kaiser's war. For him, this wrong ethical judgement queried the whole theological basis on which it was made. For Forsyth, pastoral concerns dealing with people's needs and troubles brought a dramatic change in his life – a form of conversion experience, from being 'a lover of love to an object of grace'.[4] For both, therefore, this meant a new approach to theology and the church, a serious critique of the predominant attitudes of the nineteenth century which were centred too much on our relation to God rather than on God's relation to us. Both saw one person exemplifying that which they had to reject as erroneous and dangerous. For Forsyth, it was R. J. Campbell of the City Temple and the New Theology he represented, a theology of sentiment and weakly love.[5] For Barth it was primarily Rudolph Bultmann's existentialism, demythologizing and radical criticism.[6]

Both had in common an opposition to system, i.e. compressing the faith into some preconceived framework of ideas.[7] Yet, they each had a unity of perspective, a holistic vision, a form of thinking based on God's revelation attested in Holy Scripture. This was combined with a remarkable depth of penetration and a form of speech and writing which had passionate commitment joined to a rigorous academic discipline. While this is so, Barth's is by far the more 'systematic' work and Forsyth's unsystematic writings in many places have been the object of critical comments. Nonetheless, there is a unity and a coherence of thought which runs through most of his writings despite its particular form. As pioneers with prophetic insight, both had to plough lonely furrows in the context of the prevailing tendencies of their times.[8]

---

[3] Karl Barth (1886–1968), *How I Changed My Mind,* introduction and epilogue by John D. Godsey (Edinburgh: Saint Andrew Press, 1966), 21–2.

[4] *Preaching,* 3rd ed., 192–3.

[5] J. H. Rodgers, *The Theology of P. T. Forsyth,* 9.

[6] *CD4/1.* In this and many other writings, Barth carried out a critical, sometimes overt, often quiet dialogue with Bultmann whom he saw as reverting to the errors of the nineteenth century.

[7] *Justification,* 2nd ed., 78ff. Barth, *The Epistle to the Romans,* trans. Edwyn C. Hoskyns (London: Oxford University Press), 10.

[8] Rodgers, 7. *CD* 4/4, xii.

A final comment may be made in this connection. Both shared a rather curious feature in that Forsyth's last work *This Life and the Next*[9] is in some ways at odds with most of the rest of his writings. His theme was more that of the immortality of the soul than of the resurrection, though he tried to combine the two and accepted some kind of view of purgatory. Barth, in his turn, went back at the last to Schleiermacher, not necessarily to agree with him, but in reminiscence and reverence, attempting after many years to see if he had understood him aright.[10] How to explain Schleiermacher remained a problem to the end.

There are three main areas where Forsyth's and Barth's theologies show a remarkable similarity, namely, the knowledge of God, the church and the sacraments, and social and political issues. We look briefly at each in turn.

1. The Knowledge of God

For Forsyth, the knowledge of God begins not with our human search, discovery or natural knowledge but with God's own action in revelation.[11] God communicates himself to us in his Son Jesus Christ and reaches out by a further act to include us in communion with himself. In one sense, this revelation is final; in another it is not so until it is received by humans through the Holy Spirit. This is sometimes spoken of by Forsyth as God's action reaching out to us in time and returning by the Spirit with those who experience his revelation and so come to know and commune with him. It is, in other words, a form of Hegelian dialectic though with a different content from that of Hegel.

Barth's view is almost identical. God is the self-revealing God who makes himself known in Jesus Christ as revealer, revelation and revealedness – subject, act and effect. For him, this is how we know God and is the basis of the doctrine of the Trinity.[12] Barth goes on

---

[9] *Life* (1918).

[10] Barth, *The Theology of Schleiermacher*, trans. Geoffrey W. Bromiley (Edinburgh: T&T Clark, 1978), 261ff.

[11] 'Revelation and the Person of Christ' (1893): 116–17.

[12] *CD* 1/1, 315ff.

to set the Trinity at the forefront of dogmatics and to give a lengthy treatment of it. Forsyth, on the contrary, while he clearly accepts the connection between revelation and the Trinity and mentions this trinitarian perspective from time to time, never gives any detailed treatment of the doctrine.

i. Revelation and Holy Scripture

This knowledge of God by revelation comes to us through Holy Scripture.[13] How are the two related? Forsyth values Scripture highly, but for him it is not *simpliciter* the Word of God. He states that, in this regard, we have three things. First, there is the incarnate fact of Jesus Christ, then the word or the interpretation of it by apostles and, thereby, the fact again, but the fact enshrined in the soul of the believing church.[14]

Scripture is the second of these. It is the word of God by the inspiration of the apostles. The risen and ascended Christ by the Holy Spirit, interprets the meaning of his own action in his life and death on the cross. Christ is thus the centre of Scripture; inspired and therefore authoritative testimony is given by the Spirit in and through Scripture and all of it is to be judged in relation to its centre.

Here are thoughts which are almost exactly mirrored in Barth. In Volume 1 of the *Church Dogmatics* he speaks of the three forms of the Word of God, revealed, written and preached;[15] all are centred in Jesus Christ as the Word and intimately interrelated. There is, for Barth, no direct identity but an indirect one between the Word spoken and the Word written in Holy Scripture. The latter is an authentic, divinely inspired testimony to the former.[16]

Barth's other statement is consistent with Forsyth's, that Scripture has an event character.[17] Its authority rests on the grace of God by which he uses this inspired testimony to bring us to himself, to give us the reality and knowledge of faith. Scripture authority is

---

[13] *Sacraments*, 2nd ed., xv–xvi.
[14] *Person*, 159.
[15] *CD* 1/1, 88ff.
[16] *CD* 1/2, 502ff.
[17] *CD* 1/2, 502ff.

therefore not tangible as a works religion but rests on the mystery and continued act of the grace of God.

ii. Revelation as Redemption

For both Forsyth and Barth, revelation is not just an epiphany or a manifestation of God in human terms; it is at one and the same time grace, redemption from sin and evil, reconciliation wrought by God in the context of our sinful human nature and the evil forces in the world. It is centred in Christ whose life and work are consummated on the cross as atonement.

Basic to this is the nature of God whose main attribute is not just love but *holy* love.[18] Forsyth strongly underlined the fact that it was only the *holy* love of God that showed up our sin and dealt adequately with it. In his redemption on the cross, God affirms and establishes his right, his own holy, steadfast nature in the conditions of disobedience and, in this way, acts with grace to sinners.

In all this, Forsyth wrote and spoke with passionate commitment and appeal, for here was the very heart of all he believed and taught. Without the *holy* love of God and the consequent crisis, judgement and atonement the moral heart goes out of the Christian gospel and leaves it seriously weakened and misunderstood. That was the essence of his objection to, and searing critique of, much of the theology of his day.

Here the real is the redemptive where God judges sin in Jesus Christ who undergoes the death of the cross and offers the perfect holiness required of us which we cannot give. This is done on a racial scale and includes all humanity and the cosmos in its scope. The exclusivity of the cross has this cosmic inclusive character.[19]

In this respect, Barth's massive treatment of reconciliation agrees to a large extent with that of Forsyth.[20] What takes place in reconciliation is exclusively God's work in Christ but has an inclusive all-embracing perspective, a concrete universal. It involves

---

[18] *Father*, 3ff.
[19] *Work*, 99ff.
[20] *CD* 41/1, 152ff. We see here how clearly Forsyth articulates a trinitarian theology though he never gives it any lengthy exposition.

what Barth calls 'the revolution of God', i.e. a total change of the whole race and cosmos in relation to God so that we live, as he puts it, in a reconciled world but one not yet redeemed.[21] For Barth, it is a fourfold *pro nobis*. The Judge is judged in our place, suffers and dies for us, does right and manifests God's righteousness in our place.[22] This is the essence of Christ's work for us in atonement.

In this context, we note that neither Forsyth nor Barth adopt any one theory of the atonement, although both views are clearly on the objective side. Forsyth goes beyond the Anselmic view of satisfying God's honour and the Reformers' view of retributive justice and the law to the view which sees Christ presenting from one side the perfect offering of righteousness to the holy, loving God. This is entirely in line with Barth who gives a lengthy biblical exposition. Again, Forsyth anticipates the note we find in Barth's later theology of the suffering, not only of Christ, but of God the Father. Forsyth writes, 'The Father did not suffer as the Son (that were too Sabellian), but He suffered with the Son.... It cost the Father at least as much as the Son.... Our redemption drew upon the whole Godhead. Father and Spirit were not spectators only of the Son's agony, nor only recipients of His sacrifice. They were involved in it.'[23] How modern and up-to-date are these words in terms of the contemporary debate, largely taking its beginnings from Barth. Like Forsyth, Barth's theology is a theology of the cross, the reality it embodies, the redemptive act of grace it encloses and also discloses to us for our salvation. Barth writes, 'All theology, both that which follows and indeed that which precedes the doctrine of reconciliation, depends upon this *theologia crucis*.'[24]

---

[21]For a good discussion of the significance of Barth's conception of 'the revolution of God', see Eberhard Jüngel, *Karl Barth, A Theological Legacy*, trans. Garrett E. Paul (Philadelphia: Westminster, 1986), 101ff. Also Ulrich Dannermann, *Theologie und Politik im Denken Karl Barths* (Munich: Ch. Kaiser, 1977), 150ff. Barth, *Against the Stream*, ed. R. Gregor Smith (London: SCM Press Ltd., 1954), 78–9.

[22]*CD* 4/1, 232ff.

[23]*Missions*, 29. Cf. *CD* 4/2, 357.

[24]*CD* 4/1, 273

iii. The Work of the Spirit

A further aspect of God's coming to us in revelation is the work of the Spirit. With Barth, Forsyth underlines the objectivity of reconciliation but goes on to state that it contains within it a proleptic element.[25] What Jesus has done for us includes our confession of faith and repentance proleptically. This is seen in Forsyth's view of the Spirit as a Spirit of the cross or the Word. In this regard, the Spirit performs a twofold role, namely, makes real the presence of Christ to us[26] and, at the same time, opens up our lives to receive him.[27] Now, this is exactly what Barth means when he too speaks of the Holy Spirit as the subjective aspect of revelation or reconciliation.[28] The Spirit makes the reality of reconciliation in all its fullness objectively present to us and subjectively actual within us. For both theologians, there is a sacramental relation between the work of Christ in reconciliation, and faith which is created by that reconciliation. This act of the Spirit is creative, miraculous, liberating. The agreement between Forsyth and Barth at this point is almost uncannily real.

Both again emphasize that we cannot respond, believe and obey by our own power. Yet, paradoxically, we must and do believe in what is a human act. Forsyth states that Christ 'had to create the very capacity for response. And that is where we are compelled to recognise the doctrine of the Holy Spirit'.[29] In other words, at one and the same time, this is both God's work by the Spirit and our work in being enabled to believe. Forsyth does not explicitly mention or deny natural theology as Barth does, but in passages such as this, it seems to be the conclusion that one should draw. Here this lack of our capacity to respond parallels Barth's opposition to natural theology[30] and the need for the work of Christ by the Spirit to give us the capacity to believe.

---

[25] *Work*, 192.
[26] *Father*, 96.
[27] *Work*, 18. *Freedom*, 13.
[28] *CD* 1/2, 203ff.
[29] *Work*, 18.
[30] *CD* 2/1, 135ff. That Forsyth was not entirely consistent at this point is probable; it may be argued that he does leave place for apologetics in a way Barth does not.

iv. Our Human Participation

One cannot, however, speak fully and properly of human faith unless one calls it a form of human knowledge. Faith is not ours unless we know God. At this point, Forsyth indicates that we know God because we are first known by him.[31] An epistemological question and answer are built into this whole framework of knowledge. God is the subject of our knowledge of him by electing love, enabling us to participate in his own self-knowledge by way of personal communion.[32] This is Forsyth's theory of the knowledge of God which is involved in his whole conception of the being and action of God and of our redemption by him. This is contrary to deism, pantheism and theism, which begins, as Forsyth writes, 'with ourselves as the subjects of knowledge, and treats God as its object'.[33]

This is, therefore, a gracious form of knowledge which does not begin with our need but with God's action which reveals that need.[34] At the same time, one can speak of it as an evangelical experience of the redeemer. Forsyth argues – in a way which is less typical of Barth – from the reality of our experience of redemption to the One who creates it.[35] This subjective experience is grounded in and flows from a prior act of God in Christ which creates and enables it. This is how Forsyth attempts to answer the charge often made against this way of thinking and speaking as pure subjectivism. As Rodgers puts it, 'Faith centres in an objective Christ and not in the subjectivity of the believer'[36] – the objectivity of the experienced Christ. Again he writes, 'there is no epistemological bridge built by man to God.'[37] We believe in order to understand. Faith is knowledge; it has both an experiential and an ontological character, based as it is in God's self-knowledge, in the word of that knowledge about himself to us in his redemptive act in Christ and the cross.

It is again very clear that there is a close proximity in Forsyth to the views of Barth in his theory and practice of the knowledge of

---

[31]*Authority*, 2nd ed., 35, 100, 149–50.
[32]*Authority*, 151–2. *Life* 2nd ed., 75.
[33]*Authority*, 151.
[34]*Authority*, 151.
[35]*Authority*, 372–3. *Sacraments*, 216.
[36]Rodgers, 210.
[37]Rodgers, 228. *Authority*, 49, 55, 331.

God, as one finds it in the *Church Dogmatics*.[38] The knowledge of God, according to Barth, comes from God alone. 'Only by God,' he states, 'is God known'.[39] So God comes before us as objective reality but, even before or as he does so, he is objective to himself in his triune life in what Barth calls his 'primary objectivity'. At the same time, he gives himself to be known in a 'secondary objectivity', i.e. as the object of our knowledge, but one in which he always remains the Lord, the subject of his action.[40] This objective reality of the being of God comes to be known by us in its character of grace. Because of our sinful rebellion we are unable otherwise to grasp it. It is received and perceived by faith and obedience and comes to us in creaturely sacramental signs and symbols, as Forsyth also states.

Barth, however, goes beyond Forsyth in a more explicit way. He emphasizes, for example, the primary objectivity in the trinitarian nature of God and the nature of knowledge as participation in the triune life of God. Second, the humanity of Jesus is the place where the human knows God, is ready for God. There is no natural readiness in our humanity, save as we are one in Christ. Further, Barth underlines the fact that the *Deus Revelatus* is also the *Deus Absconditus*, the God revealed is the God concealed in the miracle and mystery of his action, a point Forsyth also accepts. He comes in human form, veiled in flesh, capable of and actually being misunderstood and rejected. Barth's views remain focused objectively in Jesus Christ and would be less accepting of experience than Forsyth, though as stated, Forsyth's view is not necessarily contrary to Barth's.

v. The Nature of Theology

For both Forsyth and Barth, implicit in this form of knowledge, is an understanding of the right way to do theology. We believe in order to understand. This was the truth which Barth learnt through his study of the Scriptures and of Anselm's views on the knowledge of God. Our knowledge and statements about God must corre-

---

[38] *CD* 2/1, 63ff.
[39] *CD* 2/1, 179.
[40] *CD* 2/1, 49ff.

spond to the object of our faith. We do not begin with a particular form of knowledge and adapt faith to it, but rather we begin with the knowledge of God which moves from God to us and only then vice versa as we are brought into that knowledge. So faith is a correspondence to this activity of God and our thinking about him. Forsyth is in agreement with this; it is the basis on which the whole theological structure of both men rests.

2. The Church

P. T. Forsyth was a Congregationalist, the inheritor of Independency with its emphasis on freedom. He repeatedly bewailed the fact of a slide into a form of religious democracy, of a conception of the church seen largely as a voluntary association of religious people. As he wrote, a church 'is not put together by consents, contract, or affinities'.[41] In a great variety of ways, he saw his own church and the others loosed from their biblical, historic, theological moorings and drifting with every new tide.

What then was needed, in his view, was a new and basically biblical conception of the nature of the church. He defines the church as 'a new creation of God in the Holy Spirit, a spiritual organism, in which we find our soul'.[42] The church is, therefore, a community, the social counterpart of what is a universal, corporate salvation. He writes, 'To be a Christian is not to attach one's salvation to a grand individual, but it is to enter Christ; and to enter Christ is in the same act to enter the Church which is in Christ. Faith in Christ is faith in One Whose indwelling makes a Church, and Who carries a Church within His corporate person.'[43] 'In Christ' means in his corporate personality the church, almost an identification yet a distinction between the two. Further, this is the action of the one Lord and so the church, by the Holy Spirit united with Christ, is one. It is a unity and community of all God's people in heaven and on earth. Forsyth often speaks of the community of saints and of the dead being the majority in the church.[44] He sees the

[41] *Sacraments*, 34.
[42] *Sacraments*, 34.
[43] *Sacraments*, 43.
[44] *Sacraments*, 63, 66.

ruling conception of this in the New Testament in what he calls the 'Great Universal Church', the one church in all places and in each place.[45] He writes, 'What the Apostles planted was not Churches but stations of the Church. What the Gospel created was not a crowd of Churches but the one Church in various places.'[46] Again, he states, 'In a word, the local Church was but the outcrop there of the total and continuous Church, one everywhere.'[47] We do not get the great church by adding together different churches but each local church is a visible representative of the one great church. It is one in many manifestations.

But since we are now separated, how can one express what Forsyth believed was a basic organic union? He felt that a first step at least was federation, an idea later to take form in the Free Church Federal Council. Unity and catholicity he believed are only possible by the true succession, the evangelical one. He was, therefore, not thinking in the first instance of a federation with Rome or Anglicans but with the other Free Churches. He believed that no one polity was to be found clearly set out in the New Testament. The successor of the apostolate of the New Testament was not an apostolic succession of ministry but the apostolic testimony of Holy Scripture and its gospel word and deed. The monopolist policies of Rome and Canterbury cannot be the conditions of church unity.[48]

For Forsyth, the church is above all a missionary society. This is what the word apostolic basically means, being sent into the world, to society, to the state. In a series of sermons,[49] Forsyth gives passionate utterance to this dynamic, apostolic outreach and, in so doing, sums up virtually the whole of his own theological programme. The exclusiveness of the gospel of redemption has this inclusive note with its thrust and charge to preach the gospel to every creature. He stated that 'the Church can only be missionary as it is remissionary' and again that the church that has ceased to be missionary has lost the Holy Spirit.[50] This great truth and this dynamic aspect of the missionary task is given and promised to a

[45] *Sacraments*, 68–9.
[46] *Sacraments*, 68.
[47] *Sacraments*, 65.
[48] *Sacraments*, 81ff., 116ff.
[49] *Missions*.
[50] *Missions*, 19, 250.

church. Social and political consequences are also included in this and flow from the central proclamation of the apostolic word, the gospel. The church's mission is not just to save souls but to be the moral authority in society, to proclaim and embody true freedom in the state, to have a free church in a free state and so to be opposed to and seek the end of an established church which is contrary to the nature of the gospel and its true relation to the state.[51]

In the realm of doctrine and summing up all the foregoing, it means faith as confession. 'A Church, as soon as it is a believing Church, must above all else be a confessing Church',[52] with a common basis of faith. Again he writes, 'The Church's first duty is to confess in some form this common faith which gave it being.'[53] Confessions arise out of some crisis of faith facing the church and drawing it back to basics. Forsyth wanted the church to draw up a simple and straightforward, intelligible confession of faith in this form.

Forsyth's view of the sacraments is fairly traditionally Reformed, with a ministry of word and sacraments. Sacraments are a means of grace, conveying what they signify and not mere memorials; he accepts the two sacraments of baptism and the Lord's supper as dominical and defends strongly the baptism of the infant children of believers.[54] At the same time, he holds that the one genuine sacrament which determines all the rest is the sacrament of the grace of God in Christ, of the gospel, of the Word.[55] Hence, preaching of the Word must be central, both definitive for, and constitutive of, all else in the church. Preaching he defines too as an act of worship where God himself confronts us with his grace and claims; it is to this extent sacramental.[56] In other words, Forsyth's views of the church were high catholic in a broadly evangelical sense with an emphasis on the church as a divine society, universal in scope, the harbinger of the kingdom of God, here and now the prolepsis of the future.[57]

---

[51] *Theology*, 133.
[52] *Theology*, 127.
[53] *Freedom*, 220.
[54] *Sacraments*, 171ff.
[55] *Preaching*, 8.
[56] *Preaching*, 1–2, 50ff.
[57] Rodgers, 59, 62–7.

The views of Karl Barth follow in many respects, though not in detail, virtually all these emphases of Forsyth. Centred and based on God's reconciliation and so corresponding to the being and work of Christ and in union with him the church has three aspects – the calling and awakening of people to faith in Jesus Christ and so to be the earthly historical form of the heavenly historical body of Christ.[58] Second, the upbuilding and growth of the body of Christ,[59] and third, its commission and sending into all the world, already *de iure* Christ's by reconciliation and now summoned to know, acknowledge and confess his victorious lordship.[60] In each of these aspects, the church is brought into being, sustained and sent into the world on the basis of God's reconciliation and by the power of the Spirit. The Holy Spirit creates community, a term Barth prefers to the church which has too many aspects of an institution. The church as a community has a dynamic or event character as has all Barth's theology. Yet one can also speak of the *being* of the church. For Barth the two are, in fact, one. There is a definite and strong combination of the ontological and the dynamic since the being of God in Christ is a being in action. Further, the church is for Barth the provisional representation of what is real for all humans. Barth's views on the apostolic succession of the church are virtually identical with those of Forsyth.[61] He wanted a free church and sought to bring the churches to confess the faith to the world and to do so together in a brief common confession similar to Barmen, but was unsuccessful.[62] While Barth was for a time highly critical of the ecumenical movement, he participated in Amsterdam in 1948 when the World Council of Churches was formed and addressed its Assembly.[63] This gave him a somewhat different view enabling him later to participate more fully in ecumenical debate.

There was, however, one area where Forsyth and Barth differed, namely in their view of the doctrine of the sacraments. Forsyth's was

---

[58] *CD* 4/1, 643ff.

[59] *CD* 4/2, 614ff.

[60] *CD* 4/3, 2, 681ff.

[61] *CD* 4/1, 719–20, 724ff.

[62] Eberhard Busch, *Karl Barth: His Life from Letters and Autobiographical Texts,* trans. John Bowden (London: SCM Press Ltd., 1976), 328–9.

[63] Busch, *Karl Barth,* 359ff. In *CD* 4/1, 669–85, Barth gives his views on the unity of the church.

a traditional one. Barth, while accepting baptism and the Lord's Supper, in later life denied that infant baptism was necessary and his final step was to reject all sacraments save the sacrament of Christ himself.[64] In other words, he radically desacramentalized the sacraments, possibly because of a strict Christological concentration. His view was that both the Word and so-called sacraments were no longer means of grace but were witnesses to grace, pointers to Christ.[65] It is he alone, who speaks and acts, who is in control and brings his word of grace to humankind and the world. As Jüngel, probably correctly, points out, if one cannot follow Barth here one may have difficulty in doing so elsewhere.[66]

3. Society and Politics

It is clear that both Forsyth and Barth believed the Christian faith had practical implications in the areas of society, politics and the world as a whole and that these were to be based on theological premises which informed a Christian ethic and moral responses. This basis was theological; God's victorious redemptive action in the cross of Christ.

Both affirm that ethics flows from this basis and so must be Christian or theological ethics which determines the church's personal and social action. Forsyth writes, 'Christian ethic is a theological ethic. There is but one ethic, which is the Christian; and it has but one source – the Cross of the Holy Love.'[67] For Barth, ethics is seen as linked concretely to his theological basis.[68] For both, the application of ethics is seen as concrete and not prescriptive; in other words as evoking, in the light of grace, a particular response to particular situations and issues. It is not based on some laws or

[64] *CD* 4/4, passim.
[65] Berthold Klappert, *Promissio und Bund: Gesetz und Evangelism bei Luther und Barth* (Göttingen: Vandenhoeck & Ruprecht, 1976), 239ff. For a comment on, and critique of, this view see also John Thompson, *The Holy Spirit in the Theology of Karl Barth* (Pittsburgh: Pickwick, 1991), 124ff.
[66] Eberhard Jüngel, 'Karl Barths Lehre von der Taufe: Ein Hinweis auf ihre Problem', in *Barth Studien* (Cologne: Benzinger Verlag, 1982), 286–7.
[67] *War*, 169.
[68] *CD* 2/2, 509ff.; *CD* 3/4; *CD* 4/4; *Ethics*, ed. Dietrich Braun, trans. G. W. Bromiley (Edinburgh: T&T Clark, 1981; orig. pub. in German, 1928–9).

principles that are laid down which are regarded as permanently valid. Neither denies general ethics but both feel that for a Christian ethic, particular decisions are made in the light of Christ and his atoning cross.

Since the Christian ethic of holy love is manifest on the cross, it is racial and cosmic in scope. It therefore is applied to the world and its life and works itself out as righteousness in nations and peoples and between them.[69] Forsyth and Barth both argue that it is only if we have this particular view of ethics and its basis that we will be able properly to apply Christian insights to national and international problems and in this way manifest the kingdom of God. The church does not exist for itself, nor as a congeries of individuals but as a society which has a corporate personality and responsibility for this form of witness to the world. The Christian witness is not simply to individuals and so to convert them, but it is at the same time so to act in national affairs that it changes the moral character of the whole.[70]

In its application to society, Forsyth believed that there was a kind of evolutionary principle at work. This was not a belief in progress where things got better all the time. Rather in the West, there was a gradual movement from one period of history, one particular form of society to another, from feudalism, through capitalism to a more social conception.[71] In the early part of this century, he saw socialism emerging and believed this was to some extent the form of future society. His early sympathies were there but as it advanced and he matured he saw that, like all social views and political ideologies, it had its egoisms and weaknesses. It could never be something to which one gave oneself absolutely.[72] In an early study he wrote, 'The moral value of Socialism ... is its idea of mutuality and service',[73] as over against private enterprise and capitalism. But after a time, and careful appraisal of the movement, he had many approving but also critical things to say of it.

The two main issues that occupied him politically were the relationship of the church to democracy and the First World War.[74]

---

[69] *Preaching,* 222ff. *Sacraments,* 32.
[70] *Society,* 9ff., 44ff.
[71] *Society,* 43.
[72] *Socialism,* 28.
[73] *Socialism,* 32.
[74] For war, see *Justification,* and *War,* and for democracy, see *Authority,* 225ff.

On the former, he was concerned to point out that Christianity was not a democracy, however much it favoured it, but a theocracy based on the sovereignty, the kingship of Christ in his holy redeeming action. It could not simply act on the basis of a democratic vote. Liberalism in politics, as it existed at that time, may be the state idea but the historic base of the church prescribes a more conservative temper where neither the majority not the minority is the calculus of the Spirit. His concern was lest the democratic principle of majority rule could so enter the church and by a liberal majority overturn the whole historic basis of redemption, of revelation, of the Trinity and of the deity of Christ. But to do so, would be to strike at the very roots of the faith, its biblical, dogmatic basis. He therefore strongly emphasized that majority rule was not the principle by which the church was governed, though in its assemblies and other institutions it had to take democratic decisions.

As far as the War was concerned,[75] he believed that God acted in grace and in judgement in the whole historical process. The latter in one sense is the manifestation of the kingdom of God. From the perspective of the centre of our faith, we can see the outworkings of the kingdom in what Barth later called parables of the kingdom.[76] By this, Forsyth meant that one could discern God's ways in the world from the perspective of faith. God acts in salvation and in judgement in history and continues to do so. The War, Forsyth felt, was God's judgement on nations and national sin, particularly on the Germans who were largely responsible for the War and, like Barth in the Second World War,[78] Forsyth was strongly partisan and saw war, however regrettable, as God preaching judgement; as Forsyth added in a homely note: 'And now God enters the pulpit, ... and his sermons are long and taxing, and they spoil the dinner.'[78] He and Barth virtually said, at these junctures in history, that to be against Kaiser and Hitler is to be for the kingdom.

A few words only may be said about Barth and politics. He was involved in this throughout the greater part of his life. In his early years in Safenwil, he was strongly involved with the Religious

[75] War, passim.
[76] CD 4/3, part 1, 112, 114, 117.
[77] Justification, 22ff. Busch, Karl Barth, 203 gives Barth's view on active resistance to Hitler.
[78] Justification, 28.

Socialist movement,[79] but a lecture at Tambach in 1919 indicated a move towards a critique of it based on Christ and the kingdom.[80] The kingdom of God is the revolution of all revolutions and while there may be 'parables of the Kingdom' in the secular order, Barth dissociated himself from the danger of 'secularising Christ ... for the sake of democracy, or pacifism, or the youth movement, or something of the sort'.[81] This difference, yet relationship, between the kingdom and the world was to be worked out in a variety of ways throughout Barth's lifetime, in his confessional stance against Nazism at Barmen;[82] in his opposition to the Cold War attitude in the world post-1945;[83] in his plea in the 1950s for unilateral nuclear disarmament;[84] in his opposition to the Vietnam War and in his critical stance towards both capitalism and communism.[85] All these were based on what he perceived to be an outworking of reconciliation in social and political affairs and were regarded as analogies of the kingdom of God.

4. Conclusion

What can one say in conclusion about Forsyth and Barth? What was it that gave them so many similarities in thought and expression? I suggest three reasons for this.

In the first place, there is their understanding of Holy Scripture. Both, in different ways, were thoroughly engrossed in penetrating biblical exegesis which formed the basis and gave the content of their dogmatic works. This is much less obvious on the surface in Forsyth

---

[79]Busch, *Karl Barth*, 77ff.

[80]Busch, *Karl Barth*, 109.

[81]Barth, *The Word of God and the Word of Man*, 277, quoted in Busch, *Karl Barth*, 111.

[82]Arthur C. Cochrane, *The Church's Confession under Hitler* (Pittsburgh: Pickwick, 1976), passim; for the Barmen Declaration see Cochrane, Appendix, 237–42.

[83]Barth, *Against the Stream*, 127–44.

[84]Rowan Williams, 'Barth, War and the State', in *Reckoning With Barth: Essays in Commemoration of the Centenary of Karl Barth's Birth*, ed. Nigel Biggar (London: Mowbray, 1988), 170–90.

[85]Barth, *Against the Stream*, 167ff.

than in Barth but it is implicit and very real nonetheless. Both argued that we should use the Scriptures in such a way that, as Forsyth said, we have some difficulty in not believing in verbal inspiration.[86] Much current thought points to a great variety of views in biblical themes, in Christology, for example, and both Forsyth and Barth accepted this. At the same time, they also saw a fundamental unity in the history of God's ongoing purpose in Israel fulfilled in Jesus Christ in what Forsyth called 'a dramatic unity of action'.[87] With regard to Forsyth, A. M. Hunter believed that he anticipated much of what is now accepted in biblical scholarship, for example, form criticism, the new emphasis on the kingdom of God as his present reign in Christ and the kerygmatic character of the earliest apostolic preaching of the gospel.[88] He writes, 'Our discussion has shown that in his task as a systematic theologian (though he could be exasperatingly unsystematic himself) Forsyth brought to matters biblical, and especially the New Testament, an insight unmatched by any of his contemporary *Systematikers.*'[89] One can, I believe, say precisely the same of Karl Barth.

A second characteristic is what Barth calls a 'christological concentration',[90] i.e. a concentration on the centre of theology in Jesus Christ crucified and risen. This did not lead, as the Roman Catholic scholar von Balthasar has said, to a Christological constriction,[91] but quite the opposite. The exclusivity of Christ's life consummated on the cross as redemption led to an all inclusive, cosmic and racial perspective which dealt at once in principle with the righteous, holy love of God in his dealings with the world and people alienated and fallen from him. The consequence was a view of the reign of God which overcame all opposition to it and had a profound spiritual and moral impact on humanity and history as a whole. In this regard, Barth's is a more balanced view based on the

---

[86]*Preaching,* 109.

[87]*Preaching,* 6.

[88]A. M. Hunter, *P. T. Forsyth: Per Crucem ad Lucem,* 31ff. See also J. S. Whale, foreword to *Work,* 2nd ed., iv.

[89]Hunter, 42.

[90]Barth, *How I Changed My Mind,* 43.

[91]John Macken, *The Autonomy Theme in the Church Dogmatics: Karl Barth and His Critics* (Cambridge: Cambridge University Press, 1990), 81, refers to this view of Von Balthasar. See also *CD* 4/1, 769 for Barth's own comments.

cross and resurrection, whereas Forsyth concentrates in his whole theology almost exclusively on the cross, though he naturally believes in the resurrection and in the Trinity. Unlike Barth, he does not give either topic any extended treatment.

A third aspect is their relation to tradition. Both saw liberal Protestantism and Roman Catholicism as similar twin dangers, but also sought to retain the truths in each. They were dangerous in the sense that too great an emphasis was put on man's part in cooperating with God to the detriment of God's sovereign action in Jesus Christ. In Barth's case, however, Roman Catholic scholars like Von Balthasar saw his theology as the completely consistent expression of the thought of the Reformers. Balthasar wrote, 'This expression was attained not only by the radical return to the sources, to Calvin and Luther, cutting right across all the "developments", deformations and dilutions of Neo-Protestantism, but what is more important, by the purification and radicalization of the sources themselves.'[92] It was this critical purification of their own Reformation traditions in the light of Scripture that sums up both their intentions and, to a great extent, their achievements. One can put it in a phrase that I have coined from Barth, 'respectful freedom in relation to tradition'.[93] There is, in the first instance, respect for the totality of tradition, whether one agrees with all of it or not, yet freedom under the Word to seek its reformation and renewal in life and thought. This capacity to affirm, yet critically to reassess, the tradition in the light of its basis in the Word of God in Jesus Christ, led not to a narrowing of perspective but rather to the broadening of it, and eventually to the possibility and actuality of ecumenical dialogue which, however fitful and slow, is still moving among us today. Both Forsyth and Barth contributed, by their radical concentration on the centre of our faith, in a large measure to this mutual meeting and encounter.

[92]As quoted in Rudolph Ehrlich, *Rome: Opponent or Partner?* (London: Lutterworth, 1965), 21–2.

[93]*CD* 1/2, 658ff.

Chapter 14

BIBLIOGRAPHY

Leslie McCurdy

Prefaratory Note: The family tree of bibliographical research with regard to Peter Taylor Forsyth includes such names as Jessie Forsyth Andrews, William Bradley, C. A. McKay, and Robert Benedetto. To all of these I am grateful, and to the last named in particular – for permission to adapt the format of his 1981 work – I am especially thankful. My thanks also to many who answered my queries, including Dean Carter, Trevor Hart, Alan Lamb, Ulrike Link-Wieczorek, Masami Kojiro, and Alan Sell. Librarians at the National Library of Scotland, the Edinburgh Public Library, and the Universities of Aberdeen, Cambridge, and Oxford were consistently helpful, and the Coward Trust provided financial assistance to enable me to consult them. Particular thanks is due to the staff of Dr Williams's Library in London, and to the InterLibrary Loans librarian at the University of Aberdeen, Katharina McCurdy.

Primary Literature

1. Books
Forsyth's books are arranged chronologically by publication date. New editions are noted, as is the most recent edition or impression. When a book includes previously published material, the title and year of publication are noted; for full details see Section 3 under the year cited.

1886
Pulpit Parables for Young Hearers. With J. A. Hamilton. Manchester: Brook & Chrystal; London: Simpkin, Marshall; London: Hamilton, Adams, n.d.

1889

Religion in Recent Art: Being Expository Lectures on Rossetti, Burne Jones, Watts, Holman Hunt, and Wagner. Manchester: Abel Heywood & Son; London: Simpkin, Marshall; London: Hamilton, Adams.

The second edition is repaginated, with eight illustrations, and in a large format. London: Hodder & Stoughton, 1901.

The third edition of 1905 was augmented in 1911 with a chapter entitled 'Art, Ethic, and Christianity'.

The latest impression is from the third edition of 1905. New York: AMS Press, 1972.

1896

The Charter of the Church: Six Lectures on the Spiritual Principle of Nonconformity. London: Alexander & Shepheard.

Includes *The Antiquity of Dissent* (1889) as chapters 5 and 6.

Latest impression. London: Alexander & Shepheard, 1905.

Intercessory Services for Aid in Public Worship. Manchester: John Heywood, n.d.

A copy amended by Forsyth is in Dr Williams's Library, London.

1897

The Holy Father and the Living Christ. Little Books on Religion. Edited by W. Robertson Nicoll. London: Hodder & Stoughton.

New edition. Silent Hour Booklets. [London]: Hodder & Stoughton, n.d.

Included in *God the Holy Father* (1957).

1899

Christian Perfection. Little Books on Religion. Edited by W. Robertson Nicoll. London: Hodder & Stoughton.

New edition. London: Hodder & Stoughton, 1909.

Included in *God the Holy Father* (1957).

Japanese translation: *Kirisuto-sha no Kanzen*, translator unknown. Tokyo: Shinkyo-shuppan-sha, 1960.

Rome, Reform and Reaction: Four Lectures on the Religious Situation. London: Hodder & Stoughton.

1901

The Taste of Death and the Life of Grace. Small Books on Great Subjects, no. 21. London: James Clarke.

Comprising 'The Taste of Death and the Life of Grace' (1900), and 'The Divine Self-Emptying' (1895).
Second edition. London: James Clark, 1906.
Included in *God the Holy Father* (1957).

1907

Positive Preaching and Modern Mind: The Lyman Beecher Lecture on Preaching, Yale University, 1907. London: Hodder & Stoughton.
The second edition is a reprint with the title *Positive Preaching and the Modern Mind.* London: Hodder & Stoughton, 1909.
The third edition is reset and repaginated. London: Independent Press, 1949.
The 1907 edition was reprinted with a Foreward by Ralph G. Turnbull. Grand Rapids, Michigan: Baker Book House, 1980.
A reprint of the 1909 edition is included in Donald G. Miller, Browne Barr, and Robert S. Paul, *P. T. Forsyth: The Man, The Preachers' Theologian, Prophet for the 20th Century: A Contemporary Assessment.* Pittsburgh, Pennsylvania: Pickwick Press, 1981.
The most recent edition, with a Publisher's Foreword by Geoffrey Bingham and a Biographical Introduction by Noel Due, is published in Blackwood, South Australia: New Creation Publications, 1993.
Summary regarding pagination: The virtually identical first and second editions (with the original pagination) appeared during Forsyth's lifetime; this was reprinted in 1980. The third edition (with new pagination) was printed several times between 1949 and 1966, and reprinted in 1993.

1908

Missions in State and Church: Sermons and Addresses. London: Hodder & Stoughton.
Incorporating 'Judgment' (1902), 'Missions as the True Imperial and Apostolic Succession' (1902), and 'The Charter of Missions' (1903).
A 'second edition' in 1908 is merely a second printing.
Socialism, the Church and the Poor. London: Hodder & Stoughton.
Containing 'Sociality, Socialism and the Church' (1907).

1909

The Cruciality of the Cross. Expositor's Library. London, New York, and Toronto: Hodder & Stoughton, n.d.

Incorporating 'Forgiveness through Atonement the Essential of Evangelical Christianity' (1908), 'The Insufficiency of Social Righteousness as a Moral Ideal' (1909), and 'What Is Meant by the Blood of Christ?' (1908).

Japanese translation: *Jujika no Jujika-sei*, trans. Takayoshi Aso. Tokyo: Nagasaki-shoten, 1933.

Second edition. London: Independent Press, 1948.

Latest impression of the second edition, with an Introduction by John E. Steely. Wake Forest, North Carolina: Chanticleer, 1983.

Latest impression of the first edition, with a Foreword [by Geoffrey Bingham]. Blackwood, South Australia: New Creation Publications, 1984.

Summary regarding pagination: The first edition was printed several times during Forsyth's lifetime, and reprinted in 1984; the second edition was printed between 1948 and 1983.

The Person and Place of Jesus Christ. The Congregational Union Lecture for 1909. London: Congregational Union of England and Wales, and Hodder & Stoughton.

Chapter 6 contains 'The Distinctive Thing in Christian Experience' (1908).

Later impressions omit the 'Advertisement by the Committee of the Congregational Union of England and Wales' on p. v, and the final paragraph of the Preface.

Japanese translation: *Iesu Kirisuto no Jinkaku to Ichi*, trans. Yojiro Kami, Tokyo: Nagasaki-shoten, 1942.

Latest impressions. London: Independent Press, 1961. Grand Rapids, Michigan: Wm. B. Eerdmans, 1965.

1910

The Power of Prayer. With Dora Greenwell. Little Books on Religion. Edited by W. Robertson Nicoll. London: Hodder & Stoughton, n.d.

'Prayer as Incessant', 53–92, was, with the exception of the opening three paragraphs, reprinted in *The Soul of Prayer* (1916), chapter 5.

'Prayer as Insistent', 93–149, which incorporated 'The Minister's Prayer' (1907), was reprinted in *The Soul of Prayer* (1916), chapters 6 and 7.

The Work of Christ. Expositor's Library. London and New York: Hodder & Stoughton.

    Reprinted with a portrait, a Foreword by John S. Whale, a Memoir of the author by Jessie Forsyth Andrews, and List of [Forsyth's] Books. London: Independent Press, 1938.

    Japanese translation: *Shokuzai-von*, translator unknown. Tokyo: Nagasaki-shoten, 1939.

    Latest impression. Fontana Library. London: Collins, 1958.

1911

Christ on Parnassus: Lectures on Art, Ethic, and Theology. London: Hodder & Stoughton, n.d.

    Japanese translation: *Geijutsu, Rinri, Shingaku*, trans. Takayoshi Aso. Tokyo: Nagasaki-shoten, 1939.

    Latest impression. London: Independent Press, 1959.

1912

Faith, Freedom and the Future. London: Hodder & Stoughton.

    Reprinted with a Foreword by Jessie Forsyth Andrews and an Appendix, 'Declaration of the Faith, Church Order, and Discipline of the Congregational, or Independent Dissenters' from 1833. London: Independent Press, 1955.

Marriage: Its Ethic and Religion. London: Hodder & Stoughton, n.d.

    Based on 'Marriage: Its Ethic and Religion' (1911).

1912

The Principle of Authority in Relation to Certainty, Sanctity and Society: An Essay in the Philosophy of Experimental Religion. London: Hodder & Stoughton, n.d.

    Chapter 13 is 'Plebiscite and Gospel' (1911), chapter 14 is 'Liberty and Its Limits in the Church' (1912), and part 1 of the Epilogue is 'Authority and Theology' (1905).

    Second edition, repaginated, with a Note by Jessie Forsyth Andrews, additional footnotes, and an Index compiled by Robert McAfee Brown. London: Independent Press, 1952.

1915

Theology in Church and State. London: Hodder & Stoughton.

1916

The Christian Ethic of War. London: Longmans, Green.

The Justification of God: Lectures for War-Time on a Christian Theodicy. Studies in Theology. London: Duckworth.

New edition, repaginated, omitting the Preface, with a Foreword by D. R. Davies. London: Latimer House, 1948.

The latest impression is a reprint of the new edition, with a Foreword by Dean J. Carter. Blackwood, South Australia: New Creation Publications, 1988.

The Soul of Prayer. London: Charles H. Kelly.

Chapter 1 is 'Prayer and Its Importunity' (1908), chapter 5 is 'Prayer as Incessant' (1910), chapter 6, part 1 is a revised version of 'The Minister's Prayer' (1907), and chapters 6 and 7 are 'Prayer as Insistent' (1910).

Japanese translation: 1933.

Second edition, repaginated. London: Independent Press, 1949.

The latest impression is a reprint of the second edition. Salem, Ohio: Schmul, 1986.

1917

Lectures on the Church and the Sacraments. With a chapter by H. T. Andrews. London: Longmans, Green.

Contains 'The United States — of the Church' (1911).

Japanese translation: *Kyokai-von*, trans. Saburo Ishibima. N.pl.: Doi-shoten, 1937.

The second edition, repaginated, with the shorter title, *The Church and the Sacraments*, has a Note by Jessie Forsyth Andrews, and a Preface by J. K. Mozley. London: Independent Press, 1947.

Latest impression, 1964.

1918

This Life and the Next: The Effect on This Life of Faith in Another. London: Macmillan.

Second edition, repaginated, with a Preface by Jessie Forsyth Andrews. London: Independent Press, 1946.

Latest impression, 1953.

2. Anthologies and Collections
1948
Peter Taylor Forsyth (1848–1921), Director of Souls: Selections from His Practical Writings. Compiled and edited by Harry Escott. London: Epworth. With a portrait, a Preface by W. F. Rowlands, 'Some Biographical and Bibliographical Notes', and 'An Appraisement'. The anthology contains short selections from Forsyth's published writings, and a chapter called 'Pastoralia' (119–31), which includes previously unpublished excerpts of notes taken at the weekday evening services Forsyth gave at Hackney College.

Revised and reissued, without the portrait, as: *P. T. Forsyth and the Cure of Souls: An Appraisement and Anthology of His Practical Writings.* London: George Allen and Unwin, 1970. The only significant additions are to the 'Pastoralia' section (107–136).

1952
Congregationalism and Reunion: Two Lectures. London: Independent Press.

Comprising *Reunion and Recognition* (1917) and *Congregationalism and Reunion* (1918).

1957
God the Holy Father. London: Independent Press.

Comprising *The Holy Father and the Living Christ* (1897), *Christian Perfection* (1899), and *The Taste of Death and the Life of Grace* (1901).

The latest impression includes a Publisher's Foreword by Geoffrey Bingham. Blackwood, South Australia: New Creation Publications, 1987.

1962
The Church, the Gospel and Society, With a Foreword by Jessie Forsyth Andrews. London: Independent Press.

Comprising 'A Holy Church the Moral Guide of Society' (1905) and 'The Grace of the Gospel as the Moral Authority in the Church' (1905).

Revelation Old and New: Sermons and Addresses. Edited with a Preface by John Huxtable. London: Independent Press.

1969

The Creative Theology of P. T. Forsyth: Selections from His Works.
Edited by Samuel J. Mikolaski. Grand Rapids: Wm. B. Eerdmans.
Includes a Selected Bibliography of primary and secondary works.

1971

*The Gospel and Authority: A P. T. Forsyth Reader: Eight Essays
Previously Published in Journals.* Edited by Marvin W. Anderson.
Foreword by Gordon Rupp. Minneapolis: Augsburg.

1987

The Preaching of Jesus and the Gospel of Christ. With a Foreword,
Biographical Sketch, and Theological Introduction by Noel
Due. Blackwood, South Australia: New Creation Publications.
Comprising six articles in the *Expositor* with the general title,
'The Preaching of Jesus and the Gospel of Christ' (1915).

3. Articles, Pamphlets, Reviews and Letters to the Editor

1876

Ordination statement. *Shipley and Saltaire Times,* 25 November
1876, 4.
'The Turkish Atrocities: Sermon by the Rev. P. T. Forsyth', *Shipley
and Saltaire Times,* 23 September 1876, 4.

1877

Letter. *English Independent,* 8 November 1877, 1231–32.
Reprinted in the Appendix to Bradley, *Forsyth: The Man and
His Work,* 279–84.
Mercy the True and Only Justice. A Sermon Preached in Shipley
Congregational Church, on the Missionary Sunday, 30 September 1877. Bradford, T. Brear, n.d. [also possibly 1878].
'Religious Communion.' Letter to *English Independent,* 1 November 1877, 1202–3.
Reprinted in the Appendix to Bradley, *Forsyth: The Man and
His Work,* 276–9.
'Rev. P. T. Forsyth on "The Workers of the Future".' *Shipley and
Saltaire Times,* 28 July 1877, 4.

1878

'A Larger Comprehension the Remedy for the Decay of Theology.'

In *Public Conference on the Terms of Religious Communion*, 18–24. London: Judd, n.d.

> A report on conferences held 16 October 1877 and 7 May 1878, and on a meeting held in Forsyth's church on 9 May 1878.

'*Maid, Arise*': *A Sermon to School Girls*. Preached in Shipley Congregational Church, Sunday, 28 July 1878. Bradford: T. Brear, n.d.

'The Rev. P. T. Forsyth, MA, on "Robert Burns".' *Shipley and Saltaire Times*, 23 March 1878, 4.

'The Rev. P. T. Forsyth, MA, on "The Sunday Question".' *Shipley and Saltaire Times*, 30 November 1878, 4.

'The Rev. P. T. Forsyth, MA, on "Contents of the [Saltaire] Institute Library".' *Shipley and Saltaire Times*, 19 October 1878, 4.

'The Strength of Weakness.' *Christian World Pulpit* 13 (6 February 1878): 85–7.

'Why am I a Liberal?' *Shipley and Saltaire Times*, 20 April 1878, 4.

1879

'"The Bible Doctrine of Hell and the Unseen": Sermon by the Rev. P. T. Forsyth, Preached in the Bradford Road Congregational Church, Shipley, Nov. 23rd.' *Shipley and Saltaire Times*, 13 December 1879, 4.

'"Milton's Paradise Lost": Lecture by the Rev. P. T. Forsyth, MA.' *Shipley and Saltaire Times*, 22 March 1879, 4.

'"Mr Gladstone on Evangelical [sic] and Tractarianism": Discourse by the Rev. P. T. Forsyth.' *Shipley and Saltaire Times*, 26 July 1879, 4.

'"The Protestantism of the Protestant Religion".' *Shipley and Saltaire Times*, 29 November 1879, 4.

'The Rev. P. T. Forsyth on "Robert Burns".' *Shipley and Saltaire Times*, 8 November 1879, 4.

The Weariness in Modern Life. No publication data.

1881

'The Obligations of Doctrinal Subscription: A Discussion. – II,' 273–81. In *Modern Review* 2 (April 1881): 252–81.

1882

Corruption and Bribery: A Sermon. Preached at the Anniversary of the Congregational Church, Shipley, Yorkshire, on Sunday, 27 November 1881. Bradford, T. Brear, n.d.

'Egypt: A Sermon for Young Men.' *Christian World Pulpit* 22 (1 November 1882): 275–8.

In Memoriam: Andrew Baden, Esq., FIA (Died 9 February). [A sermon preached at] St Thomas Square Chapel, Hackney, 19 February 1882. For private circulation. Bradford: William Byles & Sons, 1882.

1883

'Discourses by Professor Bouvier.' With M. Forsyth. Review of *Le Divin d'après les Apôtres and Paroles de Foi et de Liberté*, by Auguste Bouvier. *Modern Review* 4 (April 1883): 410–13.

'Pfleiderer's View of St Paul's Doctrine.' Review of *Paulinism: A Contribution to the History of Primitive Christian Theology*, by Otto Pfleiderer. *Modern Review* 4 (January 1883): 81–96.
    Reprinted as a pamphlet. London: W. Speaght, n.d.

1884

'Baldwin Brown: A Tribute, a Reminiscence, and a Study.' In *In Memoriam: James Baldwin Brown*, 133–42. Edited by Elizabeth Baldwin Brown. London: James Clarke, 1884.
    Reprinted as a 20-page pamphlet. London: James Clarke, 1884.

'Nouvelles Paroles de Foi et de Liberté.' Review of *Nouvelles Paroles de Foi et de Liberté*, by Auguste Bouvier. *Modern Review* 5 (April 1884): 379–81.

'Pessimism.' *Christian World Pulpit* 25 (16 January 1884): 42–4.

1885

'The Argument for Immortality Drawn from the Nature of Love: A Lecture on Lord Tennyson's "Vastness".' *Christian World Pulpit* 28 (2 December 1885): 360–4.

'Liberal Education.' Signed, 'Publicola'. *Manchester Examiner and Times*, 15 December 1885, 8.

'Liberal Education.' Signed, 'Publicola.' *Manchester Examiner and Times*, 18 December 1885, 8.

'O sweet the song that in the deep, grey shade.' Poem. *Manchester Evening Gazette*, 11 December 1885.
    Reprinted on a small card.

The Pulpit and the Age. Manchester: Brook & Chrystal, 1885.

1886

'Dissent: Mr Lyulph Stanley's Address.' Signed, 'Publicola.' *Manchester Examiner and Times*, 23 December 1886, 5.

'Liberal Imperialism.' Signed, 'Publicola.' *Manchester Examiner and Times*, 30 June 1886, 5.

Socialism and Christianity in Some of their Deeper Aspects. Manchester: Brook & Chrystal, 1886.

'Society, Church and Dissent.' Signed, 'Publicola.' *Manchester Examiner and Times*, 13 December 1886, 5.

1887

'Bribery and Legislation.' Signed, 'Publicola.' *Manchester Examiner and Times*, 11 February 1887, 5.

'God send you health and bless your wealth.' Poem. Cheetham Hill Congregational Church, Manchester, 1 January 1887.

'Nonconformity and Home Rule.' Signed, 'Publicola.' *Manchester Examiner and Times*, 28 November 1887, 6, and 2 December 1887, 6.

'Preachers and Politics.' Signed 'Publicola.' *Manchester Examiner and Times*, 29 December 1887, 5.

'Sunday Schools and Modern Theology.' *Christian World Pulpit* 31 (23 February 1887): 123–7.

1888

'Ministers and the Sunday Question.' *Manchester Examiner and Times*, 23 January 1888, 7.

'Mr Balfour as a Theologian.' Signed, 'Publicola'. *Manchester Examiner and Times*, 8 October 1888, 8.

'The New Year.' *Congregational Monthly* 1 (January 1888): 13.

'The Relation of the Church to the Poor.' *Congregational Monthly* 1 (March 1888): 64.

1889

The Antiquity of Dissent. Leicester and Birmingham: Midland Educational; Manchester: Brooke [sic] & Chrystal, n.d.
    Included in *Charter*, chapters 5 and 6.

1890

'Preaching and Poetry.' *Expository Times* 1 (September 1890): 269–72.

1891

'Above the belt of darkling pines.' Poem. Clarendon Park Congregational Church, Leicester, 1 January 1891.

'Henrik Ibsen.' Review of *The Life of Henrik Ibsen*, by Henrik Jaeger, trans. Clara Bell. *Independent*, literary supplement, 6 March 1891, 1.

'The Historian of Rationalism as Poet.' Review of *Poems*, by W. E. H. Lecky. *Independent and Nonconformist*, literary supplement, 20 November 1891, 2.

The Old Faith and the New. Leicester, Birmingham, and Leamington: Midland Educational Company; Manchester: Brook & Chrystal, n.d.

'The Prevalent Distress: A Warning.' Letter. *Leicester Daily Mercury*, 19 January 1891, 4.

'A Prince of Critics on English Literature.' Review of *Essays on English Literature*, by Edmund Scherer. *Independent and Nonconformist*, literary supplement, 20 November 1891, 2.

'Teachers of the Century: Robert Browning.' *Modern Church*, 15 October 1891, 451–2.

'Theosophy and Theology.' *Independent*, 30 October and 6 November 1891, 777–8 and 798.

1892

'Art Wrestling with Death.' *Independent and Nonconformist*, 3 June 1892, 381.

'Faith and Charity.' *Congregational Monthly* 5 (January 1892): 13–17.

'A Fancy: Concerning the Critic's Inversion of Old Testament History.' Poem. *Independent and Nonconformist*, 27 May 1892, 365.

Letter. *Congregational Monthly* 5 (January 1892): 2–3.

'Origin of the Conception of God.' Review of *Lectures on the Origin and Growth of the Conception of God, as illustrated by Anthropology and History: The Hibbert Lecture for 1891*, by Count Goblet d'Alviella. *Independent and Nonconformist*, 19 and 26 August 1892, 554 and 571.

'"Revelation and the Bible": Mr Horton's New Book – A Symposium.' Review of *Revelation and the Bible*, by R. F. Horton. *Independent and Nonconformist*, 28 October 1892, 127.

'Shelley.' *Independent and Nonconformist*, 5 August 1892, 523.

1893

'John Norris, of Bemerton.' Review of *A Dissertation on John Norris, of Bemerton,* by Frederick J. Powicke. *Independent and Nonconformist,* 14 December 1893, 498–9.

'Is Christianity Played Out?' Leaflet published by Clarendon Park Congregational Church, February 1893.

'Old Testament Theology.' Review of *Old Testament Theology: The Religion of Revelation in its Pre-Christian Stage of Development,* by Hermann Schultz. *Independent and Nonconformist,* 9 February 1893, 107–8.

'Revelation and the Person of Christ.' In *Faith and Criticism: Essays by Congregationalists,* 95–144. London: Simpson Low Marston, 1893.

'A Theological Pathfinder: Dr Fairbairn's New Book.' Review of *Christ in Modern Theology,* by A. M. Fairbairn. *Evangelical Magazine* 101 (London, May 1893): 247–256.

'Thos. Campbell Finlayson, D.D.' Review of *Essays, Addresses, and Lyrical Translations,* by Thomas Campbell Finlayson. *Independent and Nonconformist,* 26 October 1893, 348; 2 November 1893, 380.

1894

'The Healing of the Paralytic.' Signed, 'F.' Poem. *British Weekly,* 25 October 1894, 4.

    Reprinted in Norah Waddington, *The First Ninety Years: Clarendon Park Congregational Church, Leicester,* 9. No publication data.

'Mystics and Saints.' *Expository Times* 5 (June 1984): 401–4.

'A Pocket of Gold.' Review of *The Way, the Truth, and the Life,* by F. A. J. [sic] Hort. *Independent and Nonconformist,* 8 March 1894, 187.

1895

'The Divine Self-Emptying.' *Christian World Pulpit* 47 (1 May 1895): 276–80.

    Also in *The Taste of Death and the Life of Grace* (1901), 89–127.

    And in *Father,* 29–44.

'Dr Dale.' *Sunday Magazine* 24 (May 1895): 331–7.

'Gain and Godliness.' In *Emmanuel Congregational Church, Cam-*

bridge: Past and Present: 1691–1895. No publication data.
In *Evangelical Magazine* 105 (1897): 482–4.
In *Congregational Quarterly* 23 (October 1945): 356–8.
'A New Year Meditation.' *Evangelical Magazine* 103 (January 1895): 29–35.

1896

'Congregationalism at Cambridge.' Letter. *British Weekly,* 24 September 1896, 356.
'Congregational Union Chairmanship.' Letter. *British Weekly,* 2 April 1896, 390.
'Dr Wendt's Picture of Christ.' Letters. *British Weekly,* 28 May and 4 June 1896, 82–3, 100.
'The Holy Father.'
As 'Annual Sermon.' *Independent and Nonconformist,* 1 October 1896 219–21.
In *Christian World Pulpit* 50 (7 October 1896): 225–9.
As 'Holy Father.' *British Weekly,* 19 and 26 November 1896, 74, 94–5.
Abstracted as 'God as Holy Father' in *Homiletic Review* 33 (March 1897): 234–6.
In *The Holy Father and the Living Christ* (1897), 1–95.
Japanese translation: *Seinaru-chichi,* trans. Masayuki Imaizumi Tokyo: YMCA, 1908.
In *Christian World Pulpit* 100 (30 November 1921): 254–9.
In *Father,* 1–27.
'A Manual of Devotion, Theological and Critical.' Review of *The Communion of the Christian with God,* by Willibald Herrmann. *Independent and Nonconformist,* 16 and 23 July 1896, 36, 54.

1897

'The Christening of Christmas.' Poem. *British Weekly,* 16 December 1897, 188.
'The Conversion of Faith by Love.' *British Weekly,* 28 October 1897, 22.
Letter. *British Weekly,* 14 October 1897, 435.
'The Living Christ.' *British Weekly,* 22 July 1897, 228–9.
In *The Holy Father and the Living Christ* (1897).
And in *Father,* 81–96.
'Theology in the Future.' *Independent and Nonconformist,* 10 June

1897, 450–2, 454.

'The Way of Life.' *Wesleyan Methodist Magazine* 120 (London, February 1897): 83–8.

1898

'The flash of arms he sees no more' [first line]. Poem. *Independent.*
Reprinted in *Poetical Tributes to the Memory of the Rt. Hon. W. E. Gladstone*, 167. Eds Samuel Jacob and Charles F. Forshaw. London: Elliot Stock, 1898.

The Happy Warrior: A Sermon on the Death of Mr Gladstone, 22 May 1898. London: H. R. Allenson, 1898.

'Sacramentalism the True Remedy for Sacerdotalism.' *Expositor*, 5th series, 8 (September, October 1898): 22–33, 262–75.

'The Solitude of Christ.' *Evangelical Magazine* 106 (October 1898): 485–91.

1899

'"The Ascent through Christ".' Review of *The Ascent through Christ*, by E. Griffith-Jones. *Puritan* 1 (March 1899): 151–4.

'The Atonement in Modern Religious Thought.' *Christian World*, 23 November 1899, 11–12.
Reprinted as an untitled essay in *The Atonement in Modern Religious Thought: A Theological Symposium*, 59–88. By Frederick Godet and sixteen others. London: James Clarke, 1900.

'The Cross as the Final Seat of Authority.' *Contemporary Review* 76 (October 1899): 589–608.
In *Living Age*, 16 December 1899, 671–87.
Part III (600–8) as 'The Evangelical Principle of Authority.' In *Volume of Proceedings of the Second International Congregational Council Held in Tremont Temple, Boston, Mass. September 20–29, 1899*, 57–63. Edited by Eugene C. Webster. Boston: Samuel Usher, 1900.
The entire article was included in *The Gospel and Authority* (1971), 148–78.

'The Dead Heart.' *Evangelical Magazine* 107 (September 1899): 435–40.

'Dr Berry: II–A Tribute by Rev. Dr Forsyth, Cambridge.' *British Weekly*, 2 February 1899, 310.

'Dr Dale.' Review of *The Life of R. W. Dale*, by A. W. W. Dale. *London Quarterly Review* 91 (April 1899): 193–222.

'A Hymn to Christ.' Poem. *British Weekly*, June 1899, 133.

Sermon on Matthew 23.39, quoted in full in Arthur Porritt, 'Leading Churches and Preachers: VI.–Emmanuel Church, Cambridge, and Dr P. T. Forsyth,' 715–19. *Puritan* 1 (October 1899): 713–19.

1900

'The Call of the New Century: I.–The Century's First Need.' *Sunday at Home* (London, 1900–1): 96–102.

'The Decay of Brain Power: The Dangers of a Cheap and Scrappy Press,' 43. Contribution to a symposium. In *Young Man* 14 (1900): 41–3.

Different Conceptions of Priesthood and Sacrifice. Report of a conference held at Oxford, 13 and 14 December 1899. [Contributions by Forsyth.] Edited by William Sanday. London: Longmans, Green, 1900.

'The Disappointment of the Cross.' *Puritan* 3 (February 1900): 135–9.

'Dr Barrett and "Higher Criticism".' Letters. *Examiner*, 30 August 1900, 580, and 20 September 1900, 650–1.

'Dr P. T. Forsyth on "The Supreme Evidence of God's Love".' *Examiner*, 20 December 1900, 167.

'Dr Martineau.' *London Quarterly Review* 93 (April 1900): 214–50.

'The Empire for Christ.' *Christian World Pulpit* 57 (16 May 1900): 303–11.

'Faith and Experience.' *Wesleyan Methodist Magazine* 123 (1900): 415–17.

'Faith, Timidity, and Superstition.' *Evangelical Magazine* 108 (March 1900): 111–6.

'Farewell Counsels to Students.' *British Weekly*, 14 June 1900, 179–80.

'Miss Overtheway.' Poem. *Christian World*, 20 December 1900, 14.

'Prayer.' *British Weekly*, 22 February 1900, 424.

'The School at the End of the Century: A Symposium on the Alleged Decline in Sunday School Attendance: Some Opinions and Suggestions.' *Sunday School Chronicle*, 13 December 1900, 849–52.

> Forsyth's contribution, subtitled 'As to the Causes of Decline', is on 850.

'A Simple Gospel.' *British Weekly*, 11 October 1900, 504.

'The Slowness of God.' *Expository Times* 11 (February 1900): 218–22.

'A Study of Dr Martineau.' Review of *James Martineau: A Biography and Study*, by A. W. Jackson. *Examiner*, 6 December 1900, 129.

'The Taste of Death and the Life of Grace.' *Christian World Pulpit* 58 (28 November 1900): 296–302.
> In *The Taste of Death and the Life of Grace* (1901).
> And in *Father*, 45–79.

'Things New and Old in Heresy.' *Examiner*, 12 July 1900, 399.

1901

'About Giving.' *Examiner*, 26 December 1901, 756.

'The Courage of Faith.' *Examiner*, 11 July 1901, 270–1.

'The Courage of Faith.' Letter. *Examiner*, 1 August 1901, 320.

'Dr G. A. Smith's Yale Lecture.' *British Weekly*, 25 April 1901, 51, 53.

'A First Primer of Apologetics.' Review of *A Primer of Apologetics*, by Robert Mackintosh. *Examiner*, 10 January 1901, 222.

'Nonconformists and the Education Bill.' Letter from Forsyth and fifteen others. *British Weekly*, 11 July 1901, 309.

'Notes from Pisgah.' *British Weekly*, 3 October 1901, 551.

'The Power of the Resurrection.' *Examiner*, 11 April 1901, 26.
> And in *Revelation*, 55–9.

'Ritschl on Justification.' Review of *The Christian Doctrine of Justification and Reconciliation*, vol. 3, by Albrecht Ritschl, translated by H. R. Mackintosh and A. B. Macauley. In *Speaker* (London), 16 February and 9 March 1901, 549–51, 629–31.

'The Significance of the Church Fabric.' *Christian World Pulpit* 59 (26 June 1901): 415–18.

'Treating the Bible Like Any Other Book.' *British Weekly*, 15 August 1901, 401–2.

1902

'The Depletion from the Ministry.' *Examiner*, 19 and 26 June 1902, 555–6, 586–7.

'The Evangelical Basis of Free Churchism.' *Contemporary Review* 81 (May 1902): 680–95.

'Evangelical Experience.' *Examiner*, 17 April 1902, 310–1.

'Judgment'. *Christian World Pulpit* 62 (1 October 1901): 209.

> And as 'Judgment unto Salvation.' *Examiner*, 2 October 1902, 332–5.

> And as 'Final Judgment Full Salvation' in *Missions*, chapter 2.

'Missions as the True Imperial and Apostolic Succession.' *Methodist Recorder*, 8 May 1902, 14–16.

> Abbreviated somewhat as 'An Allegory of the Resurrection.' *Christian World Pulpit* 61 (14 May 1902): 312–19.

> The longer version slightly revised as a pamphlet, *Holy Christian Empire*. London: James Clarke, n.d.

> Reprinted in *Missions*, chapter 10.

'Preachers and Politics.' *Examiner*, 6 and 13 February 1902, 107, 129.

'Revelation and Inspiration.' *Sunday Magazine* (1902): 178.

> Brief excerpt from a sermon called 'How to Read the Bible.'

1903

'The Charter of Missions.' *Christian World Pulpit* 63 (20 May 1903): 305–12.

> Revised as 'The Fatherhood of Death' for *Missions*, chapter 1.

> Abridged as *The Glorious Gospel.* 1795–1945 Triple Jubilee Papers, no. 3. London: Livingstone Press, n.d. [1943].

'The Church, the State, the Priest, and the Future.' *Examiner*, 9 and 16 July 1903, 27, 54.

The Courage of Faith. Glasgow: William Asher, 1903.

'Dumb Creatures and Christmas: A Little Sermon to Little Folk.' *Christian World*, 24 December 1903, 13.

'Dr Forsyth and the "Delegate".' Letter. *Examiner*, 12 November 1903, 476.

'The Need for a Revival of Personal Religion.' *Examiner*, 26 March 1903, 291–2.

> Revised for *Preaching*, chapter 5.

'Our Need of a Positive Gospel.' *Examiner*, 5 and 12 November 1903, 462–3, 486–7.

'The New Congregationalism and the New-Testament Congregationalism.' *Examiner*, 4 and 11 June 1903, 551–2, 575–6.

> Also published as a pamphlet. Introduction by W. Cunliffe-

Jones and J. Mullens. Sydney [Australia]: William Brooks, 1903.

A copy of the pamphlet, corrected by Forsyth, is in Dr Williams's Library, London.

'The Problem of Forgiveness in the Lord's Prayer.' In *The Sermon on the Mount: A Practical Exposition of the Lord's Prayer*, 181–92, 193–207. By E. Griffith-Jones and five others. Manchester: James Robinson, 1903.

'Sanctity and Certainty.' Letter. *Examiner*, 23 July 1903, 86.

'The Spiritual Reason for Passive Resistance.' *Examiner*, 8 October 1903, 338.

1904

'The Need for a Positive Gospel.' *London Quarterly Review* 101 (January 1904): 64–99.

'The Paradox of Christ.' *London Quarterly Review* 102 (June 1904): 111–38.

'The Scotch Church Case: "How It Strikes a Contemporary".' *Examiner*, 18 August 1904, 144–5.

'Self-Sacrifice.' Letter. *Examiner*, 7 January 1904, 5.

1905

'The Attacks on the Churches.' Letter. *British Weekly*, 23 and 30 March 1905, 614, 638.

'Authority and Theology.' *Hibbert Journal* 4 (October 1905): 63–78.

In *Living Age*, 6 January 1906, 18–27.

In *Authority*, Epilogue, part 1.

And in *The Gospel and Authority* (1971), 130–47.

'Dr Forsyth and Mysticism.' Letter. *Examiner*, 9 November 1905, 434.

'Dr Forsyth's Address.' Letter. *British Weekly*, 18 May 1905, 143.

'Dr Forsyth's Appeal to the Archbishop of Canterbury.' Letter. *Examiner*, 19 October 1905, 358–9.

And as 'Appeal to the Primate.' *Christian World*, 19 October 1905, 21–22.

'The Evangelical Churches and the Higher Criticism.' *Contemporary Review* 88 (October 1905): 574–99.

In *The Gospel and Authority* (1971), 15–52.

'Federate on the Gospel of Grace.' *Christian World*, 30 November 1905, 21.

As 'A Rallying Ground for the Free Churches: The Reality of Grace.' *Hibbert Journal* 4 (July 1906): 824–44.

And as 'A Rallying Ground for the Free Churches.' In *The Gospel and Authority* (1971), 95–117.

'The Grace of the Gospel as the Moral Authority in the Church.' *Examiner*, 12 October 1905, 319–25.

As a pamphlet. London: Congregational Union of England and Wales, [1905].

And, with the addition of a Preface, 57–59, in *Congregational Year Book 1906*, 57–97. London: Congregational Union of England and Wales, n.d.

And in *Society*, 65–127.

'A Holy Church the Moral Guide of Society.' *Examiner*, 11 May 1905, 441–9.

An excerpt in *British Weekly*, 11 May 1905, 129–31.

As a pamphlet. London: Congregational Union of England and Wales, n.d.

In *The Congregational Year Book 1906*, 15–56. London: Congregational Union of England and Wales, n.d.

And in *Society*, 5–64.

'Message from Principal Forsyth, D.D.' *Congregational Monthly*, new series, vol. 6 (July 1905): 74–5.

'A New Year Message to the Churches.' *Examiner*, 5 January 1905, 7–8.

'Our Colleges.' Letter. *Examiner*, 29 June 1905, 620.

'Preaching Christ and Preaching for Christ.' *Examiner*, 21 December 1905, 574.

As 'Message for the Times' in *British Missionary*, January 1906.

'The Sects and the Public.' *Examiner*, 23 March 1905, 262.

'Some Christian Aspects of Evolution.' *London Quarterly Review* 104 (October 1905): 209–39.

In *Living Age*, 11 November 1905, 325–41.

And as *Christian Aspects of Evolution*. London: Epworth, 1950.

'Reminiscences of the School-days of Two Distinguished F. P.'s [Former Pupils].' [Aberdeen] *Grammar School Magazine* 8 (March 1905): 48–50.

With the exception of the first sentence, reprinted as 'When We Were Boys'. In *Bon Record: Records and Reminiscences of Aberdeen Grammar School from the Earliest Times by many*

Writers, 259–61. Edited by H. F. Morland Simpson. Aberdeen, D. Wyllie & Son, 1906.

1906

'The Catholic Threat of Passive Resistance.' *Contemporary Review* 89 (April 1906): 562–7.

'The Chairman's Mantle: Dr Forsyth to Mr Jowett.' Poem. *Examiner*, 11 January 1906, 28.

'Chinese Labour in the Transvaal.' Letters. *Times* (London), 18 January 1906, 4; 20 January, 12; 25 January, 11; 26 January, 7; 29 January, 7.

'Church and University.'

'Principal Forsyth on Church and University: A Striking Address.' *Aberdeen Free Press*, 24 September 1906, 11.

And in *British Congregationalist*, 27 September 1906, 201–2.

And, incorporating the order of service, as 'Service in the University Chapel.' In *Record of the Celebration of the Quartercentenary of the University of Aberdeen*, 315–25. Edited by P. J. Anderson. Aberdeen: Aberdeen University Press, 1907.

'The Church's One Foundation.' *London Quarterly Review* 106 (October 1906): 193–202.

In *Living Age*, 10 November 1906, 351–6.

And in *The Gospel and Authority* (1971), 118–29.

'Church, State, Dogma and Education.' *Contemporary Review* 90 (December 1906): 827–36.

'"The Cruciality of the Cross".' Letter. *British Weekly*, 12 July 1906, 344.

'The Ideal Ministry.' *British Congregationalist*, 18 October 1906, 283–5.

As 'The Ideal Ministry of the Church.' *Christian World*, 18 October 1906, 22.

And in *Revelation*, 93–114.

'The Place of Spiritual Experience in the Making of Theology.' *Christian World*, 15 March 1906, 12.

In *Christian World Pulpit* 69 (21 March 1906): 184–7.

And in *Revelation*, 68–80.

1907

'The Address from the Chair.' *British Congregationalist*, 16 May 1907, 489.

'After Graduation What? New Series – No. V: The Congregational Church.' *Alma Mater: Aberdeen University Magazine* 25 (Aberdeen: Student's Representative Council, 18 December 1907): 110–12.

'The Apostolate of Negation.' *British Congregationalist*, 21 March 1907, 271.

Article. *Daily Chronicle*, 16 January 1907.

'Is Anything Wrong with the Churches?: A Symposium,' 46. In *British Congregationalist*, 19 January 1907, 46–8.

'The Minister's Prayer.' *British Congregationalist*, 6 June 1907, 561.
> As a pamphlet. London: National Council of Evangelical Free Churches, n.d.
> Revised and slightly expanded for *The Power of Prayer*, 95–106.
> And for *Prayer*, chapter 6, section 1.
> The *British Congregationalist* article was reprinted in *Revelation*, 120–4.

'Motherhood'. *British Congregationalist*, 26 September 1907, 255–6.

'The Newest Theology.' *British Weekly*, 7 March 1907, 581–2.

'The New Theology: I.–Immanence and Incarnation.' *British Congregationalist*, 24 January 1907, 77–78.
> As 'Immanence and Incarnation.' In *The Old Faith and the New Theology*, 47–61. Edited by C. H. Vine. London: Sampson Low Marston, 1907.

'The "New Theology": Mr Campbell's Teaching Criticised: A Repudiation.' *Daily Chronicle* (London), 4 February 1907.

'The Pastoral Duty of the Preacher.' *British Congregationalist*, 28 March 1907, 297–8.
> Revised for *Preaching*, 1st ed., 100–10.

Prayer and its Importunity. Also titled, 'The Preacher in Prayer.' Pamphlet (privately printed by the Minister's Prayer Union of the United Free Church of Scotland, 1907).
> In *London Quarterly Review* 110 (July 1908): 1–22.
> In *The Power of Prayer* (1910), 95–149.
> And in *Prayer*, chapters 6 and 7.

'Principal Forsyth on Preaching.' *British Weekly*, 31 October 1907, 83.

'Sentiment and Sentimentalism.' *British Congregationalist*, 28 November 1907, 487–8; 5 December, 509–10; 12 December, 534–5; 19 December, 561–2.
> Revised for *Socialism*, part 1.

'The Union and the Railway Dispute.' *British Congregationalist*, 24 October 1907, 361.

'The Unrest in the Churches: Dr Forsyth's Statement.' *Tribune* (London), 22 January 1907, 7–8.

1908

'Christ at the Gate.' *Christian World Pulpit* 73 (18 March 1908): 177–82.

'The Distinctive Thing in Christian Experience.' *Hibbert Journal* 6 (April 1908): 481–99.

>   In *Person*, chapter 7.

>   And in *The Gospel and Authority* (1971), 54–74.

'Dr Forsyth on "The Blood of Christ".' Reply to a letter by W. L. Walker. *Christian World*, 10 September 1908, 3.

'The Faith of Congregationalism: "Our Unwritten Belief as Progressive Evangelical Churches".' With A. E. Garvie. *British Congregationalist*, 18 June 1908, 593.

'Forgiveness Through Atonement the Essential Evangelical Christianity.' Full text.

>   In *Proceedings of the Third International Congregational Council*, Edinburgh, 1908, 28–53. Edited by J. Brown. London: Congregational Union of England and Wales, 1908.

>   Slightly revised for *Cruciality*, chapters 1 and 2.

'Forgiveness Through Atonement the Essential of Evangelical Christianity'. Abstract.

>   In *British Congregationalist*, 2 July 1908, 8.

>   And in *Revelation*, 60–7.

Introduction to *The Inspiration and Authority of Holy Scripture*, by John Monro Gibson, vii–xviii. Christian Faith and Doctrine Series, vol. 1. London: Thomas Law, 1908. New York: Fleming H. Revell, 1912.

'Law and Atonement: Dr Forsyth and Rev. W. L. Walker: Dr Forsyth's Rejoinder.' Letter. *Christian World*, 24 September 1908, 9.

Letter. *Christian World*, 10 September 1908, 3.

Letter. *Christian World*, 26 March 1908, 11.

'The Love of Liberty and the Love of Truth.' *Contemporary Review* 93 (February 1908): 158–70.

>   And in *Living Age*, 28 March 1908, 771–89.

'Some Christmas Thoughts.' *British Congregationalist*, 24 December 1908, 553.

'To the Congregational Churches of England and Wales.' *British Weekly*, 27 February 1908, 556.

'What Is Meant by the Blood of Christ?' *Expositor*, 7th series, 6 (September 1908): 207–25.

Revised and slightly expanded in *Cruciality*, chapter 4.

'What is the Evangelical Faith?' *British Congregationalist*, 10, 17 and 24 September 1908, 217–18, 239–40, 257–8.

1909

'Authority in Religion.' Review of *Authority in Religion*, by J. H. Leckie. *British Congregationalist*, 23 December 1909, 538.

'The Churches and Bible Study: Present-Day Needs.' *Christian World*, 18 February 1909, 5.

'Dr Forsyth on Modernism.' Abstract of a speech. *Christian World*, 14 October 1909, 22–3.

'The Evidential Value of Miracles.' *London Quarterly Review* 112 (July 1909): 1–7.

'The Faith of Jesus.' *Expository Times* 21 (October 1909): 8–9.

'The Insufficiency of Social Righteousness as a Moral Ideal.' *Hibbert Journal* 7 (April 1909): 596–613.

In *Living Age*, 26 June 1909, 779–89.

Expanded for *Cruciality*, chapter 3.

'The Interest and Duty of Congregationalists in the Present Crisis. (A Symposium.)' By Forsyth and others. *British Congregationalist*, 23 December 1909, 539.

Lay Religion', *British Congregationalist*, 29 April and 6 May 1909, 337–8, 357–8.

In *Person*, 3–25.

And in *Revelation*, 125–44.

'Milton's God and Milton's Satan.' *Contemporary Review* 95 (April 1909): 450–65.

And in *Living Age*, 29 May 1909, 519–30.

'Miraculous Healing, Then and Now.' *British Congregationalist*, 11 March 1909, 194.

'Modernism: Home and Foreign.' *British Congregationalist*, 14 October 1909, 303, 323–6.

Monism. London Society for the Study of Religion. Letchworth: Garden City Press, n.d.

'"Nonconformity and Politics."' Review of *Nonconformity and Politics*, 'by a Nonconformist minister.' *British Congregationalist*,

4 February 1909, 85–6.

'An Open Letter to a Young Minister on Certain Questions of the Hour.' *Christian World*, 27 May 1909, 11; 3 June, 14.

'The Peers or the People.' Symposium. *Christian World*, 16 December 1909, 4.

'The Roman Road of Rationalism: What Do the Advanced Critics Ask Us to Give Up?' *Christian World*, 26 August 1909, 6; 2 September, 3.

'Sir Joseph Compton-Rickett's New Book.' Review of *Origins and Faith*, by Sir Joseph Compton-Rickett. *British Weekly*, 13 May 1909, 150.

'The Work of Christ.' Abstract of five lectures. In *Mundesley Bible Conference, 1909: Verbatim Report of Sermons and Lectures*, 123–43. London: Westminster Chapel and Morgan & Scott, [1909].

    The full lectures, with additional material, were published as a book with the same title; see Section 1 above.

1910

'The Attitude of the Church to the Present Unrest.' *British Congregationalist*, 17 March 1910, 214–15.

'Calvinism and Capitalism.' *Contemporary Review* 97 (June 1910): 728–41, and 98 (July 1910): 74–87.

'Dr Forsyth and Mr Campbell.' Letter. *British Weekly*, 19 May 1910, 172.

    And as 'Dr Forsyth and the Rev. R. J. Campbell.' Letter. *British Congregationalist*, 19 May 1910, 418.

'"God Takes a Text and Preaches."' *British Weekly*, 14 April 1910, 36.

'Intellectual Difficulties to Faith.' *Record* (London), 22 and 29 July 1910, 708–10, 744–5.

'Messages from the Progressive Leaders: Principal Forsyth.' *British Weekly*, 6 January 1910, 421.

'Missions the Soul of Civilisation.' *Christian World Pulpit* 77 (4 May 1910): 273–7.

'Orthodoxy, Heterodoxy, Heresy and Freedom.' *Hibbert Journal* 8 (January 1910): 321–9.

'Theological Liberalism v. Liberal Theology.' *British Weekly*, 17 February 1910, 557–8.

'Welfare and Charity.' Letter. *British Weekly*, 10 February 1910, 533–4.

1911

'Christ and the Christian Principle.' In *London Theological Studies*, 133–66. By members of the Faculty of Theology in the University of London. London: University of London Press, 1911.

'Christ our Sanctification.' *Wesleyan Methodist Magazine* 134 (October 1911): 732–4.

'Church Statistics.' *British Weekly*, 15 June 1911, 284.

'The Duty of the Christian Ministry.' *British Congregationalist*, 13 July 1911, 27.

'The Goodness of God.' *British Congregationalist*, 10 August 1911, 97.
> And in *Revelation*, 81–5.

Letter. *British Weekly*, 26 October 1911, 100.

'The Majesty and the Mercy of God.' *British Congregationalist*, 4 May 1911, 367.
> Expanded as 'Majesty and Mercy.' *Christian World Pulpit* 79 (17 May 1911): 305–7.
> The shorter version was included in *Revelation*, 86–9.

'Marriage: Its Ethic and Religion.' *British Congregationalist*, 30 November 1911, 403.
> Expanded as *Marriage* (1912).

'Plebiscite and Gospel.' *Contemporary Review* 100 (July 1911): 60–76.
> And in *Authority*, chapter 13.

'Revelation and Bible.' *Hibbert Journal* 10 (October 1911): 235–52.
> And as 'Revelation and the Bible' in *The Gospel and Authority* (1971), 75–94.

Revelation Old and New. Edinburgh: William Blackwood & Sons, 1911.
> And in *Revelation*, 9–22.

'The Soul of Christ and the Cross of Christ.' *London Quarterly Review* 116 (October 1911): 193–212.
> And in *The Gospel and Authority* (1971), 179–99.

'The United States of the Church.' In *A United Free Church of England*, 15–47. With J. H. Shakespeare. London: National Council of Evangelical Free Churches, n.d.
> And in *Sacraments*, chapter 6.

Untitled address. In *The Story of the Scottish Congregational Theological Hall, 1811–1911*, 20–22. Edinburgh: Morrison & Gibb, 1911.

1912

'The Divorce Commission Report: Opinions of Prominent Congregationalists.' *British Congregationalist*, 21 November 1912, 847.

'The Doctrinal Method [of Bible Study]: The Theology of Hebrews.' *Westminster Bible Record* 3 (September 1912): 202–12.

'Faith and Mind.' *Methodist Review Quarterly* 61 (Nashville, October 1912): 627–43.

'The Home Rule Bill: Some Representative Opinions.' *British Congregationalist*, 18 April 1912, 259.

'Liberty and Its Limits in the Church.' *Contemporary Review* 101 (April 1912): 502–12.

And in *Authority*, chapter 14.

'Mackintosh on the Person of Christ.' Review of *The Doctrine of the Person of Jesus Christ*, by H. R. Mackintosh. In *British Weekly*, 28 November 1912, 281–2.

'New Year's Messages: How Congregationalists Should Meet 1912.' *British Congregationalist*, 4 January 1912, 3–4.

'The Pessimism of Mr Thomas Hardy.' *London Quarterly Review* 118 (October 1912): 193–219.

And in *Living Age*, 23 November 1912, 458–73.

'Self-Denial and Self-Committal.' *Expositor*, 8th series, 4 (July 1912): 32–43.

'Tributes to Andrew Martin Fairbairn.' *Westminster Gazette*, 12 February 1912.

As 'Appreciations and Tributes.' *British Congregationalist*, 15 February 1912, 116.

'Tributes to Principal Fairbairn: II.' *British Weekly*, 15 February 1912, 568, 574.

1913

'The Church and Divorce: Principal Forsyth's Memorandum.' *British Congregationalist*, 30 October 1913, 885.

'The Church and Society.' *Westminster Gazette*, 6 September 1913, 3; 13 September, 13; 20 September, 2.

'The Church and Society–Alien or Allied?' *British Weekly*, 9 October 1913, 43.

And as 'Christianity and Society.' *Methodist Review Quarterly* 63 (Nashville, January 1914): 3–21.

'The Church and the Children.' Letter. *British Weekly*, 15 May 1913, 169.

'Congregationalism and the Principle of Liberty.' *Constructive Quarterly* 1 (September 1913): 498–521.

'The Fund and the Faith.' Poem. *British Weekly*, 29 May 1913, 219.

'Intellectualism and Faith.' *Hibbert Journal* 11 (January 1913): 311–28.
'Land Laws of the Bible.' *Contemporary Review* 104 (October 1913): 496–504.
'The Religious Strength of Theological Reserve.' *British Weekly*, 13 February 1913, 576–8.
'Things New and Old.' *Christian World Pulpit* 84 (29 Oct 1913): 273–6.

1914

Address to students, Stockwell College, 17 June [1914]. *Educational Record: Proceedings of the British and Foreign School Society* (October 1914): 106–12.
'Christianity and Nationality.' *British Weekly*, 9 July 1914, 385–6.
'The Church and the Nation.' *Westminster Gazette*, 12 May 1914, 1–2.
> And in *British Congregationalist*, 14 May 1914, 383.
'The Church and the Nation–In Education, for Instance.' *Westminster Gazette*, 6 July 1914, 1–2.
> Extracts in 'Church and State: Dr Forsyth's Further Explanations.' *British Congregationalist*, 9 July 1914, 40.
'The Effectiveness of the Ministry.' *British Congregationalist*, 12 March 1914, 198–9.
> Expanded for *London Quarterly Review* 122 (July 1914): 1–20.
> Slightly revised for *Sacraments*, chapter 7.
'The Late Rev. C. S. Horne–A Tribute.' *British Weekly*, 7 May 1914, 140.
> As 'The Late Silvester Horne: Memorial Service at the City Temple. Dr Forsyth's Address.' *British Congregationalist*, 21 May 1914, 420–2.
> Quoted in full in W. B. Selbie, *The Life of Charles Silvester Horne* (London: Hodder & Stoughton, 1920), 302–5.
Letter. From Forsyth and others to Adolf von Harnack. *British Weekly*, 3 September 1914, 557.
'The Man and the Message.' *London Quarterly Review* 121 (*Jan* 1914): 1–11.
'Music and Worship.' *Homiletic Review* 67 (January 1914): 18–22.
> And in *Congregational Quarterly* 33 (October 1955): 339–44.
'Our Experience of a Triune God.' *Cambridge Christian Life* 1 (June 1914): 240–6.

A Radiant Life: In Memory of Charles Silvester Horne. Privately printed, 1914.

'Regeneration, Creation, and Miracle.' *Methodist Review Quarterly* 63 (Nashville, October 1914): 627–43, and 64 (January 1915): 89–103.

'Welding the Churches: A World Congress for Christian Unity.' *Daily Chronicle* (London), 19 February 1914, 6.

1915

Churches, Sects and Wars.' *Contemporary Review* 107 (May 1915): 618–26.

'The Colleges and Recruiting.' Letter from Forsyth, A. E. Garvie, W. B. Selbie and W. H. Bennett. *British Weekly,* 18 November 1915, 134.

'The Conquest of Time by Eternity.' *Christian World Pulpit* 87 (17 February 1915): 104–8.

    Also included in *Justification,* chapter 12.

'Dr Forsyth and Mr Campbell.' Letter. *British Weekly,* 4 November 1915, 93.

'Faith, Metaphysic, and Incarnation.' *Methodist Review* 97 (New York, September 1915): 696–719.

'History and Judgment.' *Contemporary Review* 108 (October 1915): 457–70.

    And in *Justification,* chapter 11.

'Ibsen's Treatment of Guilt.' *Hibbert Journal* 14 (October 1915): 457–70.

'Lay Religion.' *Constructive Quarterly* 3 (December 1915): 767–89.

'Prayer.' *London Quarterly Review* 124 (October 1915): 214–31.

    And in *Prayer,* chapter 1.

'The Preaching of Jesus and the Gospel of Christ.' *Expositor,* 8th series, volume number indicated:

    I. 9 (April 1915): 325–35.

    II. 9 (May 1915): 404–21.

    III. 'The Mind of Christ on His Death.' 10 (July 1915): 66–89.

    IV. 'Christ's Offering of His Soul for Sin.' 10 (August 1915): 117–38.

    V. 'Moral Finality and Certainty in the Holiness of the Cross.' 10 (October 1915): 340–64.

    VI. 'In What Sense Did Jesus Preach the Gospel?' 10 (November 1915): 445–65.

VII. See 1923.

The first six articles were published as *The Preaching of Jesus and the Gospel of Christ* (1987); see Section 2.

'Veracity, Reality, and Regeneration.' *London Quarterly Review* 123 (April 1915): 193–216.

1916

'Christ–King or Genius?' *Methodist Review* 65 (Nashville, July 1916): 433–47.

'Church, Ministry and Sacraments.' In *The Validity of the Congregational Ministry*, 33–52. With J. Vernon Bartlett and J. D. Jones. London: Congregational Union of England and Wales, n.d.

'The Conversion of the "Good".' *Contemporary Review* 109 (June 1916): 760–71.

'The First and Second Adam.' *Methodist Review* 98 (New York, May 1916): 347–51.

'Mr Campbell's Book: Dr Forsyth on the Status of Free Churches.' Letter. *Christian World*, 2 November 1916, 4.

'The Rev. R. J. Campbell.' Letter. *British Weekly*, 6 January 1916, 284.

'The Spiritual Needs in the Churches.' *Christian World Pulpit* 89 (3 May 1916): 251–55.

'The Truncated Mind.' Signed, 'F.' *Manchester Guardian*, 4 November 1916, 5.

'The Truncated Mind.' Letter. *Manchester Guardian*, 16 November 1916, 7.

1917

'Christ's Person and His Cross.' *Methodist Review* 66 (Nashville, January 1917): 3–22.

'Comments on a Paper at the Congregational Union.' *British Congregationalist*, 19 October 1917, 297–8.

'The Condition of Evangelicalism.' From a correspondent. *Christian World*, 13 December 1917, 11.

'The Cross of Christ as the Moral Principle of Society.' *Methodist Review* 99 (New York, January 1917): 9–21.

'The Efficiency and Sufficiency of the Bible.' *Biblical Review* 2 (January 1917); 10–30.

'The Future of the Ministry: A Talk with Dr Forsyth.' Interview. *Christian World*, 23 August 1917, 4.

'The Moralization of Religion.' *London Quarterly Review* 128 (October 1917): 161–74.
'The Need of a Church Theory for Church Union.' *Contemporary Review* 111 (March 1917): 357–65.
    Expanded for *Sacraments*, chapter 3.
'The Preacher and the Publicist.' *London Quarterly Review* 127 (January 1917): 1–18.
Reunion and Recognition. London: Congregational Union of England & Wales, n.d.
    Reprinted in *Congregationalism*, 5–41.
'A Tribute to the Rev. Dr John Hunter.' Four-page leaflet, 19 September 1917.
    Reprinted in Leslie S. Hunter, *John Hunter*, D.D.: *A Life*, 289–91. London, Hodder and Stoughton, 1922.
'The Village Churches and the War.' Letter. *British Weekly*, 29 March 1917, 496.

1918
'The Christianity of Christ and Christ our Christianity.' *Review and Expositor* 15 (July 1918): 249–65.
Congregationalism and Reunion. London, Congregational Union of England and Wales, n.d.
    This pamphlet is comprised of an expanded version of an address given at the May meeting of the Congregational Union of England and Wales, and an addendum delivered to the London Congregation Board.
    Omitting Forsyth's original preface, reprinted in *Congregationalism*, 43–78.
'Evangelicals and Home Reunion.' *Churchman* 32 (September 1918): 528–36.
'A Few Hints about Reading the Bible.' *Biblical Review* 3 (October 1918): 530–44.
    And as a pamphlet. New York: Association Press, 1919.
'The Reality of God: A War-time Question.' *Hibbert Journal* 16 (July 1918): 608–19.
'Reconstruction and Religion.' *Westminster Gazette*.
    And in *Problems of Tomorrow: Social, Moral and Religious*, 15–23. Edited by Fred A. Rees. London: James Clark, 1918.
The Roots of a World-Commonwealth. London: Hodder & Stoughton, 1918. New York: George H. Doran, 1918.

Reprinted. London: Independent Press, 1952.

'Some Effects of the War on Belief.' *Holborn Review* 9 (January 1918): 16–26.

'Testamentary Ethics.' *London Quarterly Review* 129 (April 1918): 169–79.

'The Unborn, the Once Born, the Twice Born and the First-Born.' *Christian World*, 14 February 1918, 9.

'The Unity Beneath Reunion.' *Challenge*, 15 and 22 February 1918.

1919

'Church and Nation: A Nonconformist on the Enabling Bill.' Letters on the Church of England National Assembly Bill. *Times* (London), 28 May 1919, 8; corrected 29 May, 8; 6 June, 8; 16 June, 8.

'The Foolishness of Preaching.' *Expository Times* 30 (January 1919): 153–4.

'The Inner Life of Christ.' *Constructive Quarterly* 7 (March 1919): 149–62.

'One Step to Reunion: Interchange of Pulpits.' Letter. From Forsyth and R. C. Gillie, J. H. Jowett, J. Scott Lidgett, W. B. Selbie, J. H. Shakespeare, and P. Carnegie Simpson. *Times* (London), 30 August 1919, 6.

'The Public Impotence of Religion.' *Westminster Gazette*, 21 February 1919, 1–2.

'Religion and Reality.' *Contemporary Review* 115 (May 1919): 548–54.

'Religion, Private and Public.' *London Quarterly Review* 131 (January 1919): 19–32.

'Unity and Theology: A Liberal Evangelicalism the True Catholicism.' In *Towards Reunion: Being Contributions to Mutual Understanding by Church of England and Free Church Writers*, 51–81. By J. Scott Lidgett and 13 others. London: Macmillan, 1919.

1920

'Does the Church Prolong the Incarnation?' *London Quarterly Review* 133 (January, April 1920): 1–12, 204–12.

1923

'The Preaching of Jesus and the Gospel of Christ. [VII:] The Meaning of a Sinless Christ.' *Expositor*, 8th series, vol. 25 (1923): 288–312.

Concludes the series begun in 1915.

1941

Letter to Albert Peel. In *Transactions of the Congregational Historical Society* 14 (November 1941): 67–8.

1943

Annotations on a paper written in 1906 by Robert Mackintosh, 'The Authority of the Cross,' in *Congregational Quarterly* 21 (July 1943): 209–18.

1964

'At the Centre of Me.' Excerpts from *Person. Decision*, June 1964, 7.

Undated Material

Coleridge's 'Ancient Mariner': An Exposition and Sermon from a Modern Text. Bradford: W. Byles and Sons, n.d.
> From 1880–83.

'Freedom.' Choral ode. Concert Programme, 13–16.

The Priesthood and Its Theological Assumptions. Free Church Tracts for the Times, no. 3. London: Thomas Law, n.d.
> From about 1898–90.

'A Point in Christian Ethics.' *Christian World*, 11.
> From 1895–1901.

'Moral Manhood.' *Young Man* (Cambridge): 151–3.
> After 1901.

'How You Can Help Your Minister.' *Congregational Magazine*, 200–1.
> From about 1900–05.
>> As 'How to Help Your Minister.' *Christian World*, 24 August 1950, 5.
>> In *Irish Christian Advocate* (Belfast), 8 September 1950, 1.
>> And in *Revelation*, 115–19.

'The Second Victory.' *Westminster Gazette*, 1–2.
> About 1918.

'The wind from the heath.' Poem.
> An annotation by Jessie Forsyth Andrews says, 'Probably to Mrs Waterhouse.'

Appendix to Part 3: Title Index to Forsyth's Articles

Chinese Labour in the Transvaal (1906)

Christ and the Christian Principle (1911)

Christ at the Gate (1908)

Christ–King or Genius? (1916)

Christ our Sanctification (1911)

Christ's Offering of His Soul for Sin. *See:* Preaching of Jesus and the Gospel of Christ (1915)

Christ's Person and His Cross (1917)

Christening of Christmas (1897)

Christian Aspects of Evolution. *See:* Some Christian Aspects of Evolution (1905)

Christianity and Nationality (1914)

Christianity and Society. *See:* Church and Society–Alien or Allied? (1913)

Christianity of Christ and Christ our Christianity (1918)

Church and Divorce (1913)

Church and Nation: A Nonconformist on the Enabling Bill (1919)

Church and Society (1913)

Church and Society–Alien or Allied? (1913)

Church and State: Dr Forsyth's Further Explanations. *See:* The Church and the Nation–In Education, for Instance (1914)

Church and the Children (1913)

Church and the Nation (1914)

Church and the Nation–In Education, for Instance (1914)

Church and University (1906)

Church as the Corporate Missionary of the Gospel. *See: Revelation,* chapter 3.

Church Statistics (1911)

Church, Ministry and Sacraments (1916)

Church, State, Dogma and Education (1906)

Church, the State, the Priest, and the Future (1903)

Churches and Bible Study: Present-Day Needs (1909)

Churches, Sects and Wars (1915)

Church's One Foundation (1906)

Coleridge's 'Ancient Mariner': An Exposition and Sermon from a Modern Text (undated)

Colleges and Recruiting (1915)

Comments on a Paper at the Congregational Union (1917)

Condition of Evangelicalism (1917)

Congregational Union Chairmanship (1896)

Congregationalism and Reunion (1918)
Congregationalism and the Principle of Liberty (1913)
Congregationalism at Cambridge (1896)
Conquest of Time by Eternity (1915)
Contents of the [Saltaire] Institute Library (1878)
Conversion of Faith by Love (1897)
Conversion of the Good (1916)
Corruption and Bribery (1882)
Courage of Faith (1901, twice; 1903)
Cross as the Final Seat of Authority (1899)
Cross of Christ as the Moral Principle of Society (1917)
Cruciality of the Cross (1906)
Dead Heart (1899)
Decay of Brain Power (1899)
Depletion from the Ministry (1902)
Different Conceptions of Priesthood and Sacrifice (1900)
Disappointment of the Cross (1900)
Discourses by Professor Bouvier (1883)
Dissent: Mr Lyulph Stanley's Address (1886)
Distinctive Thing in Christian Experience (1908)
Divine Self-Emptying (1895)
Divorce Commission Report (1912)
Doctrinal Method of Bible Study: The Theology of Hebrews
    (1912)
Does the Church Prolong the Incarnation? (1920)
Dr Barrett and Higher Criticism (1900)
Dr Berry: A Tribute (1899)
Dr Dale (1895, 1899)
Dr Forsyth and Mr Campbell (1910, 1915)
Dr Forsyth and Mysticism (1905)
Dr Forsyth and the Delegate (1903)
Dr Forsyth and the Rev. R. J. Campbell. *See:* Dr. Forsyth and Mr
    Campbell (1910)
Dr Forsyth on Modernism (1909)
Dr Forsyth on 'The Blood of Christ' (1908)
Dr Forsyth's Address (1905)
Dr Forsyth's Appeal to the Archbishop of Canterbury (1905)
Dr G. A. Smith's Yale Lecture (1901)
Dr Martineau (1900)
Dr P. T. Forsyth on 'The Supreme Evidence of God's Love' (1900)

Dr Wendt's Picture of Christ (1896)

Dumb Creatures and Christmas: A Little Sermon to Little Folk (1903)

Duty of the Christian Ministry (1911)

Effectiveness of the Ministry (1914)

Efficiency and Sufficiency of the Bible (1917)

Egypt: A Sermon for Young Men (1882)

Empire for Christ (1900)

Evangelical Basis of Free Churchism (1902)

Evangelical Principle of Authority. *See:* Cross as the Final Seat of Authority (1899)

Evangelicals and Home Reunion (1918)

Evidential Value of Miracles (1909)

Faith and Charity (1892)

Faith and Experience (1900)

Faith and Mind (1912)

Faith of Congregationalism: Our Unwritten Belief as Progressive Evangelical Churches (1908)

Faith of Jesus (1909)

Faith, Metaphysic, and Incarnation (1915)

Faith, Timidity, and Superstition (1900)

Fancy: Concerning the Critic's Inversion of Old Testament History (1892)

Farewell Counsels to Students (1900)

Fatherhood of Death. *See:* Charter of Missions (1903)

Federate on the Gospel of Grace (1905)

Few Hints about Reading the Bible (1918)

First and Second Adam (1916)

First Primer of Apologetics (1901)

Flash of arms he sees no more (1898)

Foolishness of Preaching (1919)

For the Fraternal. *See:* Unborn, the Once Born, the Twice Born and the First-Born (1915)

Forgiveness Through Atonement the Essential of Evangelical Christianity (1908)

Freedom (undated)

Fund and the Faith (1913)

Future of the Ministry (1917)

Gain and Godliness (1895)

Glorious Gospel. *See:* Charter of Missions (1903)

God as Holy Father. *See:* Holy Father (1896)
God send you health, and bless your wealth (1887)
God Takes a Text and Preaches (1910)
Goodness of God (1911)
Grace of the Gospel as the Moral Authority in the Church (1905)
Happy Warrior: A Sermon on the Death of Mr Gladstone (1898)
Healing of the Paralytic (1894)
Henrik Ibsen (1891)
Historian of Rationalism as Poet (1891)
History and Judgment (1915)
Holy Christian Empire. *See:* Missions as the True Imperial and
    Apostolic Succession (1902)
Holy Church the Moral Guide of Society (1905)
Holy Father (1896)
Home Rule Bill (1912)
How to Help Your Minister. *See:* How You Can Help Your
    Minister (undated)
How to Read the Bible. *See:* Revelation and Inspiration (1902)
How You Can Help Your Minister (undated)
Hymn to Christ (1899)
Ibsen's Treatment of Guilt (1915)
Ideal City. *See in* Revelation Old and New (1962)
Ideal Ministry (1906)
Ideal Ministry of the Church. *See:* Ideal Ministry (1906)
Immanence and Incarnation. *See:* New Theology: Immanence and
    Incarnation (1907)
In Memoriam: Andrew Baden (1882)
In What Sense Did Jesus Preach the Gospel? *See:* Preaching of Jesus
    and the Gospel of Christ (1915)
Inner Life of Christ (1919)
Inspiration and Authority of Holy Scripture (1908)
Insufficiency of Social Righteousness as a Moral Ideal (1909)
Intellectual Difficulties to Faith (1910)
Intellectualism and Faith (1913)
Interest and Duty of Congregationalists in the Present Crisis (1909)
Is Anything Wrong with the Churches? (1907)
Is Christianity Played Out? (1893)
John Norris, of Bemerton (1893)
Judgment (1902)
Judgment unto Salvation. *See:* Judgment (1902)

Land Laws of the Bible (1913)

Larger Comprehension the Remedy for the Decay of Theology (1878)

Late Rev. C. S. Horne–A Tribute (1914)

Late Silvester Horne ... Dr Forsyth's Address. *See:* Late Rev. C. S. Horne–A Tribute (1914)

Law and Atonement (1908)

Lay Religion (1909, 1915)

Letter to Adolf von Harnack (1914)

Letter to Albert Peel (1941)

Letter to *British Weekly* (1897)

Letter to *British Weekly* (1911)

Letter to *Christian World* (1908, twice)

Letter to *Congregational Monthly* (1892)

Letter to *English Independent* (1877)

Liberal Education (1885, twice)

Liberal Imperialism (1886)

Liberty and Its Limits in the Church (1912)

Living Christ (1897)

Love of Liberty and the Love of Truth (1908)

Mackintosh on the Person of Christ (1912)

Maid, Arise: A Sermon to School Girls (1878)

Majesty and Mercy. *See:* Majesty and the Mercy of God (1911)

Majesty and the Mercy of God (1911)

Man and the Message (1914)

Manual of Devotion, Theological and Critical (1896)

Marriage: Its Ethic and Religion (1911)

Meaning of a Sinless Christ. *See:* Preaching of Jesus and the Gospel of Christ (1923)

Mercy the True and Only Justice (1877)

Message for the Times. See: Preaching Christ and Preaching for Christ (1905)

Message from Principal Forsyth (1905)

Messages from the Progressive Leaders (1910)

Milton's God and Milton's Satan (1909)

Milton's 'Paradise Lost' (1879)

Mind of Christ on His Death. *See:* Preaching of Jesus and the Gospel of Christ (1915)

Minister's Prayer (1907)

Ministers and the Sunday Question (1888)

Miraculous Healing, Then and Now (1909)
Miss Overtheway (1900)
Missions as the True Imperial and Apostolic Succession (1902)
Missions the Soul of Civilisation (1910)
Modernism: Home and Foreign (1909)
Monism (1909)
Moral Finality and Certainty in the Holiness of the Cross. *See:*
    Preaching of Jesus and the Gospel of Christ (1915)
Moral Manhood (undated)
Moral Peril of the Frontier Life (1900)
Moralization of Religion (1917)
Motherhood (1907)
Mr Balfour as a Theologian (1888)
Mr Campbell's Book: Dr Forsyth on the Status of Free Churches (1916)
Mr Gladstone on Evangelical and Tractarianism (1879)
Music and Worship (1914)
Mystics and Saints (1894)
Need for a Positive Gospel (1904)
Need for a Revival of Personal Religion (1903)
Need of a Church Theory for Church Union (1917)
New Congregationalism and the New-Testament Congregationalism
    (1903)
New Theology: Immanence and Incarnation (1907)
New Theology: Mr Campbell's Teaching Criticised: A Repudiation
    (1907)
New Year (1888)
New Year Meditation (1895)
New Year Message to the Churches (1905)
New Year's Messages: How Congregationalist Should Meet 1912
    (1912)
Newest Theology (1907)
Nonconformists and the Education Bill (1901)
Nonconformity and Home Rule (1887)
Nonconformity and Politics (1909)
Notes from Pisgah (1901)
Nouvelles Paroles de Foi et de Liberté (1884)
O sweet the song that in the deep, grey shade (1885)
Obligations of Doctrinal Subscription (1881)
Old Faith and the New (1891)
Old Testament Theology (1893)

One Step to Reunion: Interchange of Pulpits (1919)
Open Letter to a Young Minister on Certain Questions of the Hour (1909)
Ordination statement (1876)
Origin of the Conception of God (1892)
Orthodoxy, Heterodoxy, Heresy and Freedom (1910)
Our Colleges (1905)
Our Experience of a Triune God (1914)
Our Need of a Positive Gospel (1903)
Paradox of Christ (1904)
Pastoral Duty of the Preacher (1907)
Pastoralia. *See in Section Two:* Escott
Peers or the People (1909)
Pessimism (1884)
Pessimism of Mr Thomas Hardy (1912)
Pfleiderer's View of St Paul's Doctrine (1883)
Place of Spiritual Experience in the Making of Theology (1906)
Plebiscite and Gospel (1911)
Pocket of Gold (1894)
Point in Christian Ethics (undated)
Power of the Resurrection (1901)
Prayer (1900, 1915)
Prayer and its Importunity (1907)
Preacher and the Publicist (1917)
Preacher in Prayer. *See:* Prayer and its Importunity (1907)
Preachers and Politics (1887, 1902)
Preaching and Poetry (1890)
Preaching Christ and Preaching for Christ (1905)
Preaching of Jesus and the Gospel of Christ (1915, 1923)
Prevalent Distress: A Warning (1891)
Priesthood and Its Theological Assumptions (undated)
Prince of Critics on English Literature (1891)
Principal Forsyth on Church and University: A Striking Address. *See:* Church and University (1906)
Principal Forsyth on Preaching (1907)
Problem of Forgiveness in the Lord's Prayer (1903)
Protestantism of the Protestant Religion (1879)
Public Impotence of Religion (1919)
Pulpit and the Age (1885)
Radiant Life: In Memory of Charles Silvester Horne (1914)

Rallying Ground for the Free Churches. *See:* Federate on the Gospel of Grace (1905)
Reality of God: A War-time Question (1918)
Reconstruction and Religion (1918)
Regeneration, Creation, and Miracle (1914)
Relation of the Church to the Poor (1888)
Religion and Reality (1919)
Religious Communion (1877)
Religious Strength of Theological Reserve (1913)
Reminiscences of the School-days of Two Distinguished F. P.'s [Former Pupils] (1905)
Reunion and Recognition (1917)
Rev. R. J. Campbell (1916)
Revelation and Bible (1911)
Revelation and Inspiration (1902)
Revelation and the Bible: Mr Horton's New Book (1892)
Revelation and the Person of Christ (1893)
Revelation Old and New (1911)
Ritschl on Justification (1901)
Robert Burns (1878, 1879)
Roman Road of Rationalism: What Do the Advanced Critics Ask Us to Give Up? (1909)
Roots of a World-Commonwealth (1918)
Sacramentalism the True Remedy for Sacerdotalism (1898)
Sanctity and Certainty (1903)
School at the End of the Century: On the Alleged Decline in Sunday School Attendance (1900)
Scotch Church Case: How It Strikes a Contemporary (1904)
Second Victory (undated)
Sects and the Public (1905)
Self-Denial and Self-Committal (1912)
Self-Sacrifice (1904)
Sentiment and Sentimentalism (1907)
Sermon on Matthew 23.39 (1899)
Service in the University Chapel. *See:* Church and University (1906)
Shelley (1892)
Significance of the Church Fabric (1901)
Simple Gospel (1900)
Sir Joseph Compton-Rickett's New Book (1909)

Slowness of God (1900)
Socialism and Christianity in Some of their Deeper Aspects (1886)
Sociality, Socialism and the Church (1907)
Society, Church and Dissent (1886)
Solitude of Christ (1898)
Some Christian Aspects of Evolution (1905)
Some Christmas Thoughts (1908)
Some Effects of the War on Belief (1918)
Soul of Christ and the Cross of Christ (1911)
Spiritual Needs in the Churches (1916)
Spiritual Reason for Passive Resistance (1903)
Story of the Scottish Congregational Theological Hall (1911)
Strength of Weakness (1878)
Study of Dr Martineau (1900)
Suffering. *See: Revelation*, chapter 9
Sunday Question (1878)
Sunday Schools and Modern Theology (1887)
Supreme Evidence of God's Love. *See:* Dr P. T. Forsyth on 'The
    Supreme Evidence of God's Love' (1900)
Taste of Death and the Life of Grace (1900)
Teachers of the Century: Robert Browning (1891)
Testamentary Ethics (1918)
Theological Liberalism v. Liberal Theology (1910)
Theological Pathfinder: Dr Fairbairn's New Book (1893)
Theological Reaction (1909)
Theology in the Future (1897)
Theosophy and Theology (1891)
Things New and Old (1913)
Things New and Old in Heresy (1900)
Thos. Campbell Finlayson (1893)
To the Congregational Churches of England and Wales (1908)
Treating the Bible Like Any Other Book (1901)
Tribute to the Rev. Dr John Hunter (1917)
Tributes to Andrew Martin Fairbairn (1912)
Tributes to Principal Fairbairn (1912)
Truncated Mind (1916, twice)
Turkish Atrocities (1876)
Unborn, the Once Born, the Twice Born and the First-Born (1918)
Union and the Railway Dispute (1907)
United States–of the Church (1911)

Unity and Theology: A Liberal Evangelicalism the True Catholi-
cism (1919)
Unity Beneath Reunion (1918)
Unrest in the Churches (1907)
Veracity, Reality, and Regeneration (1915)
Village Churches and the War (1917)
Way of Life (1897)
Weariness in Modern Life (1879)
Welding the Churches: A World Congress for Christian Unity
(1914)
Welfare and Charity (1910)
What Is Meant by the Blood of Christ? (1908)
What is the Evangelical Faith? (1908)
When We Were Boys. *See:* Reminiscences of the School-days of
Two Distinguished F.P.'s [Former Pupils] (1905)
Why am I a Liberal? (1878)
Wind from the Heath (undated)
Word and the World (1910)
Work of Christ (1909)
Workers of the Future (1877)

4. Unpublished Manuscripts and Letters

*Unless otherwise indicated in square brackets, these item s are held at Dr
William's Library, London. NCL indicates the New College London
materials at Dr Williams's Library.*

Dated Material:
'"Shall I from the Christmas mart?"' Poem. Christmas 1886.
'God was in Christ reconciling.' Sermon manuscript. Text: 2
Corinthians 5.19. Christmas 1896.
'Freedom our vocation; freedom our temptation; freedom our
education.' Sermon manuscript. Text: Galatians 5.13. 6 No-
vember 1898.
'The Joy that was before him.' Sermon manuscript. Text: Hebrews
2.12. 2 July 1899.
Letter to Edith Roper, 28 October 1900 [David Bebbington,
Stirling].

Lecture notes on Christology, 1901ff. NCL ms.

Midsummer examination apologetics, set by Forsyth, 1902. NCL ms 244/2.

Letter to M. Auchterlonie, 8 July 1904 [James Gordon, Aberdeen].

Notes of addresses by Forsyth for Wednesday evening devotional services at Hackney College; valedictory address, June 1909; and ordination address, 20 October 1909.

> Excerpts published in Escott (See Section 2 above).

Letter to Matthew Stanley, 27 July 1908.

Sermon manuscript. Text: 1 Corinthians 1.24. June 1909.

Letter to A. C. Headlam, 30 March 1912.

> Held at Lambeth Palace Library, London.

'Martyrdom not come yet but threatened.' Sermon manuscript. Text: Hebrews 12.4-11. Hackney College, January 1913.

Letter to James Shepheard, 23 July 1913. NCL ms 536/22.

Letter to H. F. Lovell Cocks, 14 August 1915 [Alan Lamb, Fort Augustus].

Letter to R. Morton Stanley, 28 April 1916.

Letter to R. Morton Stanley, 19 June 1916.

Letter to R. Morton Stanley, 6 December 1919.

Undated material:

'A Dramatic Lyric.' Poem.

'Be ye reconciled to God.' Sermon manuscript. Text: 2 Corinthians 5.20.

'Glory in Cross.' Sermon manuscript. Text: Galatians 6.14.

'Prayer and its Answer: An Apologue.' Poem.

'Spring.' Sermon manuscript. Readings: Matthew 24.32–33, Hebrews 5.12–14, and Galatians 4.

'Thy kingdom come.' Poem.

Sermon manuscript. Text: Genesis 3.9–10.

Secondary Literature

5. Books about Forsyth

Benedetto, Robert. *P. T. Forsyth Bibliography and Index.* Foreward by Donald G. Miller. Bibliographies and Indexes in Religious Studies, no. 27. Westport, Connecticut: Greenwood Press, 1993.

Bradley, W. L. *P. T. Forsyth: The Man and His Work.* London: Independent Press, 1952.

Brake, George Thompson. *Peter Taylor Forsyth: An Introduction.* Theology Starters, no. 2. Ilford, Essex: Robert Odcombe, [1990].

Brown, R. M. *P. T. Forsyth: Prophet for Today.* Philadelphia: Westminster, 1952.

Griffith, Gwilym O. *The Theology of P. T. Forsyth.* London: Lutterworth, 1948.

Hunter, A. M. *P. T. Forsyth: Per Crucem and Lucem.* SCM Book Club, no. 217. London: SCM Press Ltd, 1974.

Ishijima, Saburo. *Gaisetsu Forsyth-shingaku* [An Introduction to the Theology of Forsyth]. Tokyo: Nagasaki-shoten, 1938.

Miller, Donald G., Browne Barr, and Robert S. Paul, *P. T. Forsyth – The Man, The Preacher's Theologian, Prophet for the Twentieth Century: A Contemporary Asessment.* With a Bibliography by Robert Benedetto. Pittsburgh Theological Monograph series, vol. 36. Pittsburgh: Pickwick, 1981.

Omiya, Hiroshi. *Fosaisu.* [The Life and Work of P. T. Forsyth. Series of Man Thought.] Tokyo: Nippon Kirisute Kyodan Shuppanbu, 1965.

Pitt, Clifford S. *Church, Ministry and Sacraments: A Critical Evaluation of the Thought of Peter Taylor Forsyth.* Washington, D. C.: University Press of America, 1983.

Rodgers, John. H. *The Theology of P. T. Forsyth: The Cross of Christ and the Revelation of God.* London: Independent Press, 1965.

6. Doctoral Theses and Dissertations

Allen, Ray Maxwell. 'The Christology of P. T. Forsyth.' Duke University, Durham, North Carolina, 1953.

Bosse, Walter. 'Theologie and Kirche bei Peter Taylor Forsyth.' Munster, 1967.

Bradley, W. L. 'The Theology of P. T. Forsyth, 1848–1921.' University of Edinburgh, 1949.
  Published as *P. T. Forsyth: The Man and His Work* (1952).

Brown, Robert McAfee. 'P. T. Forsyth and the Gospel of Grace.' Columbia University, New York, 1951.
  Revised and condensed as *P. T. Forsyth: Prophet for Today* (1952).

Gardner, Harry M. 'The Doctrine of the Person and Work of Jesus Christ in the Thought of Peter Taylor Forsyth and Emil Brunner.' Boston University, 1962.

Gardom, James T. D. 'The Cross in Time and the Hidden Hand of God: [Theology and the Problem of Evil with Reference to the Work of Peter Taylor Forsyth and Austin Farrer].' University of London, 1992.

Hsü, John Dao-Luong. 'Peter Taylor Forsyth's Concept of Spirituality.' Aquinas Institute of Theology, Dubuque, Iowa, 1974.

Jackson, George D. 'The Biblical Basis of the Theology of P. T. Forsyth.' Princeton Theological Seminary, Princeton, New Jersey, 1952.

Jones, Frank F. 'The Christological Thought of Peter Taylor Forsyth and Emil Brunner: A Comparative Study.' University of St Andrew's, 1970.

McCurdy, Leslie Charles. 'Attributes and Atonement: The Holy Love of God in the Theology of P.T. Forsyth.' University of Aberdeen, 1994.

McKay, Clifford Anderson. 'The Moral Structure of Reality in the Theology of Peter Taylor Forsyth.' Vanderbilt University, Nashville, Tennessee, 1970.

Mikolaski, Samuel J. 'The Nature and Place of Human Response to the Work of Christ in the Objective Theories of the Atonement Advanced in Recent British Theology by R. W. Dale, James Denney and P. T. Forsyth.' Oxford University, 1958.

Newman, Guy Douglas, 'The Theology of P. T. Forsyth with Special Reference to his Christology.' Southwestern Baptist Theological Seminary, Fort Worth, Texas, 1952.

Norwood, D. W. 'The Case for Democracy in Church Government: A Study in the Reformed Tradition, with Special Reference to the Congregationalism of Robert William Dale, Peter Taylor Forsyth, Albert Peel and Nathaniel Micklem.' King's College, London, 1983.

Parker, Gary Edmund. 'A Comparison of the Concept of Proclamation in the Writings of Peter Taylor Forsyth and Rudolf Bultmann.' Baylor University, Waco, Texas, 1984.

Pitt, Clifford S. 'Church, Ministry and Sacraments: A Critical Evaluation of the Thought of Peter Taylor Forsyth.' New College, London, 1977.

    Published under the same title (1983).

Rodgers, John H. 'The Theology of P. T. Forsyth: The Cross of Christ and the Revelation of God.' University of Basle, 1963. Published under the same title (1965).

Rosenthal, Klaus. 'Die Stellung des Kreuzes in der Theologie von Forsyth.' Heidelberg, 1956.

Rosser, William Ray. 'The Cross as the Hermeneutical Norm for Scriptural Interpretation in the Thought of Peter Taylor Forsyth.' Southern Baptist Theological Seminary, Louisville, Kentucky, 1990.

Simpson, A. F. 'Certainty Through Faith: An Examination of the Religious Philosophy of Peter Taylor Forsyth.' New College, London, 1949.

Stewart, Winthrop R. 'The Biblical Foundations and Insights of P. T. Forsyth's Theology.' University of Aberdeen, 1965.

Sturm, William A. 'The Self-Authenticating Character of Revelation: Authority and Certitude Studied in Twentieth Century English Nonconformist Thought, with Special Reference to the Works of P. T. Forsyth, John Oman and H. Wheeler Robinson.' Oxford University, 1959.

Thompson, Robert Franklin. 'Peter Taylor Forsyth: A Pre-Barthian.' Drew University, Madison, New Jersey, 1940.

Vicchio, Stephen J. 'The Problem of Evil with Special Reference to P. T. Forsyth, John Wisdom and Ludwig Wittgenstein.' University of St Andrew's, 1985.

Wilson, Reginald A. 'The Problem of Religious Authority in Contemporary Theological Thought with Particular Reference to the Interpretations of John Oman, P. T. Forsyth, and A. E. J. Rawlinson.' Columbia University, New York, 1960.

Wismar, Don Ray. 'A Sacramental View of Preaching as Seen in the Writings of John Calvin and P. T. Forsyth and Applied to the Mid-Twentieth Century.' Pacific School of Religion, Berkeley, California, 1963.

Articles and Pamphlets

This section includes articles which focus specifically on P. T. Forsyth, but does not include short items of an historical nature (e.g. obituaries, appreciations, reminiscences; see Section 12) or prefaces, introductions, and forewords to Forsyth's reprinted works, anthologies, and collections (see Sections 1 and 2). Review articles, some substantial, are included in Section 10.

Anderson, K. C. 'Dr Forsyth and Reaction.' *Message Extra*, no. 1. [Bristol, c. 1905.]
    Available at Mansfield College, Oxford.
Anderson, Marvin W. 'P. T. Forsyth: Prophet of the Cross.' *Evangelical Quarterly* 47 (July 1975): 146–61.
Andrews, Jessie Forsyth. 'Memoir.' In *The Work of Christ*, by P. T. Forsyth, vii–xxviii. London: Independent Press, 1938.
Barr, Browne, 'P. T. Forsyth: The Preachers' Theologian–A Witness and Confession.' In Miller, Barr, and Paul, *P. T. Forsyth: The Man, The Preachers' Theologian, Prophet for the Twentieth Century: A Contemporary Assessment*, 31–42.
Barth, Markus. 'P. T. Forsyth: The Theologian for the Practical Man.' *Congregational Quarterly* 17 (October 1939): 436–42.
Bergh, O., ed. 'The Missiological Legacy of P. T. Forsyth.' *Japan Christian Quarterly* 51 (Spring 1985): 69–74.
    Quotations from *Missions*.
Binfield, Clyde. 'Principal when Pastor: P. T. Forsyth, 1876–1901.' In *The Ministry: Clerical and Lay*, 397–414. Edited by W. J. Sheils and Diana Wood. Studies in Church History, vol. 26. Oxford: Basil Blackwell, 1989.
Bishop, John. 'P. T. Forsyth: "Preaching and the Modern Mind."' *Religion in Life* 48 (Autumn 1979): 303–8.
Bradley, W. L. 'Forsyth's Contributions to Pastoral Theology.' *Religion in Life* 28 (Autumn 1959): 546–56.
Brown, Robert McAfee. 'The "Conversion" of P. T. Forsyth.' *Congregational Quarterly* 30 (July 1952): 236–44.
——— 'P. T. Forsyth.' In *A Handbook of Christian Theologians*, 144–65. Edited by Martin E. Marty and Dean G. Peerman. Cleveland: World Publishing, 1965.
    Enlarged edition. Nashville: Abingdon, 1984.
Camfield, F. W. 'Peter Taylor Forsyth.' *Presbyter* 6 (April 1948): 3–10.
Cave, Sydney. 'Dr P. T. Forsyth: The Man and His Writings.' *Congregational Quarterly* 26 (April 1948): 107–119.
Child, R. L. 'P. T. Forsyth: Some Aspects of His Thought.' *Baptist Times*, 20 May 1948, 9; 27 May, 7; 3 June, 9.
Church, Leslie F. 'Principal P. T. Forsyth.' *London Quarterly and Holborn Review* 174 (January 1949): 2–4.

Cocks, H. F. Lovell. 'Two Theological Prophets of the Nineteenth Century.' BBC Third Programme, 20 July 1948, 9:45–10:25p.m.

Cocks's presentation on Forsyth occupied the second half of the programme; the script, entitled 'A Nineteenth-Century Prophet: Peter Taylor Forsyth,' is in the Lovell Cocks papers held at Dr Williams's Library, London.

—— 'The Message of P. T. Forsyth.' *Congregational Quarterly* 26 (July 1948): 214–21.

—— Address delivered at Commemoration. In *New College London Report for Session, 1976–1977*, 8–11.

Excerpt in Miller, Barr, and Paul, *P. T. Forsyth: The Man, The Preachers' Theologian, Prophet for the Twentieth Century: A Contemporary Assessment*, 71–72.

Craston, R. C. 'The Grace of a Holy God: P. T. Forsyth and the Contemporary Church.' In *Authority in the Anglican Communion: Essays Presented to Bishop John Howe*, 47–64. Edited by Stephen S. Sykes. Toronto: Anglican Book Centre, 1987.

Cunliffe-Jones, H. 'P. T. Forsyth: Reactionary or Prophet?' *Congregational Quarterly* 27 (October 1950): 344–56.

[Davies, D. R.] 'The Watch Tower.' Signed, 'Agro.' *Record*, 1 December 1944, 479.

Douglas, Crerar. 'The Cost of Mediation: A Study of Augustus Hopkins Strong and P. T. Forsyth.' *Congregational Journal* 3 (1978): 28–35.

Duthie, Charles S. 'The Faith of P. T. Forsyth.' Also entitled 'Fireworks in a Fog?' *British Weekly*, 17 December 1964, 9.

Floyd, Richard L. 'The Cross and the Church: The Soteriology and Ecclesiology of P.T. Forsyth.' *Andover Newton Review* 3 (1992): 1–16.

Forster, John. 'Dr Forsyth on the Authority of Grace.' *Primitive Methodist Quarterly Review* 29 (London, April 1907): 286–300.

Forsyth Society. *Forsyth-kenkyu* [Forsyth Studies], vols. 1–35 (Tokyo, 1932–5).

Garrett, John. 'Forsyth, Forsooth.' In *Studies of the Church in History: Essays Honoring Robert S. Paul on His Sixty-fifth Birthday*, 243–52. Edited by Horton Davies. Pittsburgh Theological Monographs new series, vol. 5. Allison Park, Pennsylvania: Pickwick Publications, 1983.

Garvie, A. E. 'Placarding the Cross: The Theology of P. T. Forsyth.' *Congregational Quarterly* 21 (October 1943): 343–52.

—— 'A Cross-Centred Theology.' *Congregational Quarterly* 22 (October 1944): 324–30.

—— 'P. T. Forsyth and Reunion.' Letter. *Congregational Quarterly* 23 (January 1945): 96.

Griffith, Gwilym O. 'Peter Taylor Forsyth.' *Christian World*, 13 May 1948, 1–2.

Griffith-Jones, E. 'Dr Forsyth on the Atonement.' *Expositor*, 7th series, 9 (1910): 307–19.

Gummer, Selwyn. 'Peter Taylor Forsyth: A Contemporary Theologian.' *London Quarterly and Holborn Review* 173 (October 1948): 349–53.

Hamilton, Kenneth. 'Love or Holy Love? Nels Ferré versus P. T. Forsyth.' *Canadian Journal of Theology* 8 (October 1962): 229–36.

Hermann, E. 'Studies of Representative British Theologians: VI.– Peter Taylor Forsyth, D.D.' *Homiletic Review* 66 (New York, July-December 1913): 178–85.
Includes a portrait on p. 178.

Higginson, R. E. 'The Authentic Word: A Study in Forsyth's Attitude to the Bible.' *Churchman* 50 (London, June 1946): 82–6.

—— 'Peter Taylor Forsyth: Prophet and Pastor, 1848–1921.' *English Churchman and St James's Chronicle*, 1 July 1955, 309, 315.

—— 'God's Seminal Word: An Enquiry into what is Fontal and Final for the Soul in the Writings of P. T. Forsyth.' Lenten series. *English Churchman and St James's Chronicle*, subtitle, date in 1959, and page number(s) indicated:
    1. 6 February, 4.
    2. 'Forsyth on Biblical Authority.' 13 February, 4.
    3. 'P. T. Forsyth on the Nature of Religious Authority.' 20 February, 7.
    4. 'The Nature of the Biblical Revelation.' 27 February, 7–8.
    5. 'Forsyth on Apostolic Inspiration.' 6 March, 5.
    6. 'Forsyth under Criticism.' 13 March, 4.
    7. 'Forsyth and the Church of Rome.' 20 March, 4.
    8. 'The Function of Biblical Criticism.' 3 April, 5.

—— 'The Theology of P. T. Forsyth and its Significance for Us Today.' *Churchman*, June 1959, 66–75.

Hughes, Philip Edgcumbe. 'Forsyth: Theologian of the Cross.' *Christianity Today*, 23 December 1957, 5–7.

Hughes, T. Hywel. 'A Barthian Before Barth?' *Congregational Quarterly* 12 (July 1934): 308–15.

—— 'Dr Forsyth's View of the Atonement.' *Congregational Quarterly* 18 (January 1940): 30–7.

Hunt, George L. 'Interpreters of our Faith: P. T. Forsyth.' *A.D.* 4 (Philadelphia, May 1975): 39–41.
    Includes excerpts from *Person* on 40–1.

Hunter, A. M. 'P. T. Forsyth Neutestamentler.' *Expository Times* 73 (January 1962): 100–6.

—— 'The Theology of P. T. Forsyth.' In *Teaching and Preaching the New Testament*, 129–87. London: SCM Press Ltd, 1963.
    Revised and expanded for *P. T. Forsyth: Per Crucem ad Lucem* (1974).

Huxtable, W. J. F. 'The Welcome Ghost Who was a Good Prophet.' *Congregational Monthly*, October 1964, 4.

—— 'P. T. Forsyth: 1848–1921.' *Journal of the United Reformed Church History Society* 4 (October 1987): 72–8.

Ishijima, Saburo. 'Forsyth-ni-tsuite' [On Forsyth]. In Forsyth, *Kirisuto-sha no Kanzen* [Christian Perfection] Tokyo: Shinkyo-shuppan-sha, 1960.

Jackson, George D. 'The Interpreter at Work: XIV. P. T. Forsyth's Use of the Bible.' *Interpretation* 7 (July 1953): 323–37.

Justice and Mercy: A Review of a Sermon Published by Rev. P. T. Forsyth, MA. By a Curious Reader. Bradford: M. Field, n.d. [likely 1878].

Kellogg, Edwin H. 'A Theologian for the Hour: Peter Taylor Forsyth.' *Bulletin of Western Theological Seminary* 6 (April 1914): 204–33.

Lambert, D. W. 'The Missionary Message of P. T. Forsyth.' *Evangelical Quarterly* 21 (July 1949): 203–8.

—— 'The Theology of Missions: The Contribution of P. T. Forsyth.' *London Quarterly and Holborn Review* 176 (April 1951): 114–17.

Leembruggen, W. H. 'The Witness of P. T. Forsyth–A Theologian of the Cross.' *Reformed Theological Review* (1945): 18–46.
    Also published as a pamphlet, *P. T. Forsyth: A Theologian of the Cross.* With a Foreword by John Gillies. Melbourne: S. John Bacon, n.d.

Mackintosh, R. 'The Authority of the Cross.' *Congregational Quarterly* 21 (July 1943): 209–18.
Annotated by Forsyth.

Meadley, Thomas D. 'The "Obscurity" of P. T. Forsyth.' *Congregational Quarterly* 24 (October 1946): 308–17.

—— 'A Preacher's Theologian: P. T. Forsyth.' *Preacher's and Classleader's Magazine* 22 (January–February 1949): 149–53, 157.

—— 'The Great Church, P. T. Forsyth, and Christian Unity.' *London Quarterly and Holborn Review* 190 (July 1965): 225–33.

—— 'The Forsyth Saga: Fifty Years On.' *Methodist Recorder* (London), 11 November 1971, 17.

Mews, Stuart. 'Neo-Orthodoxy, Liberalism and War: Karl Barth, P. T. Forsyth and John Oman 1914–1918.' In *Renaissance and Renewal in Christian History*, 361–75.
Edited by Derek Baker. Studies in Church History, vol. 14. Oxford: Basil Blackwell, 1977.

Mikolaski, S. J. 'The Theology of P. T. Forsyth.' *Evangelical Quarterly* 36 (January 1964): 27–41.

—— 'P. T. Forsyth on the Atonement.' *Evangelical Quarterly* 36 (April 1964): 78–91.

—— 'P. T. Forsyth.' In *Creative Minds in Contemporary Theology*, 307–39. Edited by P. E. Hughes. Grand Rapids: Wm. B. Eerdmans, 1966. 2nd ed., 1969.

Miller, Donald G. 'P. T. Forsyth: The Man.' In Miller, Barr, and Paul, *P. T. Forsyth: The Man, The Preachers' Theologian, Prophet for the Twentieth Century: A Contemporary Assessment*, 1–29.

'Ministerial Libraries: V. Principal Forsyth's Library at Hackney College.' *British Monthly* 4 (May 1904): 267–70.

Mozley, J. K. 'The Theology of Dr Forsyth.' *Expositor*, 8th series, 23 (February, March 1922): 81–98, 161–80.
Reprinted in *The Heart of the Gospel*, 66–109. London: SPCK, 1925.

—— 'Forsyth–The Theologian.' *British Weekly*, 21 November 1946, 110.

Omiya, Hiroshi. 'P. T. Forsyth–no Shokuzai-von' [The Doctrine of Atonement of P. T. Forsyth]. *Shingaku Journal of Theology* 16 (1959): 26–67; and 18 (1960): 119–44.

Paul, Robert S. 'P. T. Forsyth: Prophet for the Twentieth Century.' In Miller, Barr, and Paul, *P. T. Forsyth: The Man, The Preachers' Theologian, Prophet for the Twentieth Century: A Contemporary*

Assessment, 43–70. Pittsburgh Theological Monograph series, vol. 36. Pittsburgh: Pickwick, 1981.

Porritt, Arthur. 'Leading Churches and Preachers: VI.–Emmanuel Church, Cambridge, and Dr P. T. Forsyth.' *Puritan* 1 (1899): 713–19.

Robinson, N. H. G. 'The Importance of P. T. Forsyth.' *Expository Times* 64 (December 1952): 76–9.

Rosenthal, Klaus. 'Die Bedeutung des Kreuzesgeschehens für Lehre und Bekenntnis nach Peter Taylor Forsyth.' *Kerygma und Dogma Zeitschrift für Theologische Forschung und kirchliche Lehre* 7 (Göttingen, July 1961): 237–59.

Shaw, J. M. 'The Theology of P. T. Forsyth.' *Theology Today* 3 (October 1946): 358–70.

Simpson, A. F. 'P. T. Forsyth: The Prophet of Judgment.' *Scottish Journal of Theology* 4 (1951): 148–56.

[Stoddart, Jane]. 'Dr P. T. Forsyth, of Cambridge: A Special Biography.' Signed 'Lorna.' *British Weekly*, 7 March 1901, 530–1.

Suzuki, Mitsutake. 'Forsyth-shingaku no konpon-mondai' [Basic Issues in Forsyth's Theology]. *St Paul University Bulletin of Theology* 1 (Tokyo, 1953).

Turner, John Munsey. 'Theologian of Righteousness: Peter Taylor Forsyth (1848–1921).' *Methodist Sacramental Fellowship Bulletin*, no. 119 (1990): 1–14.

Waddell, H. C. 'Is P. T. Forsyth Coming to His Own?' *Biblical Theology* 7 (January 1957): 35–9.

Warschauer, J. '"Liberty, Limited": A Rejoinder to Dr Forsyth.' *Contemporary Review* 101 (June 1912): 831–9.

Webster, Douglas. 'P. T. Forsyth's Theology of Missions.' *International Review of Missions* 44 (April 1955): 175–81.

Wiersbe, W. W. 'Theologian For Pastors.' *Moody Monthly*, May 1975, 97–101.

Wood, Ralph C. 'Christ on Parnassus: P. T. Forsyth Among the Liberals.' *Literature and Theology* 2 (March 1988): 83–95.

Worrall, B. G. 'The Authority of Grace in the Theology of P. T. Forsyth.' *Scottish Journal of Theology* 25 (February 1972): 58–74.

Ziegler, Robert E. 'P. T. Forsyth and His Theology.' *Methodist Quarterly Review* 62 (Nashville, July 1913): 455–63. Introduction reprinted in *Baptist World*, 31 July 1913.

8. Excerpts from Books and Articles

This section is comprised of books and articles which discuss Forsyth's life or work within a broader context than the articles listed in the previous part, which are specifically concerned with Forsyth. Not included here are materials which only mention his contribution or cite his works. Page references are not exhaustive.

Bloesch, Donald G. *Essentials of Evangelical Theology*, 2 vols., passim. San Francisco: Harper & Row, 1978 and 1979.

—— *Jesus Is Victor! Karl Barth's Doctrine of Salvation.* Nashville: Abingdon, 1976, 53–8.

Carpenter, James. *Gore: A Study in Liberal Catholic Thought.* London: The Faith Press, 1960, 226–7.

Cave, Sydney. *The Doctrine of the Person of Christ.* London: Duckworth, 1925, 222–4.

Clements, Keith W. 'An Indefinable Something: R. J. Campbell and the "New Theology,"' 39–41. In *Lovers of Discord: Twentieth-Century Theological Controversies in England.* London: SPCK, 1988, 19–48.

Corner, Mark A. '"The Umbilical Cord": A View of Man and Nature in the Light of Darwin,' 128–32. *Scottish Journal of Religious Studies* 4 (Autumn 1983): 121–37.

Davie, Donald. *A Gathered Church: The Literature of the English Dissenting Interest, 1700–1930.* Clark Lectures, 1976. London: Routledge & Kegan Paul, 1978, 141–3.

Davies, Rupert E. *Religious Authority in an Age of Doubt.* London: Epworth, 1968, 166–83.

Dawe, Donald. 'Kenosis and the Moralizing of Dogma.' In *The Form of a Servant: A Historical Analysis of the Kenotic Motif.* Philadelphia: Westminster, 1963, 131–41.

Dillistone, F. W. *The Christian Understanding of Atonement.* Digswell Place: James Nisbet, 1968, 293–5.

Essex, E. C. 'The Atonement in Post-Reformation Writers,' 252–6. In *The Atonement in History and in Life: A Volume of Essays.* Edited by L. W. Grensted. London: Society for Promoting Christian Knowledge, 1929, 236–63.

Ferré, Nels. *The Christian Understanding of God.* New York: Harper, 1951, 116–17.

Fuller, Peter. *Theoria: Art, and the Absence of Grace.* London: Chatto & Windus, 1988, 144–6.

Garvie, Alfred E. *The Christian Certainty amid the Modern Perplexity: Essays, Constructive and Critical, towards the Solution of Some Current Theological Problems.* London: Hodder & Stoughton, 1910, 460–74.

Glover, Willis B. *Evangelical Nonconformists and Higher Criticism in the Nineteenth Century.* London: Independent Press, 1954, 272–82.

Gordon, James W. *Evangelical Spirituality [:From the Wesleys to John Stott].* London: SPCK, 1991, 229–54.

Grant, John. W. *Free Churchmanship in England 1870–1940: With Special Reference to Congregationalism.* London: Independent Press, n.d, 227–53.

Greeves, Frederix, *Theology and the Cure of Souls: An Introduction to Pastoral Theology.* The Cato Lecture of 1960. London: Epworth, 1960, 161–7.

Gunton, Colin E. *The Actuality of Atonement: A Study of Metaphor, Rationality and the Christian Tradition.* Edinburgh: T&T Clark, 1988, 106–9.

—— *Yesterday and Today: A Study of Continuities in Christology.* London: Darton, Longman & Todd, 1983, 169–73.

Hamilton, Kenneth. 'Created Soul–Eternal Spirit: A Continuing Theological Thorn,' 27–8. *Scottish Journal of Theology* 19 (1966): 23–34.

Hanshell, Deryck. 'Christian Worship: Catholic and Evangelical,' 266–7. *Downside Review* 90 (1972): 260–7.

Hanson, Anthony Tyrrell. *The Wrath of the Lamb.* London: SPCK, 1957, 187–8.

Hardy, Daniel W. 'Created and Redeemed Sociality,' 38–41. In *On Being the Church: Essays on the Christian Community.* Eds Colin E. Gunton and Daniel W. Hardy. Edinburgh: T&T Clark, 1989, 21–47.

Hart, Trevor A. 'Sinlessness and Moral Responsibility: A Problem in Christology.' *Scottish Journal of Theology* (forthcoming).

Hendry, George S. *The Gospel of the Incarnation.* Philadelphia: Westminster, 1958, 92–8.

Hick, John. *Evil and the God of Love.* London: Macmillan, 1966, 246–50.
  Forsyth is not mentioned in the second edition of 1977.

Hinchliff, Peter. 'Off with the New and On with the Old: R. J. Campbell and the New Theology,' 212–17. In *God and History:*

Aspects of British Theology 1875–1914. Oxford: Clarendon, 1992, 198–222.

Hughes, Thomas Hywel. *The Atonement: Modern Theories of the Doctrine.* London: George Allen & Unwin, 1949, 38–46.

Huxtable, John. *The Bible Says.* London: SCM Press Ltd, 1962, 82–7.

—— 'National Recognition of Religion,' 304–310. In *Congregational Quarterly* 35, no. 4 (1957): 297–310.

Jenkins, Daniel. *Congregationalism: A Restatement.* London: Faber & Faber, 1954, 48–50.

Johnson, Robert Clyde. *Authority in Protestant Theology.* Philadelphia: Westminster, 1959, 100–7.

Jones, Edgar DeWitt. *The Royalty of the Pulpit: A Survey and Appreciation of the Lyman Beecher Lectures on Preaching [etc.].* New York: Harper & Bros., 1951, 128–34.

    Reprinted. Freeport, N.Y.: Books for Libraries Press, 1970.

Jones, J. D. *Three Score Years and Ten.* London: The Book Club, 1940, 279–82.

Jones, Peter d'A. *The Christian Socialist Revival 1877–1914: Religion, Class, and Social Concern in Late-Victorian England.* Princeton, New Jersey: Princeton University Press, 1968, 419–21.

Kiek, Edward S. *The Modern Religious Situation.* Edinburgh: T&T Clark, 1926, 151–60.

Langford, T. A. *In Search of Foundations: English Theology 1900–1920.* Nashville: Abingdon, 1969, 170–5.

MacKinnon, Donald M. 'Aspects of Kant's Influence on British Theology,' 354–58. In *Kant and His Influence.* Eds George MacDonald Ross and Tony McWalter, Bristol: Thoemmes, 1990, 348–66.

—— 'Philosophy and Christology,' 285–7. In *Essays in Christology for Karl Barth.* Ed. T. H. L. Parker. London: Lutterworth, 1956, 269–97.

    Reprinted as 'Philosophy and Christology,' 70–1. In *Borderlands of Theology and Other Essays.* Edited and introduced by George W. Roberts and Donovan E. Smucker. London: Lutterworth, 1968, 55–81.

Mackintosh, H. R. *The Doctrine of the Person of Jesus Christ.* Edinburgh: T&T Clark, 1912, 465–66, 472–5.

Maxwell, Jack M. 'A Conversation with Robert Paul,' 4–6, 8–10. In

Studies of the Church in History: Essays Honoring Robert S. Paul on His Sixty-fifth Birthday. Ed. Horton Davies. Pittsburgh Theological Monographs, new series, vol. 5. Allison Park, Pennsylvania: Pickwick Publications, 1983, 3–26.

McDonald, H. D. *The Atonement of the Death of Christ: In Faith, Revelation, and History.* Grand Rapids, Michigan: Baker Book House, 1985, 250–57.

—— *Theories of Revelation: An Historical Study 1860–1960.* London: George Allen & Unwin, 1963, 87–9, 304–5.

Mozley, J. K. 'Christology and Soteriology,' 182–4. In *Mysterium Christi: Christological Studies by British and German Theologians.* Eds G. K. A. Bell and D. Adolf Deissmann. London: Longmans, Green, 1930, 167–90.

—— *The Doctrine of the Atonement.* London: Gerald Duckworth, 1915, 182–9.

—— *The Doctrine of the Incarnation.* London: Geoffrey Bles, 1936, 93–4, 105–9.

—— *The Gospel Sacraments.* London: Hodder & Stoughton, 1933, 98–100.

—— *Some Tendencies in British Theology: From the Publication of* Lux Mundi *to the Present Day.* London: SPCK, 1951, 45–6.

Pattison, George. *Art, Modernity and Faith: Towards a Theology of Art.* London: Macmillan, 1991, 78–99.

Paul, R. S. *The Atonement and the Sacraments.* London: Hodder & Stoughton, 1961, 227–40.

Porritt, Arthur. *The Best I Remember.* London: Cassell, 1922, 128–32.

Robinson, N. H. G. *Christ and Conscience.* London: James Nisbet, 1956, 132–43.

Rogers, Jack B., and Donald K. McKim. *The Authority and Interpretation of the Bible: An Historical Approach.* San Francisco: Harper & Row, 1979, 393–8.

Sell, Alan P. F. 'Anabaptist-Congregational Relations and Current Mennonite-Reformed Dialogue,' 321–9. *Mennonite Quarterly Review* 61 (July 1987): 321–34.

    Also published in Sell, *Dissenting Thought and the Life of the Churches: Studies in an English Tradition.* San Francisco: Mellen Research University Press, 1990, 578–99.

—— *Aspects of Christian Integrity* and passim. Louisville, Kentucky: Westminster/John Knox, 1990, 46–7.

—— *A Reformed, Evangelical, Catholic Theology: The Contribution of the World Alliance of Reformed Churches, 1875–1982*. Grand Rapids, Michigan: William B. Eerdmans, 1991, 33–6.

—— *Saints: Visible, Orderly and Catholic: The Congregational Idea of the Church*. Geneva: World Alliance of Reformed Churches, 104–5.

—— *Theology in Turmoil: The Roots, Course and Significance of the Conservative-Liberal Debate in Modern Theology*, passim. Grand Rapids, Michigan: Baker, 1986.

Stott, John R. W. *The Cross of Christ*. Leicester: Inter-Varsity, 1986, 129–32.

Sturch, Richard. *The Word and the Christ: An Essay in Analytic Christology*. Oxford: Clarendon, 1991, 37–9, 182–4, 199–200, 254–5.

Surin, K. *Theology and the Problem of Evil*. Signposts in Theology. Oxford: Basil Blackwell, 1986, 132–6.

Suzuki, Mitsutake. 'Kiristo-von josetsu' [An Introduction to Christology]. *St Paul University Bulletin of Theology* 2 (Tokyo, 1954).

—— 'Kiristo-von no ichi-kosatsu' [A Reflection on Christology]. *Shukyo-kenkyu* [Religious Studies] 143 (1955).

—— 'Kiristo-von kara Kyokai-von-e' [From Christology to Ecclesiology]. *St Paul University Bulletin of Theology* 3 (Tokyo, 1955).

Swanton, R. 'Scottish Theology and Karl Barth,' 23–5. In *Reformed Theological Review* (1974): 17–25.

Sykes, S. W. 'Theology through History,' 6–11. In *The Modern Theologians: An Introduction to Christian Theology in the Twentieth Century*. Edited by David F. Ford. Oxford: Basil Blackwell, 1989, 3–29.

Thomas, J. Heywood. 'Influence on English Thought,' 167–71. In *The Legacy and Interpretation of Kierkegaard*. Edited by Niels Thulstrup and M. Mikulová Thulstrup. Bibliotheca Kiekegaardiana Edenda Curaaverunt, vol. 8. Copenhagen: C. A. Reitzels Boghandel, 1981, 160–77.

Thomas, John. *Christ in Perspective: Christological Perspectives in the Theology of Karl Barth* and passim. Edinburgh: Saint Andrew Press, 1978, 164–5.

Turnbull, Ralph G. *A History of Preaching*, vol. 3, *From the Close of the Nineteenth Century to the Middle of the Twentieth Century*. Grand Rapids, Michigan: Baker Book House, 1974, 474–7.

Tuttle, George M. *So Rich a Soil: John McLeod Campbell on Christian Atonement.* Edinburgh: Handsel, 1986, 115–16.

Wallace, Ronald S. *The Atoning Death of Christ,* chapters 7–9 passim. Foundations for Faith. Ed. Peter Toon. Westchester, Illinois: Crossway Books, 1981.

Welch, Claude. *Protestant Thought in the Nineteenth Century,* vol.2, 1870–1914. New Haven: Yale University Press, 1985, 236–8.

Wickham, E. R. *Church and People in an Industrial City.* London: Lutterworth, 1957, 200–9.

Williams, R. R. *Authority in the Apostolic Age: With Two Essays on the Modern Problem of Authority.* London: SCM Press Ltd, 1950, 119–22.

9. Dictionary and Encyclopedia Articles about Forsyth

Signed articles:

Albright, Raymond W. In *Twentieth Century Encyclopedia of Religious Knowledge: An Extension of the New Schaff-Herzog Encyclopedia of Religious Knowledge.* Ed. Lefferts A. Loetscher. Grand Rapids, Michigan: Baker Book House, 1955.

—— In *New Twentieth-Century Encyclopedia of Religious Knowledge.* 2nd ed. Ed. J. D. Douglas. Grand Rapids, Michigan: Baker Book House, 1991.

Anderson, Andrew F. In *Dictionary of Scottish Church History and Theology.* Ed. Nigel M. de S. Cameron. Edinburgh: T&T Clark, 1993.

Bloesch, D. G. In *Evangelical Dictionary of Theology.* Ed. Walter A. Elwell. Grand Rapids, Michigan: Baker Book House, 1984.

Bowden, John, In *Who's Who in Theology.* London: SCM Press Ltd, 1990.

Brown, R. In *New Dictionary of Theology.* Eds Sinclair B. Ferguson and David F. Wright. Downers Grove, Illinois: Inter-Varsity, 1988.

Hannah, W. In *New Catholic Encyclopedia.* New York: McGraw-Hill, 1967.

Huxtable, John. In *Dictionary of National Biography: Missing Persons.* Ed. C. S. Nicholls. Oxford: Oxford University Press, 1993.

Lane, Tony. In *The Lion Book of Christian Thought.* Oxford: Lion, 1992, 190–2.

Miller, Donald G. In *Encyclopedia of the Reformed Faith.* Ed. Donald K. McKim. Louisville, Kentucky: Westminster/John Knox, 1992.

Rodgers, John H. In *Encyclopedia of Christianity*. Ed. Philip E. Hughes. Marshallton, Delaware: National Foundation for Christian Education, 1972.

Schrey, H.H. In *Religion in Geschichte und Gegenwart: Handwörterbuch für Theologie und Religionswissenschaft*. 3rd ed. Eds Hans Frhr. v. Campenhausen et al. Tübingen: J. C. B. Mohr (Paul Siebeck), 1958.

Sell, Alan P. F. In *Dictionary of Biblical Interpretation*. Nashville: Abingdon, forthcoming.

Toon, Peter. In *Who's Who in Christian History*. Eds J. D. Douglas and Philip W. Comfort. Wheaton, Illinois: Tyndale House, 1992.

Willmer, Haddon. In *New International Dictionary of the Christian Church*. 2nd ed. Gen. ed. J. D. Douglas. Exeter: Paternoster, 1978.

Unsigned articles:

Blackwell Encyclopedia of Modern Religious Thought. Ed. Alister E. McGrath. Oxford: Blackwell, 1993.

Chambers Biographical Dictionary. 5th ed. Gen. ed. Magnus Magnusson. Edinburgh: Chambers, 1990.

Chambers Dictionary of Beliefs and Religion. Ed. Rosemary Goring. Edinburgh: Chambers, 1992.

Concise Dictionary of the Christian Tradition. Eds J. D. Douglas, Walter A. Elwell, and Peter Toon. London: Marshall Pickering, 1989.

Concise Oxford Dictionary of the Christian Church. Ed. Elizabeth A. Livingstone. Oxford: Oxford University Press, 1977.

Corpus Dictionary of Western Churches. Ed. T. C. O'Brien. Washington, D. C.: Corpus Publications, 1970.

Dictionary of Bible and Religion. Ed. William H. Gentz. Nashville: Abingdon, 1986.

Encyclopaedia Britannica. 11th ed. Cambridge University Press, 1910. Updated in 12th ed., 1922, and 13th ed., 1926.

Encyclopedic Dictionary of Religion. Eds Paul K. Meagher, Thomas C. O'Brien, and Consuelo Maria Ahernee, Washington, D. D.: Corpus Publications, 1979.

New Encyclopaedia Britannica. 15th ed., 1989.

New Schaff-Herzog Encyclopedia of Religious Knowledge. Ed. Samuel Macauley Jackson et al. New York: Funk & Wagnalls, 1909.

Oxford Dictionary of the Christian Church. 2nd ed. Eds F. L. Cross and E. A. Livingstone. London: Oxford University Press, 1974.

Westminster Dictionary of Church History. Ed. Jerald C. Brauer. Philadelphia: Westminster, 1971.

Who Was Who 1916–1928. 4th ed. London: Adam & Charles Black, 1967.

Wycliffe Biographical Dictionary of the Church. Ed. Elgin Moyer. Revised and enlarged by Earle E. Cairns. Chicago: Moody, 1982.

10. Reviews of Forsyth's Writings

Forsyth's books are listed alphabetically, and pamphlets or books to which he contributed have the publication date added. Within each section, the reviews are listed in chronological order. Titles of the reviews are only occasionally included.

The Atonement in Modern Religious Thought (1900)

Duff, Prof. Arch. In *Christian World,* 3 January 1901, 16, 18.

The Charter of the Church

[Denney, James.] 'I Will Build My Church.' *British Weekly,* 21 May 1896, 65.

Russell, F. A. 'For Christ and His Church.' *Independent and Nonconformist,* 4 June 1896, 400.

Expository Times 7 (July 1896): 447.

Primitive Methodist Quarterly Review 18 (October 1896): 774–7.

Presbyterian and Reformed Review 7 (October 1896): 757.

In 'The Problem of Christian Unity,' 205. *London Quarterly Review* 87 (January 1897): 205–29.

The Christian Ethic of War

Times Literary Supplement, 24 August 1916, 408.

'Cromwellian Religion.' In *Times Literary Supplement,* 7 September 426.

Holborn Review (London, October 1916): 593.

London Quarterly Review 126 (October 1916): 300.

Expository Times 28 (November 1916): 55–6.

Lyman, Eugene W. 'Discussions of War and Christianity,' 469–70. In *American Journal of Theology* 21 (July 1917): 467–70.

Farmer, J. H. In *Review and Expositor* 14 (April 1917): 264–5.

Ethics 27 (Chicago, 1916–17): 399.

Christian Perfection
London Quarterly Review 92 (April 1899): 383.
Puritan 3 (1900): 420.
Wesleyan Methodist Magazine 123 (1900): 878.

Christ on Parnassus
Art Journal, n.s. [no volume number] (1899): 128.
Church Quarterly Review 75 (October 1912): 226–7.
Expository Times 23 (November 1916): 74.
London Quarterly Review 117 (April 1912): 362.
Times Literary Supplement, 5 October 1911, 371.
Robertson, A. T. In *Review and Expositor* 9 (January 1912): 130.
Bedford, Basil. In *Church of England Newspaper,* 10 February 1961, 12.
Cope, Gilbert. In *Church Quarterly Review* 162 (July 1961): 387–8.
Aberdeen Press and Journal, 4 March 1967.

The Church and the Sacraments, [Lectures on]
Times Literary Supplement, 24 May 1917, 251.
London Quarterly Review 128 (July 1917): 131–2.
Expository Times 28 (August 1917): 497–8.
Hamilton, Harold. In *Journal of Theological Studies* 19 (October 1917): 91–4.
Wilson, Charles. In *Churchman* 31 (1917): 632–4.
Griffith-Thomas, W. H. In *Bibliotheca Sacra* 74 (1917): 638–9.
Christie, Francis A. In *American Journal of Theology* 22 (January 1918): 143–5.
Methodist Review 101 (New York, May 1918): 462–4.
McConnachie, John. 'His Work was a Bell Heard Ringing in the Night.' *British Weekly,* 22 July 1949, 4.
Smith, C. Ryder. In *London Quarterly and Holborn Review* 173 (October 1948): 377.
Expository Times 60 (*Dec* 1948): 63.

The Church, the Gospel and Society
Preston R. In *Modern Churchman* n.s., 6 (April 1963): 245–6.
Times Literary Supplement, 10 May 1963, 346.

Congregationalism and Reunion

Times Literary Supplement, 28 November 1952, 783.
Hughes, G. W. In *Baptist Quarterly* 15 (January 1953): 46–7.

The Cruciality of the Cross

Expository Times 21 (November 1909): 84.
Glasgow Herald, November 1909.
London Quarterly Review 113 (January 1910): 145.
Child, R. L. In *Baptist Quarterly* 13 (January 1949): 44–5.
Gossip, A. J. In *Expository Times* 60 (March 1949): 149.
Smith, C. Ryder. In *London Quarterly and Holborn Review* 174 (1949): 92.
Smith, L. B. In *Faith and Mission* 1 (Spring 1984): 86–7.

Faith and Criticism (1893)

'Modern Congregational Theology,' 12–18. In *London Quarterly Review* 81 (October 1893): 1–24.
Somerville, D. In *Critical Review of Theological and Philosophical Literature* 3 (Edinburgh, 1893): 418–24. See especially 420–1.
Warfield, B. B. In *Presbyterian and Reformed Review* 5 (April 1894): 354–7.

Faith, Freedom and the Future

Times Literary Supplement, 21 March 1912, 119.
Expository Times 23 (June 1912): 411–12.
Mozley, J. K. In *Journal of Theological Studies* 14 (October 1912): 132–3.
Whitley, W. T. In *Review and Expositor* 9 (October 1912): 573–4.
Church of England Newspaper, 23 December 1955.
Joyful News, 5 January 1956. Signed, 'R. P.'
Huxtable, John. In *British Weekly*, 5 January 1956.
Towlson, Clifford W. In *Yorkshire Observer*, 14 January 1956.
Duthie, Charles. S. In *Expository Times* 67 (April 1956): 202–3.
Smith, C. Ryder. In *London Quarterly and Holborn Review* 181 (1956): 157.
Bradley, William L. In *Religion in Life* 26 (Spring 1957): 310–12.
Huxtable, John. In *Congregational Quarterly* 36 (October 1958): 270.

God the Holy Father

Cocks, H. F. Lovell. In *Congregational Quarterly* 36 (June 1958): 169–70.

Flew, R. Newton. In *London Quarterly and Holborn Review* 183 (1958): 78.

Christian World, 14 December 1978.

Cumbers, Frank. In *Methodist Recorder,* 18 January 1979, 6.

Holy Christian Empire (n.d.)

Wesleyan Methodist Magazine 125 (1902): 800.

The Holy Father and the Living Christ

Expository Times 8 (November 1896): 53–5.

Expository Times 9 (April 1898): 269–70.

London Quarterly Review 90 (April 1898): 179.

Intercessory Services for Aid in Public Worship

Independent and Nonconformist, 10 December 1896, 443.

The Justification of God

Times Literary Supplement, 23 November 1916, 564.

Expository Times 28 (January 1917): 177.

Methodist Review 99 (New York, July 1917): 650–3.

Boston Transcript, 12 September 1917, 6.

New York Times, 25 November 1917, 500.

Cook, E. Albert. 'The Defense of God and Other Problems.' *American Journal of Theology* 22 (April 1918): 303–5.

Davies, D. A. 'On Re-Reading T. P. [sic] Forsyth's *Justification of God.'* *British Weekly,* 19 October 1939, 31.

London Quarterly Review 173 (July 1948): 280.

Gardner, J. In *Journal of Bible and Religion* 20 (January 1952): 44–5.

Dillistone, F. W. In *Anglican Theological Review* 35 (January 1953): 63–4.

Marriage: Its Ethic and Religion

Expository Times 24 (November 1912): 79.

Eager, George B. In *Review and Expositor* 10 (January 1913): 146–7.

Helm, Mary, In *Methodist Quarterly Review* 62 (Nashville, July 1913): 609.
Greene, William Brenton, Jr. In *Princeton Theological Review* 11 (1913): 546–8.
Strange, E. H. In *Ethics* 24 (1913–14): 115.

Missions in State and Church
Denney, James. In *British Weekly*, 15 October 1908, 50.
Expository Times 20 (November 1908): 86.
Westminster Gazette, 23 January 1909, 6.
Primitive Methodist Quarterly Review 51 (January 1909): 166–7.
London Quarterly Review 111 (April 1909): 355–6.
Church Quarterly Review 70 (April 1910): 208.

The Old Faith and the New (1891)
'The Cross and the Kingdom.' *Independent and Nonconformist*, 2 October 1891, 682.
Congregational Monthly 4 (December 1891): 320–4.

The Person and Place of Jesus Christ
Mackintosh, H. R. In *British Weekly*, 21 October 1909, 57–8.
Glasgow Herald, November 1909.
Expository Times 21 (April 1910): 320.
Exley, C. A. 'The Person and Place of Christ.' *American Journal of Theology* 14 (April 1910): 313.
Boutwood, Arthur. In *Hibbert Journal* 8 (May 1910): 686–90.
New York Times: Saturday Review of Books 15 (16 July 1910): 400.
Independent 69 (28 July 1910): 197.
Eager, George B. In *Review and Expositor* 7 (July 1910): 435–6.
Lamar, A. J. *Methodist Quarterly Review* (Nashville, July 1910): 618–21.
Nation 91 (US, 20 October 1910): 367.
Hodge, Charles W. In *Princeton Theological Review* 8 (October 1910): 688–93.
Hodge, Charles W. In *Bibliotheca Sacra* 67 (1910): 363–4.
Mozley, J. K. 'The Person and Place of Jesus Christ.' *Journal of Theological Studies* 12 (January 1911): 298–300.
Mozley, J. K. In *Theology* 42 (April 1941): 229–35.
Lawton, J. S. "Salute to Forsyth." *Guardian*, 18 July 1947, 318.

Stewart, R. W. 'Old soldiers Never Die.' *Expository Times* 58 (August 1947): 289.

Lambert, D. W. 'A Great Theologian and his Greatest Book.' *London Quarterly and Holborn Review* 173 (July 1948): 244–7.

Cocks, H. F. Lovell. 'Books on the Person of Christ: P. T. Forsyth's *The Person and Place of Jesus Christ.*' *Expository Times* 64 (April 1953): 195–8.

Positive Preaching and [the] Modern Mind

Denney, James. 'Principal Forsyth on Preaching.' In *British Weekly*, 24 October 1907, 57–8.

Times Literary Supplement, 19 December 1907: 387.

Expository Times 19 (December 1907): 98–9.

Davison, W. T. 'The Changeless Gospel and the Modern Mind,' 1–17. In *London Quarterly Review* 109 (January 1908): 1–20.

Outlook 88 (7 March 1908): 560.

Nation 86 (26 March 1908): 284.

New York Times: Saturday Review of Books 13 (9 May 1908): 267.

Methodist Review 90 (New York, May 1908): 491–2.

Biblical World 31 (May 1908): 400.

Saturday Review 106 (4 July 1908): 400.

Saturday Review 106 (4 July 1908): 24.

Independent 65 (20 August 1908): 436.

Bibliotheca Sacra 65 (1908): 596–7.

Smith, Gerald Birney. In 'The Modern-Positive Movement in Theology.' *American Journal of Theology* 13 (January 1909): 92–9.

Erdman, Charles P. 'Practical Theology.' *Princeton Theological Review* 7 (1909): 519–21.

Public Opinion (May 1949): 333.

Barnes, I. J. In *Baptist Quarterly* 13 (October 1949): 190–1.

Harris, S. B. In *Presbyter* 7 (1949): 27–8.

Fallows, W. G. In *Modern Churchman* 40 (June 1950): 166–7.

Coggan, F. D. In *Expository Times* 72 (August 1961): 324–6.

Aho, G. In *Springfielder* 30 (1966): 67–9.

Rossow, F. C. In *Concordia Journal* 7 (November 1981): 260–1.

Independent (U. S.), no date.

The Principle of Authority

'Theology and the Church.' *Expository Times* 24 (February 1913): 213.

London Quarterly Review 119 (April 1913): 340–1.

Grover, Delo C. In *Methodist Quarterly Review* (Nashville, July 1913): 587–8.

Mullins, E. Y. In *Review and Expositor* 10 (October 1913): 584–7.

Whateley, A. R. In *Hibbert Journal* 12 (July 1914): 936–41.

Johnson, George. In *Princeton Theological Review* 12 (1914): 125–7.

Cunliffe-Jones, Hubert. In *London Quarterly and Holborn Review* 172 (October 1947): 316.

Argyle, A. W. In *Baptist Quarterly* 14 (October 1952): 378–9.

Stewart, R. W. 'Unrusted Claymore.' In *Expository Times* 63 (August 1952): 329–30.

Cocks, H. F. Lovell. In *Congregational Quarterly* 31 (January 1953): 75–6.

Religion in Recent Art

Scotsman, 11 February 1889.

Manchester Examiner and Times, 16 February 1889, 5.

Liverpool *Daily Post*, 28 February 1889.

Bradford Observer, 1 March 1889.

British Weekly, 9 March 1889.

Manchester Guardian, 14 August 1889.

Art Journal (London, 1889): 128.

Spectator 62 (1889): 639.

London Quarterly Review 97 (January 1902): 201.

New York Times: Saturday Review of Books, 7 June 1902, 379.

Nation 74 (1902): 472.

Outlook 72 (1902): 463–4.

Christian World, no date.

Rome, Reform and Reaction

Bennett, J. H. In *British Weekly*, 11 January 1900, 306.

Banks, J. S. In *London Quarterly Review* 93 (April 1900): 352–5.

Socialism, the Church and the Poor

London Quarterly Review 110 (July 1908): 171.

Garvie, Alfred E. In *Review of Theology and Philosophy* 4 (Edinburgh, 1908–9): 421–2.

The Soul of Prayer

London Quarterly Review 127 (January 1917): 130–1.

The Taste of Death and the Life of Grace
Expository Times 12 (June 1901): 367.

Theology in Church and State
'The Charter of the Church.' *Times Literary Supplement*, 30 December 1915, 495.
Springfield Republican, 5 March 1916, 15.
Expository Times 27 (March 1916): 276–7.
Kellogg, Edwin H. In *Biblical World* 47 (May 1916): 341–2.
Boston Transcript, 17 June 1916, 6.
New York Times: Saturday Review of Books, 6 August 1916, 312.
Methodist Review 98 (New York, September 1916): 816–18.
Starratt, Frank Aubrey. 'Dogma and Theology.' *American Journal of Theology* 20 (October 1916): 615–16.
DuBose, H. M. In *Methodist Quarterly Review* 65 (Nashville, October 1916): 782–5.
Hodge, C. W. In *Princeton Theological Review* 14 (1916): 674–6.
Murray, R. H. In *Quarterly Review of Literature* 266 (Princeton, 1944): 205.

This Life and the Next
London Quarterly Review 130 (April 1918): 121.
American Library Association Booklist 14 (18 July 1918): 313.
Van Dyke, Tertius. In *Boston Transcript*, 24 August 1918, 3.
Springfield Republican, 27 August 1918, 6.
Van Dyke, Tertius. In *Bookman* 47 (August 1918): 653.
Keith, Hhodadad E. In *Churchman* 32 (September 1918): 575
Methodist Review 101 (New York, September 1918): 807–10.
Times Literary Supplement 17 (September 1918): 175.
Griffith-Thomas, W. H. In *Bibliotheca Sacra* 75 (1918): 604–7.
Griffith-Thomas, W. H. In *Biblical World* 53 (1919): 204.
Lawton, J. S. 'Salute to Forsyth.' *Guardian*, 18 July 1947, 318.
Stewart, R. W. 'Old Soldiers Never Die.' *Expository Times* 58 (August 1947): 289.
Child, R. L. In *Baptist Quarterly* 13 (January 1949): 44–5.

Towards Reunion (1919)
Holborn Review 11 (January 1920): 1–12.

The Work of Christ
Denney, James. *British Weekly,* 10 (November 1910).
Expository Times 22 (November 1910): 84.
Carver, W. O. In *Review and Expositor* 8 (January 1911): 122–3.
London Quarterly Review 115 (January 1911): 151.
London Quarterly and Holborn Review 164 (1939): 111.
Stewart, R. W. *Expository Times* 59 (January 1948): 92.
Smith, C. Ryder. In *London Quarterly and Holborn Review* 173 (July 1948): 185.

11. Reviews of Secondary Literature
Reviews are arranged chronologically for each title.

Anderson, Marvin W., *The Gospel and Authority: A P. T. Forsyth Reader.*
Pfatteicher, P. H. In *Lutheran Quarterly* 24 (May 1972): 210–12.
Galloway, Allan. In *Expository Times* 84 (November 1972): 57–8.
Choice 9 (1972): 660.

Benedetto, Robert, *P. T. Forsyth Bibliography and Index.*
McCurdy, Leslie C. *Evangelical Quarterly* (forthcoming)

Bradley, W. L., *P. T. Forsyth: The Man and His Work.*
Lofthouse, W. F. 'A Great Theologian.' *Church Quarterly Review* 153, no. 309 (London, October 1952): 516–20.
Jenkins, Daniel. 'Forsyth and Our Time.' *Christian Century,* 3 December 1952, 1409.
Cave, Sydney. In *Congregational Quarterly* 31 (January 1953): 73–4.
Hough, Lynn Harold. In *Religion in Life* 22 (Summer 1953): 469–70.
Gamble, C. In *Interpretation* 8 (October 1954): 490–1.

Brown, Robert McAfee, *P. T. Forsyth: Prophet for Today.*
Kirkus 20 (15 September 1952): 633.
Lawson, O. G. In *Library Journal* 77 (15 October 1952): 1804.
Jenkins, Daniel. 'Forsyth and Our Time.' *Christian Century,* 3 December 1952, 1409.
Saturday Review 36 (21 February 1953): 58. [By K. D. M.]

Hough, Lynn Harold. In *Religion in Life* 22 (Summer 1953): 469–70.

Shaw, J. M. In *Theology Today* 10 (October 1953): 429–31.

Cully, K. B. In *Interpretation* 8 (January 1954): 99–100.

Bromiley, G. W. In *Scottish Journal of Theology* 9 (December 1956): 447.

Escott, Harry., P. T. Forsyth: Director of Souls.
Gossip, A. J. In *Expository Times* 60 (March 1949): 149.

Church, Leslie F. In *London Quarterly and Holborn Review* 174 (1949): 2–4.

Griffith, Gwilym O., The Theology of P. T. Forsyth.
Cocks, H. F. Lovell. 'P. T. Forsyth, 'A Voice from a Better Future.' *British Weekly*, 6 May 1948, 7.

London Quarterly Review 173 (July 1948): 280.

Thomas, John Newton. In *Theology Today* 7 (July 1950): 268–9.

Hunter, A. M., P. T. Forsyth: Per Crucem ad Lucem.
Worrall, B. G. In *Theology* 77 (October 1974): 544–5.

Gillespie, Neal C. In *Church History* 44 (June 1975): 274–5.

Scott, Geoffrey D. In *Perkins School of Theology Journal* 29 (Winter 1976): 45–6.

McClain, Frank M. In *Anglican Theological Review* 59 (July 1977): 349–50.

A. M. Hunter, Teaching and Preaching the New Testament.
Cunliffe-Jones, H. In *Scottish Journal of Theology* 16 (1963): 435–8.

Mikolaski, Samuel J., The Creative Theology of P. T. Forsyth.
Robinson, William Childs. 'A Movable Feast.' *Christianity Today*, 1 August 1969, 16.

Bos, W. H. In *Reformed Review* 23 (Fall 1969): 29–30.

McKay, C. A., Jr. In *Journal of the American Academy of Religion* 38 (September 1970): 342–3.

Harman, A. M. In *Westminster Theological Journal* 33 (November 1970): 111–12.

Wood, A. S. In *Evangelical Quarterly* 42 (1970): 247–8.

Miller, Donald G., Browne Barr, and Robert S. Paul, P. T. Forsyth: The Man, the Preacher's Theologian, Prophet for the Twentieth Century: A Contemporary Assessment.
Ford, D. W. C. In *Expository Times* 94 (March 1983): 184.

Rodgers, John H., The Theology of P. T. Forsyth: The Cross of Christ and the Revelation of God.
Daane, James. 'Apostle of Grace.' *Christianity Today*, 24 September 1965, 20–21.
Woodyard, D. O. In *Christian Century*, 6 October 1965, 1230–31.
Baker, J. P. In *Churchman* 80 (March 1966): 49–50.
Aldwinckle, R. F. In *Canadian Journal of Theology* 12 (April 1966): 141–2.
Greeves, Frederic. In *London Quarterly and Holborn Review* 191 (April 1966): 164–5.
Coggan, Donald. In *Expository Times* 77 (June 1966): 268–9. [signed, Donald Ebor].
Roberts, J. D. In *Journal of Religious Thought* 23 (1966–7): 187–8.
Robinson, N. H. G. In *Journal of Theological Studies*, n.s., 18 (April 1967): 288–9.

12. Items of Historical Interest

While the bibliography as a whole intends to present a comprehensive picture of the theological writings by and about Forsyth, this section is an eclectic selection of shorter items of mainly historical interest: news reports, accounts of unpublished sermons, interviews, obituaries, reminiscences, etc. They are listed in chronological order of their connection with Forsyth's life.

Records of the Arts Class, 1864–8, University of Aberdeen, 66–7. Edited by W. S. Bruce. Aberdeen: Central Press, 1912.
Record of the Arts Class, 1865–9, University of Aberdeen, 25–6. Edited by James B. Duncan and William Smith. Aberdeen: Milne and Hutchison, 1913.
Wicks, Sidney F. 'He Loved the Children in Cheetham Hill.' *Manchester City News*, 23 Sept 1949.
'Manchester Free Library Lectures: Rev. P. T. Forsyth on Popular Religious Literature.' *Manchester Examiner and Times*, 26 January 1888, 6.

Waddington, Norah. 'The Rev. P. T. Forsyth 1888–94,' and 'Appendix I.' In *The First Ninety Years: Clarendon Park Congregational Church, Leicester*, 4–9, 55–6. No publication data, [c. 1976].

'First Impressions: Dr P. T. Forsyth at Cambridge.' Signed, 'A Country Cousin.' *Christian World*, 15 December 1898.

Manning, B. L. *This Latter House: The Life of Emmanuel Congregational Church, Cambridge, from 1874–1924*, 10–13. Cambridge: W. Heffer & Sons, 1924.

[Stoddart, Jane]. 'Dr P. T. Forsyth, of Cambridge: A Special Biography.' Signed, 'Lorna.' *British Weekly*, 7 March 1901, 530–1.

'Cambridge Character Sketches: The Rev. Dr P. T. Forsyth.' *Cambridge Graphic*, 23 March 1901, 1, 4.

'How to Read the Bible.' *Examiner*, 21 November 1901, 647.

[Stoddart, Jane]. 'Principal Forsyth's Impressions of America.' Signed, 'L[orna].' *British Weekly*, 27 April 1907, 59.

'The Modern Ministry: Its Duties and Perils.' Interview. Signed, 'E. C.' *British Congregationalist*, 30 December 1909, 559–60.

Sell, Alan P. F. 'Theology for All: The Contribution of H. F. Lovell Cocks,' 304–5. In *Commemorations: Studies in Christian Thought and History*, 303–40. Calgary: University of Calgary Press, 1993.

'Roosevelt of Modern Theology.' Editorial. *Literary Digest* 47 (23 August 1913): 289.

And in 'Principal Forsyth: The Roosevelt of Modern Theology.' *British Weekly*, 4 September 1913, 549.

These articles are largely composed of quotations from Ziegler's article–see Section 7.

'Death of Principal Forsyth, an Original Thinker.' *Times* (London), 12 November 1921, 14.

Report of Forsyth's funeral. *Times* (London), 16 November 1921, 13.

Nicoll, W. R. 'Principal Forsyth: A Memoir.' *British Weekly*, 17 November 1921, 145–6.

Mozley, J. K. 'A Personal Tribute.' *British Weekly*, 17 November 1921, 146.

D[arlow], T. H. 'A Cedar Has Fallen.' *British Weekly*, 17 November 1921, 146.

Jowett, J. H. 'Dr P. T. Forsyth.' *British Weekly*, 17 November 1921, 146–7.

Glegg, A. J. Tribute to Forsyth. *Christian World*, 17 November 1921, 4.

'Dr Forsyth.' *Australian Christian Commonwealth* (Adelaide), 18 November 1921, 1.

Ruhu, H. Vincent. Letter. *British Weekly*, 24 November 1921.

Cave, Sydney. 'Dr P. T. Forsyth: His Influence in Congregationalism.' *Christian World*, 24 November 1921.

Aberdeen Grammar School Magazine 25 (November 1921): 25–6.

Bruce, [W. S.] 'Leading Minds in Modern Times: Principal Forsyth.' *Aberdeen Daily Journal*, 2 December 1921.

Correspondence on Forsyth's style. Manchester *Guardian*, 12 and 13 December 1921.

Cave, Sydney. 'Dr Forsyth: "A Student Tribute."' Letter. *Christian World*, no date, December 1921.

Rowe, Gilbert T. 'The Passing of Peter Taylor Forsyth.' *Methodist Quarterly Review* 71 (January 1922): 104–6.

Scullard, H. H. 'Principal Forsyth.' *London Quarterly Review* 137 (January 1922): 104–6.

Peake, A. S. 'Peter Taylor Forsyth.' *Holborn Review* (January 1922). Reprinted in *Recollections and Appreciations*, 192–5. Edited by W. F. Howard. London: Epworth, 1938.

Hackney College: The Addresses Delivered at the Unveiling of the Tablet, May 11th, 1922, Erected in the College Library, to the Memory of Rev. Peter Taylor Forsyth. Addresses by James Carmichael, Alex Glegg, T. Yates, R. Macleod, and R. J. Campbell.

Aberdeen University Review 9 (March 1922): 186.

A[ndrews], H. T. Obituary. *Congregational Year Book 1922*, 104–5.

Thomas, H. Arnold. 'Preachers I Have Known,' 60. *Congregational Quarterly* (January 1923): 51–62.

B[inns], J. B. 'Peter Taylor Forsyth.' *New College London: Report for Session 1945–1946*, 14–18. London: Independent Press, 1946.

Green, Alan. 'Personal Memories of P. T. Forsyth.' *British Weekly*, 13 May 1948, 11.

McMurray Adams, R. H. 'Postman's Son Who Became Church Leader.' Aberdeen *Press and Journal*, 21 May 1948.

13. Unpublished Manuscripts

Binfield, Clyde. 'In Celebration of Peter Taylor Forsyth 1848–1921, Minister of Emmanuel Church, Cambridge, 1894–1901.' Sermon Preached at Emmanuel Church, Cambridge, 15 November 1981.

'Dr Peter Taylor Forsyth.' Coward Trust ms 16, 142–5, including 142a. Dr Williams's Library, London.

Garvie, Alfred E. 'Placarding Jesus Christ the Crucified: The Theology of the Late Dr Peter Taylor Forsyth.' 97-page manuscript from the library of New College, London (NCL ms 537/1), now in Dr Williams's Library, London.

McKim, Donald K. 'The Authority of Scripture in P. T. Forsyth.' Pittsburgh, 1973.

Mozley, J. K. Letter to Forsyth, 20 January 1909. NCL ms 536/22.

Price, Charles. 'Introduction to the Theology of P. T. Forsyth.' Notes of lectures given at the Protestant Episcopal Theological Seminary in Alexandria, Virginia, 1960.

INDEX

331